A BUFF LOOKS AT THE AMERICAN CIVIL WAR

A look at the United States' greatest conflict
from the point of view of a Civil War buff

By: Shon Powers

authorHOUSE®

AuthorHouse™
1663 Liberty Drive
Bloomington, IN 47403
www.authorhouse.com
Phone: 1-800-839-8640

First published by AuthorHouse 4/16/2011

ISBN: 978-1-4567-5549-2 (e)
ISBN: 978-1-4567-5550-8 (dj)
ISBN: 978-1-4567-5551-5 (sc)

Library of Congress Control Number: 2011904109

Printed in the United States of America

Introduction:

There are literally thousands of books published on the American Civil War each year. Historians, such as James McPherson, Jay Winik, and William C. Davis, write new books while works from past greats like Bruce Catton are reprinted with regularity. There are now thousands, if not millions of websites devoted to the conflict, including web logs and discussion forums. Interactive disks take viewers to a bird's eye view of the battlefields. Games are constantly being released, in both board and electronic form. Tour groups are taken around battlefields by day and lectured at night by well-known historians. Thousands don reproduction uniforms and equipment and stage mock battles every year. Whole industries have sprung up to satisfy our thirst to learn about a war that split this nation in two for a while with repercussions that still exist today. Interest has grown with the Lincoln Bicentennial of 2009 and the Civil War Sesquicentennial of 2011-2015.

I started this project in 2005 as a way to learn about Civil War events. After about six months, it started to get a life of its own. I started putting in other bits of information, such as camp life, some of the food that was eaten, and health issues. Next thing I knew, I had 400 pages of material, and that is when the book idea was born.

You see, of all the books on the Civil War that I have read (about 300 at last count), I have not seen one by a regular Civil War buff. I consider myself an amateur Civil War historian (I don't make a living by it) and a newbie to the world of reenacting. Otherwise, I read all the books I can get my hands on, see all the documentaries I can, and watch all the movies that Hollywood puts out.

How did I get interested? My father took me to Gettysburg in 1972 and it was there that I was exposed to the Civil War. At the gift shop, a copy of the American Heritage *History of the American Civil War* was purchased and I literally wore that book out. Sometimes, I would read it twice a day. (It's still on my bookshelf, in tatters).

In the course of time my interest waned. I grew up, entered the United States Air Force, got married while stationed in the United Kingdom, and was having fun when, while on a visit to my parents in San Antonio, TX, I saw the trailer for the movie *Gettysburg*. Soon after returning to the UK, I discovered magazines such as *America's Civil War* and *Civil War Times Illustrated* at the base bookstore. After seeing *Gettysburg*, I was bitten again by the CW bug. I began to read more and more and I started to understand the conflict in a way that I never knew before.

What also sparked my interest was the fact that I have three ancestors that fought in the war:

Private Arnuah Norton, Union Army, 60th Ohio.

Captain Thomas Morrow, Confederate Army, 29th Texas Cavalry

Lieutenant George Morrow, Confederate Army, 31st Texas Cavalry

Private Norton, my Great-Great-Great Grandfather on my father's side, was captured during operations along the Weldon Railroad, south of the siege lines at Petersburg, VA. He was taken to the prison camp at Salisbury, NC where he died in November 1864

Captain Morrow, a Great-Great-Great Uncle, and Lieutenant Morrow, a Great-Great-Great Grandfather, both on my mother's, father's, mother's side, survived the war.

I hope you enjoy reading the book as much as I've had fun writing it.

Forward the colors!

Shon Powers
San Antonio, Texas
2011

Table of Contents

Civil War Timeline

The events depicted here include notes and quotes from people such as:

John Beauchamp Jones, a clerk in the Confederate War Department.

Robert Knox Sneeden: a Private in the 40th New York who was a mapmaker for III Corps and a prisoner in Andersonville.

John Ransom, a Sergeant in the 9th Michigan Cavalry who was a prisoner at Andersonville.

Sam Watkins, a Private in the 1st Tennessee.

Mary Chesnut, the wife of US Senator and Confederate Congressman James Chesnut.

Arthur Freemantle, Lieutenant Colonel of the British Royal Army's Coldstream Guards, who spent three months in the CSA.

Judith McGuire, a resident of Alexandria and Richmond, VA.

November 6: Abraham Lincoln elected 16th President of the United States.

December 19:

> *Secession is not intended to break up the present Government, but to perpetuate it. We do not propose to go out by way of breaking up or destroying the Union as our fathers gave it to us, but we go out for the purpose of getting further guarantees and security for our rights*
> *—A.H. Handy, Representative from*
> *Mississippi, at a speech in Baltimore*

December 20: South Carolina secedes from the Union.

> *"We the people of South Carolina, in convention assembled, to declare and ordain, and it is hereby declared and ordained, that the ordinance adopted by us in convention on the twenty third day of May in the year of our Lord one thousand seven hundred and eighty eight, whereby the Constitution of the United States of America was ratified, and also all acts and parts of acts of the General Assembly of this State, ratifying amendments of the said Constitution, are hereby repealed: and the union now subsisting between South Carolina and other States, under the name "United States of America" is hereby dissolved. Done at Charleston the twentieth day of December in the year of our Lord one thousand eight hundred and sixty"*
> *--South Carolina Secession Proclamation*

December 25: Under cover of darkness, Union Major Robert Anderson moved his troops and supplies to Fort Sumter, in the middle of Charleston Harbor.

1861

January 1: As the year 1861 began, tension and excitement had gripped the nation. South Carolina was the only state so far that had seceded while several other states were considering Articles of Secession. The Administration of President James Buchanan had adopted a "wait and see" attitude towards the situation (probably wanted to push the whole thing onto the incoming Lincoln Administration). It was felt in Washington DC that even though they believed secession was illegal the government did not have the power to prevent it. The US Constitution spelled out the procedures for making new states, but was silent on what to do if a state wanted to leave the Union.

In Charleston, newly formed militia units drilled under the Palmetto flag while glaring at the US flag that still flew over Fort Sumter. On Christmas Day, 1860, the US Army garrison was relocated to the fort to avoid a confrontation with the locals but the move only angered them instead. The garrison troops felt that they had become pawns in a game in which the rules had yet to be written. They also knew that the stalemate would last as long as their provisions.

The question this New Years morning was: will the United States of America remain a loose collection of states where some find it OK to keep 4,000,000 African-Americans in bondage, or a new nation in which the promises of the Founding Fathers will finally become a reality?

January 2: South Carolina troops seized Fort Johnson in Charleston Harbor.

January 3: Georgia troops seized Fort Pulaski, near Savannah (in anticipation of the state's secession).

Delaware voters rejected secession. (Yes, Delaware was a Slave state).

January 4: Alabama State troops seized the arsenal at Mouth Vernon (in anticipation of the state's secession).

January 5: The merchant ship *Star of the West* left New York to resupply Fort Sumter's garrison.

Senators of several Southern states met in Washington to discuss the secession crisis.

January 6: New York City Mayor Fernando Wood urged ties be kept with South Carolina and any other state that secede. Then he suggested that NYC itself should be independent. (What is it about these NYC mayors?)

January 8: US Secretary of the Interior Jacob Thompson of Mississippi resigned.

President Buchanan called for compromise in order to preserve the Union (which fell on increasingly deaf ears).

January 9: Mississippi secedes.

Star of the West was fired upon while attempting to deliver supplies to the Fort Sumter garrison. The ship departed without reaching the fort.

January 10: Florida secedes.

William T. Sherman resigned his position as head of the Louisiana Military Academy (now Louisiana State University).

January 11: Alabama secedes.

New York voters approved a pro-Union state constitution.

January 14: Louisiana militia seized Fort Pike, near New Orleans (in anticipation of the state's secession).

January 16: The Crittenden Compromise, a last attempt to ease Southern fears, failed in the Senate.

January 18: There were reports of death threats against US President-elect Lincoln. One such report mentioned that a body of armed men would come to the Inauguration and prevent Lincoln from taking the oath.

January 19: Georgia secedes.

January 20: Ship Island seized by Mississippi troops.

Mississippi Senator Jefferson Davis resigned his seat in response to his state's secession.

January 24: Georgia troops seized the US Arsenal at Augusta.

January 26: Louisiana secedes.

January 29: Kansas is admitted as the 34th US state.

January 31: An editorial in Cincinnati, OH decried the effect of secession on trade with Southern cities. (Nation was falling apart and some people still thought about their pocketbooks).

February 1: Texas secedes.

February 4: A convention of Southern secessionists began meetings in Montgomery, AL.

Southern peace commissioners arrived in Washington for a conference (a last ditch attempt at a resolution that would fail).

February 8: Convention in Montgomery approved a Provisional Constitution for the Confederate States of America.

February 9: Former Senator Davis was elected Provisional President of the CSA until a permanent government could be established.

February 11: US President-elect Lincoln left his home in Springfield, IL for Washington, DC.

> *I now leave, not knowing when, or whether ever, I may return, with a task before me greater than that which rested upon Washington. Without the assistance of that Divine Being who every attended him, I cannot succeed. With that assistance I cannot fail.*
> *—Lincoln in his speech before departing Springfield.*

February 15: Commander Rafael Semmes resigned from the US Navy.

> *Washington D.C.*
> *February 15th 1861*
> *Sir,*
> *I respectfully tender, through you, to the President of the United States, this, my resignation of the commission, which I have the honor to hold, as a Commander in the Navy of the United States. In severing my connection with the government of the United States, and with the Department over which you now preside, I pray you to accept my thanks, for the kindness which has characterized your official deportment towards me.*
> *I have the honor to be*
> *Very respectfully*
> *Your Obt. Svt*
> *Raphael Semmes, Commander U.S. Navy*

February 18: Davis was inaugurated as CSA Provisional President.

> *We have entered upon the career of independence, and it must be inflexibly pursued....As a necessity: not a choice, we have resorted to the remedy of separation and henceforth our energies must be directed to the conduct of our own affairs, and the perpetuity of the Confederacy which we have formed.*
> *CS President Jefferson Davis, Inaugural Address*

February 21: Diarist Mary Chesnut wrote in her diary, ...*our wise men say that if the President (Buchanan) had left us there to fret & fume a while with a little wholesome neglect we would have come back in time— certainly nobody would have joined us. But Fort Sumter in Anderson's hands united the cotton states…*

February 22: California declared itself for the Union (even though they were too far away to do anything).

US President-elect Lincoln spoke at Independence Hall, Philadelphia, while en route to Washington.

February 23: Lincoln arrived in Washington, supposedly in a sealed railroad car and in disguise because of the security threat. That made for a few derisive woodcut pictures in the papers.

February 25: Diarist Mary Chesnut wrote in her journal expressing pride that her husband, James, became the first US Senator to resign his seat.

February 28: Chesnut wrote …*these men* (leaders in the new Confederate government) *have brought old hatreds & grudges & spites from the old Union. Already we see they are will willing injure our cause to hurt Jeff Davis.* (Nothing new under the sun).

March 1: Chesnut wrote about having met Varina Davis, the Confederate First Lady.

March 4: Abraham Lincoln was inaugurated as the 16th President of the United States.

In your hands, my dissatisfied fellow countrymen, and not in mine is the momentous issue of civil war. The government will not assail you. You can have no conflict without being yourselves the aggressors. You have no oath registered in Heaven to destroy the government. While I shall have the solemn oath to "preserve, protect, and defend" it.
  US President Lincoln, First Inaugural Address.

The "Stars and Bars" (Confederate First National Flag) was raised for the first time.

> *South Carolina slave holder as I am my very soul sickened— it is too dreadful. I tried to reason— this is not worse than the willing sale most women make of themselves in marriage— nor can the consequences be worse.*
>
> —*Mary Chesnut, diary entry.*

March 11: Confederate Congress adopted a Constitution almost exactly like the US Constitution, except that slavery was endorsed.

> *We the people of the Confederate States, each state acting in its sovereign and independent character, in order to form a permanent government, establish justice, insure domestic tranquility, and secure the blessings of liberty and our posterity—invoking the favor and guidance of Almighty God—do ordain and establish this Constitution for the Confederate States of America.*
>
> —*Confederate Constitution Preamble*

March 16: US Army Lieutenant Colonel Robert E. Lee was promoted to Colonel in charge of 1st US Cavalry.

March 18: Texas Governor Sam Houston refused to take Confederate Oath of Allegiance, he was immediately removed from office by the Texas Legislature.

> *Let me tell you what is coming...Your fathers and husbands, your sons and brothers, will be herded at the point of the bayonet...You may, after the sacrifice of countless millions of treasure and hundreds of thousands of lives, as a bare possibility, win Southern independence.... but I doubt it. I tell you that, while I believe with you in the doctrine of States rights, the North is determined to preserve this Union. They are not a fiery, impulsive people as you are...they move with a steady momentum and perseverance of a mighty avalanche.*
>
> —*Texas Governor Sam Houston, before his removal from office.*

March 19: Forts Clark, Inge, and Lancaster were surrendered to Texas authorities.

March 21: In what became known as "The Cornerstone Speech," CS Vice-President Alexander Stephens, in Savannah, GA, defended the position taken by the South concerning Slavery.

March 29: US President Lincoln ordered a relied expedition to Fort Sumter (finally, somebody was acting).

April 4: Virginia voted to reject secession (The issue will be revisited following US President Lincoln's call for volunteers).

April 6: An envoy was sent to South Carolina Governor Francis Pickens to inform him that Fort Sumter will only be resupplied, not reinforced.

April 8: The *Harriet Lane*, with supplies for Fort Sumter, left New York. The message concerning the resupply was delivered to SC Governor Perkins.

John Beauchamp Jones, the editor of the *Southern Monitor*, a pro-southern newspaper based in Philadelphia, began his diary with news of the relief expedition to Fort Sumter and that he must flee his house in Burlington, NJ, leaving his family for the time being.

April 9: Charleston newspaper editorials called for war if Fort Sumter is resupplied, while the Confederate government urged caution.

John Beauchamp Jones departed New Jersey with other Southerners who feared hostility from vengeful Northerners. He was delayed in Baltimore because his baggage was not placed on the connecting train.

April 10: USS *Pawnee* sailed from Hampton Roads, VA toward Fort Sumter.

Confederate Secretary of War Leroy Walker instructed Gen P.G.T. Beauregard to either force the surrender of Fort Sumter or reduce it by force (time to end the stalemate).

John Beauchamp Jones arrived in Washington, DC and wrote that he did not see too much of a military presence.

April 12: Seeing the situation as grave, Union Major Anderson offered to evacuate Fort Sumter on April 15, when supplies were slated to run out. Confederate authorities demanded that he surrender immediately or they would open fire. Citing no instructions from Washington, Anderson refused. He had no way of knowing that a relief fleet was approaching.

At 4:30 a.m., according to legend, Virginia secessionist Edmund Ruffin was given the honor of firing the first artillery shot towards Fort Sumter. **The American Civil War has begun.** (It is now disputed whether or not Ruffin actually pulled the lanyard.)

> *The news-boys are rushing in all directions with extras announcing the bombardment of Fort Sumter! This is an irrevocable blow! Every reflecting mind here should know that the only alternatives now are successful revolution or abject subjugation.*
> —*John Beauchamp Jones, diary entry*

Federal troops occupied Fort Pickens, near Pensacola, FL.

April 13: After hours of bombardment with surprisingly no causalities, Union Major Anderson agreed to surrender Fort Sumter and leave on the transports that had just arrived. He asked for and received permission to fire a 100-gun salute as the US flag was lowered. Halfway through the salute, a spark landed on a pile of powder bags, causing an explosion that killed Private Daniel Hough, the first to die in the Civil War. The salute was halted and the garrison left Fort Sumter.

April 14: Word of the surrender of Fort Sumter reached Washington.

April 15: US President Lincoln issued a call for 75,000 volunteers for three-month service in order to fight the rebellion.

BY THE PRESIDENT OF THE UNITED STATES, A PROCLAMATION

WHEREAS: The laws of the United States have been for some time past, and now are opposed, and the execution thereof obstructed in the States of South Carolina, Georgia, Alabama, Florida, Mississippi, Louisiana, and Texas, by combinations too powerful to be suppressed by the ordinary course of Judicial proceedings, or by the powers vested by the Marshals in law—now, therefore, I, ABRAHAM LINCOLN, President of the United States, in virtue of the power vested in my by the Constitution and the laws, have thought fit to call forth, and hereby do call forth, the militia of the several States of the Union to the aggregate number of seventy-five thousand, on order to suppress said combinations, and to cause the laws to be duly executed.

The details for this object will be immediately communicated to the State authorities through the War Department. I appeal to all loyal citizens to favor, facilitate, and aid this effort to maintain the honor, the integrity and the existence of out national Union and the perpetuity of popular government, and to redress wrongs already long enough endured.

I deem it proper to say that this service assigned to the forces hereby called forth will probably be to repossess the forts, places and property which have been seized from the Union, and in every event the utmost care will be observed, consistently with the objects aforesaid, to avoid ant devastation, any destruction of, or interference with property, or any disturbance of peaceful citizens in any part of the country, and I hereby command the persons composing the combinations aforesaid to disperse and retire peaceably to their respective abodes, within twenty days from this date.

Deeming that the present condition of public affairs presents an extraordinary occasion, I do hereby, in virtue of the power in me vested by the Constitution, convene both houses of Congress. The Senators and Representatives are therefore summoned to assemble at their respective Chambers, at 12 o' clock, on Thursday, the fourth day of July next, then and there to consider and determine such measure as in their wisdom the public safety and interest may seem to demand.

In witness whereof, I have hereunto set my hand, and caused the seal of the United States to be affixed.

Done at the City of Washington, this fifteenth day of April, in the year of out Lord one thousand eight hundred and sixty-one, and of the Independence of the United States, the eighty-fifth.

BY THE PRESIDENT   ABRAHAM LINCOLN
William H. Seward, Secretary of State.

John Beauchamp Jones wrote that he had learned of the sacking of his *Southern Monitor* offices. The crowd had a rope in which to hang him. Finding no "secesh" to hang, they trashed the offices instead. He also wrote about the mood in Richmond as the Virginia Secession Convention was about to meet for the second time.

April 16: Tennessee Governor Isham Harris rejected US President Lincoln's call for troops and announced that his state was now part of the Confederacy. He proclaimed, *"Tennessee will not furnish a single man for coercion, but 50,000, if necessary, for the defense of our rights, or those of our Southern brethren."*

April 17: Virginia secedes (their answer to Lincoln's call for volunteers).

> *Well, my dearest one, Virginia has severed her connection with the Northern hive of abolitionists, and takes her stand as a sovereign and independent state.*
>
> *—Former US President John Tyler.*

April 18: First Union troops reached Washington.

> *As they marched from the railroad stations, they were escorted by crowds cheering vociferously. Merchants and clerks rushed out from stores, bareheaded, saluting them as they passed. Windows were flung up: and women leaned out into the rain, waving flags and handkerchiefs. Horse-cars and omnibuses halted for the passage of the soldiers and cheer upon cheer leaped forth from thronged doors and windows.*
>
> *—Mary A. Livermore describing a scene in Boston, MA in her book* My Story of the War.

Colonel Lee was offered command of the entire Union war effort. He refused.

Union troops abandoned Harpers Ferry, VA.

US Army Quartermaster General Joseph Johnston resigned his commission.

John Beauchamp Jones wrote that word of the secession of Virginia has spread through the streets of Richmond and the issue would go to a popular vote.

April 19: The 6th Massachusetts infantry regiment, marching through

Baltimore, was attacked by a pro-Southern mob. The soldiers fired on the crowd, killing 12 civilians while losing 4.

US President Lincoln declared a blockade on the ports of seceded states; problem was the US Navy had enough ships to block one, maybe two, ports.

John Beauchamp Jones wrote that volunteers were already pouring into Richmond to join the Virginia Army. He also mentioned sending a letter to his wife, telling her to bring the family to Virginia.

April 20: US Navy personnel, while evacuating Gosport Naval Yard, set fire to USS *Merrimac*. Upon taking over the base, Confederate personnel succeed in raising the hulk, which would become CSS *Virginia*.

Colonel Lee resigned from the US Army (it was really painful for him to be breaking his oath).

> *Save in defense of my native state, I never desire again to draw my sword.*
> —*Robert E. Lee.*

Sam Watkins joined the Bigby Grays, a volunteer unit formed in response to President Lincoln's call for troops, except that this response is the opposite of what Lincoln anticipated.

John Beauchamp Jones wrote that the new Confederate flag was already flying over the Virginia capital building and gun salutes were firing in celebration. "*I think they had better save the powder, etc. At night. We have a gay illumination. This too is wrong. We had better save the candles.*" (Did he have a feeling of what's to come?)

April 21: All rail and telegraph connections at Baltimore were cut, isolating Washington.

April 22: Union troops garrisoned Cairo, IL, a strategic town at the junction of the Mississippi and Ohio Rivers. (This was a really good move on the Federal's part).

John Beauchamp Jones wrote that he had a meeting with Virginia Governor Wise and told him about the call for volunteers that US President Lincoln had made.

April 23: Union General Benjamin Butler offered the use of his troops to restore order in Baltimore.

Brigadier General Lee formally assumed command of the Virginia State Provisional Army.

John Beauchamp Jones wrote about the slowness of several other states in seceding (North Carolina had not seceded yet) and of the military preparations. He seemed impressed with a Professor Jackson at the Virginia Military Institute and predicted a successful career if he took to the field.

> *But the gay uniforms we see to-day will change their hue before the advent of another year. All history shows that fighting is not only the most perilous pursuit in the world, but the hardest and the roughest work one can engage in.*
> — *John Beauchamp Jones, diary entry.*

April 25: A Unionist Captain named Stokes led a raid on the Arsenal at St Louis, MO, and seized 10,000 muskets before local Confederate supporters could get them.

The 7th New York Infantry Regiment, among the first Union reinforcements, arrived in Washington, DC.

The Prairie du Chien (WI), *Courier*, reported on a town meeting in which there was support for the Union.

VMI Professor Thomas Jackson joined the Virginia Army with the rank of Colonel.

April 26: Virginia General Joe Johnston was assigned command of troops in the Richmond area.

The State Government of Georgia canceled all debts owed to Northern interests. (Why would one pay a debt to an enemy?)

Communications were restored between Washington, DC and the North.

April 27: Federal naval blockade extended to include the Virginia coastline.

US President Lincoln suspended civilian laws in the Baltimore area in order to let the military restore order.

Richmond was formally offered as a permanent capital for the Confederacy.

John Beauchamp Jones wrote about a panic in Richmond over rumors of a US warship coming up the James River to shell the city.

An article in the New York *Anglo-African* featured a speech by Wendell Phillips who proclaimed the new war as a war against Slavery (well before it became politically acceptable).

April 28: Unrest in Baltimore continues.

John Beauchamp Jones decided to continue his diary throughout the coming war. He also decided to go to Montgomery, AL, the present Confederate capital, to seek a government job.

April 29: Maryland voted against secession.

CS President Davis makes the case for secession in a speech to the Second Provisional Congress of the Confederacy.

April 30: Federal forces abandoned forts in Indian Territory (present day Oklahoma), allowing the region to fall under Confederate control.

The New York *Herald* printed an article about women drilling as soldiers in Mississippi. This and other such articles stoked the opinion that the rebellion would be quashed quickly.

May 1: Virginia Army commander General Lee sent Colonel Jackson to Harper's Ferry to secure the area.

US Naval forces blockaded the mouth of the James River.

Call for Union volunteers goes out in Nebraska.

John Beauchamp Jones wrote about the amount of troops arriving at Richmond and of the agreement between Virginia and the CSA concerning the capital moving there.

May 2: Virginia Army Colonel Jackson organized his army on the basis of ability instead of the old method of letting the soldiers elect their officers. He also began a training and discipline program that would turn a mob of militia into one of the best brigades in Confederate service, the 1st Virginia Brigade (or the Stonewall Brigade, as they were soon to be called).

May 3: Union Military Department of the Ohio, covering Ohio, Indiana, and Illinois, was created with General George McClellan in command.

US President Lincoln called for an additional 42,000 troops to serve three years (those 90-day troops mustered earlier might leave before they see action).

Missouri Governor Claiborne Jackson declared his state as part of the Confederacy.

Union General Winfield Scott revealed his "Anaconda" plan for defeating the Confederacy. This plan called for Union forces seizing the Mississippi River and blockading the coasts. The plan, derided at first, would become the overall Union war plan.

John Beauchamp Jones wrote that he has not heard from his wife. He thinks that his family might have gone to Maryland.

The Confederate Congress passed a Declaration of War on the United States. (The US would not do the same thing because they did not recognize the Rebel government).

May 4: *Harper's Weekly* reported on the vulnerability of Washington, DC since the city was surrounded by either Confederate or Southern-leaning territory.

William H. Lee of Alabama wrote a letter to CS President Davis that called for the Confederacy to either lock up their slaves or put them into the army (quite a radical thought).

May 5: Virginia forces abandoned Alexandria, VA, across the Potomac River from Washington, DC.

John Beauchamp Jones wrote that he received a letter from Former US President Tyler to CS President Davis, recommending Jones for a government position.

May 6: Arkansas secedes.

William Howard Russell, a correspondent for the London *Times* arrived in Montgomery and gave an account of a meeting of the Confederate Congress which detailed tobacco chewing, banquets, and a clergyman's prayer for divine judgment on the US.

May 7: The Federals stepped up their recruiting campaign in Western Virginia and Kentucky.

May 8: Union Major Anderson, former Fort Sumter commander, was selected to head recruiting efforts along the Border States (Missouri, Kentucky, Maryland, and Delaware).

John Beauchamp Jones wrote that five Virginians had been selected to go to Montgomery as Members of Congress.

May 9: US Naval Academy was evacuated from Annapolis due to the political instability in Maryland.

USS *Yankee* exchanged fire with Confederate gun emplacements at Gloucester Point, VA.

May 10: Union Captain Nathaniel Lyon jailed 700 Confederate sympathizers in St Louis, sparking a riot in which 28 were killed.

CS President Davis and Confederate Navy Secretary Mallory sent instructions to Admiral Bulloch in London to begin purchasing ironclad warships. (The UK and France already had ironclads in their navies and had the technological experience to build them).

Judith McGuire, a resident of Alexandria, VA wrote in her diary about her fears concerning a possible Union takeover of the city.

May 11: Unrest continued in St Louis as seven rioters were killed in clashes with US troops.

May 12: Union General Butler moved troops into Baltimore without authorization in order to prevent major unrest.

John Beauchamp Jones departed Richmond for Montgomery.

May 13: The Government of Great Britain announced that they were staying neutral in the growing conflict in the US. They also declared the CSA a belligerent, which afforded it rights under International treaties.

May 14: William T. Sherman reentered the US Army as commander of the 13th US Infantry.

Irvin McDowell was promoted to Brigadier General of Volunteers in the Federal army (and probably still a Major in the Regular Army).

US President Lincoln pledged support for Unionists in Kentucky despite that state's official neutrality stance.

John Beauchamp Jones arrived in Montgomery. Spent the night in the Montgomery Hotel and was bitten by mosquitoes all night.

> *Make your plans for a long war.*
> —*Robert E. Lee as he accepted a commission*
> *as a Confederate Brigadier General.*

May 15: Union General Butler continued the occupation of Baltimore due to the presence of pro-Confederates in the city.

Sam Watkins transferred to the Maury Grays, from Maury County, TN. This unit will become Co. H of the 1st Tennessee Infantry.

May 16: Confederate Provisional Congress passed a bill that authorized the recruitment of 400,000 troops.

Union Naval Commodore John Rodgers took command of US Navy river operations in the West.

Kentucky Legislature submitted a bill that would codify its neutrality stance.

John Beauchamp Jones was introduced to Leroy Walker, the new Confederate Secretary of War. Jones was promised a meeting with President Davis the next day.

May 17: John Beauchamp Jones had his meeting with CS President Davis, who does not believe that the war would be a large affair.

May 18: Union troops engaged Confederate artillery positions at Sewall's Point, VA.

May 19: Union troops began improving the defenses around Washington.

John Beauchamp Jones received a job offer as a clerk in the CS War Department. (Hereafter identified as CS War Department clerk John B. Jones).

May 20: North Carolina secedes.

Telegraph offices throughout the North were raided in order to find any messages sent by spies.

May 21: Plans were finalized to move the Confederate capital from Montgomery to Richmond.

May 22: Union General Butler arrived at Fortress Monroe, VA and took command of Union efforts to seize the Confederate Atlantic coast.

May 23: Virginia formally joined the Confederacy.

May 24: At Fort Monroe, Union General Butler declared that escaped slaves that crossed into Union lines were "contraband of war." His rationale for this action was reports he had received stating that slaves were being used to construct fortifications for the Confederates. Using that rationale, he would not need to enforce the Fugitive Slave Law.

Alexandria, VA seized by Union forces. During the capture of the town, the commander of the 11th New York Infantry (known as the "Fire Zouaves" because they were comprised of NYC firefighters), Colonel Elmer Ellsworth, spotted a Confederate flag flying from a hotel. Taking two soldiers, he raced to the roof and took the flag down. On the way down the stairs, Ellsworth was met by the hotel owner, James Jackson, who killed him with a shotgun. Jackson was killed by one of the soldiers. Both men become symbols to both sides. (The private who killed the hotel owner was immediately promoted to 2nd Lieutenant).

> *The Secessionists in Alexandria naturally did not relish the capture of their city by the Federals, and the proprietor of the Marshall House showed the resentment by refusing to take down the Confederate flag flying in his roof. Seeing this, Colonel Ellsworth, with one or two of his zouaves, rushed up the stairs and pulled down the offending colors. As they descended with the flag in their hands the tavern keeper picked up a gun and shot the gallant young colonel dead, only to be immediately killed himself by one of the zouaves.*
> —*account printed in* Frank Leslie's Illustrated Newspaper

CS War Department clerk John B. Jones wrote about hearing of the proposed move to Richmond, but that CS President Davis had vetoed it.

May 25: Union forces seized Hampton, VA.

May26: US Postmaster General Montgomery Blair announced that postal service to the Southern states would cease on May 31.

Author Nathaniel Hawthorne wrote about the surge in patriotism in the North but wondered what the aim of the war should be.

CS War Department clerk John B. Jones wrote about meeting several members of the Confederate government.

May 27: Union General McClellan crossed the Ohio River into Western Virginia in support of the 1st Virginia (US).

May 28: Union General McDowell was named Commander of the Department of Northeastern Virginia.

CS War Department clerk John B. Jones wrote that the government has begun their movement to Richmond. He also received word that his wife and children were there. (That must have been a load off his mind).

May 29: Dorothea Dix received authorization to establish military hospitals in the Washington DC area.

Union troops under General Butler occupied Newport News, VA.

May 31: Confederate General Beauregard was appointed Commander of the Confederate Army of the Potomac. This was the force being gathered to counter any Union moves to stop the rebellion.

Union troops move from Indian Territory (modern day Oklahoma) to Fort Leavenworth, KS on a route that will become the Chisholm Trail, which will be the route for massive cattle drives after the war.

CS War Department clerk John B. Jones wrote about reaching Richmond and securing space for the War Department at the Customs House. At the same time he was reunited with his family.

June 1: Confederate cavalry defeated a Federal force near Fairfax Court House, VA.

He spoke some bitter words against the National Government, and after saying that there was "not one true son of the South who was not ready to shoulder his musket, to bleed, to die or to conquer in the cause of liberty here," he declared: "We have now reached the point where, arguments being exhausted, it only remains for us to stand by our weapons. When the time and occasion serve, we shall smite the smiter with manly arms, as did our fathers before us and as becomes their sons. To the enemy we leave the base acts of the assassin and incendiary. To them we leave it to insult helpless women, to us belongs vengeance upon man."
—*CS President Jefferson Davis' speech in Richmond, VA, as reported in* Frank Leslie's Illustrated Newspaper.

CS War Department clerk John B. Jones wrote about a dispute between the War and Treasury departments about office space in the Customs House.

June 2: 3000 Union troops under General McClellan moved toward Philippi, Western Virginia.

CS War Department clerk John B. Jones wrote that his family was boarding at a place called Carleton House.

June 3: Union troops in Western Virginia surprised Confederate troops near Philippi. The resulting pursuit became known as the "Philippi Races." This would instill an over confidence in the Union that Confederate troops had no stomach for a fight.

Stephen Douglas, the Northern Democrat candidate in the 1860 Presidential Election, and US President Lincoln's opponent in a famous series of debates, died.

June 5: A shipment of munitions that was slated to go south was seized at the DuPont works in Delaware.

June 6: The Federal Government announced that they would fund war expenditures as the states' fulfilled their quota of volunteers.

June 7: Union General McClellan's victories in Western Virginia gave hope to the anti-secession faction there.

June 8: Tennessee secedes.

All Virginia State forces were transferred to the Confederate government. Its commander, Robert E. Lee, became an advisor to CS President Davis.

US Sanitary Commission was set up in Washington, DC. This group would render great assistance to the troops and was an ancestor of today's support and morale agencies for the military.

June 9: Union troops under General Butler began their movement towards a Confederate outpost at Little Bethel Church, VA.

June 10: The rebuilt ship that was once USS *Merrimack* was rechristened CSS *Virginia*.

The first serious battle of the Civil War took place at Big Bethel, VA with a repulse of Union troops.

June 11: Pro-Unionists held a meeting in Wheeling to discuss seceding from seceded Virginia.

There was a meeting between Union General Nathaniel Lyon, commander of the US Army Department of the West, Missouri Governor Jackson, and Missouri Militia commander General Sterling Price. Both Jackson and Price demanded that the state be declared neutral and for US troops to leave. Lyon, armed with the intelligence that Jackson and Price have raised an army in order to take over Missouri and turn it over to the Confederacy, refused. Meanwhile, troops from Texas under Ben McCulloch crossed into Missouri and were headed for Springfield.

Harriet Beecher Stowe, author of *Uncle Tom's Cabin*, wrote a letter about meeting her son, who had joined a Massachusetts regiment.

CS War Department clerk John B. Jones wrote about hearing the noise of battle from Big Bethel the previous day.

June 12: Missouri Governor Jackson called for 50,000 volunteers to fight the Union "invasion." Union forces under General Franz Sigel moved toward Springfield in order to block Confederate troops under General McCulloch.

June 13: Union General Lyon took 1500 men and headed for Jefferson City, MO. Upon hearing of this, the pro-Confederate state government fled with some local troops.

June 14: Confederates abandoned Harper's Ferry, VA in the face of two Union forces.

June 15: Confederate forces were gathering strength in western Missouri.

At Los Angeles, CA a dinner party was given for a small group of officers who had resigned their commissions and planned on joining the CS Army. The hosts were Captain and Mrs. Winfield S. Hancock (Captain Hancock will become a Union corps commander). The guests included Colonel Albert Johnston (who will die at Shiloh), Major Lewis Armistead, and Captain Richard Garnett (who will both lead brigades against Hancock at Gettysburg and die in the process).

June 16: Union General Lyon decided to attack Confederate forces in Missouri before they could concentrate.

June 17: Thaddeus Lowe demonstrated his balloon for use as an observation and artillery fire direction platform.

Confederate cavalry came to within sight of Washington DC. On the way back, that same troop ambush a Federal train at Vienna, VA.

Union General Lyon's troops had advanced on Boonville, MO and drew the Confederates into the range of his own artillery. This forced the Confederates to withdraw with some losses.

June 18: Skirmish at Camp Cole, MO.

June 19: Francis H. Pierpont was named provisional governor over the breakaway northwestern counties of Virginia.

June 20: Efforts were underway to concentrate Confederate forces in the south of Missouri.

June 21: Union forces under General Samuel Sturgis were stopped at the Osage River, MO as retreating Confederates burned the bridge across the swollen river.

June 22: Missouri Governor Jackson fled Boonville and headed south to join other Confederate forces.

June 23: Confederate Army of the Potomac, under General Beauregard, was deployed at Manassas Junction, VA while the Army of the Shenandoah, under General Joe Johnston, was deployed to the Shenandoah Valley.

June 24: The world's first machine gun was demonstrated in front of US President Lincoln. Its cost and the views of senior military leaders ensured that few were produced and fewer were deployed.

Union gunboats shelled Virginia artillery batteries at Mathias Point, VA.

June 25: Union General Robert Patterson's forces advanced toward Winchester, VA. Most of this army was made up of three-month enlistees who were about to leave when their enlistments expire, no matter where they were.

June 26: Skirmish at Patterson Creek (Kelley's Island), VA.

June 27: Army and Navy costal survey experts met in Washington, DC to examine problems that might be encountered during costal operations.

June 28: New York *Tribune* published an article under the headline "On to Richmond" which became the battle cry in Washington, DC. This placed pressure on the US Army to end the rebellion before the Confederates were strong enough.

CS War Department clerk John B. Jones wrote about seeing a comet, which was interpreted as an omen of the coming war and the dissolution of the United States.

June 29: Union General McDowell finalized his plan to seize Manassas Junction.

CS War Department clerk John B. Jones wrote that he could not support his family on his clerk's salary, so he was sending them to a Dr Custis, Jones' wife's cousin, in North Carolina.

June 30: CSS *Sumter*, under the command of Commander Semmes, breached the Union blockade at the mouth of the Mississippi River and escaped into the Gulf of Mexico.

July 1: US War Department announced a recruitment effort in Tennessee and Kentucky. There were two problems with that: Kentucky had declared neutrality and Tennessee had joined the Confederacy.

CS War Department clerk John B. Jones wrote that the War Department had been moved to Mechanics' Hall. The dispute at Customs House over office space seems to have been resolved.

July 2: US President Lincoln suspended the writ of *habeas corpus* as regards to any military railroad lines between Washington, DC and New York, NY.

Union General Patterson moved his army into the Shenandoah Valley to counter any possible moves by Confederate General Joe Johnston's forces.

July 3: Union troops under General Patterson approached Martinsburg, VA, which forced Confederate General Joe Johnston to pull his troops back toward Winchester.

July 4: US Congress met in session and heard US President Lincoln press his case for putting down the rebellion. Secretary of War Simon Cameron called for three-year enlistments for incoming volunteers. Secretary of the Treasury Chase asked for $240,000,000 for war expenses and $80,000,000 for other governmental expenses. Secretary of the Navy Gideon Welles began to push his expansion plans that would include ironclad vessels.

A newspaper published at Camp Pennsylvania, Baltimore, called *The National Guard* published a series of caricatures about camp life.

July 5: Union General Sigel's forces attacked Confederates under Missouri Governor Jackson at Carthage. Union troops were forced back and Confederates escaped to join up with the army of General Price.

July 6: CSS *Sumter* arrived at Cienfuegos, Cuba with seven Union ships in tow.

July 8: Confederate forces under General Henry Sibley moved into New Mexico Territory to secure it for the CSA. Sibley had been appointed Governor of the territory.

July 9: Confederate camp at Florida, MO was broken up by a small Union force.

July 10: US President Lincoln sent a letter to the Kentucky Inspector General of Militia, Simon Bolivar Buckner, stating that Union troops would respect the states neutrality stance.

July 11: Union forces under General Rosecrans defeated Confederates at Rich Mountain, Western VA.

At Laurel Hill, Western Virginia, Union General T.A. Morris forced Confederates under General Robert Garnett to abandon their positions.

July 12: Union forces under General Jacob Cox moved into the Great Kanawha Valley in Western Virginia.

July 13: At Carrick's Ford, Western Virginia, Confederate General Robert Garnett became the first general officer to die in the Civil War. His death and the surrender of 555 troops cleared the northern part of Western Virginia of Confederates.

July 14: Union troops under General McDowell prepared to move into Virginia with Fairfax Court House as the main line of advance.

July 15: Union troops under General Patterson clashed with Confederates near Winchester.

USS *Daylight* had been stationed off Wilmington, NC as a single ship blockade force. It was apparent that more warships were needed.

July 16: 30,000 men, at the time the largest army on the North American continent, under the command of Union General McDowell, began their movement toward Manassas Junction.

July 17: Union forces reached Fairfax Court House.

> *They stopped every moment to pick blackberries or get water: they would not keep in the ranks, order as much as you please. When they came where water was fresh, they would pour the old water out of their canteens and fill them with fresh water. They were not used to denying themselves much: they were not used to journeys on foot.*
> —*Union General Irwin McDowell.*

Union General Patterson was ordered to leave Winchester, which allowed Confederate General Joe Johnston to move his army toward Manassas in order to support General Beauregard.

July 18: Union and Confederate troops clashed at Centerville, VA. Union troops were forced to retreat.

Confederate General Joe Johnston left a force at Winchester to hold up any Union troops while he marched the rest of his army through Ashby's Gap in order to take the railroad to Manassas Junction.

July 19: As Union General McDowell's forces arrived at Fairfax Court House; they did not find any Confederates. McDowell decided to proceed to a creek called Bull Run. The motivation for continuing this was the fact that many of his troops were 90-day volunteers and their enlistments would end in a couple of days. McDowell found a crossing and decided to use it in a flanking movement against the Confederate's right. He did not know that reinforcements were coming to the aid of the Southerners.

Judith McGuire had fled her Alexandria home and was living with friends in Manassas. The war was about to catch up with her.

July 20: Confederate General Joe Johnston's army completed their move to Manassas Junction, meanwhile 2000 Union troops have departed as their 90-day enlistments had expired and they couldn't be persuaded to stay.

Confederate Congress met for the first time in Richmond.

July 21: First Battle of Bull Run (First Manassas): Union commander: General Irwin McDowell. Confederate commander: General Joseph Johnston. Two armies of green troops tried flanking each other until General Jackson's troops arrived and were able to stiffen the collapsing Confederate line near Henry House Hill. Jackson ordered a full charge which sent the Union troops into a rout. A cavalry charge led by Colonel James Ewell Brown "Jeb" Stuart added to the panic. The panic was compounded by the presence of civilians who were there to watch the battle. Confederate victory, but they were too disorganized to press an attack toward Washington, DC.

July 22: There were two state governments in Missouri. The pro-Union government in Jefferson City and the pro-Confederate government in southwest Missouri.

> *Mrs. Davis came in, sat by me. Kissed me, said a great battle had been fought at Manassas— Jeff Davis led the centre—Beauregard the right wing— Johnston the left. Beauregard's staff safe. What a load from my heart. Wade Hampton wounded— Leiut. Col. Johnson killed— Gen Bee killed— Kirby Smith killed (wounded). Poor Col. Bartow— killed gallantly leading his men into action.*
> —*Mary Chesnut, diary entry.*
>
> In actuality, CS President Davis did not arrive until late in the day, so he never led troops in battle. General Smith was wounded, so she made that correction later.

July 23: Union General John Fremont was named commander of the Department of Missouri.

July 24: Union General Jacob Cox attacked the Confederate garrison, commanded by General Henry Wise, at Charleston, Western VA, and forced them to retreat.

July 25: Union General Nathaniel Banks assumed command of Union forces in the Shenandoah Valley.

US Congress passed a resolution that the preservation of the Union, not the abolishment of slavery, was the main war aim.

Federal troops at Fort Fillmore, New Mexico Territory repelled Confederates invading the area.

July 26: Union Major Isaac Linde withdrew from Fort Fillmore despite enjoying a 2 to 1 advantage.

July 27: The remnants of the Union army that lost at First Bull Run were reorganized and redesignated the Army of the Potomac. General McClellan was given command of the new army. (Union armies were named after rivers. Confederate armies were named after states or regions.)

> *He at once became so popular in this position that when, a few months afterward (November 1ˢᵗ) General [Winfield] Scott resigned his place as general in chief of the armies, on account of old age and ill health, McClellan was appointed to that officer. He immediately set to work to reorganize the army, which had been shattered by the terrible blow at Bull Run.*
>
> —*from* Frank Leslie's Illustrated History of the Civil War

---

CS War Department clerk John B. Jones wrote that there were people wondering why Generals Joe Johnston and Beauregard were not marching on Washington City.

July 28: US Seventh Infantry surrendered to Confederates at Augustine Springs, New Mexico Territory.

CS President Davis called for a follow-up action on the heels of the Confederate victory at Manassas Junction.

July 29: CS President Davis decided to send his military advisor, General Lee, to Western Virginia to take command of Confederate forces there and attempt to retake the area from the Union.

July 30: Union General Butler at Fort Monroe had about 900 runaway slaves on his hands and was waiting for orders from Washington, DC on what to do with them.

July 31: Union Colonel Ulysses S. Grant was appointed Brigadier General of Volunteers.

Richmond *Enquirer* printed an article about the Union sympathies of Elizabeth Van Lew. Little did the paper's staff know that Van Lew was a spy for the Union and leader of the Union Resistance in Richmond. Her greatest coup was placing a spy (an African-American servant) in the Confederate White House.

August 1: Brazil recognized the CSA as a belligerent.

> *When you left America last, you left also*
> *A free Press—prosperity—A Constitution*
> *Habeas Corpus*
> *Peace*
> *I hope you may come back and find them. There is now—*
> *No freedom of the Press—A passport system—Domiciliary visits*
> *Police surveillance—Fort Lafayette—a bastille—*
> *No freedom of the person—*
> *War calamity and distress*
> *Irresponsible Govt.*
>
> — *London* Times *reporter William Russell*
> *to a friend living in Paris.*

August 2: Union General Fremont sent reinforcements for General Lyon who was engaging Confederates near Dug Springs.

Confederates took Fort Stanton, New Mexico Territory.

US Congress passed a bill establishing an income tax, affecting those who earned $800 or over a year.

August 3: Union reinforcements reached General Lyon at Dug Springs.

Skirmish at Mesilla, New Mexico Territory with Union troops getting the upper hand.

A Federal balloon was successfully launched from a vessel at Hampton Roads.

August 4: US Government advertised for proposals to improve the Navy, especially in ironclads.

> *If the abundance of heaven only sends us a fair share of light &*
> *conscience, we shall redeem America for all its sinful years since the*
> *century began.*
>
> — *Ralph Waldo Emerson, letter to a friend*

August 5: Union General Lyon's troops were forced back from Dug Springs in the face of heavy Confederate pressure.

Confederate blockade-runner *Alvarado* was captured and burned by USS *Vincennes* off the Florida coast.

Henry Brooks Adams wrote to a friend from London, England of the humiliation Americans living in Britain felt when news of the Battle of Bull Run hit the front pages of UK papers.

August 6: US Congress passed a law that allowed for the confiscation of any and all property that was used for insurrection. This included slaves used in the construction of Confederate fortifications. US President Lincoln signed the bill: although he felt by doing so he was giving belligerent status to the CSA, and therefore recognition.

August 7: Hampton, VA was burned by Confederate General John Magruder upon hearing that Union General Butler had planned to use the town as a holding center for runaway slaves.

CS War Department clerk John B. Jones wrote about hearing that a recent edition of the New York *Herald* contained an article listing Confederate forces in the area and several general officers. He documented the uproar and his feelings that the culprit must be a clerk that worked in Washington and moved south when his native state seceded (Such a clerk must have been influenced by the Yankees).

August 8: US Congress approved $1,500,000 for construction of ironclad warships, including USS *Monitor.*

CS Congress officially recognized Kentucky, Missouri, Maryland, and Delaware as Confederate states, allowing citizens of those states to be mustered into Confederate service, even though those states were not controlled by Richmond (it was a symbolic move, really).

Union General Butler was ordered by Secretary of War Cameron to adhere to fugitive slave laws, but only in states not in rebellion.

August 9: Union General Lyon headed for Wilson's Creek, MO in order to delay advancing Confederates.

> *Prince Napoleon, he is very stout & as he reviewed our troops— it was so hot. John Manning says "en avant," "Allons" is all he heard him say.*
>
> —*Mary Chesnut, diary entry.*
>
> This is in reference to the French Crown Prince paying a visit to the CSA.

August 10: Battle of Wilson's Creek, MO: Union commanders: Generals Nathaniel Lyon and Franz Sigel. Confederate commander: General Ben McCulloch. In the first major battle in the West, the Union troops were sent in a two-pronged attack. Sigel's attack on the Confederate rear was repulsed with heavy losses and Lyon was killed leading a charge. Union troops held off three Confederate charges. Confederates withdrew, but Union troops did not pursue due to lack of ammunition. The Federals pulled back to Rolla, which left the Confederates in control of a large part of Missouri. Confederate victory because they were left on the field.

August 11: Union General McClellan urged the formation of a massive army that would totally crush the rebellion.

August 12: A Confederate patrol was attacked by Apaches in West Texas. Local militias were now guarding the frontier, a job that the US Army used to do.

August 13: The popular opinion at this time was that it would take longer to build a pontoon bridge then to defeat the CSA. The Union army was learning that it would not be the case.

August 14: Martial law was imposed in St Louis and two pro-Southern newspapers were closed by order of Union General Fremont.

A mutiny in the 79th New York was put down.

August 15: Former Fort Sumter commander, Union General Anderson, was named commander of the Department of the Cumberland, covering Kentucky and Tennessee.

Another mutiny, this time in the 2nd Maine, was put down.

US President Lincoln ordered reinforcements to Missouri.

August 16: US President Lincoln formally declared the Southern states in rebellion.

Skirmishing at Fredericktown and Kirkville, MO.

August 17: Union Departments of Northeastern Virginia, Washington DC, and the Shenandoah were merged into the Army of the Potomac.

Skirmish at Brunswick, MO.

August 18: Any Northern newspaper publishing pro-Southern opinions was targeted either for legal action or violence by outraged citizens. (Sound familiar?)

Union General Butler was relieved as commander, Department of Virginia but remained at Fort Monroe.

August 19: Confederate Congress declared an alliance with Missouri.

August 20: Confederate Congress appointed commissioners who will be sent to Europe to buy supplies and weapons for the CS Army.

August 21: With Fort Monroe as a secure Union base, operations along the Confederate Atlantic coast were being planned.

August 22: The Augusta (GA) *Chronicle and Sentinel* published an editorial calling for the strengthening of costal defenses against any Union seaborne attack.

August 23: Confederate forces in Western Virginia receive reinforcements under General John Floyd. This would prove a disaster for the Confederate effort there. Floyd was an incompetent officer who had a newspaper editor as his chief-of-staff and a farmer as his cavalry commander.

Rose O'Neal Greenhow, a Washington, DC socialite, was arrested for spying for the Confederacy when it was found that she had sent details of Union General McDowell's movements to the Confederates.

> *She wants us to know how her delicacy was shocked and outraged. That could be done only by most plain-spoken revelations. For eight days she was kept in full sight of men—her rooms wide open—and sleepless sentinels watching by day and by night. Soldiers tramping— looking in at her leisurely by way of amusement.*
> *Beautiful as she is, at her time of life few women like all the mysteries of their toilette laid bare to the public eye.*
> *She says she was worse used than Marie Antoinette when they snatched a letter from the poor queen's bosom.*
> *—Mary Chesnut, diary entry about Rose O'Neal Greenhow.*

August 24: CS President Davis named James Mason as commissioner to Great Britain, John Slidell as commissioner to France, and Pierre Rost as commissioner to Spain. All three had been tasked with seeking diplomatic recognition as well as arms and equipment from the three European powers.

In an example of some of the wild rumors floating around, CS War Department clerk John B. Jones wrote about hearing that the Union was training 600,000 for battle and building iron-clad vessels.

August 25: Union General McClellan continued to improve the Union Army but would not take the offensive as the public was demanding. He believed that only a trained army with an intricate plan would defeat the Confederates with one massive blow. He did not seem to understand that 1). One of the first rules of war is that the plan will last until contact with the enemy, and 2). The nature of war had changed and a single victory would not end this war.

August 26: Union forces defeated at Cross Lanes (Summerville), Western Virginia.

Action at Wayne Court House and Blue's House, both in Western Virginia.

Eight Union vessels departed Hampton Roads for Hatteras Inlet, NC.

August 27: Skirmishing at Ball's Cross Roads, VA.

August 28: A Union force was landed at Hatteras Inlet to attack two Confederate forts, Hatteras and Clark. Fort Clark was evacuated but Fort Hatteras would take a little longer to subdue.

Union General Grant was appointed commanded of Union forces in southern Illinois and southeastern Missouri.

August 29: Fort Hatteras fell to Union troops in the first successful Federal incursion into Confederate territory. In one of the ironies of the war the fort's commander, Commodore Samuel Barron, noticed as he was going into captivity that one of the ships in the Union fleet was USS *Wabash*. Barron was that ship's commander six months previously.

Skirmish at Lexington, MO.

Mary Chesnut expressed her anger in her diary about William Russell's account on the Battle of Manassas in the London *Times*. She was expressing the feeling that most Southerners had about Russell's articles.

August: 30: Union General Fremont declared martial law in Missouri and declared all slaves in the state free.

Union General Butler proposed that Fort Hatteras be kept as a base for future Union operations along the Confederate Atlantic Coast.

Frederick Douglass wrote to a minister of the fear he had that the US Government would not declare emancipation of slaves a war aim.

August 31: Confederate Government promoted Samuel Cooper, Albert Sidney Johnston, Robert E. Lee, Joseph Johnston, and Pierre Beauregard to the rank of General, equivalent to four-star rank in today's military. The US Army would not use that rank until 1866.

CS War Department clerk John B. Jones wrote that his family had returned with the news of the Union seizure of Fort Hatteras.

September 1: Union offensive in Western Virginia continued as engagements occur at Boone's Court House, Blue Creek, and Burlington.

Union General Grant arrived at Cape Girardeau, MO as skirmishing occurred at Bennet's Mills, MO.

September 2: US President Lincoln rescinded General Fremont's order freeing slaves in Missouri.

Leonidas Polk, Episcopalian Bishop of Louisiana, was made a Confederate General and given command of troops in Arkansas and Missouri.

September 3: Confederate troops under General Gideon Pillow entered Kentucky on their way to occupy the town of Columbus, violating the proclaimed neutrality of Kentucky.

September 4: Columbus, KY occupied by Confederate troops.

September 5: Union General Grant moved on Paducah, KY in response to the Confederate occupation of Columbus.

US President Lincoln had doubts that General Fremont could handle the situation in Missouri.

CS War Department clerk John B. Jones wrote about the CS Congress approving appropriations for 400 regiments. This while rumors circulated that the North had 1,000,000 volunteers.

September 6: Union General Grant's troops seized Paducah, KY. He placed General Charles Smith in command while Grant returned to Cairo, IL.

September 7: Union General Rosecrans began his movement against Confederates in Western Virginia. The Confederate force was now under the overall command of General Lee.

CS War Department clerk John B. Jones wrote an entry that gave insight into his prejudices concerning Jews.

September 8: Union troops defeated Confederates at Summersville, Western Virginia.

September 9: Union General David Hunter was sent to Missouri to assist General Fremont over the furor over his handling of the situation in the state.

September 10: Confederate General Albert Sidney Johnston was given command of Confederate armies in the West.

Union General Rosecrans attacked Confederate positions at Carnifix Ferry, Western Virginia, which forced a withdrawal of Confederate troops from the region.

September 11: Confederate General Lee launched an attack on Union forces at Cheat Mountain, Western Virginia, but bad weather and poor coordination of troops caused the attack to fail.

> *All at once everything was a scene of consternation and confusion: no one seemed equal to the emergency. We did not know whether to run or stand, when Captain Field gave the command to fire and charge the bushes. We charged the bushes and saw the Yankees running through them, and we fired on them as they retreated. I do not know how many Yankees were killed, if any. Our company (H) had one man killed, Pat Hanley, an Irishman, who had joined out company at Chattanooga. Hugh Padgett and Dr. Hooper, and perhaps one of two others, were wounded.*
> *--Sam Watkins, Private, 1ˢᵗ Tennessee, CS Army*

US President Lincoln sent Judge Joseph Holt to St Louis in order to convince General Fremont to soften his stand on freeing Missouri's slaves.

September 12: Confederate General Price besieged Union forces at Lexington, MO.

Maryland legislators, suspected of secessionist leanings, were arrested between 12 and 17 September. The state would remain loyal to the Union.

Confederate General Lee had managed to concentrate his forces at Meadow Bridge, Western Virginia in order to counter Union General Rosecrans' moves.

September 13: Confederate Generals Lee and Wise were recalled to Richmond, leaving in command, General John Floyd, who ordered his army into winter quarters.

September 14: USS *Colorado* sank the blockade-runner *Judah* off Pensacola, FL.

September 15: Confederate General Price continued his assault on Lexington, MO. The Union commander, a Colonel Mulligan, had called for reinforcements but all the couriers had been intercepted.

September 16: Confederate forces at Lexington halted their assault in order to get supplies sent in.

Confederates evacuate Ship Island, MS.

September 17: Federal naval forces destroyed Confederate defenses at Ocracoke Inlet, NC.

Federal naval forces seized Ship Island for use as a base.

There was a shakeup in the Confederate Cabinet as Leroy P. Walker resigned as Secretary of War. Following this, Judah Benjamin resigned as Attorney General and was named the new Secretary of War. Thomas Bragg was named the new Attorney General.

September 18: There was a clamor to have Union General Fremont replaced as commander of Union forces in Missouri.

Confederate General Price managed to get his troops resupplied and resumed the assault on Lexington.

September 19: Confederate forces attacking Lexington have not only surrounded the town, but have sealed off river traffic to the town, which prevented the Union defenders from being supplied.

September 20: Lexington, MO fell to Confederates.

CS War Department clerk John B. Jones wrote that Colonel J. W. Washington, a descendant of George Washington, was killed in a recent skirmish.

September 22: Pro-Union raiders burned the town of Osceola, MO.

Skirmishes at Papinsville and Elliot's Mills, MO

September 23: Skirmish at Hanging Rock, Western Virginia.

September 24: Adding to the list of things to be held against him, Union General Fremont ordered the St Louis *Evening News* closed and the editor arrested after an editorial was printed chiding him for his inaction concerning the Union defeat at Lexington. (He was not making himself popular in any way).

September 25: US Navy Secretary Welles gave orders that "contrabands" (escaped slaves) could enlist in the Navy, almost two years before the same would be authorized for the Army.

Skirmish at Chapmanville, Western Virginia.

Skirmish at Canada Alamosa, New Mexico Territory.

Skirmish at Lewinsville, VA.

September 26: Skirmish at Lucas Bend, KY.

September 27: Union General McClellan met with US President Lincoln and the Cabinet about a new offensive into Virginia.

September 28: An early indication of how Union General McClellan operated was made apparent when he stated that he could not conduct an offensive with any less than 150,000 men. McClellan cited reports that the Confederates have at least 150,000 (in fact, they did not have even 50,000).

September 29: Munson's Hill, VA was occupied by Federal troops. A friendly fire incident occurred nearby when the 69th Pennsylvania fired on the 71st Pennsylvania, killing nine.

Robert Knox Sneeden, a private who had joined the Union Army as a member of the 40th New York, started his diary by writing about participating in an exercise that ended in a fistfight between members of the regiment.

September 30: Things have settled down, but there were still problems. Skirmishing was taking place in Missouri and Union General Fremont was causing a firestorm with recent actions. Kentucky was about to become a major war zone and Western Virginia was turning out in favor of the Union. Above all this, there was still that public clamor for a Union offensive into Virginia.

October 1: There was a conference between US President Lincoln, the Cabinet, and Generals Scott and McClellan discussing strategy for operations along the Confederate Atlantic coast.

Union General Butler was appointed commander of the Department of New England and tasked with recruitment.

CS President Davis met with his commanders in Centerville, VA about dealing with any new Federal threats.

CS War Department clerk John B. Jones wrote about writing passports so that "alien enemies" can depart the CSA.

October 2: A Confederate force was repulsed at Chapmanville, Western Virginia.

Skirmish at Charleston, MO.

October 3: The Confederate Government began their plan to force diplomatic recognition from Britain and France by halting cotton shipments. Louisiana Governor Thomas Moore banned cotton shipments from going to New Orleans. This plan would backfire due to new supplies of cotton from Egypt and India reaching European mills.

Union forces won a minor engagement at Greenbriar, Western Virginia.

October 4: USS *South Carolina* captured two Confederate blockade-runners carrying almost 5000 weapons between them.

US President Lincoln observed a balloon flight made by Thaddeus Lowe.

Confederate Government signed treaties with several Native-American nations.

Two Confederate blockade-runners were captured by USS *South Carolina* off the Louisiana coast.

October 5: Contract between the Federal Government and John Ericson to build USS *Monitor* was signed.

Union troops left Los Angeles, CA to investigate reports of Confederate supporters operating in the Santa Ana Mountains.

October 6: Confederate strategy at this point was to close the Potomac River to river traffic, isolate Washington, DC, and cut the Baltimore and Ohio railroad.

October 7: Union General Fremont left St. Louis to fight Confederate General Price, unknowing that US President Lincoln and Secretary of War Cameron have decided to remove him from command.

Union Private Sneeden observed a prisoner exchange at Fort Monroe involving soldiers captured at the Battle of Bull Run.

> *War is surely the results of man's ambitions. How clearly it shows the folly of the human heart. Can we still hope for success? Our counter, I fear, is lost, forever is lost to me. Can we still be encouraged to fight for a much loved, but now ruined country?*
> —*Corporal James E. Hall, Confederate States Army, 31st Virginia.*

October 8: Union General Sherman was given command of the Department of the Cumberland after General Anderson retired due to ill health.

Skirmish at Hillsborough, KY.

October 9: Confederates attempted to take Fort Pickens, FL but were repulsed.

CS War Department clerk John B. Jones wrote about the contributions of clothing and provisions made by citizens, to the amount of $20,000.

October 10: CS President Davis rejected an early proposal to allow the enlistment of African-Americans into the Confederate Army. This decision would lock into place the numerical superiority of the North.

October 11: Union forces have extended their lines from Harper's Ferry, Western Virginia in order to stop any Confederate movement towards Maryland.

October 12: CSS *Manassas* and two steamers attacked Union ships in the Mississippi River Delta south of New Orleans. USS *Richmond* and USS *Vincennes* were forced aground.

Confederate commissioners Mason and Slidell departed for Cuba on board the blockade-runner *Theodora*.

US Navy launched its first river ironclad, USS *St. Louis* at Carondelet, MO.

Skirmishing at Bayles Cross Roads, LA and Upton Hill, KY.

Fighting at Clintonville, Pomme de Terre, Cameron, and Ironton, MO.

October 13: Union garrison at Harper's Ferry assaulted by Confederate cavalry under Colonel Turner Ashby with little success other than psychological. (That means the Federals got rattled.)

October 14: Former Mayor of St Louis Jeff Thompson, vowed to drive the Federals out of southeastern Missouri.

October: 15: Union gunboats scrambled on reports of a blockade-runner that was carrying Confederate commissioners to Europe. That vessel was not found.

Confederates destroyed Big River Bridge near Potosi, MO.

Skirmish at Lime Creek, MO.

October 16: Confederate General Nathan Evans moved four regiments to Leesburg, VA. His force was outnumbered but managed to convince Federal troops in the area that it was they who were outnumbered. During this day there was a skirmish at Bolivar Heights, VA.

Federal troops recaptured Lexington, MO without a shot.

Skirmish at Warsaw, MO.

October 17: Skirmishing around Fredericktown and Ironton, MO.

October 18: Union General McClellan's name was being considered to replace General Scott as General-in-Chief.

Federal gunboats began a movement down the Mississippi River from Cairo, IL.

Skirmish at Ironton, MO.

October 19: Fighting continued at Ironton.

Skirmish at Big Hurricane Creek, MO.

October 20: Confederate General Nathan Evans forces at Leesburg moved toward Ball's Bluff as Union forces attempted to cross the Potomac River there.

October 21: Battle of Ball's Bluff, VA: Union commander: General Charles Stone. Confederate commander: General Nathan Evans. An ill advised crossing of the Potomac River failed to establish a secure bridgehead and allowed a Confederate response, which resulted in the death of large numbers of Union troops, including Edward Baker, a personal friend of US President Lincoln. Confederate victory.

CS War Department clerk John B. Jones wrote about Northern newspaper reports that put the CS presence in Kentucky at 80,000 men. Truth was the number was less than 30,000.

October 22: US President Lincoln's cabinet had a meeting to discuss the Ball's Bluff debacle and the concerns about General Fremont's activities in Missouri.

October 23: Piracy trial of officers and men of CSS *Savannah* began in New York, NY. This was an attempt by the Union government to stop privateering by the Confederacy.

October 24: Union General R.S. Curtis received orders to remove General Fremont from command. General Hunter was selected to replace Fremont. Fremont, however, was still out on his mission to find Confederate General Price, so he did not know what was happening.

The Transcontinental Telegraph was completed, linking the West and East coasts (and ending the Pony Express).

October 25: USS *Monitor's* keel laid in New York.

Skirmish at Springfield, MO.

October 26: Skirmish at Romney, Western Virginia.

Skirmish at Saratoga, KY.

October 27: Union General Fremont arrived in Springfield but did not find Confederate General Price; he had already gone to Neosho.

October 28: Confederate General Albert S. Johnston assumed command of the Army of Central Kentucky.

Confederate General Price made an impassioned appeal for 50,000 to join him while five Federal divisions were searching Missouri for him.

October 29: 77 Union ships departed Fort Monroe, VA en route to attack Port Royal, SC.

October 30: The Union fleet t heading for Port Royal ran into bad weather along the North Carolina coast.

October 31: Union General Scott asked to be relieved as General-in Chief.

November 1: Union General Fremont finally received the order relieving him, but he ordered the messenger arrested!

Union Naval fleet sailing for Port Royal runs into more weather problems off Cape Hatteras, NC, losing one transport (USS *Sabine*) in the process.

Union General Winfield Scott retired from the US Army.

A British paper called *British Worker* published an article against the continuing practice of Slavery in the US. This article included a description of a slave market.

November 2: Union General Fremont finally saw the light and gave up command of the Department of Missouri.

November 4: Union fleet regrouped off Port Royal Sound.

Union General McClellan has been organizing and training the Army of the Potomac, making himself popular with the troops in the process. He ignored calls from the Lincoln Administration to do any kind of offensive action. McClellan also began criticizing the President, both publicly and privately.

Confederate General Jackson began moving his forces toward the Shenandoah Valley.

November 5: Because of inclement weather, the Port Royal assault was postponed until November 7.

November 6: Jefferson Davis was elected 1st (and only) President of the Confederate States. (Changing his status from Provisional to Permanent President).

November 7: A Union force under General Grant attacked Confederate positions near Belmont, MO. Confederate General Polk was slow to send aid at first because he thought that the main target of the attack was Columbus, KY. Reinforcements were later sent and Grant had to withdraw in the face of 13,000 men and heavy artillery fire.

> *Skirmish! Hell and damnation! I'd like to know what he calls a battle.*
> —*Confederate Major General Leonidas Polk in response to a message from Union Brigadier General Ulysses S. Grant.*

A Union fleet went up the channel between Hilton Head and St Philip's Island, SC and engaged the Confederate's Fort Beauregard. By 11 a.m. the fort was silenced. Another fort, Fort Walker, was silenced by noon. That afternoon, both islands were in Union hands, which gave the Federals a base to support the blockade of the South Carolina Coast.

November 8: Confederate commissioners Mason and Slidell left Cuba aboard the British mail steamer *Trent*. In international waters, the *Trent* was stopped by USS *San Jacinto*, boarded, and Mason and Slidell taken aboard the Union warship in violation of international treaty. This began the *Trent* Incident. (This would surely tick off the British).

November 9: Union General Henry W. Halleck is assigned command of the Department of the Missouri.

Union General Sherman was relieved of command after reporting numerous Confederate movements and stating that 200,000 troops were needed to win in the Mississippi valley. Sherman was reassigned to the Department of the Missouri amid accusations of insanity.

Union troops captured Beaufort, SC cutting off communications between Savannah, GA and Charleston.

> *Yankee invaders have succeeded in establishing themselves on our soil—Oh God help us!*
> —*Mary Chesnut, diary entry.*

Pro-Union uprising in eastern Kentucky was causing concern for Confederates there who wanted to hold the state for the CSA.

November 11: Celebrations marking the appointment of General McClellan as General-in-Chief of the Union Army included a torchlight parade through the streets of Washington, DC.

An article in the Keokuk, IA, *Daily Gate City* highlighted the work of women in the US Sanitary Commission and called for men not to limit them.

November 12: Union General McClellan reformed the Union command structure with a series of departments. The overall Department of the West was divided into the Department of New Mexico (Colonel Canby), Department of Kansas, consisting of Kansas, the Indian Territory (Oklahoma), Nebraska, Colorado, and Dakota Territory (General Hunter), and the Department of Missouri, consisting of Missouri, Iowa, Minnesota, Arkansas, and Western Kentucky (General Halleck). Other departments include the Department of the Ohio (Eastern Kentucky, Ohio, Michigan, Indiana, and Tennessee) under General Don Carlos Buell and the Department of Western Virginia under General Rosecrans. General McClellan took control of the Department of the Potomac, which included Virginia.

The blockade-runner *Fingal* arrived at Savannah, where she would be converted into an ironclad and renamed CSS *Atlanta*.

November 13: US President Lincoln visited General McClellan at his home. Not only did the general ignore the President, he went to bed!

Dr Mary Walker wrote a letter home that described conditions in her hospital, located in the US Patent Office in Washington, DC. She had 80 patients in her care.

November 14: Union General McClellan ordered General Halleck to clean up the corruption he believed was rampant in General Fremont's former command.

November 15: USS *San Jacinto* reached Hampton Roads, VA and the ship's commander, Captain John Wilkes, reported the capture of Confederate commissioners Mason and Slidell.

Young Men's Christian Association (YMCA) was organizing assistance for Union hospitals at this time.

November 16: Upon the report of the captured Confederate commissioners reaching Washington, DC, US President Lincoln was urged to release them immediately to avoid diplomatic trouble with Britain. Lincoln refused to do so.

Union Private Sneeden wrote about a theatre being built for the entertainment of Union soldiers in Alexandria, VA. He also described the daily whiskey ration. (Didn't know they actually issued rations of whiskey, did you?)

November 17: Provisional Confederate Congress gathered in Richmond.

Union General McClellan wrote a letter to his wife in which he made disparaging remarks about US President Lincoln and Secretary of State Seward.

November 18: As the Confederate Congress opened its session in Richmond, all was not united in the CSA as pro-Union groups meet in North Carolina and a secessionist government was formed in Kentucky, which meant that state had two governments.

Union Commodore David Dixon Porter was assigned the task of amassing the vessels needed for the attack on New Orleans.

I remarked that it would bring the Eagle cowering to the feet of the Lion.
— John Beauchamp Jones writing about the capture of Commissioners Mason and Slidell.

November 19: CS President Davis gave a message calling for the building of additional rail links throughout the Confederacy in order to aid the war effort.

Union General Halleck assumed command of the Department of the Missouri in St Louis, MO.

The report is that Mason & Slidell are in Fortress Monroe— taken from under the British flag. Oh that we could hear a growl from the British Lion.
—Mary Chesnut, diary entry.

November 20: Union General McClellan reviewed 60,000 troops in Washington, DC.

Union troops battled Confederate sympathizers southeast of Los Angeles, CA.

November 21: Judah Benjamin was replaced as Confederate Secretary of War by Leroy Walker.

Confederate General Lloyd Tlighman was given command of Forts Henry and Donelson in Tennessee.

CSS *Nashville* arrived at Southampton, UK, the first visit of a Confederate warship to a foreign port.

November 22: Union held Fort Pickens, outside Pensacola, FL exchanged fire with Confederate batteries in the area.

November 23: A second day of artillery fire at Fort Pickens convinced the Confederates that they could not take the fort. This fort remained in Union hands for the remainder of the war.

November 24: Union forces took Tybee Island near Savannah.

Confederate commissioners Mason and Slidell were taken to Boston, MA and imprisoned.

November 25: First load of armor needed to transform CSS *Virginia* into an ironclad vessel reached Norfolk Navy Yard.

November 26: Pro-Union delegates at Wheeling, Western Virginia called for the formation of the State of West Virginia.

At Savannah, Confederates at Fort Pulaski exchanged fire with Federal warships with no effect.

Another Union merchant ship fell to CSS *Sumter* in the Atlantic.

November 27: British steamer *Trent* arrived in England and reports about her boarding by USS *San Jacinto* were sent to London.

Preparations were made for the assault on New Orleans with plans made to fortify Ship Island, off Gulfport, MS, as a first step.

Union Secretary of War Simon Cameron received a letter from William Jones of Oberlin, OH expressing the desire of many African-Americans to serve in the Union Army and Navy.

> *My inclination is to whip the rebellion into submission, preserving all Constitutional rights. If it cannot be whipped any other way than through a war against slavery, let it come to that legitimately. If it is necessary that slavery should fall that the Republic may continue its existence, let slavery go.*
> — *Ulysses S. Grant, letter to his father*

November 28: Union troops at Port Royal seized slaves and foodstuffs in accordance with the Confiscation Act.

November 30: The British Government was in an extreme uproar about the boarding of the vessel *Trent*. Lord Russell, the Foreign Secretary labeled it an "act of aggression" and prepared to recall Lord Richard Lyons, UK Minister (Ambassador) to the US.

A Quaker group published an article stating their opposition to war for any reason, even emancipation (not exactly a new thing).

John Sullivan Dwight, a Boston, MA music critic, wrote an article that called for people to go on with cultural pursuits as if no war is going on.

December 1: British government sent a message demanding the release of Confederate commissioners Mason and Slidell and an apology for the boarding of the *Trent*, or the UK would declare war on the US. The Lincoln Administration had 10 days to respond (about the time it took a message to cross the Atlantic).

US President Lincoln, growing frustrated with General McClellan's inaction, sent a letter demanding to know when he could expect the army moving.

US Cabinet was split over the *Trent* incident. Secretary of State Seward proposed the notion that a war with Britain could reunite the country. US President Lincoln's response was, *"one war at a time."*

December 2: Union Secretary of the Navy Welles reported that the blockade so far had resulted in the capture of 153 blockade-runners.

US President Lincoln authorized General Halleck to suspend the writ of *habeas corpus* in Missouri.

CSS *Patrick Henry* was damaged by Federal gunboats off Newport News. This vessel would go on to serve as the Confederate States Naval Academy.

December 3: US President Lincoln gave a State of the Union Address to the 37th Congress.

USS *Constitution* carried the 26th Massachusetts and the 9th Connecticut to Ship Island. The presence of the Massachusetts troops would lead to the fort being named Fort Massachusetts.

December 4: UK announced a trade embargo against the US in retaliation for the *Trent* incident.

Union General Halleck approved the death penalty for those caught aiding Confederates.

December 5: Confederate General William Hardee assumed command of the Central Army of Kentucky.

December 6: US Secretary of the Treasury Salmon Chase announced that there was sufficient revenue to fund the war, provided that the war ended by mid-1862.

December 7: USS *Santiago de Cuba* stopped the British vessel *Eugenia Smith* at the mouth of the Rio Grande River, Texas/Mexico border, Confederate agent J.W. Zacherie was removed and placed into Union custody.

December 8: Sam Watkins wrote about the 1st Tennessee deploying to Winchester, VA to join Confederate General Jackson's forces.

> *The first night we arrived at this place, the wind blew a perfect hurricane, and every tent and marquee in Lee's and Jackson's army was blown down. This is the first sight we had of Stonewall Jackson, riding upon his old sorrel horse, his feet drawn up as if his stirrups were much too short for him, and his old dingy military cap hanging well forward his head, and his nose erected in the air, his old rusty sabre rattling by his side.*
> *—Sam Watkins, Private, 1st Tennessee, CS Army*

December 9: US Congressional Joint Committee on the Conduct of the War was created to look into the actions of Union army leaders.

Pro-Union Native-Americans clashed with pro-Confederate Native-Americans at Chusto-Talasah, Indian Territory (Oklahoma).

December 10: Union forces took control of an abandoned Confederate fort on the Ashepoo River in South Carolina.

December 11: Fire swept through the business district of Charleston, which worsened supply shortages already caused by the blockade.

December 12: Southern coastal planters were burning cotton crops rather than see them taken by Union troops.

December 13: Union and Confederate forces engaged at Buffalo Mountain, Western Virginia, with no clear outcome.

December 14: Prince Albert of Great Britain died as he was urging calm during the furor over the *Trent* Affair.

The *Illustrated London News* publishes an article called "Our Controversy with America" referring to the *Trent* Affair.

December 15: US Congress began to take up the issue of slavery, which would result in new proposals and laws.

Union General John Pope was attempting to prevent Confederate General Price's forces from moving into Kansas.

December 16: Confederate General Jackson began his Shenandoah Valley Campaign by leaving Winchester and marching north.

Union General Pope's troops disrupted a Confederate recruit camp on the Osage River in Missouri.

December 17: Confederate troops under General Jackson destroyed Dam No.5 on the Baltimore and Ohio canal, which rendered the canal useless.

Skirmishes at Rockville and Hilton Head, SC.

Another Confederate recruit camp was taken by Federals at Milford, MO.

December 18: Josiah Patterson, a soldier in a Georgia regiment, wrote a letter that expressed his anguish about spending Christmas away from home.

December 19: US Secretary of State Seward received the official protest message from the UK Government concerning the *Trent*. Although Seward was an Anglophobe (he hated Brits), he seemed receptive to the UK's position. US President Lincoln wanted the situation to blow over and Ambassador Charles Francis Adams was busy smoothing ruffled feathers in London.

December 20: 8000 British troops and two warships arrived in Canada to reinforce the garrison there in the event of a war with the US (Surprisingly, things ended up getting so calm between the two countries that some British troops were allowed to transit through Maine en route to Canada).

Two hulks were sunk in Charleston Harbor in order to assist the fledgling blockade.

December 21: Confederate General Jackson's troops returned to Winchester and went into winter quarters.

US Secretary of State Seward met with Lord Lyons to discuss the British demands.

December 22: Union General Halleck issues General Orders No. 32, promising swift retribution for any Confederate attacks in Missouri.

December 23: The Lincoln Administration received advice from Massachusetts Senator Charles Sumner to yield to the British demands in order to avoid another war, or worse, that the UK would enter the current war on the side of the CSA. Even though the seizing of the *Trent* might have been lawful, how it was handled afterwards was not.

December 24: US Congress passed a tax on sugar, molasses, tea, and coffee to help pay for the war.

December 25: US President Lincoln and the cabinet discussed the *Trent* situation with a deadline for an answer to the British demands due the next day.

Have had snow for past eight hours. It laid six to eight inches deep on everything. Many tents had to be taken down and repitched. Could not have dress parade or drill today. All were eating and drinking all they could get. Rations of whiskey were served to the brigade and the 40th guardhouse was full of drunken soldiers before sundown. Many officers got leave yesterday to go to Washington for forty-eight hours. General Sedgwick never leaves camp and insists in brigade drill every fine afternoon...

—*Robert Knox Sneeden, diary entry.*

December 26: US President Lincoln and the Cabinet decided to release Confederate commissioners Mason and Slidell, effectively ending the *Trent* affair.

Union General Halleck declared martial law in St Louis. This order was applied to all railroads in Missouri.

December 27: Skirmishing at Hallsville and Mount Zion, MO.

December 30: Confederate commissioners Mason and Slidell were handed over to UK Ambassador Lord Lyons, who got them on the first British vessel headed for London. Despite lingering differences of opinion, relations between the US and the UK began to return to normal.

December 31: US President Lincoln learned that two of his commanders, Generals Don Carlos Buell and Henry Halleck, might not cooperate with him. At the same time, General McClellan had fallen ill.

1862

January 1: Federal artillery on Fort Pickens shelled Pensacola. FL.

> *Seward has cowered beneath the roar of the British Lion, and surrendered Mason and Slidell, who have been permitted to go on their errand to England. Now we must depend upon our own strong arms and stout hearts for defense.*
> —*John Beauchamp Jones, diary entry.*

January 3: CS President Davis realized how dangerous the Union occupation of Ship Island had become; with New Orleans 65 miles away and Mobile 50 miles away, both cities are within striking range of any Federal force stationed on the island.

Confederate General Jackson's brigade began moving toward Romney, VA in order to cut the Baltimore and Ohio railroad.

January 4: Confederate General Jackson captured the town of Bath, VA while other engagements took place at Great Cacapon Bridge, VA and Hancock, MD.

January 5: Authorities in Hancock refused to surrender to Confederate General Jackson, so he ordered the town shelled.

January 6: Union reinforcements reached Hancock, which forced General Jackson to pull back his army.

US President Lincoln resisted demands that Union General McClellan be replaced. At the same time he was urging General Buell to move into Tennessee.

January 7: Confederate General Jackson withdrew into Virginia after a skirmish at Hanging Rock Pass, MD.

Federal gunboats *Essex, Lexington,* and *Tyler* headed down the Mississippi River toward Columbus, KY.

January 9: Union General Grant began operations against Columbus, KY.

CS War Department clerk John B. Jones began chronicling the cost of living in Richmond. He wrote about butter being .50 cents a pound, bacon at .25 cents a pound, beef at .30 cents a pound, and wood at $8 a cord in Richmond.

January 10: Confederate General Jackson's forces approached Romney, VA, causing Union troops there to pullout.

At Middle Creek, KY there was an engagement between Union troops under Colonel James Garfield and Confederates under Colonel Humphrey Marshall. Both sides claimed victory but both were also in retreat. (Colonel Garfield would one day become President Garfield.)

There were inconsistent procedures for handling escaped slaves who made it to Union encampments. Some were pressed into service with the army as teamsters, cooks, and laborers. Some were allowed to pass to the North. Others were held and turned over to locals and Confederate officers who claimed them as property in accordance with the Fugitive Slave Act. One of those units who disregarded the Fugitive Slave Act was the 14th New York who was harboring a runaway named John Boston.

January 11: US Secretary of War Simon Cameron resigned amid charges of corruption.

Union Naval force of over 100 ships and 15,000 men under General Ambrose Burnside left Hampton Roads and headed south to reinforce Port Royal, SC.

Union General John McClernand began a probe toward Columbus, KY.

Union Private Sneeden wrote about starting a new job as a mapmaker.

Despite the fact that mapmakers were officers, his talent for drawing had caught the attention of Union General Samuel Heintzelman and he was assigned to the general's staff.

January 12: In the nine months since the war began, the US Navy had grown from 76 vessels to 264.

January 13: Roanoke Island assault fleet was stalled off Hatteras Inlet due to storms. This will last until Jan 20.

Union Naval Lieutenant John Worden assumed command of USS *Monitor*, under construction in New York.

Edwin Stanton was named the new US Secretary of War.

January 14: Union General McClernand concentrated his troops at Blandville, KY.

January 15: Union General Grant concentrated his forces at Milburn, KY. Confederates were now wondering if the axis of attack was Columbus, or if the attack was going somewhere else.

January 16: Five Confederate regiments and 12 cannon were posted at Mill Springs, KY to watch for any Union attacks through the Cumberland Gap.

I pray God that I be one of the men who will pull the rope to hang Jeff Davis and that the Spirits of Washington, Jefferson, and Jackson, and Adams may look over the Batalments of Heaven down upon the Bleeding Carcuss as the flesh Drops from the Bones and Listen to the Winds Whistleing Hail Columbia and Yankee doodle through the Decaying ribs which once enclosed his corrupt and Traititous heart— for causing this war and Still Caring on this Wicked and Cruell War and Keeping W. E. Limbarker from his Dear Wife and Daughter
—*Private William Limbarker, Union Army*
(He was not happy to be in the war.)

January 17: Union General George Thomas stopped at Somerset, KY, near Mill Springs in order to gather his strung out forces.

January 18: Confederate General Jackson ordered the Stonewall brigade into winter quarters.

USS *Kearsarge* departed Cadiz, Spain to search for Confederate Captain Raphael Semmes and CSS *Sumter.*

CSA Territory of Arizona was created.

Former US President and Confederate Congressman John Tyler died at Richmond.

General George Crittenden took command of Confederate forces in the Cumberland Gap and planned to take the battle to Union General Thomas.

January 19: Battle of Mill Springs (Logan's Cross Roads), KY: Union commander: General George H. Thomas. Confederate commander: General Felix Zollicoffer. Fighting started at dawn as the 15th Mississippi encountered two companies from the 10th Indiana. At first, Confederate assaults pushed back the Union troops, who were running out of ammunition. During one such attack Zollicoffer was killed. At one point troops from both sides were firing at each other over a single fence. In the afternoon, Thomas got in some artillery and proceeded to pummel the Southern line. A flanking movement followed by a bayonet charge finally routed the Confederates, who reformed at Beech Grove, 10 miles away.

January 20: A planned Union assault on the regrouped Confederates at Beech Grove was called off when it was discovered that the Southern lines had been deserted. Battle of Mill Springs ended in a Union victory.

US Navy sunk vessels filled with stones in order to bottle up the harbor at Charleston.

CS War Department clerk John B. Jones wrote that there was an order from the CS Treasury Department that the interest on some government bonds was to be paid in specie (coin).

January 21: Union General Grant pulled his forces back to Cairo, IL in order to execute the real mission, an attack on Forts Henry and Donelson in Tennessee.

January 22: Confederate General Wise was given command of forces at Roanoke Island, NC in order to counter the growing Union presence at nearby Port Royal.

January 23: More ships were filled with stones and sunk at Charleston.

January 24: Union General Halleck ordered the arrest of any who opposed his enforcement of martial law in St Louis.

January 25: Union General Burnside's forces reached Pamlico Sound and began maneuvering toward Roanoke Island.

January 26: Union naval force off Cape Hatteras entered Pamlico Sound. This action created another jumping off point for Union attacks on the North Carolina coast.

January 27: Confederate commander at Roanoke Island, General Wise, was ordered to hold the island at all costs.

US President Lincoln issued General War Order 1, ordering an offensive on all fronts on February 22.

January 30: USS *Monitor* was launched in New York.

Confederate Commissioners Mason and Slidell arrived in London, UK.

February 1: Confederate General Albert S. Johnston found out that he could expect no more reinforcements for his army in Tennessee. Meanwhile General Beauregard arrived from Virginia.

Union Private Sneeden observed a discussion in which it was suggested that live shells could be dropped on Confederate formations from a balloon. It was rejected because it was not in line with the rules of war.

February 2: Confederate General Albert S. Johnston received word of Union activity in Tennessee but believed that they were not ready to attack him.

February 3: The US Federal government declared captured Confederate privateers to be prisoners of war.

The Forts Henry and Donelson campaign began as four gunboats and troop carriers with 23 regiments under the command of Union General Grant left Cairo.

US President Lincoln urged General McClellan to launch an offensive on Richmond, McClellan instead proposed moving the Army of the Potomac to the James River Peninsula and attack Richmond from that direction.

USS *Tuscarora* attempted to intercept CSS *Nashville* off Southampton, UK but was stopped by HMS *Shannon*.

February 4: Union General Grant's forces are landed south of Fort Henry.

February 5: Union General Grant halted his forces at Bailey's Ferry, TN so that all of his army could be present when nearby Fort Henry was assaulted. Grant ordered Commodore Andrew Foote to begin shelling the fort the next morning. Confederate General Tlighman ordered all of his forces within the walls of the fort.

Federal fleet left Pamlico Sound, NC.

February 6: Federal gunboats *Essex, Carondelet, Cincinnati, St Louis, Conestoga, Tyler,* and *Lexington* approached Fort Henry, causing Confederate General Tlighman to order his garrison to evacuate to Fort Donelson, with the exception of the artillery. At noon, the Federal vessels opened fire, starting an engagement that dismounted 13 of the fort's 17 guns. Despite damaging the *Essex*, Tlighman was forced to surrender, which allowed General Grant to take the fort without an infantry assault. Commodore Foote ordered his flotilla back to Cairo.

February 7: Confederate reinforcements were rushed to Fort Donelson as Union General Grant began moving his forces towards the fort. At the same time Fort Henry was renamed Fort Foote.

Union assault on Roanoke Island began with the signal, *"This day our country expects every man to do his duty."*

February 8: Union forces under General Burnside succeed in capturing Roanoke Island, ensuring Union control over most of the NC coast.

February 9: Confederate General Gideon J. Pillow assumed command of Fort Donelson.

Federal warships begin crossing Albemarle Sound, NC in order to search for Confederate vessels.

February 10: USS *Delaware* engaged a Confederate flotilla, known as the "Mosquito Fleet" off Roanoke Island, sinking one, capturing another, and forcing the Confederates to burn the remaining three.

Six Confederate steamships were burned on the Tennessee River in order to prevent them from falling into Union hands while three others were captured.

February 11: Confederate General Simon Bolivar Buckner arrived at Fort Donelson with more troops.

Union Commodore Foote's flotilla sailed from Cairo in support of Union General Grant's operations against Fort Donelson. Union General McClernand marched his troops overland to the Confederate fort.

February 12: Union General Grant's forces reached Fort Donelson and proceed to surround the fort.

February 13: Confederate General Floyd arrived at Fort Donelson and assumed command as Union General Grant's first attack was driven back. Grant then proceeded to bombard the fort. That night, a snowstorm made life rough for the defenders.

CSS *Virginia*, the ironclad warship built on the hull of the USS *Merrimack*, was launched.

February 14: Additional Union reinforcements arrived, which allowed General Grant to begin his assault on Fort Donelson in earnest. Gunboats began shelling the fort at 3:00 p.m. but after *St Louis* and *Louisville* were damaged, Grant decided to wait until more reinforcements arrived before renewing the attack. Confederate General Gideon Pillow had planed to attack the Federal right flank, break out of the fort, and then go south.

February 15: Confederate General Pillow attempted to break through the Union lines but failed. That night he and General Floyd, a former US Secretary of War, fled the fort. General Nathan B. Forrest also departed the fort with his cavalry. General Buckner was left in command.

February 16: Fort Donelson surrendered to Union General Grant, who wrote to Confederate General Buckner, a West Point classmate, in response to the question about terms of surrender.

Yours of this date proposing an armistice and appointment of commissioners to settle the terms of capitulation is just received. No terms other than an unconditional and immediate surrender can be accepted. I propose to move immediately upon your works.
—Union Major General Ulysses S. Grant answering Confederate General Simon Buckner.

While the exchange of letters was going on, Union Flag Officer Foote's gunboats were busy destroying the Tennessee Iron Works.

February 17: Provisional Congress of the CSA met for the last time.

Sam Watkins' 1st Tennessee was transferred to the Confederate Army of Tennessee.

> *Virginia, farewell! Away back yonder, in good old Tennessee, our homes and loved ones are being robbed and insulted, our fields laid waste, our cities sacked, our people slain.*
> --*Sam Watkins, Private, 1ˢᵗ Tennessee, CS Army*

February 18: First elected Confederate Congress met in Richmond.

News of the Union victory at Forts Henry and Donelson reached Washington, DC and Union General Grant was being referred to in the press as "Unconditional Surrender" Grant.

February 19: Confederate forces evacuated Clarksville, TN as a result of the Confederate losses of Forts Henry and Donelson.

February 20: Tennessee state government was moved from Nashville to Memphis.

Columbus, KY was evacuated as Confederates attempted to form a defensive line to counter any Federal moves toward the Tennessee capital.

Union Admiral David Farragut arrived at Ship Island, MS, the staging area for the assault on New Orleans.

US President Lincoln's son William died of typhoid fever.

CS War Department clerk John B. Jones wrote a large entry covering Feb 8-20. He mentioned the death of former US President John Tyler, the fall of Fort Henry and the assault on Fort Donelson.

February 21: Tons of Confederate supplies in Nashville were destroyed.

Battle of Val Verde, NM: Union commander: Colonel Edward Canby. Confederate commander: General Henry Sibley. A Confederate incursion into the New Mexico Territory reached Fort Craig, on the Rio Grande River. Canby hoped to make the Confederates besiege the post and let their lack of supplies drive them off. Sibley instead orders his troops to seize the Val Verde fords up river. A detachment of Union troops held the Confederate (mainly Texas) troops in a ravine, but reinforcements under the command of Confederate Colonel Tom Green arrived and drove the Federals off, which allowed the fords to be taken. Confederate victory.

February 22: Union gunboats isolate Fort Pulaski, GA.

Jefferson Davis was inaugurated as President of the permanent Confederate Government.

Union Private Sneeden wrote about going to Washington, DC on errands and while there observed officers at the various hotel bars around the city. He attended a play and had an oyster supper afterwards.

The feature in this day's *Richmond Enquirer* included CS President Davis' Inaugural Address. In the lower right corner of the front page, the evacuation of Nashville was mentioned.

February 23: Confederate troops in Missouri continued their retreat into Arkansas.

CS War Department clerk John B. Jones wrote about the mood in Richmond upon hearing the news that Fort Donelson had fallen.

February 24: Union troops under General Buell reached the Cumberland River opposite Nashville.

Union troops under General Banks occupied Harpers Ferry.

Skirmishing at Pohick Creek and Mason's Neck, VA.

February 25: Nashville, TN fell to Union troops.

Union troops were moving into Arkansas in pursuit of Confederate General Price's army.

February 26: Skirmish at Keytesville, MO.

February 27: CS Congress gave President Davis the right to suspend the writ of habeas corpus if necessary. Davis asked to impose martial law at Norfolk and Portsmouth.

USS *Monitor* departed New York.

February 28: A Day of Fasting was held throughout the Confederacy.

March 1: Union General Grant began moving his troops from Fort Donelson to Pittsburg Landing, on the Tennessee River, where Union gunboats have destroyed a Confederate battery.

Union Private Robert Sneeden wrote about working on maps for the Peninsular Campaign.

Harper's Weekly featured a woodcut picture called *"The Surrender of Fort Donelson, February 18, 1862."*

March 2: Confederate General Leonidas Polk completed his evacuation of Columbus which left all of Kentucky in Union hands.

Confederate General Earl Van Dorn assumed command of CS forces along the Mississippi River upon reaching the Confederate encampment in the Boston Mountains, AR.

March 3: Skirmish at New Madrid, MO

March 4: Union General John Pope led an assault on New Madrid and Island No. 10 on the Mississippi River.

Union Flag Officer Andrew Foote arrived in Columbus, KY to find that Confederate forces had already left.

Union General Halleck relieved General Grant for allegedly being drunk on duty.

Andrew Johnson was appointed military governor of Tennessee.

Confederate General Lee was recalled from South Carolina to Richmond.

Confederate General Van Dorn began his operation against Union forces in northern Arkansas.

March 5: Union General Banks moved against Confederate General Jackson at Winchester, VA (1st Shenandoah Valley Campaign begins).

Union General William Sooey Smith's troops were concentrated at Savannah, TN.

Confederate General Beauregard was given command of Confederate troops in the Mississippi River Valley.

Union General Sigel avoided getting surrounded by Confederate General Van Dorn's troops by pulling back to Sugar Creek, AR.

March 6: Union General Samuel Curtis concentrated his forces to face Confederate General Van Dorn near Pea Ridge, AR. Meanwhile, Van Dorn's soldiers launched an attack on Union lines at Sugar Creek.

CS Congress approved a scorched earth policy for Confederate forces in Virginia.

US President Lincoln advocated funding to help states that were considering emancipation laws.

March 7: Battle of Pea Ridge (Elkhorn Tavern), AR: Union commander: General Samuel Curtis. Confederate commander: General Earl Van Dorn. Day One: Confederate forces attacked on a two-pronged front, which threatened any possible Union retreat route, but Federal forces managed to turn the right wing attack back. Confederates lost two generals (McCulloch and McIntosh) in the process. Fighting ended at sundown.

USS *Monitor* encountered storms while enroute to VA.

There was a skirmish between Union General Banks and Confederate General Jackson at Winchester.

March 8: CSS *Virginia* sailed into Hampton Roads, sinks USS *Cumberland* and USS *Congress*, and forces USS *Minnesota* aground. The vessel was withdrawn up the James River after the *Virginia's* commander, Commander Franklin Buchanan, was wounded. USS *Monitor* arrived about 1a.m.

Union General McClellan received approval to launch a campaign against Richmond from the coast by way of the York Peninsula.

Battle of Pea Ridge: Day Two. Union forces opened the second day with an artillery bombardment of Confederate lines followed by an infantry assault. This attack forced the Confederates to retreat from the area. Union victory.

Union Private Sneeden wrote about visiting Mount Vernon, George Washington's home, and finding the place a little run down.

March 9: Battle of Hampton Roads, VA: First battle between ironclad ships began after dawn as CSS *Virginia* reentered Hampton Roads intending to finish off USS *Minnesota*. Union commander: Naval Lieutenant John Worden aboard USS *Monitor*. Confederate commander: Lieutenant Catsby ap R Jones aboard CSS *Virginia*. During the battle both ships sustained damage and the *Monitor's* commander was wounded. Both ships pulled back, each crew believed they had defeated the other. (Officially a draw).

Union troops advanced toward suspected Confederate positions in northern Virginia, but failed to find any enemy troops to engage.

March 10: Skirmish at Burke's Station, VA.

Skirmish at Jacksbobough, TN.

March 11: US President Lincoln relieved Union General McClellan as commander-in-chief of the Union Armies, but left him in command of the Army of the Potomac.

Confederate General Jackson's forces withdrew to the south of Winchester.

Confederate Generals Floyd and Pillow were sacked for their actions at Fort Donelson.

March 12: Skirmish at Lexington, MO.

March 13: Confederate troops evacuated New Madrid and moved to Island #10, up the Mississippi River.

Union General Burnside moved his troops from Roanoke Island to the North Carolina mainland.

Union General McClellan received a reminder from US President Lincoln that any plans for an offensive from the tip of the York Peninsula to Richmond must take into account the defense of Washington, DC.

Union troops under General Pope seized Point Pleasant, MO.

March 14: Union forces captured New Berne, NC, defeating a larger Confederate army.

March 15: Union Generals Sherman and Stephen Hurlbut reach Pittsburg Landing. Union General Don Carlos Buell was also ordered to Pittsburg Landing with his Army of the Ohio. Meanwhile, Union General C. F. Smith injured his leg and as a result Grant was restored to command of the Union armies massing there.

March 16: Skirmish at Black Jack's Forest, TN.

CS War Department clerk John B. Jones wrote about the exploits of CSS *Virginia*.

Martial Law declared in San Francisco, CA in response to suspected Confederate activity.

March 17: The Union Army of the Potomac began boarding their transports for the trip to the York Peninsula. This was the start of the Peninsular Campaign.

March 18: Judah Benjamin was named Confederate Secretary of State while George W. Randolph was named Confederate Secretary of War.

Confederate troops under General Albert Johnston arrived in Corinth, MS.

March 19: The Confederate strategy in Tennessee was to prevent Union forces from opening avenues of invasion into the heart of the Confederacy. General Beauregard's army would join General Albert Johnston's at Corinth to attack a reported Union force under General Grant at Pittsburg Landing.

March 20: Union General Butler assumed command of Army units assigned to the assault on New Orleans.

Confederate General Jackson moved his troops toward Winchester in pursuit of fleeing Federal troops.

March 21: Skirmish at Mosquito Inlet, FL.

March 22: Confederate General Jackson's troops met Union forces near Winchester.

Forney's War Press featured a woodcut picture of the engagement between USS *Monitor* and CSS *Virginia*.

March 23: Battle of Kernstown (First Winchester), VA: Union commander: General John Shields. Confederate commander: General Thomas Jackson. Confederates were repulsed by superior forces, but the action resulted in commanders in Washington, DC redeploying troops from General McClellan's army to support operations in the Shenandoah Valley. Union victory.

Union General Burnside's troops head toward Fort Macon, near Beaufort, NC.

Union forces under General Sherman encamped at Pittsburg Landing while General Grant established headquarters at Savannah, eight miles away. No one was aware to the growing Confederate force only a day's march away at Corinth.

March 24: Confederate General Jackson's troops marched to Mt. Jackson, VA.

Wendell Phillips, an abolitionist speaker, was attacked at a rally at Cincinnati, OH and a riot broke out.

Union troops besieged Fort Macon when a surrender demand was refused.

March 25: Union troops pursuing Confederate General Jackson's forces stopped at Woodstock, VA.

March 26: Skirmishes at Hammondsville and Warrensburg, MO.

March 27: Union forces at Apache Canyon fell back to Glorieta Pass, New Mexico Territory.

March 28: Battle of Glorieta Pass, NM: Union commander: Colonel John Slough. Confederate commander: Colonel W. R. Scurry. Confederate General Sibley continued his attempt to seize New Mexico for the Confederacy. Southeast of Santa Fe, they run into Scurry's Colorado troops. While the Confederates were busy, a Union force of 400, under command of Major J. M. Chivington moved west and managed to destroy the Confederate supply wagons. Sibley was forced to withdraw his entire force back into Texas, ending any dreams of Confederate westward expansion. Union victory.

Union troops captured Shipping Point, VA.

March 29: Skirmish at Middleburg, VA. First recorded use of a machine gun in battle.

Confederate General Albert Sidney Johnston assumed command of the army that was being assembled at Corinth.

March 30: Confederate General Jackson's troops pulled back to Harrisonville, VA.

March 31: Union troops were concentrated at Pittsburg Landing.

April 1: Union General McClellan's headquarters was established at Fort Monroe.

> *One wharf was piled with gunpowder in kegs and grape and canister. I saw a soldier rolling some of the kegs and smoking his pipe at the same time. I got off that wharf as soon as I could...*
> *— Private Robert Knox Sneeden, diary entry.*

April 2: US Senate considered President Lincoln's plan to provide Federal funding support to states that freed their slaves.

Confederate General Albert S. Johnston began moving troops from Corinth toward Pittsburg Landing.

Skirmish at Doniphan, MO.

April 3: US Senate voted to abolish slavery in the District of Columbia.

Union Private Sneeden wrote about preparing "skeleton maps" to be used by officers as the Army of the Potomac begins marching from Fort Monroe.

> *I have put you in motion to offer battle to the invaders of your country. With the resolution and disciplined valor becoming men fighting, as you are, for all worth living or dying for, you can but march to a decisive victory over agrarian mercenaries, sent to subjugate and despoil you of your liberties, property, and honor. Remember the precious stake involved. Remember the dependence of your mothers, your wives, your sisters, and our children on the result. Remember the fair, broad, abounding land, the happy homes, and ties that will be destroyed by your defeat. The eyes and hopes of 8,000,000 of people rest upon you. You are expected to show yourself worthy of your valor and lineage: worthy of the women of the South, whose noble devotion in this war has never been exceeded in any time. With such incentives to brave deeds and with the trust that God is with us your generals will lead you confidently to the combat, assured of success.*
> —*Confederate General Albert S. Johnston in a proclamation to the Army of Mississippi.*

April 4: Union troops were landed at the mouth of the Mississippi River.

A canal, bypassing Confederate guns at Island No. 10, was completed.

Union General McClellan began moving his troops toward Yorktown, VA. The Peninsular Campaign has begun.

CS War Department clerk John B. Jones wrote about hearing news of the shelling at Yorktown.

April 5: At Yorktown, Confederate General John Magruder held back Union General McClellan's army, despite the Federals having a 5 to 1 superiority.

There was skirmishing at the edge of Union lines at Pittsburg Landing. Union commanders did not believe reports of a massed Confederate advance.

The Military Governor of Tennessee, Andrew Johnson, suspended Nashville's city government for not taking the oath to the Union.

April 6: Battle of Shiloh (Pittsburg Landing), TN: Union commander: General Ulysses S. Grant. Confederate commander: General Albert S. Johnston. Day One. In the early morning hours, the Confederates launched a surprise attack on Union encampments. The Federals were pushed back until Generals Stephen Hurlbut and W.H.L. Wallace organized a defense in a line of trees that afterwards was named The Hornets Nest. Assisted by General Benjamin Prentiss, the Union army was given time to form up a stronger defensive line and to get General Don Carlos Buell's army from the landing. While rallying his troops, Johnston was wounded and bled to death. Command was passed to General Beauregard, but everything was disorganized and the attack stopped, but not before the Hornet's Nest was captured and W.H.L. Wallace was wounded.

I had heard and read of battlefields, seen pictures of battlefields, of horses and men, of cannons and wagons, all jumbled together, but I must confess that I never realized the "pomp and circumstance" of the thing called glorious war until I saw this. Men were lying with their eyes wide open, the wounded begging piteously for help, and some waving their hats and shouting to us to go forward. It all seemed to me a dream: I seemed to be in a sort of haze, when siz, siz, siz, the Minnie balls from the Yankee line began to whistle around our ears, and I thought of the Irishman when he said, "Sure enough, those fellows are shooting bullets!"
—Sam Watkins, Private, 1ˢᵗ Tennessee, who was at Shiloh.

Gen. Sidney Johnston having fallen in battle, the Command in the West devolved on Gen. Beauregard, whose recent defense at Island No. 10 on the Mississippi, has revived his popularity. But, I repeat, he is a doomed man.
—John Beauchamp Jones, diary entry.

April 7: Battle of Shiloh: Day Two: General Grant, supported by Generals Buell and Lew Wallace launched a counterattack and regained all the ground lost on April 6. General Beauregard ordered his army to retreat back to Corinth, MS. Battle of Shiloh ends with a Union victory, but at a cost of 24,000 killed, wounded and missing on both sides.

Federal gunboats ran past Island No. 10 and landed troops to its south.

Union Private Sneeden wrote about the Union forces approaching Yorktown, but not receiving an order to attack. There are, according to Sneeden, 53,000 men with 42,000 ready for battle, and 13,000 Confederates opposing them.

> *But by McClellan's orders, no general is permitted to bring on a battle until all out forces are up. One corps alone could take the place in an hour. Disgust at the inactivity is very manifest among most officers of all grades...*
> —*Robert Knox Sneeden, diary entry.*

April 8: Union forces made an assault on Island No. 10, capturing the position and forcing the Mississippi River open as far south as Memphis.

April 9: Skirmish at Owen's River, CA (yes, the war got that far west).

April 10: Union forces under Colonel Quincy Adams Gilmore attacked Fort Pulaski, near Savannah. The fort was taken after 30 hours.

US Congress passed a joint resolution that called for the end of Slavery.

Union General W.H.L. Wallace died of wounds suffered at the Battle of Shiloh.

April 11: Union General Halleck arrived at Pittsburg Landing and assumed command of Union forces in the area, supplanting General Grant.

At Newport News, CSS *Virginia* and USS *Monitor* are near each other but no shot is fired.

US House of Representatives passed a resolution to abolish slavery in the District of Columbia.

April 12: Confederate Captain Semmes ordered CSS *Sumter* abandoned at Gibraltar due to boiler problems that could not be fixed.

In what became known as the Great Locomotive Chase, Union operatives under James Andrews stole a Confederate train, the *General*, at Big Shanty (Kennesaw), GA. The *General's* crew gave chase until they were able to commandeer another train, the *Texas*. The chase continued until the *General* ran out of fuel. The operatives were eventually captured. Andrews and seven others were hung as spies. The others were paroled after a time in prison.

Union Private Sneeden wrote about an observation balloon getting loose with General Fitz-John Porter in it. General Porter rose to 2000 feet and momentarily came under Confederate rifle fire. He managed to open the gas valve but could not close it again. Finally he crashed into a tree but was not injured. It was found that a sergeant with the 50th New York Engineers smeared the ropes with acid to get back at a captain who chewed him out the day before (Fragging officers was not unique to the 20th Century).

CS War Department clerk John B. Jones wrote about a government commission investigating the Confederate loss of Roanoke Island and the blame seems to be fixed to "Gen. Huger and Judah P. Benjamin."

April 13: Union troops began to force Confederates to leave New Mexico Territory.

Union Private Sneeden wrote about going up in a balloon and observing Confederate positions.

April 14: Minor skirmish near Pollocksville, NC.

Skirmishes reported near Montavallo, Diamond Grove, and Walkersville, MO.

CS War Department clerk John B. Jones wrote about the coming fight on the Peninsula.

April 15: Union 1ˢᵗ California Cavalry engaged Confederates near Pechacho Pass, Arizona Territory.

April 16: US President Lincoln signed the bill that outlawed slavery in the District of Columbia into law.

CS President Davis approved a law making all white males between the ages of 18 and 35 liable for a military draft.

Skirmish at Lee's Mills, VA.

Skirmish at White Marsh, GA.

Skirmish at Savannah, TN.

> *So now I am minus a leg! But never mind, dear parents, I suffer but little pain, and will be home in a few weeks, I think.*
> —*Private Julian Scott, 9ᵗʰ New York, in a letter to his parents.*

April 17: Skirmish at Holly River, VA.

April 18: Union naval forces began their bombardment of Forts Jackson and St Philip, on the Mississippi river southeast of New Orleans.

Falmouth, VA was taken by Federal cavalry.

April 19: The Union naval assault on Forts Jackson and St Philip continued.

Proof that not all Northerners were for freeing the slaves. A newspaper called the *New York Caucasian* had this headline: *FREE NEGROISM: or the Results of Emancipation in the North and the West India Islands with Statistics of the Decay of Commerce, Idleness of the Negro, His Return to Savagism, &c.*

April 20: Union sailors attempted to breach an obstacle across the Mississippi River below Forts Jackson and St Philip.

Union Private Sneeden wrote that on this Easter, no Easter eggs but plenty of broken shells from enemy guns.

April 21: Despite 4000 shells hitting Forts Jackson and St Philip, the commander of the Federal ground assault on New Orleans, General Butler, felt that his troops would be needed to take those forts.

April 22: Union Flag Officer David Farragut decided to run his ships past Forts Jackson and St Philip upon learning that the obstacles across the Mississippi River had been breached.

Union Private Sneeden wrote about seeing the Prince de Joinville and the duc de Chartres, French observers on Union General McClellan's staff. He also noted that newspaper reports included accurate maps. Perhaps they thought that New York papers did not make it South.

> *No one but McClellan could have hesitated to attack.*
> *—Confederate General Joseph Johnston in a letter to*
> *General Robert E. Lee written on this date.*

The Charleston *Tri-Weekly Mercury* publishes an article featuring the *"New Flag of the Confederacy."*

April 23: Skirmish at Grass Lick, Western Virginia.

April 24: Union Admiral Farragut sent his fleet past Forts Jackson and St Philip, driving off the Confederate flotilla that was guarding New Orleans.

April 25: New Orleans surrendered to Union forces.

Fort Macon, NC fell to Federal troops.

April 26: Forts Jackson and St Philip surrendered to Union forces.

Union Army of the Potomac advancing on Yorktown.

Skirmishes at Turnback Creek and Neosho, MO.

CS War Department clerk John B. Jones wrote that he was impressed with Confederate General Lee's efforts to rush reinforcements to Richmond.

April 27: Skirmish at Horton's Mills, NC.

Confederate forts to the north of New Orleans surrendered.

April 28: Union General Butler arrived in New Orleans as the Union flag was hoisted above the Customs House, City Hall, and the Mint.

At Nassau, British Bahamas, the vessel *Oreto* was outfitted and rechristened CSS *Florida*.

CS War Department clerk John B. Jones wrote about his disbelief that Yorktown and Norfolk were to be abandoned and that Confederate troops were falling back towards Richmond.

April 29: Skirmish at Bridgeport, AL ends in favor of the Union.

April 30: The unofficial Southern anthem "Dixie" was published.

Confederate General Richard Ewell's division reached the Shenandoah Valley to reinforce General Jackson's army.

Skirmishes at Cumberland Mountain and Monterey, TN.

May 1: Union General Butler formally assumed command of the Union garrison of New Orleans.

Laura Lee, a resident of Winchester wrote about the scarcity of fresh food in the area.

May 2: Confederate General Joe Johnston prepared to evacuate Yorktown in the face of approaching Union troops.

Union Private Sneeden wrote about the Union having 103,378 soldiers to the Confederates 50,000 on the York Peninsula, but a full press was not being done.

The New Orleans *Daily Delta* printed a profile on Major General Benjamin Butler, the US Army commander in New Orleans.

May 3: Confederate troops evacuated Yorktown and began pulling back towards Richmond.

CS War Department clerk John B. Jones wrote about rumors that the entire Peninsula was to be given up. He also reported that the Secretaries of War and the Navy were in Norfolk.

May 4: Union forces reached Yorktown and continued their advance on Williamsburg, where Confederate forces under Generals James Longstreet and D.H. Hill were waiting.

Union Private Sneeden wrote a full description of the entry of Union troops into Yorktown. He described the area being bobby-trapped, with explosions killing several troops before the engineers could disarm them.

Confederate General Jackson moved his troops to Staunton, VA to counter an expected Union move.

May 5: Union forces engaged Confederates at Williamsburg, VA.

US President Lincoln visited Fort Monroe in order to see how General McClellan's offensive is going.

Mexican troops, under Benito Juarez, defeated French troops at Puebla. This development would have been watched with interest in Washington, DC.

May 6: Union troops captured Williamsburg.

May 7: Union General McClellan transported four divisions up the York

River to Eltham's Landing, VA. There they engaged Confederate troops who were retreating from Yorktown.

May 8: Union forces captured the arsenal at Baton Rouge, LA.

Battle of McDowell, VA: Union commander: General John Fremont. Confederate commander: General Thomas Jackson. Fremont attempted to take on Jackson, but was repulsed and chased toward Franklin, VA. Confederate victory.

CS War Department clerk John B. Jones wrote about the evacuation of Norfolk and the plans to destroy CSS *Virginia*.

May 9: Union Flag Officer Foote was relieved of command due to injuries suffered in the Battle of Fort Donelson.

Norfolk Navy Yard retaken by Union forces.

> *All devices, signs, and flags of the Confederacy shall be suppressed. So says Picayune Butler. Good. I devote all my red, white, and blue silk to the manufacture of Confederate flags. As soon as one is confiscated, I make another, until my ribbon is exhausted, when I will sport a duster emblazoned in high colors. Hurrah! For the Bonny blue flag! Henceforth, I will wear one pinned to my bosom—not a duster, but a little flag: the man who says take it off will have to pull it off himself: the man who dares attempt it—well! A pistol in my pocket fills up the gap. I am capable too.*
> *—Baton Rouge resident Sarah Morgan Dawson, diary entry.*

May 10: Union forces occupied Pensacola, FL.

Union General Butler stole $80,000 in gold from the Dutch Consulate in New Orleans (adding to his already tarnished reputation).

Union General Fremont's retreating army linked up with General Huston Milroy's army and together they managed to stop Confederate General Jackson's advance.

Engagement between USS *Cincinnati*, USS *Mound City*, and Confederate batteries at Fort Pillow, TN.

May 11: CSS *Virginia* was destroyed on the James River to prevent her falling into Federal hands.

Skirmish at Bloomfield, MO.

May 12: Union Naval forces under Admiral David Farragut captured Natchez, MS.

Beaufort, NC, Port Royal, SC, and New Orleans were reopened to shipping since they were back in Union control.

Baton Rouge taken by Federal troops.

May 13: Citizens began fleeing Richmond, as Union forces approached.

Confederate vessel *Planter* was seized by its crew of African-Americans and surrendered to the Union blockading force at Charleston. The crew's leader, Robert Smalls, would one day become a US Congressman.

May 14: Confederate General Jackson concentrated his army at Harrisonburg, VA in order to strike divided Union forces in the Shenandoah Valley.

CS War Department clerk John B. Jones wrote about the anxiety in Richmond as Federal forces approached the city.

May 15: Union General Butler, in command of the New Orleans garrison, issued Order No. 28, declaring that any woman who insulted Union troops *"shall be regarded and held liable to be treated as a woman of the town plying her avocation,"* meaning as a prostitute. This was in response to an attack on a Union Admiral in which the contents of a chamber pot (toilet) was dumped on him. This order resulted in fierce anger throughout the Confederacy.

> *General Orders No. 28: As the Officers and Soldiers of the United States have been subjected to repeated insults from the women calling themselves ladies of New Orleans, in return for the most scrupulous non-interference and courtesy on out part, it is ordained that hereafter when any Female shall, by word, gesture, or movement, insult or show contempt for any Officer of the United States, she shall be regarded and held liable to be treated as a woman of the town plying her avocation.*
> —*Major General Benjamin F. Butler, May 15, 1862.*

A Union flotilla was stopped at Drewry's Bluff, eight miles from Richmond.

CS War Department clerk John B. Jones heard about the engagement at Drewry's Bluff and mentioned it in his diary.

Confederate General Joe Johnston pulled his army back to within three miles of Richmond.

May 16: Fighting raged around Princeton, Western Virginia.

> *In giving publicity to order No. 28, from Gen. Butler, we have little apprehension that our readers will suspect that we do so with any other feelings but these which pervade this whole community. Such publicity may not be unproductive of good results.*
> — *New Orleans* Daily Delta, *editorial.*

May 17: Union troops under General Irwin McDowell advanced on Richmond from the north.

Skirmishing near Corinth, MS.

May 18: Suffolk, VA fell to Union troops.

US Naval forces under Flag Officer Farragut headed up the Mississippi River toward Vicksburg.

May 19: CS President Davis showed uncertainty in the ability of the CS Army to defend Richmond in a letter to his wife.

Skirmish at Searcy Landing, AR.

US President Lincoln revoked an emancipation order made by Union General Hunter in South Carolina.

May 20: CS President Davis declared that Richmond will be held at all costs.

Confederate General Jackson's forces in the Shenandoah Valley were reinforced by those of General Ewell.

The Union advance toward Richmond came to a halt within sight of the city's church spires.

US President Lincoln signed the Homestead Act, opening large areas of the West to settlement.

Confederates repulsed at Searcy Landing, AR.

May 21: Confederate General Jackson moved his army across Massanutten Mountain to avoid Union forces under General Banks.

Union General McClellan asked for General McDowell's troops to join his army, claiming that the Confederates outnumbered his forces. (McClellan actually had at least a 3 to 1 superiority.)

CS War Department clerk John B. Jones wrote that skirmishing can be heard and that houses on the eastern edge of Richmond were being hit by musket fire.

Skirmish at Phillip's Creek, MS.

May 22: Confederate General Jackson moved his forces toward Front Royal.

Skirmish at New Berne, NC.

Skirmish at Florida, MO.

May 23: Battle of Front Royal, VA: Union commander: General Nathaniel Banks. Confederate commander: General Thomas Jackson. Jackson's maneuver placed his forces in a position to capture a number of Banks' forces. Confederate victory.

US President Lincoln met General McDowell at Fredericksburg, VA.

Skirmish at Fort Craig, New Mexico Territory.

CS War Department clerk John B. Jones wrote about the prices being charged in Richmond: all kinds of meat at .50 cents a pound, butter at .75 cents a pound, tea at $10 a pound, boots at $30 a pair, shoes at $18 a pair, ladies shoes at $15 a pair, and shirts for $6.00 each. The yearly rent on a house was $1000 and to stay in a boarding house would cost a tenant $40 a month.

May 24: Union General Banks were moving to Winchester in a panic, leaving behind tons of supplies that the Confederates were very happy to take advantage of.

US President Lincoln ordered Generals Fremont and McDowell to press their attack on Confederate General Jackson in the Shenandoah Valley.

May 25: Union General Banks made a stand at Winchester, but his troops were routed and fled towards Harpers Ferry. Confederates, noting another capture of Federal supplies, begin to refer to the Union commander as "Commissary" Banks.

Diarist Laura Lee expressed her glee at her town's liberation.

US President Lincoln ordered General McClellan to either attack Richmond or aid in the defense of Washington, DC.

Union General Halleck finally had his whole army at Corinth, after taking 26 days to march a mere 20 miles, usually a day's journey.

May 26: Confederate General Jackson kept up the pursuit of Union General Banks, briefly engaging him near Loudoun Heights, VA. Banks managed to escape across the Potomac River.

CS War Department clerk John B. Jones wrote that General Lee was still gathering reinforcements for General Joe Johnston.

May 27: Union forces under General Porter attacked Confederates near Hanover Court House, VA, routing them.

Skirmish near Searcy Landing, AR.

May 28: Skirmish at Wardensville, VA.

May 29: Skirmish at Seven Pines, near Richmond.

Union forces were massing near Harper's Ferry to counter Confederate General Jackson. This positioning of forces took away troops that Union General McClellan needed for operations in the Peninsula.

Union troops occupied Ashland, VA.

May 30: Confederate troops under General Beauregard pulled out of Corinth, which left the important crossroads town to Union General Halleck, but also leaving a Confederate army in the field.

Confederate General Jackson's troops skirmished with Union General James Shields' forces at Front Royal.

May 31: Battle of Fair Oaks (or Seven Pines), VA: Union commander: General George McClellan. Confederate commander: General Joseph Johnston. Johnston ordered an attack while McClellan's army was split along the Chickahominy River. Union General Edwin Sumner moved his command, without orders, in order to stop Johnston. During the fighting Johnston was severely wounded and General Lee, on an inspection tour for CS President Davis, was placed in command of what will soon become the Army of Northern Virginia.

Confederate General Jackson's forces used the cover of a heavy rainstorm to march south in the Shenandoah Valley, avoiding the trap being set by Union Generals Fremont and McDowell.

Skirmishing at Neosho, MO.

June 1: Confederate General Lee assumed command of the Richmond defenses.

Confederate troops renewed the assault on Union lines at Fair Oaks, but were repulsed with heavy losses.

Ohio Representative Samuel Sullivan Cox gave a speech on the House floor in opposition to any emancipation measures.

June 2: Confederate General Jackson's troops clashed with Union General McDowell's forces near Strasburg, VA as the Confederates continue their retreat.

CS War Department clerk John B. Jones wrote about hearing of the news of General Joe Johnston's wounding.

June 3: Skirmishing at Legare's Point, near Charleston, SC.

Union forces at Corinth, began their advance on Memphis, TN.

CS War Department clerk John B. Jones wrote about General Lee taking command of the army. Jones saw this at a *"harbinger of bright fortune."*

June 4: Confederates evacuated Fort Pillow, TN, which opened the way for Union forces to reach Memphis.

Confederate General Jackson's forces continue their withdrawal in the Shenandoah Valley.

June 5: Union troops entered Fort Pillow, and found the place deserted.

<blockquote>
$5000 will be given by one man for BUTLER'S head/ Columbus, Miss, June 2, 1862. Editor Mississippian: I like the suggestion of your correspondent on offering a reward for the head of the infamous General BUTLER. I will be good for $5000. Let the money go to the family of the party who succeeds in the undertaking if he should forfeit his life in so doing. B.
— *Jackson, MS* Daily Mississippian, *letter to the editor.*
</blockquote>

June 6: Battle of Memphis, TN: Union commander: Commodore Charles Davis. Confederate commander: Captain James Montgomery. In a full-scale river battle, Union naval forces destroyed a Confederate flotilla tasked with protecting Memphis. By mid-day the city surrendered to Union forces, opening the Mississippi River as far as Vicksburg.

In a minor skirmish near Harrisonburg, VA, Confederate Colonel Turner Ashby, General Jackson's cavalry commander was killed.

June 7: In New Orleans, Union garrison commander General Butler ordered William Munford hanged for cutting down a US flag from the Mint building.

June 8: Battle of Cross Keys, VA: Union commanders: Generals John Fremont, John Shields, and Irwin McDowell. Confederate commander: General Thomas Jackson. Union forces launched a two-pronged (Fremont and Shields) attack that was uncoordinated. What didn't help was McDowell basically stayed out of the fight. Fremont's troops attacked Confederate General Richard Ewell's forces, but were partially repulsed. Confederate victory.

June 9: Battle of Port Republic, VA: Union commander: General John Fremont. Confederate commander: General Thomas Jackson. Having dealt with Shields, Jackson turned his attention to Fremont's column. He pulled General Richard Ewell's forces back, and then launched a massive attack that broke the Union line and forced them out of the Shenandoah

Valley. The Shenandoah Valley Campaign was effectively over at this point with a victory for the Confederates.

June 10: At this point in time, the Federal Army of the Potomac was within four miles of Richmond, but was split into two groups. Confederate General Lee planed to take advantage of this by weakening the Richmond defenses and going on the offensive.

June 11: Minor action at Monterey, KY.

An Atlanta newspaper printed an article about large families sending all of their able-body sons into the CS Army.

June 12: Confederate General Jackson's army crossed the South Fork of the Shenandoah River, so they could rest before joining the Army of Northern Virginia. There was no threat to Richmond from the north for the time being, so the focus can be placed on Union General McClellan and the Army of the Potomac.

Confederate General Stuart took his cavalry force on a mission that would take them in a circle around the Union Army of the Potomac.

> *Gentlemen, in ten minutes every man must be in his saddle!*
> *—Confederate Major General J.E.B. Stuart, order to his troopers.*

June 13: Skirmish at James Island, SC.

June 14: Confederate General Stuart's troopers attacked Union supply points, as well as a train, creating confusion throughout the Union operational area.

June 15: Confederate General Stuart received a hero's welcome in Richmond for his ride, which circled the area where Union General McClellan's army was positioned. The tally of the raid was 165 prisoners and 300 horses. This boosted Southern morale but also served to alert McClellan to his army's weaknesses. Confederate General Lee ordered Jackson to join his troops, while he sent 10,000 toward the Shenandoah

Valley in order to trick the Federals into thinking that Jackson was being reinforced.

> *What a change! No one now dreams of the loss of the capital.*
> *—John Beauchamp Jones, diary entry.*

June 16: Union General Henry Benham launched an attack on Confederate positions at Secessionville, SC against orders and was repulsed with heavy losses.

June 17: A Union assault on Confederate positions at St Charles, AR, resulted in Federal control of the White River. During this battle, the highest naval combat losses in the war occurred when USS *Mound City* suffered a boiler explosion, killing over 100.

Union General Pope assumed command of the newly created Army of Virginia, composed of Union armies that had fought in the Shenandoah Valley.

Confederate General Jackson began moving his army south to join General Lee's army, ending the Shenandoah Valley Campaign.

Confederate General Order 17 issued. This regulated "independent" commands.

> *Keep cool, obey orders and aim low.*
> *—Confederate Lieutenant General James Longstreet,*
> *advice given to his troops.*

June 18: US President Lincoln wrote General McClellan, urging him to attack. McClellan still believed he was outnumbered but in truth the Union forces outnumber the Confederates.

Union troops under General George Morgan occupy the Cumberland Gap, TN.

June 19: US President Lincoln began focusing on the end of slavery as the main war aim as he announced his intention to outlaw slavery in all states currently in rebellion.

CS War Department clerk John B. Jones wrote about taking on the additional duty of preparing passports for those who wanted to travel beyond CSA borders.

June 20: Union General Thomas Williams departed Baton Rouge and headed for Vicksburg.

June 21: Skirmish at Battle Creek, TN.

June 22: US President Lincoln met with now retired General Winfield Scott for advice on running the war.

Skirmish at Algiers, LA (across the Mississippi River from New Orleans).

Fannie Christian, a Virginia resident, wrote CS Secretary of War Randolph asking that her husband be discharged from the army. It was refused and her husband will be killed the following year. CS War Department clerk John B. Jones probably would have seen that letter.

Members of the Sisters of Charity arrived at Fortress Monroe to help sick and wounded Union soldiers.

June 24: Union General McClellan received intelligence from a Confederate deserter that General Jackson was coming to join General Lee.

Union General Williams reached Vicksburg but did not have enough troops to take the city.

June 25: Union General McClellan sent a corps under General Samuel Heintzelman to determine Confederate General Lee's intentions. This force ran into Confederate troops under General Ben Huger, who stopped the probe. Lee decided to go ahead and launch his planned attack. The Seven Days Battles had begun.

June 26: Union Admiral Farragut's gunboats shelled Vicksburg.

Battle of Mechanicsville, VA: Union commander: General McClellan. Confederate commander: General Lee. Lee moved Longstreet and A.P. Hill's troops overnight to position them in order to attack McClellan. Lee wanted to wait until Jackson's troops had arrived, but Hill grew impatient and ordered an attack. Union forces were then forced into additional prepared positions while Longstreet's troops joined in the attack. The defensive line, commanded by Union General Fitz-John Porter, withstood the Confederate attack. Union victory, but McClellan ordered Porter to withdraw. Lee decides to continue the advance.

CS War Department clerk John B. Jones wrote about seeing dispatches between Lee and the War Department. That night, he, his son, and a few friends went to a hill where they could hear the sounds of the battle.

June 27: Battle of Gains Mill, VA: Union commander: General McClellan. Confederate commander: General Lee. Union forces were in improved positions. Lee ordered an attack, but was repulsed. Jackson arrived late in the day while Longstreet prepared another attack. The Union line was breached but it was too late in the day to exploit it, which allowed McClellan to withdraw. Confederate victory.

Union Admiral Farragut ran his vessels past the batteries at Vicksburg.

Confederate General Bragg was named as commander of the Army of the Mississippi, replacing General Beauregard.

June 28: Union General McClellan ordered a withdrawal to Harrison's Landing on the James River. Much of the supplies at White House Landing were destroyed in order to keep it from Confederate hands.

> *If I save the army now, I tell you plainly that I owe no thanks to you or any other persons in Washington.*
> *—Union Major General George McClellan in a letter to US Secretary of War Edwin Stanton.* (This part was deleted from a larger dispatch before being sent, so Stanton never saw this.)

CS War Department clerk John B. Jones wrote that thousands of Federal prisoners were marched through the streets of Richmond.

June 29: Battle of Savage Station, VA: Union commander: General McClellan. Confederate commander: General Lee. After some uncertainty, Lee figured out where McClellan was heading and decided to follow. Lee sent out a force under General John Magruder to keep the Union forces occupied while Jackson attacked the flank. Jackson did not arrive and Magruder was repulsed. Union victory, however they were the ones who retreated.

> *Our lines stood as firm as a rock, 5,000 were simultaneously pointed and discharged with a terrific crash! To this the enemy replied by double the numbers, when all in front was hid by smoke.*
> *—Union Private Robert Knox Sneeden, diary entry.*

June 30: Battle of Glendale, VA: Union commander: General McClellan. Confederate commander: General Lee. Lee was trying to give McClellan a knock out blow but his commanders were delayed by various factors. When the attack finally began, Longstreet and A.P. Hill were repulsed while Jackson had fallen asleep and did not order his troops in. Union victory, but McClellan again ordered his army to retreat, this time to Malvern Hill.

July 1: Battle of Malvern Hill, VA: Union commander: General McClellan. Confederate commander: General Lee. Lee had problems getting his entire army in place and it was the afternoon before he could attack. The battle was preceded by an artillery duel that rendered the Confederate artillery ineffective. Lee decided anyway to launch a massive infantry attack on the Union positions, but the expert employment of artillery by Union General Henry Hunt was instrumental in repulsing the Confederates. Union victory. This ended the Seven Days Battles. McClellan won all but one, but still withdrew to Harrison's Landing, where he was planning to pull out his entire force!

> *Night came, yet the fight went on...The lurid flashes of artillery...the crackle of musketry, with flashes seen in the distance like fireflies: the hoarse shriek of the huge shells from the gun-boats...made it a scene of terrible grandeur. The ground in front...was literally covered with the dead and wounded. At nine o'clock the sounds of the battle died away, and cheer after cheer went up from the victors on the hill.*
> —*Union Private Warren Lee Goss.*

> *About 6 p.m. by pushing out about twenty pieces of artillery from their front, followed by four lines of solid infantry colors flying, as if on parade, they advanced at a run with terrifying yells, heard all above the crash of musketry and roar of artillery. We now opened on them with terrible effects...*
> —*Union Private Robert Knox Sneeden.*

> *We retreated like a parcel of sheep, and a few shots from the rebels would have panic-stricken the whole command.*
> —*Union Major General Joseph Hooker.*

Union Admiral Farragut's fleet was united with the fleet of Flag Officer Davis below Vicksburg.

Union cavalry under General Philip Sheridan defeated Confederate forces south of Corinth.

July 2: Union Army of the Potomac completed their retreat to Harrison's Landing.

US President Lincoln called for 300,000 men to volunteer for three years.

US Congress approved the construction of the Transcontinental Railroad as well as the Morrill Land Grant Act, opening up lands in the West for settlement. US President Lincoln signed them into law.

July 3: Union General McClellan ordered fortification of the Army of the Potomac's positions around Harrison's Landing.

Skirmish at Ellington Heights, Western Virginia.

July 4: Confederate General John Hunt Morgan began a raid into Union territory in Kentucky with a force of Georgians, Texans, and Tennesseans.

July 6: Union General Burnside moved his forces from Roanoke Island and New Bern, NC in order to reinforce McClellan in Virginia, leaving behind a garrison.

Skirmish at Grand Prairie, AR.

July 7: Union General McClellan wrote US President Lincoln, blaming him for the "difficulties" his army is facing. He claimed that massive Confederate forces were at his front when in fact, Confederate General Lee had begun a pullback.

Skirmish at Cotton Plant, AR.

July 8: Confederate General Lee continued to pull his troops back toward Richmond while employing a deception tactic that kept Union General McClellan in the dark (usually that meant leaving a regiment to keep the campfires burning and marching up and down the roads to give the impression of a larger force maneuvering).

Skirmish at Black River, MO.

Union Private Robert Sneeden wrote about a visit by US President Lincoln to Harrison's Landing, describing him as looking *"ungainly on horseback."*

July 9: Confederate General John Morgan escaped capture at Tompkinsville, KY.

Confederate General Lee had his artillery attempt to drive away Union gunboats on the James River with no success.

Skirmish at Aberdeen, AR.

July 10: Union General Pope, commander of the Army of Virginia, declared that he will be harsh with Confederate supporters in the Shenandoah Valley.

July 11: Union General Halleck assumed duties as Commander in Chief of Union forces in the field.

Skirmish at Williamsburg, VA.

Confederate General Morgan's troops attacked Lebanon, KY but fail to prevent Union forces from destroying the supplies there.

July 12: Confederate General Morgan's forces succeeded in taking Lebanon.

Skirmish at Culpepper, VA.

July 13: Confederate forces under General Nathan B. Forrest captured the Union garrison at Murfreesboro, TN.

Confederate General Lee began moving his army to the north towards Manassas Junction.

Confederate General Morgan's forces were advancing on Cynthiana, KY.

July 14: Confederate General Morgan's forces reached Cynthiana, placing Ohio and Indiana under threat.

Union Army of Virginia advanced towards Gordonsville, VA.

> *I hear constantly of taking "strong positions and holding them," or "lines of retreat" and of "bases of supplies." Let us discard such ideas. The strongest position a soldier should desire to occupy is one from which he can most easily advance against the enemy.*
> *—Union Major General John Pope, commanding the Army of Virginia, speech to his troops.*

Skirmish at Batesville, AR.

July 15: Union Flag Officer Farragut sailed his fleet by Vicksburg and received heavy fire from the artillery emplacements guarding the city. Meanwhile, CSS *Arkansas* attacked two Union ships on the Yazoo River north of Vicksburg, and then faced heavy Union fire as the ship was sailed to Vicksburg.

Small Confederate force defeated at Fayetteville, AR.

Skirmish at Apache Pass, Arizona Territory.

July 16: Union Flag Officer Farragut was promoted to the rank of Rear Admiral, the first in US Navy history.

France declined to give diplomatic recognition to the CSA.

July 17: Union General Grant assumed command of all Union armies in the West.

US Congress passed a lifetime pension plan for disabled naval personnel.

July 18: Skirmish at Memphis, MO.

July 19: Confederate General Morgan's troops clashed with Federals at Paris, KY.

A group of Confederates raided Brownsville, TN.

A court-martial cleared Confederate Flag Officer Josiah Tattnall of any wrong doing in the scuttling of CSS *Virginia* on May 11.

Confederate forces were mostly expelled from Missouri, but concerns about guerilla activity continued.

July 20: Union Department of Missouri, under command of General John Schofield, launched an anti-guerilla campaign.

July 21: Union General Pope failed to seize Gordonsville, but still presented a considerable threat to central Virginia. Confederate General Lee dispatched General Jackson to Gordonsville to keep an eye on things. Lee was waiting on what Union General McClellan would do before reinforcing Jackson.

July 22: Confederate General Morgan's troops reached Livingston, TN.

Two Union ships attacked CSS *Arkansas* near Vicksburg but fail to sink her.

Union and Confederate governments signed an accord regulating the exchange of prisoners of war.

US President Lincoln presented the first draft of the Emancipation Proclamation to his Cabinet. After some debate, it was decided that they would wait until a Union victory.

July 23: Major General Halleck assumed duties as Commander-in-Chief of Union forces.

Confederate General Bragg began his movement of his army from Tupelo, MS to Chattanooga, TN, but had to go by way of Mobile and Montgomery, AL due to the state of the railroads.

Skirmishes at Florida and Columbus, both in MO.

July 24: Skirmishes at Trinity, AL and Santa Fe, MO.

July 25: Union troops departed Natchez, MS.

Confederates captured 100 Union troops at Courtland Bridge, AL.

July 26: Skirmishes at Mountain Store and Big Piney, both in MO.

July 27: Skirmishing continued in Missouri in Brown's Spring, Carroll County, Ray County, and Livingstone County.

Skirmish at Fort Gibson, Indian Territory (Oklahoma).

July 28: Confederate guerillas lost a short battle at Moore's Mills, MO.

Skirmish at Bayou Bernard, Indian Territory (Oklahoma).

July 29: Confederate spy Belle Boyd was captured at Warrenton, VA and taken to Old Capital Prison at Washington, DC.

Steamer *290*, the soon to be CSS *Alabama*, left Liverpool, UK for the Azores where she would receive guns and munitions.

Skirmishes at Russellville, KY and Brownsville, TN.

CS War Department clerk John B. Jones wrote about the reported destruction in Culpepper and Orange counties by Union General Pope's troops.

July 30: Union General McClellan began pulling his army out of Harrison's Landing. Meanwhile, General Pope had placed his Army of Virginia (the only Union army to be named after a state) on the Rappahannock River and 12000 troops under General Burnside were near Fredericksburg.

Skirmish at Paris, KY.

July 31: Confederate General D.H. Hill had his artillery send 1000 shells into the Union lines at Harrison's Landing with little effect.

August 1: In response to Union General Pope's order to treat harshly anyone who gave aid to the Confederate cause, the CS Government issued General Order #54, declaring that Pope and his officers were not entitled to prisoner-of-war status and could be hanged.

US President Lincoln signed the Second Confiscation Act into law. One of the provisions was that any slave that reached Union territory would be automatically freed.

Union Private Sneeden wrote about Union troops destroying a plantation that served as an observation post for Confederates.

August 2: US Minister to the UK, Charles Francis Adams, received instructions to refuse any British offer of mediation. Adams was the son of President John Quincy Adams and the grandson of President John Adams.

Union forces seized Orange Court House, VA.

Skirmishes at Ozark and Clear Creek, both in MO.

August 3: Union General Halleck ordered General McClellan to move his army back to Alexandria, VA.

Skirmish at Chariton Bridge, MO.

Action at Jonesboro and Lauguelle Ferry, both in AR.

At a meeting of the Federal Cabinet, Secretary of the Treasury Salmon Chase expressed the opinion that emancipation should be the main war aim.

New York *Herald* led its news with a report on the capture of Confederate spy Belle Boyd, "the betrayer of our forces at Front Royal." She had tipped Confederate General Jackson to the disposition of Federal forces in the area.

Jennie Hodgers assumed the name of "Albert Cashier" and enlisted in the 95th Illinois.

August 4: Union General Burnside had moved his troops from Fredericksburg, fearing an attack by Confederate General Lee.

Indiana offered two African-American regiments but was declined by US President Lincoln, despite a problem with raising troops. There was resistance to three-year enlistments and a nine-month enlistment had been offered.

Skirmish at Sparta, TN.

August 5: Confederate forces under General John Breckenridge launched an attack on the Union garrison at Baton Rouge. Before the assault was made, a group of Confederate partisans mistook them for Union infantry and opened fire. Among those killed was Captain Alexander Todd, brother-in-law of US President Lincoln. The attack itself had initial success but it was also dependent on supporting fire from CSS *Arkansas*, which never arrived. Breckenridge was forced to pull back. Among the Federal dead was the garrison commander, General Thomas Williams.

Iowa Governor Samuel Kirkwood sent a letter to Union General-in-Chief Halleck calling on him to allow African-Americans to join the Army, but only as cooks and laborers, not as soldiers.

August 6: CSS *Arkansas*, while attempting to assist in the assault on Baton Rouge lost her engines south of Vicksburg. USS *Essex* appeared and attacked. *Arkansas's* commander decided to scuttle the vessel in order to prevent her from falling into Union hands. During the attack, Confederate forces under General Breckenridge contended with thick fog and Union gunboat support and had to withdraw.

Confederate partisans north of Athens, AL ambushed Union General Robert McCook, mortally wounding him.

Skirmishes at Beech Creek, Western Virginia, Thornburg, VA, and Tazewell, TN.

August 7: Confederate General Lee found out that Union General McClellan had totally pulled out of the Malvern Hill area. His attention turned to the north.

Confederate Generals Jackson and A.P. Hill reached Gordonsville and spotted Union troops. Upon reporting this to General Lee, the order came to attack. Jackson moved his army to Orange and prepared to cross the Rapidan River.

Confederates forced from Fort Fillmore, New Mexico Territory.

August 8: Union General Pope ordered General Banks to deploy his troops south of Culpepper, VA in order to stop Confederate General Jackson.

US Congress passed a law making it a criminal offense to avoid conscription.

August 9: Battle of Cedar Mountain, VA: Union commander: General Banks. Confederate commander: General Thomas Jackson. Confederate infantry struck Banks while on the march from Culpepper to the Rapidan River. Union forces successfully flanked the Confederates in several places, one of those attacks resulting in Confederate General Charles Winder being killed. The timely arrival of General A.P. Hill's troops allowed the Confederates to push Banks back. Union troops withdrew but Jackson kept up the pursuit until midnight. Confederate victory.

Banks is in front of me, and he is always ready to fight. And he generally gets whipped.
—Confederate Major General Thomas Jackson.

August 10: Donelson, LA was shelled by Union gunboats.

Union General Banks, retreating from Cedar Mountain was reinforced by troops under Generals Sigel and McDowell, with General Burnside's troops on the way. Union forces now outnumbered General Jackson's Confederate army.

Skirmishes in Missouri at the following locations: Grand River, Lee's Ford, Chariton River, Walnut Creek, Compton Ferry, Switzler's Mills, and Yellow Creek.

A group of Unionists, mostly Germans, were attacked and massacred on the Nueces River in Texas. (A monument to them can be found in Comfort, TX).

August 11: Confederate General Jackson, seeing that the odds were now against him, pulled his army back to Gordonsville, VA.

Skirmish at Wyoming Court House, WV.

Union General Grant issued an order that any fugitive slaves in his area of operations would be employed by the military.

Action at Independence, MO and Helena, AR.

August 12: Confederate General Morgan raided Gallatin, TN capturing the Union garrison there.

August 13: Confederate General Lee sent General James Longstreet to Gordonsville to assist General Jackson while sending General John Hood to Hanover Junction to watch Union General Burnside's troops at Fredericksburg.

Confederate General Morgan's army fled Gallatin in the face of a large Federal force.

Fighting at Grand River, MO and Clarendon, AR.

August 14: Confederate General Edmund Kirby Smith led a force from Knoxville towards the Kentucky River valley.

August 15: Skirmish at Merriweather's Ferry, TN.

August 16: Most of the Union Army of the Potomac had begun to leave Harrison's Landing when General McClellan received orders to link up with General John Pope's army and try again to capture Richmond.

Skirmish at Lone Jack, MO.

August 17: Confederate General Stuart's cavalry were surprised at Clark's Mountain, VA. In his escape, he lost his hat with plume, cape, and a satchel containing General Lee's plans.

August 18: CS President Davis delivered a "State of the Nation" address before the Confederate Congress.

Confederate General Lee began a series of probes to seek a weakness in Union General Pope's lines. Pope's army was wedged between the Rappahannock and Rapidan Rivers and managed to cross the Rappahannock before Lee could entrap him. Pope then sent a call to General McClellan for reinforcements.

Confederate ship *Fairplay* captured near Milliken's Bend, LA.

CS War Department clerk John B. Jones wrote of his belief that 20,000 mounted troops will come from Texas, Louisiana, and Arkansas to aid Generals Lee and Jackson.

August 20: Union and Confederate cavalry clashed at Brandy Station, VA. This alerted General Pope that the Army of Northern Virginia was on the move and coming at him.

August 21: Confederate General Bragg's army departed Chattanooga, TN to campaign in Kentucky. Union General Buell responded by deploying his troops to Murfreesboro, TN.

Union and Confederate artillery exchange fire along the Rappahannock River as Confederate General Lee tries to find a way across.

August 22: Confederate General Stuart's cavalry raided Union General Pope's headquarters in which Pope's book containing copies of all his orders was taken.

Horace Greeley, editor of the New York *Times*, published an open letter to US President Lincoln called "The Prayer of Twenty Millions" which called for a declaration that the main aim of the war will be to free the slaves.

> *If I could save the Union without freeing any slaves, I would do it: and if I could save it by freeing all of the slaves, I would do it: and if I could save it by freeing some and leaving others alone, I would also do that.*
> —*President Lincoln's response to Greeley's editorial.*

August 23: The Rappahannock River, swollen by rainstorms, prevented both armies from crossing. Confederate General Lee decided to use Union General Pope's orders book against him. A small force would keep Pope occupied while Lee took the rest of his army around and into the Federal rear, which would cut Pope off from communications with Washington, DC and prevent reinforcements from arriving.

August 24: CSS *Alabama* arrived at Terceira, Azores and was officially commissioned into the CS Navy.

August 25: Confederate General Jackson began a flanking movement in order to draw Union General Pope out. Pope received information that Jackson had 30 regiments plus cavalry moving around him. The truth was that Jackson had 66 regiments.

Confederate forces attacked Fort Donelson and the Cumberland Iron Works, both in TN.

August 26: Confederate General Jackson's troops reached the Union supply depot at Manassas Junction and proceed to loot the place. Confederate General Longstreet began moving his corps to join Jackson. Union General Pope decided to head for Manassas.

> *By God, General Jackson, I will be a major general or a corpse before this war is over.*
> —*Confederate Brigadier General Isaac Trimble to Major General Thomas Jackson.*

August 28: Second Battle of Manassas: Union commander: General John Pope. Confederate commander: General Thomas Jackson, but Generals Lee and Longstreet would arrive later. Day One: Jackson began the battle by hitting a single Federal brigade at Brawner's Farm (That brigade became known as the Iron Brigade for their stubborn defense).

Union Private Sneeden wrote about moving from Alexandria to Manassas to join General John Pope's forces.

Confederate spy Belle Boyd released from prison due to lack of evidence.

Confederate General Bragg moved his troops in support of General Edmund Kirby Smith's troops, who were advancing into Kentucky.

August 29: Second Battle of Manassas; Day Two: Pope ordered troops under Generals McDowell and Porter to move against Jackson, whose line starched from Brawner's Farm to Sudley Springs and included an unfinished railroad cut. At midday, Pope himself was on the field. Longstreet and Lee arrived on the field in the early afternoon and saw the developing situation. Jackson's troops ran low on ammunition and were forced to throw rocks at one point (repulsing a Federal attack). Lee ordered Longstreet to attack, but Longstreet stated there might be Union reinforcements nearby (he was right, McDowell and Porter were near). At 4:30, Pope ordered Porter to hit Jackson's right and rear. At 5:30, the attack was ordered on Jackson's left, which turned the flank and forced a pullback of several Confederate divisions. Neither side had left the field but Pope sent a victory telegram to Washington and asked for reinforcements.

I saw the head of one of our artillerymen taken off, shot within fifty feet of my position. His blood spattered his gun. He was pulled up by his arms a few paces away, the blood gushing in streams from his neck.... The other artillerymen kept on loading and firing without giving him further notice....Having seen enough of the terrible fighting, I returned to our headquarters...
—*Private Robert Knox Sneeden, diary entry.*

August 30: Second Battle of Manassas: Day Three: The fighting continued with Union General Pope renewing his attack on Jackson. At midday, Union General Porter's corps advanced forward to hit Confederate

General Jackson's lines, but Confederate General Longstreet had placed his troops in a position to hit Porter on his left. Longstreet's attack crushed Porter and forced the Federals to withdraw at sundown. Battle ends. Confederate victory.

> *The sparkling lines of musketry shone in the darkness like fireflies in a meadow, while the more brilliant flashes of artillery might have been mistaken for swamp meteors. The show continued for an hour, the advancing and receding fires indicating distinctly the surge of the battle tide...It seemed at length that the fire of the enemy's line began to extend and thicken, while ours wavered and fell back...Between eight and nine o'clock it ceased entirely...*
> *—D. H. Strother, witnessing the battle while at Union General Pope's headquarters.*

August 31: Heavy rain in the area prevented Confederate General Jackson from pursuing the defeated Union Army of Virginia. Union General Pope had not given up yet. Upon hearing that Jackson had started marching on Fairfax, Pope sent three corps (Generals McDowell, Heintzelman, and Reno) to counter the Confederate's move. Meanwhile, two corps from General McClellan arrived to assist Pope, but far too late.

Federal troops evacuated Fredericksburg.

Clara Barton, a volunteer nurse, helped attend to wounded Union soldiers brought back from the Second Manassas battlefield.

September 1: Battle of Chantilly, VA: Union commanders: Generals I.I. Stevens and Phil Kearney. Confederate commander: General Thomas Jackson. Jackson's troops were in pursuit of General Pope's army when they ran into a blocking force under Stevens and Kearny. The ensuing battle took place in a thunderstorm, which created a lot of confusion during which both Stevens and Kearny were killed. Jackson was forced to halt his attack and the Federals continued their withdrawal. Confederate victory because the Union forces left the field. As a result, General Lee began forming his plan to take the war into the North.

September 2: US President Lincoln ordered General McClellan to leave the field and take command of the Washington. defenses. Lincoln did complement the general by saying, *"If he can't fight himself, he excels in making others ready to fight."* McClellan had not much time to pull the army together as the Confederates began their strike north.

Union General Buell's troops moving towards Nashville.

Union troops withdrew from the Shenandoah Valley leaving a large amount of supplies for the Confederates.

September 3: Confederate troops under General Edmund Kirby Smith occupied Frankfort, KY.

USS *Essex* was fired on by batteries at Natchez, MS. The Federals return fire caused the town's surrender.

Union General Pope issued a report blaming everyone but himself for the defeat at Manassas. This would result in his removal and reassignment.

CS War Department clerk John B. Jones wrote about hearing that General Ewell was not only wounded, but he had lost a leg. Rejoiced that General Lee had captured 10,000 muskets and 50 cannon.

September 4: Confederate General Edmund Kirby Smith's forces were reinforced in Lexington, KY by General Morgan's raiders.

CSS *Florida* reached Mobile Bay, AL despite the Federal blockade and that some of the crew were ill with yellow fever.

September 5: CSS *Alabama* captured a Union merchant vessel off the Azores.

Confederate Army of Northern Virginia began their march into Maryland.

Meta Morris Grimball wrote in her diary that several families that she knew have learned to read and write in order to communicate with their sons in the Confederate Army.

September 6: Between September 6-9, CSS *Alabama* will destroy four more Union ships.

Union General McClellan began moving his army to shield Washington, DC from Confederate General Lee's army. No one has figured out yet what Lee was doing.

Lee, meanwhile, was crossing the Potomac River into Maryland, hoping to get support and volunteers from the state. Lee, Longstreet and Jackson were suffering from minor injuries while A.P. Hill and John Bell Hood were under arrest.

Union General Pope was given command of troops in the Northwest and tasked with putting down a Sioux uprising in Minnesota.

September 7: Union General Buell left Nashville with five divisions to protect the Federal supply base at Bowling Green, KY.

Union Army of the Potomac was sent to Rockville, MD while panic gripped Washington, DC.

> *The slave oligarchy has organized the most unnatural, perfidious and formidable rebellion known to history.*
> —*L. B. Otis, chairman of the Christian Men of Chicago in a letter to US President Lincoln.*

September 8: Union General Banks was given command of the Washington DC defenses while General McClellan takes to the field.

Confederate General Lee issued a proclamation to Maryland that the Army of Northern Virginia was here to liberate the state and to call on Marylanders to rally to the Confederate flag.

September 9: The proclamation that Confederate General Lee issued the previous day had fallen on deaf ears. No one showed up to join the CS

Army. At Frederick, Lee issued General Order 191, which ordered his army split into three groups. General Jackson would take Harpers Ferry. General Lafayette McLaws would take Maryland Heights. General Longstreet would move on Boonsboro. Army would then reunite after Harpers Ferry had fallen. Afterwards they would then press into Pennsylvania. Copies of the order were made and distributed. One of those copies was used as a wrapper for three cigars. That package was lost!

September 10: Union General McClellan began moving his army toward Frederick, as Confederate General Lee's army departed. General Jackson attacked Harpers Ferry as Generals James Longstreet and D.H. Hill were heading for Hagerstown.

US President Lincoln wrote to a group of clergymen based in Chicago who sent him a letter stating that is was God's Will that the slaves be freed. Lincoln was impatient with ministers who claim to speak for God in certain matters, and he told them that he would seek the "will of Providence" in the matter of emancipation.

September 11: CS President Davis appointed General Van Dorn commander of Confederate forces in Missouri, except that the army he was supposed to take over, still led by General Price, was marching on Iuka, MS, intending to head into Tennessee.

September 12: Union General McClellan's army entered Frederick, to the delight of its citizens.

September 13: Confederate troops under General W.W. Loring forced the Federals to abandon Charleston, Western Virginia.

As Federal troops reached Frederick when Private Billy W. Mitchell found three cigars wrapped in a piece of paper. The paper looked official, so it was given to his lieutenant. (No one knows what happened to the cigars.) The paper ended up at General McClellan's headquarters, where it was determined to be a copy of Confederate General Lee's Special Order 191, outlining the Confederate battle plan. McClellan proclaimed,

"I now have a paper in which if I can not whip Bobby Lee, I'm willing to go home."

> *We came up close to the fight at Frederick [Maryland], and, forming line of battle, went in at double-quick through cornfields, potato patches, gardens, and backyards—the German washer-woman of the 103d New York regiment going in with us on the run.*
> *—Private David Thompson, United States Army, 9th New York.*

September 14: Union General Buell reached Bowling Green, KY.

Confederate General Price's army entered Iuka, MS.

Union General McClellan implemented his own plan to destroy Confederate General Lee's army by attacking General D.H. Hill's position at South Mountain, MD. The Confederate line broke but General Longstreet's timely arrival prevented a rout. However the southernmost pass, Crampton's Gap was in Union hands by evening.

Confederate General McLaws' troops reached Maryland Heights but were attacked by Union forces under General William Franklin. The Confederate line broke but the Federals did not pursue.

> *We are flanked, boys, but let us die in out tracks.*
> *—Confederate Colonel B.B. Gayle, commander, 12th Alabama, shortly before he was killed at South Mountain.*

Confederate General Lee, seeing that his plan was unraveling, ordered his army to concentrate near Sharpsburg.

September 15: Confederate General Jackson captured Harpers Ferry and left a division under General A.P. Hill while he took the rest of his force toward Sharpsburg.

Lettie Kennedy, a resident of Jasper County, MS wrote to the Confederate War Office asking for troops to guard their town because all of the men were away in the Army.

September 16: Union Army of the Potomac and Confederate Army of Northern Virginia gathered near Sharpsburg as long-range artillery duels take place.

September 17: Battle of Antietam Creek (Sharpsburg, MD): Union commander: General George McClellan. Confederate commander: General Robert E. Lee. At dawn, General Joseph Hooker's corps began to advance but was held up by artillery fire. Meanwhile a brigade under Union General Gibbon attacked Confederates in a cornfield but failed to drive them out. The Confederates refused to budge and with reinforcements coming in for both sides, losses were heavy. (This field became known as The Cornfield.) Confederates were finally driven off by 9 a.m. From 9:30 a.m. and 1 p.m., Union troops under General Sumner made repeated attacks on Confederate General D.H. Hill's troops, who were in a sunken road (afterwards known as Bloody Lane). Those attacks failed to dislodge the Confederates until a mistake allowed Federal troops to flank that position, allowing crossfire. The Federal troops advanced until stopped by General James Longstreet's corps. At 10 a.m. a Union corps under General Burnside attempted to cross the Antietam at Rohrbach Bridge (now called Burnside's Bridge), southeast of Sharpsburg. It took three hours and several attacks to finally cross the creek. The amazing thing was that the ridges across the creek were lightly held by Georgia troops. General Lee was beginning to think that his army might be destroyed when A.P. Hill's troops arrived and helped drive back Burnside's advance. Fighting died away at dusk. Battle ended as a Union victory. This became the bloodiest day in US history with 23,000 causalities, followed only by the attacks of 11 September 2001 and the attack on Pearl Harbor, HI on 7 December 1941.

In a second the air was full of the hiss of bullets and the hurtle of grape-shot. The mental strain was so great that I saw at that moment the singular effect mentioned, I think in the life of Goethe on a similar occasion—the whole landscape for an instant turned slightly red.
— Private David Thompson, United States Army, 9ᵗʰ New York.

Confederate General Bragg captured Mumfordville, KY.

September 18: Confederate General Lee learned that the Federals near Sharpsburg have 30000 fresh troops, while his army had been fully used up.

September 19: Confederates begin pulling back from Sharpsburg, into Virginia. Union General McClellan does not order a pursuit.

Battle of Iuka, MS: Union commanders: Generals Edward Ord and William Rosecrans. Confederate commander: General Sterling Price. Ord attacked Price from the north of the town, but Rosecrans was delayed, which allowed Price to escape. Union victory.

CS War Department clerk John B. Jones wrote about hearing of the Confederate capture of Harper's Ferry, but he had not yet heard about the battle at Sharpsburg.

September 20: Union armies under Generals Thomas and Buell linked up at Bowling Green, KY and began their movement toward Louisville.

Union General McClellan still had not moved from Sharpsburg.

Confederate troops under General Price began their withdrawal from Iuka.

CS War Department clerk John B. Jones heard about the battle at Sharpsburg, but he believed the Confederates had driven the Federals off the field.

September 21: A Federal reconnaissance force crossed the Potomac River at Blackford's Ford and skirmished with elements of Confederate General A. P. Hill's corps that was covering the Confederate retreat back into Virginia.

Confederate General Bragg's troops left Mumfordville, KY for Bardstown in order to link up with General Smith's forces. This move left the door open for Union General Buell to advance on Louisville.

September 22: US President Lincoln issued his Emancipation

Proclamation, citing the recent Union victory at Sharpsburg. On January 1, 1863, all slaves in areas still in rebellion would be declared free. This placed the Union war effort as both the restoration of the Union and the freeing of the slaves. This also placed the US on the moral high ground and closed the door on any British or French recognition of the CSA.

September 23: Union General McClellan had stopped his army on the Potomac River near Harper's Ferry. He believed that Confederate General Lee would force another crossing. In fact, Lee had no other plans than to reassemble his army near Winchester.

September 24: Troops under Union General Buell reached Louisville, KY.

US President Lincoln suspended the *writ of habeas corpus* in cases involving interference with recruitment and draft efforts.

Fourteen Northern governors met at Altoona, PA and gave a rousing endorsement for freeing the slaves.

September 25: Union General McClellan sent demands for supplies, uniforms, and reinforcements. Supplies and uniforms were sent, but not a single man was released from the Washington defenses.

CS War Department clerk John B. Jones wrote that blankets were selling for $25 a pair, sheets for $15 a pair, and bleached cotton for shirts for $1 a yard.

September 26: The Confederate Foreign Policy Committee issued a report calling for the Mississippi River to be kept open for trade, following a Confederate victory in the war, and that favored trade status to be given to the Northwestern States.

Confederate General Bragg issued a proclamation calling on Northwest states to force the US government to stop the war.

September 27: There was panic in Louisville, KY as Confederate

General Bragg's forces approached and there was no confidence that Union General Buell's troops would arrive in time.

September 28: Union General McClellan was still under the assumption that he was outnumbered, not realizing that he had 100,000 troops and that Confederate General Lee only had 53,000.

September 29: In Louisville there was a duel between Union Major Generals Jefferson C. Davis (no relation to CS President Davis) and William Nelson. Nelson was killed. The incident never comes to trial. This happen on the same day that General Buell's forces reached the city.

> *Send for a clergyman, I wish to be baptized. I have been basely murdered.*
> *—Union Major General William Nelson after he was shot.*

September 30: Photographer Matthew Brady opened an exhibit of photographs taken on the Antietam battlefield. Called "The Dead of Antietam," this exhibit allowed civilians to view the aftermath of a battle for the first time.

Skirmish at Newtonia, MO.

October 1: Union gunboats on the Mississippi River were transferred from Army to Navy command and placed under the command of newly promoted Rear Admiral Porter.

Command of the Vicksburg defenses was given to Confederate General John C. Pemberton, a Northerner who decided to go with the South when the war began.

Confederates under General Thomas Hindman crossed into Arkansas but were stopped by Union troops under General Schofield.

Confederate General Price's troops reached Ripley, MS and joined General Van Dorn's forces. They attempted to launch an attack on Corinth, MS but ran into Union cavalry.

Union troops under Generals Buell and Thomas began their movement toward Frankfort, KY.

The Southern press called US President Lincoln's Emancipation Proclamation an invitation to start a slave revolt.

Skirmish at Sheppardstown, MD as US President Lincoln met with General McClellan to discuss post-Antietam strategy.

October 2: Confederate General Van Dorn's troops met Federal troops ten miles from Corinth; he decided to press the attack.

October 3: Battle of Corinth, MS: Union commander: General William Rosecrans. Confederate commander: General Earl Van Dorn. Day One: Confederates launched an all out attack and managed to drive the Federals out of the outer defensive line. Troops on the second line of defenses halted the Confederate advance. Fighting ended at sundown with no decision.

October 4: Battle of Corinth: Day Two: General Van Dorn ordered a massive artillery attack followed by a massed infantry assault, which broke the Union line. Federals reformed their lines and withstood further attacks. Confederates were forced to withdraw but Rosecrans did not order a pursuit. Union victory.

October 5: Confederate General Van Dorn held off Federals at the Big Hatchie River, MS, and then resumed his retreat.

US President Lincoln gave General McClellan a direct order to "cross the Potomac, give battle to the enemy, and drive him south." McClellan's answer was to demand more troops and supplies and that he would move when he was good and ready.

October 6: Union troops under General Buell occupied Bardstown, KY.

October 7: Union troops under General Buell reached Perryville, KY and found Confederates there.

CS War Department clerk John B. Jones wrote about paying .80 cents for a pound of sugar, .25 cents for a quart of milk, .37 ½ cents for a pound of sausage meat, four loaves of bread the size of his fist (dinner rolls?) for .80 cents, and a pound of coffee for $2.50.

> *Jefferson Davis and other leaders of the South have made an army: they are making, it appears, a navy: and they have made what is more than either: they have made a nation.*
> —*William E. Gladstone, UK Chancellor of the Exchequer, at a meeting at Newcastle.*

October 8: Battle of Perryville, KY: Union commander: General D.C. Buell. Confederate commander: General Braxton Bragg. There was confusion on both sides: Buell thought he was hitting Bragg's main force, but was only hitting part of it. Bragg thought he was hitting a part of Buell's force, but was engaging the main force. Union attack was spearheaded by General Sherman's troops, who gained the heights that dominated the area. Buell, however, was slow to gather his forces. Confederate General Polk attacked Buell's left flank with some success. Neither side gained the advantage and Bragg withdrew after sundown. Union victory because they kept the field.

October 9: Confederates began their withdrawal from Perryville with the result that all Confederate forces were now out of Kentucky.

Confederate General Stuart led 1800 cavalry behind Federal lines in Virginia so he could create some havoc.

CS War Department clerk John B. Jones wrote that the latest substitute for coffee, toasted corn meal, could be bought for .06 cents a pound.

October 10: Confederate General John Magruder was assigned command of the District of Texas, Arizona, and New Mexico.

CS President Davis made a request for 4500 slaves to be used in building fortifications around Richmond.

October 11: CSS *Alabama* captured the Union ship *Manchester* off Nova

Scotia. They found the dispositions of Union gunboats by reading a captured New York newspaper.

Skirmish at LaGrange, AR.

October 12: Confederate General Stuart completed another ride around the Union Army of the Potomac, which caused a stir in Washington, DC about General McClellan's inactivity.

October 13: US President Lincoln once again urged General McClellan to get moving.

October 14: Union General Stephen Hurlbut was given command of the military district of Mississippi. His field command was given to General James McPherson.

The Midwest states held their Congressional mid-term elections with Democrats winning most of them.

The only success in the Confederate attempt to take Kentucky was the amount of supplies taken. That was according to the Richmond *Examiner.*

CS War Department clerk John B. Jones wrote about General J.E.B. Stuart's raid into Pennsylvania.

October 15: Union forces made a reconnaissance along the Potomac River into Western Virginia.

It was around this time that Union Private Sneeden was sent to Washington, DC when General Samuel Heintzelman was assigned the command of the District of Washington.

October 16: US President Lincoln sent yet another message to General McClellan telling him to do something, anything, just make an attack!

October 17: Confederate General Morgan's forces defeated Union troops near Lexington, KY.

October 18: Skirmish at Haymarket, VA.

October 19: Confederate General Van Dorn had managed to regroup his troops near Holly Springs, MS.

The administration of Union General Butler at New Orleans continued to astonish and anger Southerners with not only the raising of three regiments of African-American soldiers, but also with the announcement that Blacks and Whites were equal under the law, at least in New Orleans.

October 20: Skirmishing at Bardstown, KY.

October 21: Union General McClernand was ordered by US President Lincoln to raise a force to assault Vicksburg.

US President Lincoln expressed his support for elections in Tennessee, at this time under a military government.

October 22: Skirmishing at Port Royal and Hilton Head, SC.

Union force left Fort Donelson, TN, headed for Waverly, TN.

Confederates captured Loudon, KY.

October 23: Small action at Waverly, TN.

October 24: Union General Buell was replaced by General Rosecrans as commander, Army of the Ohio.

Skirmishes at Brownsville, TN and Morgantown, KY.

Skirmish at Grand Prairie, MO.

October 25: US President Lincoln was getting very annoyed that General McClellan had not moved an inch from his position. In response to a complaint that the Army's horses were worn out and that remounts were needed, Lincoln wrote, *"Will you pardon me for asking what the horses of your army have done since the Battle of Antietam that fatigues them anything?"*

October 26: Union Army of the Potomac **finally** began their movement across the Potomac River into Virginia.

October 27: Federals win a skirmish at Labadieville, LA.

October 28: Confederate General Lee moved his army up the Shenandoah Valley to check Union General McClellan's movements.

Confederate General Breckenridge assumed command of the Army of Middle Tennessee.

October 29: Union Army of the Potomac, about 130,000 men, moved across the Potomac River and into the Shenandoah Valley. All of this under observation of Confederate Generals Lee and Jackson.

October 30: US Navy offered a $500,000 reward for the capture of CSS *Alabama*.

Union General Rosecrans formally assumed command of the Department of the Cumberland.

October 31: Union General Grant began gathering his troops at Grand Junction, TN with the aim to attack Vicksburg.

November 1: Confederates fled Plymouth, NC as Union naval forces seized the town.

Skirmish at Philomont, VA.

An article in the Cincinnati, OH *Gazette* called for the mechanization of farming to ease the labor shortage that was caused by many farmers joining the Union Army.

November 2: CSS *Alabama* left Nova Scotia for the waters near Bermuda.

Cavalry skirmish at Bloomfield, VA.

Union General Grant moved his forces toward Holly Springs, MS to engage Confederate General Van Dorn's troops.

November 3: Skirmish in Loudon County, VA.

November 4: Union forces seized Hamilton, NC. They ended up chasing the same Confederates who fled Plymouth.

US Congressional elections concluded with Democrats gaining in many states, but Republicans maintained control of the US House of Representatives.

An article in the Philadelphia, PA *Public Ledger* illustrated the effect of the shortage of cotton on other industries, such as paper manufacturing.

An article in the Charleston *Mercury* called on Confederate citizens to save their rags for industrial use.

CS War Department clerk John B. Jones wrote that government agents were buying flour at $12 a barrel and selling it for $24.

November 5: Union task force continued up the Roanoke River, but turned back when illness struck the troops.

US President Lincoln ordered General McClellan's removal from command of the Army of the Potomac. General Burnside was assigned the command, even though he did not want it.

Skirmishing at Barbee's Cross Roads and Chester's Gap, VA.

Confederate attack on Nashville repulsed.

November 6: Confederate Generals Longstreet and Jackson were promoted to Lieutenant General and assigned as commanders of First and Second Corps of the Army of Northern Virginia.

November 7: Union General McClellan received the order that relieved him of his command.

November 8: Union General Butler ordered New Orleans breweries closed, not knowing that General Banks had just been appointed to succeed him as commander.

November 9: Blockade-runner *Robert E. Lee* was captured off the North Carolina coast.

Union General Burnside officially assumed command of the Army of the Potomac.

November 10: Union General McClellan left the camps of the Army of the Potomac with much ceremony.

November 10th, 1862.—In accordance with General orders, No. 182, issued by the President of the United States, I hereby assume command of the Army of the Potomac. Patriotism, and the exercise of my every energy in the direction of this army, aided by the full and hearty co-operation of its officers and men, I hope, under the blessing of God, insure its success. Having been a sharer of the privations, and a witness of the bravery of the old Army of the Potomac in the Maryland campaign, and fully identified with them in their feelings of respect and esteem for General McClellan, entertained through a long and most friendly association with him, I feel that it is not as a stranger I assume command.
A. E. BURNSIDE, Major General Commanding
—Burnside's proclamation as printed in
Frank Leslie's Illustrated Newspaper

November 11: Union General Burnside's first act as army commander was to change the plan General McClellan had formed for an assault on Richmond by advancing on the Confederate Capital by way of Fredericksburg.

November 12: Union victories in Tennessee had left General Rosecrans overextended, fortunately for him, the Confederates did not have a commander that could take advantage of the situation, they had General Bragg!

November 13: Confederate General Bragg advanced on Murfreesboro, TN while some of his troops clashed with Union forces near Nashville, TN.

Union forces under General Grant took Holly Springs, MS.

November 14: Union General Burnside organized the Army of the Potomac into three "Grand Divisions." Right Grand Division (General Sumner), made up of II Corps (General Couch) and IX Corps (General Wilcox), Center Grand Division (General Hooker), made up of III Corps (General Stoneman) and V Corps (General Butterfield), and the Left Grand Division (General Franklin), made up of I Corps (General Reynolds) and VI Corps (General Smith). Detached units include the XI Corps at Manassas Junction, and the XII Corps at Harper's Ferry.

November 15: Union General Ambrose Burnside began moving his army from Warrenton, VA to Fredericksburg.

November 16: Union General Burnside's reasoning for going through Fredericksburg was simple: Washington, DC could still be covered, supply routes were shorter, and the distance to Richmond was only 75 miles. The only question is whether he could pull it off.

November 17: Union vanguard reached Falmouth, opposite Fredericksburg and found the Rappahannock River too deep to march across. Pontoon bridges were needed. A Confederate battery gave the Union troops a welcome that was soon suppressed. An idea was floated to send troops across to find suitable fords but General Burnside would not hear of it. He ordered no action to be taken until the bridging material and the rest of the army arrived. Meanwhile, Confederate General Lee was not idle: he was sending artillery and cavalry to the area to hold things until the rest of the army could get there.

CSS *Alabama* arrived at Martinique.

November 18: USS *San Jacinto* arrived off Martinique in order to prevent CSS *Alabama* from leaving. The Confederate ship does anyway.

Skirmish at Rural Hills, TN.

Confederate General Stuart had confirmed that the Union army had left Warrenton, VA and was headed for Fredericksburg. General Lee ordered General Longstreet to march there immediately.

November 19: James Seddon appointed Confederate Secretary of War.

Confederate General Jackson ordered to march his troops to Fredericksburg in order to aid General Lee.

November 20: Confederate General Lee arrived at Fredericksburg.

On the South Carolina Sea Islands, newly freed African-Americans were being educated with great success.

CS War Department clerk John B. Jones wrote about salt being sold at $1.30 a pound.

November 21: Confederate General Bragg sent General Forrest on a mission to cut Union communications.

Union General Burnside sent a letter to the Mayor of Fredericksburg ordering the town's surrender. The mayor's reaction was to evacuate the town.

CS War Department clerk John B. Jones wrote that cotton for shirts and calico were selling for $1.75 a yard.

November 22: Union General Edwin Sumner sent his own message, promising not to fire on Fredericksburg unless he was fired at.

November 23: The entire Union Army of the Potomac was on the bank of the Rappahannock River, opposite Fredericksburg, but none of the bridging material had arrived. The time for an easy occupation of the town has now passed.

November 24: Skirmish at Beaver Creek, MO.

US President Lincoln wrote to Union General Carl Schurz in which he criticized fellow Republicans for trying to run the war for him.

November 25: Union General Grant restored his lines of communication and was resuming the offensive against Vicksburg.

November 26: Skirmish at Summerville, MS.

November 27: US President Lincoln visited the Army of the Potomac campsite near Fredericksburg and conferred with General Burnside.

November 28: Union General Grant continued his advance against Confederate General Van Dorn in Mississippi. Grant was now receiving assistance in the form of a Union column under General Alvin Hovey that was coming in from Arkansas.

November 29: Confederate Army of Northern Virginia adopted a formal corps structure with General Longstreet commanding I Corps and General Jackson commanding II Corps.

Union troops were building a supply base at Aquila Creek in order to support the Fredericksburg operation.

Holly Springs, MS was captured by Union troops.

Skirmish at Cane Hill, AR.

An article in the Chicago *Times* reported on a meeting in Dixon, IL scheduled for December 1 to address what was felt to be an unfair advantage that Easterners had in getting military contracts and tax breaks.

CS War Department clerk John B. Jones wrote that shirts could be bought for $12 each.

November 30: Confederate Captain Semmes moved his base of operations to the Leeward Islands. While in transit his ship, CSS *Alabama*, was approached by USS *Vanderbilt* but the Federal vessel did not catch her.

Confederate General Jackson's corps arrived at Fredericksburg.

December 1: US President Lincoln gave a State of the Union Address, in which he pledged that the full might of the Union would be used to bring about the abolition of Slavery.

Skirmishes at Charleston and Berryville, VA.

CS War Department clerk John B. Jones wrote that there were rumors concerning a coming battle on the Rappahannock River.

December 2: There was skirmishing along the Rappahannock River in Virginia, but Union troops still did not have the pontoon bridging they needed in order to cross the river. Confederates were digging in to meet any attack.

December 3: Granada, MS fell to Federal troops.

Skirmishing along the Hardin Pike, near Nashville, TN.

Harper's Weekly printed a poem by a Union soldier entitled "Thanksgiving."

December 4: Confederate General Joe Johnston assumed command of the Department of the West.

Winchester, VA taken by Federal troops.

Rebecca Usher, a Union nurse, wrote her sister on her experiences at a hospital at Chester, PA.

December 5: Confederate General Thomas Hindman defied orders to withdraw from Arkansas and marched against Union General James Blunt's forces at Fayetteville. Blunt called for reinforcements and General

Francis Herron's troops began a forced march from 100 miles to reinforce Blunt.

December 6: Confederate General Hindman, upon hearing of Union reinforcements coming to Fayetteville decided to attack those reinforcements first, and then deal with the others.

December 7: Battle of Prairie Grove, AR: Union commanders: Generals James Blunt and Francis Herron. Confederate commander: General Thomas Hindman. Herron's forces arrived in the area but were too tired to do much more than hold off Hindman's attacks. Blunt brought in his forces but did not break the Confederate line. Battle ended in a draw, but Hindman pulled out during the night.

Confederate General Morgan attacked the Union garrison at Hartsville, TN and captured it.

December 8: Confederate General Hindman pulled his troops back from the Union lines at Prairie Grove.

December 10: Pontoon bridging finally arrived so that the Army of the Potomac could cross the Rappahannock River at Fredericksburg.

US Congress passed the bill that created the State of West Virginia.

Confederate General Lee wrote a letter to his daughter-in-law, Charlotte (wife of Fitzhugh) in which he expressed his sorrow on the death of her second child.

December 11: Union General Burnside ordered Fredericksburg shelled as the pontoon bridges were put across. Bridging units came under fire by Confederate General William Barksdale's Mississippi troops. Union troops finally grabbed some pontoon boats and rowed across. They established a bridgehead and drove off the Confederates, which allowed the bridges to be completed. This also allowed a small detachment to occupy the town.

Confederate General Forrest led 2500 cavalry from Columbia, TN in order to disrupt Union General Grant's communication lines.

December 12: Union troops crossed the Rappahannock River under the cover of fog and entered Fredericksburg. There was no fighting and the Union forces proceed to loot the town.

December 13: Battle of Fredericksburg, VA: Union commander: General Ambrose Burnside. Confederate commander: General Robert E. Lee. Battle opened as General Meade's corps attacked the Confederate right, but was held up by Confederate artillery commanded by Major John Pelham, who kept shifting his two guns in order to confuse the Federals. By mid-morning, Confederate artillery shelled the town, which caused havoc amongst the Union forces. At noon, the first of six frontal assaults on the Confederate line on Marye's Heights, west of the town, commenced and resulted in three brigades getting shattered. At the same time, Meade's advance was again halted by artillery fire. Meade attacked through an area previously thought impassable and found Confederate troops under General Maxey Gregg. Gregg believed the advancing troops were friendly and ordered his troops to hold their fire. He paid for the mistake for his life. Meade found himself unsupported and had to pull back. At 1a.m., a second assault, including the famed Irish Brigade, went up Marye's Heights and was repulsed with heavy losses. At 2 p.m. another two divisions were sent up the heights, at this time carpeted with the dead and dying, and they were also shattered. At 3p.m. and 5p.m. more attacks were sent up the heights but to no avail, the Confederates were behind a stone wall that allowed almost absolute protection. Burnside decided to make one more attack, this time with him leading it, but was talked out of it. Union forces were pulled back into the town, but many were trapped on the slope and could not be evacuated until the next day. Confederate victory.

> *I saw one man with gun in hand, walking with a firm step and a cheerful countenance, having been struck by a piece of shell in the forehead, laying bare the brain so I could see every pulsation.*
> *—Unknown Union soldier at Fredericksburg.*

December 14: Union General Burnside ordered all of his troops to pull out of Fredericksburg.

Skirmish at Kingston, NC.

CS War Department clerk John B. Jones wrote, *"Yesterday was a bloody day"* referring to the Battle of Fredericksburg.

December 15: Confederate General Forrest disrupted Union General Grant's communication lines as Grant moved his army toward Vicksburg.

Union General Banks arrived in New Orleans to take command of Union troops there.

December 16: Union troops reached Whitehall, NC and, after a skirmish, destroyed two ironclads under construction.

December 17: Union forces destroyed rail lines and bridges near Goldsboro, NC, but were driven off by a Confederate counterattack.

Union General Grant issued General Order 11, which expelled Jews from his area of operations. This did not go over well in Washington, DC.

December 18: Union General Grant reorganized his army into four corps, commanded by Generals Sherman, Stephen Hurlbut, James McPherson, and John McClernand.

Confederate General Forrest defeated Union cavalry near Lexington, TN.

December 19: US President Lincoln refused an offer by Secretary of State Seward to resign amid trouble amongst the Cabinet.

Skirmishes at Spring Creek and Jackson, TN.

December 20: Confederate General Van Dorn's troops launched an attack on Union General Grant's supply base at Holly Springs, which captured 1800 prisoners and destroyed $1,500,000 of materiel.

Union General Sherman began the Vicksburg, Campaign by departing Memphis and attempting to approach Vicksburg by the swamps to the north of the town.

Confederate General Forrest eluded Union pursuers near Jackson, TN, while tearing up nearby rail lines.

US Secretary of the Treasury Chase offered to resign. US President Lincoln refused.

December 21: Near Holly Springs, MS, Confederate General Van Dorn was stopped at a river crossing by a force of only 200 Union troops.

US Congress authorized the award of the Medal of Honor to naval personnel.

Confederate General Morgan launched a raid behind Union lines in Tennessee.

Skirmish at Davis Mills, MS.

December 22: Union General Rosecrans moved his command to Nashville.

December 23: CS President Davis declared Union General Butler, the former commander in New Orleans, an outlaw and authorized immediate hanging if captured.

December 24: Union General John Foster's North Carolina expedition reached New Berne.

December 25: Confederate General Van Dorn moved his forces back into Mississippi following a small victory at Ripley, TN.

Confederate forces under General Morgan skirmished with Union forces at Green's Chapel and Bear Wallow, both in Kentucky.

CS War Department clerk John B. Jones wrote on this Christmas Day, turkeys could be bought for $11 each and salt for .33 cents a pound. To pay for Christmas dinner and to buy a few gifts, he had to sell a silver watch for $75.

December 26: Union General Rosecrans began moving his troops from Nashville in pursuit of Confederate General Bragg's troops near Murfreesboro, TN.

Union General Sherman's troops reached the Yazoo River, north of Vicksburg.

December 27: Union garrison of Elizabethtown, TN surrendered to Confederate General Morgan's raiders.

Union General Rosecrans forces approached Murfreesboro and began meeting resistance from Confederates.

December 28: Confederate General Hindman was forced to pull out of Arkansas in the face of Federal cavalry attacks.

Union General Sherman's troops crossed the Yazoo River but ran into Confederate defenders on high bluffs. The only avenue of attack was covered by Confederate artillery.

Frederick Douglass delivered a speech in Rochester, NY about the fall of slavery.

December 29: Union General Sherman, supported by gunboats, attempted to hit Chickasaw Bluffs north of Vicksburg, but was turned back.

December 30: Union General Rosecrans maneuvered his army in line outside Murfreesboro.

Union General Sherman made plans to try again to hit Chickasaw Bluffs north of Vicksburg, this time with naval support.

USS *Monitor* sank in heavy seas off Cape Hatteras, NC.

December 31: Battle of Murfreesboro (Stone's River), TN: Union commander: General William Rosecrans. Confederate commander: General Braxton Bragg. Union and Confederate left flanks were attacked at the same time. Union line gave way first but the line was reinforced. Union line held firm but were out of their original lines as darkness falls. Battle will end on January 2, 1863.

> *The spectacle was grand. With cheers and shouts they charged up the hill, shooting down and bayoneting the flying cannoneers. General Cheatham, Colonel Field and Joe Lee cutting and slashing with their swords. The victory was complete. The whole left wing of the Federal army was driven back five miles from their original position. Their dead and wounded were in our lines, and we captured many pieces of artillery, small arms, and prisoners.*
> *-Sam Watkins, Private, 1ˢᵗ Tennessee, CS Army, who was wounded at Murfreesboro*

US President Lincoln met with General Ambrose Burnside and discussed the defeat at Fredericksburg.

> *The closing day of 1862 will always be a dark one in our history, for just on the threshold of its birth the pet monster of our ironclads went down off Hatteras, with our flag flying on its tower, and in the midst of a furious storm. Its sudden and unlooked-for fate recalled to every mind that memorable Sunday in March when it signaled its advent to war by driving back to its Norfolk retreat the terrible Merrimac.*
> *—quoted from* Frank Leslie's Illustrated Newspaper

1863

January 1: US President Abraham Lincoln issued the Emancipation Proclamation.

> *That on the first day of January, in the year of our Lord, one thousand eight hundred and sixty-three, all persons held as slaves within any state or designated part of a state, the people whereof shall there be in rebellion against the United States, shall be then, thenceforth, and forever free...*
> —*Emancipation Proclamation, opening paragraph.*

Union General Burnside, taking responsibility for the defeat at Fredericksburg, offered to resign, but was refused.

Battle of Stones River: Day Two: Not much fighting took place but Union General Rosecrans and Confederate General Braxton Bragg maneuvered their troops for another fight the next day.

January 2: Battle of Stones River: Day Three: Confederate General Bragg resumed his attack by launching a massive artillery bombardment on the Union lines. A Union counterattack threatened to outflank the Confederate lines. That attack was halted but another Union assault caused the Confederates to pull back from the line in general. Union victory.

January 3: Confederate General Bragg pulled his army from Murfreesboro.

January 4: Confederate General Roger Hanson, commander of the Kentucky Orphan Brigade, died of wounds suffered at Stones River.

Union General McClernand started an expedition against Fort Hindman

(Arkansas Post), AR, against the wishes of General Grant, who needed the troops for the Vicksburg campaign.

USS *Quaker City* captured a blockade-runner off Charleston.

January 5: Confederate General Bragg's recent withdrawal to Chattanooga has left Central and Western Tennessee under Federal control.

January 6: Union General McClernand continued his expedition to Fort Hindman. The force was made up of two corps, his and General Sherman's.

January 7: Three Confederate blockade-runners broke through the Federal cordon and reached Charleston.

CS Secretary of the Navy Stephen Mallory sent a dispatch to Commander James Bulloch in the UK that urged the buying of new ironclad vessels as quickly as possible. Funding the vessels, however, had become an issue.

CS War Department clerk John B. Jones wrote about a article in a Northern newspaper that detailed a letter that Confederate General Stuart sent to Washington stating, *"Gen. Meigs will in future please furnish better mules: those you have furnished recently are very inferior."* (Stuart did not like the mules he had stolen from the Union).

January 8: Confederate attack on Springfield, MO was repulsed by a scratch Union defense force.

John Usher was named US Secretary of the Interior.

January 9: Union General McClernand's forces, backed by US Navy river boats, reached Fort Hindman.

Skirmish at Ripley, TN.

CS War Department clerk John B. Jones wrote that living in Richmond was getting very expensive (by 19th Century standards): $60 a month got a person a room at a boarding house while a house rented for $1800 a year, almost ¼ of a years salary for clerks.

January 10: Federal gunboats shelled Fort Hindman.

Federal forces shelled Galveston, TX.

Skirmishes at Suffolk and Fairfax Court House, VA.

France offered mediation of peace talks between the US and CS while the UK postponed any such move.

January 11: CSS *Alabama* attacked and sunk USS *Hatteras* off Galveston, TX.

Battle of Arkansas Post, AR: Union commander: General John McClernand. Confederate commander: General Thomas J. Churchill. McClernand sent his two brigades, under Generals Sherman and George Morgan against Confederate defenses backed onto the Arkansas River. The area was dominated by Fort Hindman. Supported by Admiral David Dixon Porter's flotilla of gunboats, the fort was surrounded. At the end of the day, the Confederates surrendered. Union victory.

Federal gunboat sunk at Memphis.

January 12: Union General Grant received a report of General McClernand's attack on Fort Hindman. He had secured authorization to remove McClernand from command but did not choose use it yet.

Third session of the Confederate Congress was convened.

January 13: Federal officials authorized the enlistment of African-Americans into the 1st South Carolina Volunteer Infantry (US) African Descent.

Fort Hindman, AR was demolished because it was of no use for Union operations.

January 14: A Union attempt to advance up the Bayou Teche, LA was stopped by determined Confederate defenses.

Ohio Representative Clement Vallandingham, a leader in the rising anti-war movement known as the Copperheads, delivered a blistering speech in the House against US President Lincoln's conduct of the war. Copperheads were so named because they wore Goddess of Liberty figures cut from copper pennies on their lapels (In one of those amazing facts, their main enemy, Lincoln, is now depicted on the penny).

January 15: CS President Davis suggested (read: ordered) that General Bragg should go on the offensive in Tennessee.

US President Lincoln viewed a demonstration of new weapons at the Washington, DC Navy Yard.

January 16: CSS *Florida* sailed out of Mobile Bay, AL and through the Federal blockade.

There was an unusual prisoner exchange as women and children who were detained in the North were allowed to travel from Washington DC to Richmond. They were searched, to their great complaint, but much material made it through the lines to be made into uniforms for Confederate soldiers.

January 17: Union General Grant left Memphis, TN for Milliken's Bend to take charge of what will become the Vicksburg Campaign.

Morale in the Union Army of the Potomac has hit a new low due to recent defeats and the fact that the Emancipation Proclamation was not popular with the army, whose members felt that they had not enlisted to free slaves.

CS War Department clerk John B. Jones wrote that beef was selling for .60 a pound, lard for $1.00 a pound, and butter for $2.00 a pound.

January 18: Union General Grant organized his Army of the Tennessee into four corps, the 13th (General McClernand), the 15th (General

Sherman), the 16th (General Hurlbut), and the 17th (General McPherson). This, along with supporting naval units, will be the force that will go after Vicksburg.

CS War Department clerk John B. Jones wrote about the price of these items: calico for $2.25 a yard, a lady's dress of the same material for $300, bleached cotton for shirts for $1.50 a yard, no ladies bonnets available, tallow candles for $1.25 a pound, soap for $1.00 a pound, ham for $1.00 a pound, opossum for $3.00 each, turkeys for $11.00 each, brown sugar for $1.00 a pound, molasses for $8.00 a gallon, and potatoes for $6.00 a bushel.

January 19: Union Army of the Potomac commander General Burnside proposed to move troops up the Rappahannock River to United States Ford in order to launch another assault on the Confederates.

An article in the Bangor, MA *Whig and Courier* highlights the exploits of Anna Etheridge, a nurse with the 5th MI. These accounts include times when she was exposed to fire, a situation considered scandalous at the time. What not many people knew at the tine was that many women were dressed as men and serving in the ranks.

January 20: The Mud March, Union General Burnside's attempt to reposition troops for a planned advance on Richmond, began.

January 21: Confederate forces recaptured Sabine Pass, TX.

Union General Fitz John Porter was dismissed from the US Army for the Union defeat at the Second Battle of Manassas. It would take 23 years to clear his name.

Thirty hours of rain made any movement of Union troops across the Rappahannock River impossible.

CS War Department clerk John B. Jones wrote about that same rainstorm.

January 22: The Mud March ended as Federal troops were ordered back to the same camps they left. The weather conditions made it impossible to move as wagons, cannon, and even horses and mules were swallowed up by deep mud.

January 23: US Army of the Potomac pulled back from Fredericksburg and into winter quarters. General Burnside now turned his attention against many of his subordinate generals.

January 24: Union General Burnside went to Washington, DC and demanded that US President Lincoln remove several senior officers from the Army of the Potomac.

Union forces arrived on the land opposite Vicksburg, MS and sent patrols up the Yazoo River.

January 25: US President Lincoln responded to General Burnside's latest demand by removing him from command of the Army of the Potomac and replacing him with General Joseph Hooker.

January 26: Union General Hooker formally assumed command of the Army of the Potomac. He was nicknamed "Fighting Joe Hooker" due to a newspaper misprint.

January 27: Editor of the Philadelphia *Journal* was arrested for printing anti-Union articles.

January 28: There was a mass meeting in St Louis in which the Emancipation Proclamation was endorsed.

As Union General Hooker took command of the Army of the Potomac, there were as many as 200 desertions per day. Many of the senior officers Hooker had to deal with were also McClellan partisans, who were not too happy with Hooker's appointment.

January 29: Skirmishes at Suffolk and Turner's Mills, VA.

January 30: Confederate General John Pemberton, commanding the

Vicksburg defenses, was asked by CS President Davis if the Yazoo River could be obstructed to prevent a Union advance from the north.

CS War Department clerk John B. Jones wrote that prices for common goods had increased at least 1000% since 1860.

January 31: Two US vessels were sunk by Confederate ramming boats in Charleston Harbor.

Skirmish at Deserted House, VA.

Union General Grant proposed that a canal be cut across the bend of the Mississippi opposite Vicksburg. The idea was to divert the Mississippi River away from Vicksburg (The project would fail, but nature would accomplish in 1876 what Grant couldn't).

Union commanders in Tennessee realized the importance of keeping the Cumberland River open in order to keep supplies moving.

February 1: Franklin, TN fell to Union troops.

February 2: USS *Queen of the West* sailed past Vicksburg, MS in broad daylight and engaged CSS *City of Vicksburg*. Neither was damaged.

Skirmish at Rappahannock Station, VA.

February 3: USS *Queen of the West* captured three Confederate supply boats that were headed for Port Hudson, MS.

A levee north of Vicksburg was blown to make a passage for Union gunboats. The passage proved too narrow.

Confederate forces attacked Fort Donelson, TN but were forced back by Union gunboat fire.

US Secretary of State Seward had a conference with the French Minister to the US, but nothing came of it.

Skirmish at Mingo Swamp, MO.

CS War Department clerk John B. Jones wrote that gold was selling in the North for .58 ½ cents an ounce while in the South it was selling for $1.75 an ounce. Cotton was selling for .96 cents a pound.

February 4: Skirmish at Lake Providence, LA.

February 5: Union General Hooker started his reorganization of the Army of the Potomac by eliminating the Grand Divisions that General Burnside had formed.

Skirmishes at Rappahannock Bridge and Grove Church, VA.

February 6: US Secretary of State William Seward formally rejected any French offer of mediation.

Union General Samuel Heintzelman was named commander of the Department of Washington and charged with protecting the Nation's Capital.

February 7: Skirmish at Williamsburg, VA.

Confederate authorities announced the reopening of the port of Galveston, TX.

As the Confederate economy continued to decline, cotton had become a medium of exchange, except that cotton exports were 1/10 of pre-war levels. Prices for goods and services were also skyrocketing, with staples such as tea reaching $500.00 a pound. Another factor that was affecting the economy was that the rail network, not very large to begin with, was deteriorating.

February 8: Union General Hooker completed his reorganization of the Army of the Potomac.

February 9: With the reorganization of the Army of the Potomac complete, Union General Hooker turned his attention to his headquarters staff.

CS War Department clerk John B. Jones wrote that he was now renting four rooms for $800 a year. Beef was selling for $1.00 a pound.

February 10: Skirmish at Chantilly, VA.

Skirmishes at Camp Sheldon, MS and Old River, LA.

February 11: Union General Hooker reformed the Army of the Potomac by replacing bad officers and improving food and living conditions. As a result the level of desertions had dropped almost to zero.

February 12: Skirmish at Bolivar, TN.

There was action at the mouth of the Atchafalaya River, LA as USS *Queen of the West* and USS *De Soto* destroyed several Confederate ammunition wagon trains on the riverbank.

USS *Conestoga* captured two Confederate ships on the White River, AR.

CSS *Florida* captured the merchant ship *Jacob Bell* in the West Indies.

February 13: Union General Hooker reorganized the cavalry in his army under a single corps command.

USS *Indianola* departed the mouth of the Yazoo River and sailed past Vicksburg without alerting the shore batteries.

February 14: On the Atchafalaya River, USS *Queen of the West* came under Confederate fire and was abandoned after she had captured the Confederate steamer *New Era Number 5*. The crew managed to board *New Era* and escape.

February 15: Action at Nolansville and Cainsville, TN.

Steamer *New Era* reached the Mississippi River while being pursued by CSS *Webb*. The timely arrival of USS *Indianola* forced the Confederate ironclad to turn back.

February 16: US Congress passed the First Conscription Act.

Skirmish at Romney, WV.

February 17: Union troops departed Lexington, TN and marched on Clifton.

USS *Indianola* took up station on the Mississippi River south of Vicksburg.

February 18: CS War Department clerk John B. Jones wrote that butter was selling for $3.00 a pound, beef is holding at $1.00 a pound, bacon at $1.25 a pound, sausage meat at $1.00 a pound, and liver at .50 cents a pound.

February 19: At Keokuk, IA, the office of a local newspaper was ransacked by Union troops who were home recovering from wounds suffered in recent battles. The paper had been publishing anti-Union articles.

February 20: Mass rallies in Liverpool and Carlisle, UK were held in support of the Emancipation Proclamation.

February 21: Even though the Union industrial advantage was making itself apparent, there was proof that war profiteering was not a new thing. Colt Firearms was selling its Model 1861 Revolver on the open market for $15 per weapon. The price the US Army was paying was $25 per weapon. Politicians steering rich war contracts to companies in their districts were not helping the situation.

February 22: Skirmish at Tuscumbia, AL.

February 23: Around the Union Army of the Potomac's operational area, the Cavalry Corps was still having trouble with Confederate cavalry raids and ambushes.

February 24: Confederates used the recovered *Queen of the West* to capture the USS *Indianola*.

The US Territory of Arizona was created.

Union troops continued their advance down the Yazoo River towards Vicksburg.

February 25: An international incident was avoided when mail seized from the British flagged blockade-runner *Peterhoff* was returned unopened.

US Congress passed the National Bank Act, which allowed the creation of a national paper currency.

February 26: Cherokee Nation declared its support for the Union, overturning their earlier declaration for the Confederacy.

Confederate General Longstreet was appointed commander of CS Department of Virginia and North Carolina.

Skirmish at Woodstock, VA.

Union Admiral Porter sent a dummy vessel down the Mississippi River past Vicksburg. The ensuing panic caused the Confederates to destroy the captured USS *Indianola* in order to prevent its recapture.

February 27: Union cavalry were ordered to be more aggressive in dealing with Confederate cavalry incursions into the Army of the Potomac's area in Virginia.

February 28: USS *Montauk* engaged and destroyed CSS *Nashville* on the Ogeechee River. The *Montauk* was commanded by Commodore John Worden, who once commanded USS *Monitor*.

March 1: Skirmish at Bradyville, TN.

March 2: US Congress approved a bill for military appointments, which included the dismissal of 30 officers.

CS War Department clerk John B. Jones wrote that he had to move his family into another house. He also wrote about making an agreement for another edition of his "Wild Western Stories." 10,000 copies were to be printed and would sell for $2.00 each. He would get .25 cents for every copy sold, or $2500 for the entire order.

March 3: US Congress approved the Enrollment Act, which made men between 20 and 45 eligible for the draft.

March 4: Confederate General Van Dorn launched an attack on Union General Rosecrans' troops near Spring Hill, TN.

March 5: Battle of Thompson's Station, TN: Union commander: Colonel John Coburn. Confederate commander: General Earl Van Dorn. Colonel Coburn saw a target of opportunity and attacked. The Confederates counterattacked and Coburn's force was taken prisoner. Confederate victory.

Union engineers began the construction of canal across the area of land opposite Vicksburg while under fire from the city.

CS War Department clerk John B. Jones wrote that his dinner consisted of 12 eggs (costing $1.25 for the dozen), corn bread, rice, and potatoes. Beef was selling for $1.25 a pound but was of bad quality. He also wrote that one ounce of gold was worth CS$4.25.

March 6: The Army of the Potomac's Calvary Corps was re-equipping with Sharps breech-loading carbines. This would give the Union mounted arm more firepower than their Confederate counterparts.

March 7: Baltimore, MD prohibited sale of "secesh" music.

Union troops under General Banks advance on Baton Rouge.

Confederate General Edmund Kirby Smith assumed command of all Confederate troops west of the Mississippi River. (Department of the Trans-Mississippi)

March 8: Confederate Colonel John Mosby led his troopers to Fairfax

Court House, VA and captured Union General Edwin Stoughton, plus 30 men and 58 horses. Ironically, that Union force had orders to seek and capture Mosby.

> *Mosby: General, have you heard of the rebel partisan, Mosby.*
> *Stoughton: Yes, do you have him?*
> *Mosby: No. But he does have you.*

Writer Nathaniel Hawthorne wrote a friend in England and expressed the war weariness that many Northerners felt.

March 9: Union General Banks concentrated his forces at Baton Rouge. This force was supposed to join General Grant's campaign to take Vicksburg but the Confederate stronghold at Port Hudson, LA was in the way.

> *I can make more brigadier generals, but I can't make more horses.*
> *—US President Lincoln after Confederate Colonel*
> *John S. Mosby's raid of March 8.*

March 10: US President Lincoln proclaimed that any Union deserter who returned to his unit by April 1 would not be punished.

Jacksonville, FL was occupied by Union troops.

March 11: A Union force heading down the Yazoo River toward Vicksburg reached Fort Pemberton and was repulsed by the defenders.

Baltimore prohibited the sale of pictures of Confederate leaders.

CS War Department clerk John B. Jones wrote that one ounce of gold was selling for CS$5.00, US Treasury notes for $2.50, and that banknotes issued by state banks were worth more than Confederate currency.

March 12: Massachusetts Senator Charles Sumner expressed his concerns about Confederate commerce raiders being built in British ports in a letter to a friend in England.

Union Admiral Farragut made plans to run his vessels past Port Hudson, LA in order to block the supply routes from northwestern Louisiana.

March 13: A second Union attack on Fort Pemberton, MS, was repulsed.

The Confederate States Laboratory on Brown's Island, Richmond, suffered an explosion, killing 69 women and children.

March 14: A Federal attempt to sail past Confederate batteries at Port Hudson, LA resulted in only two ships making it past. Despite this, Union naval forces were now between Port Hudson and Vicksburg.

A Confederate attack on Union positions at Fort Anderson, on the Neuse River, NC, was repulsed.

CS War Department clerk John B. Jones wrote that bacon was selling for $1.50 a pound, butter for $3.00 a pound, potatoes at $12 a bushel, chickens for $3.00 each. He has decided to start a garden to supplement the family's groceries but seeds are scarce. His youngest daughter had put a pair of earrings on sale for $25 but Jones was not optimistic.

March 15: USS *Mississippi*, grounded in the attempt to sail past Port Hudson, LA was destroyed in order to prevent the gunboat falling into Confederate hands.

Authorities in San Francisco, CA seize the vessel *J.M. Chapman*, preventing the transport of six Dahlgren cannon, presumably to the Confederacy.

March 16: The Steele's Bayou expedition was launched to find another way to Vicksburg from the northeast. This would end on March 22 in failure.

Union General William Averill planed a cavalry raid in response to Confederate raids and taunting by General Fitzhugh Lee, Averill's West Point classmate. General Hooker approved the raid, noting the attitude in the Union army at the time was that no one had "seen a dead cavalryman." (Cavalry was getting no respect).

March 17: The Yazoo Pass expedition ended in failure, another way to get to Vicksburg was needed.

At Kelly's Ford, VA, Union cavalry under General Averill engaged Confederate cavalry under General Fitzhugh Lee, son of General Lee. When told that General Stuart was approaching, Averill sounded retreat and forfeited the opportunity to destroy Lee. Among the Confederate dead was Major John Pelham ("the Gallant Pelham"), one of the best artillery officers the Army of Northern Virginia had.

Members of the 116th Pennsylvania put out this advertisement, "*To come off the 17th of March, rain or shine, by horses the property of, and to be ridden by, commissioned officers of that brigade. The prizes are a purse of $500: second horse to save his stakes: 2 1/2 mile heat, best two in three, over four hurdles four and a half feet high, and five ditch fences including two artificial rivers fifteen feet wide and six deep: hurdles to be made of forest pine and braced with hoop.*" This became known as the "Grand Irish Steeple Chase."

March 18: In Paris, France, the Erlanger Bank lent the Confederacy 3,000,000 British Pounds Sterling. The bank would never recoup the losses.

March 19: Union forces, retreating from Fort Pemberton, north of Vicksburg, met reinforcements and would try another assault on the fort.

USS *Hartford* and *Albatross* sailed past Confederate batteries at Natchez and Grand Gulf, MS and positioned themselves below Vicksburg.

CS War Department clerk John B. Jones wrote that one ounce of gold was selling for CS$10.00.

March 20: A Union attempt to take Vicksburg by way of Steele's Bayou was repulsed.

March 21: Confederates hit a Federal train between Bolivar and Grand Junction, TN.

Skirmishing at Salem, TN.

March 22: Confederate General Morgan's raiders captured Mount Sterling, KY.

Confederate General John Pegram's troopers conducted several raids into Kentucky.

CS War Department clerk John B. Jones wrote on the following prices: cornmeal for $8.00 a bushel, chickens at $5.00 each, turkeys at $20.00 each, turnip greens for $8.00 a bushel, bacon for $1.50 a pound, bread at .20 cents a loaf, and flour for $38 a barrel.

March 23: Massachusetts Governor Andrew Curtin pledged to local African-American businessman George T. Dowling that blacks would receive equal treatment in the Union Army (sadly that was not the case).

USS *Hartford* and USS *Albatross* bombarded Confederate batteries at Warrenton, MS.

March 24: The last Federal attempt to take Vicksburg by a water route failed as General Sherman's troops were repulsed in the Black Bayou.

March 25: Confederate cavalry under General Forrest attacked a small Union garrison at Paducah, KY.

Union General Burnside appointed commander of the Department of the Ohio.

March 26: West Virginia approves emancipation measure.

Confederate Congress passed an act allowing the government to seize private property for military use.

March 27: US President Lincoln met with a delegation of Native-Americans.

March 28: Confederates improved their batteries at Grand Gulf, MS.

March 29: Union General Grant ordered General McClernand from Milliken's Bend to New Carthage in order to bypass Vicksburg.

Skirmish at Kelly's Ford, VA.

March 30: Confederate General A.P. Hill moved his forces to Washington, NC in order to besiege the Union garrison there.

US President Lincoln proclaimed April 30 a Day of Prayer.

Fighting at Dutton's Hill, KY.

CS War Department clerk John B. Jones wrote that cornmeal was selling for $12.00 a bushel and potatoes at $16 a bushel. On this day, no meat was to be had and butter was selling for $3.50 a pound, putting it out of the reach of some families.

March 31: Skirmish at Dranesville, VA.

Union troops departed Jacksonville, FL

Federal warships *Hartford*, *Albatross*, and *Switzerland* ran past the Grand Gulf, MS batteries.

CS War Department clerk John B. Jones wrote that the price of cornmeal went up to $17.00 a bushel, while coal is priced at $20.50 a ton and wood for $30.00 a cord.

April 1: Union troops routed a Confederate cavalry unit near the Ware River, VA.

CSS *Nashville* was sunk in the Savannah River, GA by a Union ironclad.

Union General Hooker requested siege equipment for the planned assault on Richmond.

Lt Col Arthur Freemantle, of HM Coldstream Guards, arrived in the port of Bagdad, Mexico. He was on leave from the British Army and intended on touring the CSA. On this day, he started to document everything he saw in his diary.

April 2: A women's protest over the cost on food in Richmond degenerated into a riot. It was quelled after CS President Davis emptied his own pockets of money and threatened to have local militia fire on them. This became known as the Bread Riots.

CS War Department clerk John B. Jones wrote about witnessing the Bread Riots.

Union General O.O. Howard succeeded General Carl Schurz as commander of the largely German XI Corps.

Small Confederate force repulsed at Snow Hill, TN.

April 3: US President Lincoln made a visit to the Army of the Potomac in order to press General Hooker to attack Confederate General Lee's Army of Northern Virginia.

Lt Col Freemantle arrived in Brownsville, TX, where he met with Confederate officials.

CS War Department clerk John B. Jones wrote about seeing correspondence from North Carolina about the state of conscription. He also noticed that none of the Richmond papers were mentioning the Bread Riots.

April 4: CSS *Alabama* captured the merchant vessel *Louisa*, whose cargo of coal was seized for the Confederate's own uses.

Union General Hooker ordered preparations for yet another assault on Richmond.

April 5: Several Confederate ships were detained at Liverpool, UK by British authorities.

April 6: US President Lincoln suggested for the first time that Confederate General Lee's army should be the target instead of Richmond.

April 7: Union flotilla attacked Fort Sumter, failing to reduce the fort and losing USS *Keokuk* in the process.

April 8: Union General McClernand's XIII Corps engaged Confederates near New Carthage, LA, which slowed his advance.

CS War Department clerk John B. Jones wrote about receiving reports about the shelling of Charleston, SC. He also addressed the belief that almost everybody was engaging in smuggling.

April 9: Union General Banks launched an expedition to Bayou Teche, LA.

Union troops under General McClernand stripped plantation houses in order to provide bridging material for a clear route towards Vicksburg from Louisiana.

April 10: There was an engagement between Union forces under General Gordon Granger and Confederate forces under General Van Dorn near Franklin, TN. Despite Union forces being driven off by General Forrest's cavalry, Van Dorn withdraws.

US President Lincoln reviewed the Army of the Potomac in Falmouth, VA.

April 11: US President Lincoln returned to Washington, not sure of General Hooker's plans.

CS War Department clerk John B. Jones wrote about CS President Davis' call for farmers to stop growing cotton and tobacco and instead grow food. Jones stated that it was his idea.

April 12: Union forces under General Banks reached Fort Bisland, LA. One division was sent to cut off any routes of retreat.

April 13: Union forces attacked Fort Bisland, backed up by US Navy gunboats. The Confederate forces evacuated during the night.

Union General Burnside published General Order 38, which allowed the death penalty for treason.

April 14: Union General Banks' troops entered Fort Bisland to find it deserted. Meanwhile, retreating Confederates ran into the Union blocking force and were driven off, despite support from CSS *Diana*.

April 15: CSS *Alabama* captured two Union whaling ships off Fernando de Noronha Island, Brazil.

Lt Col Freemantle wrote that he met Confederate General Magruder before departing for San Antonio, TX.

April 16: Union transport ships ran the gauntlet at Vicksburg. Only one vessel was sunk and the rest reached Grand Gulf, MS.

Confederate forces seized Fort Huger, near Suffolk, VA.

Confederate General A.P. Hill abandoned the siege of Washington, NC due to lack of supplies.

April 17: Union Colonel Benjamin Grierson led his troops out of La Grange, TN on a mission into Mississippi. This would last 16 days and cover 600 miles.

Union forces under General Banks clashed with Confederate forces under General Richard Taylor at Vermillion Bayou, LA. Confederates were forced to continue retreat.

April 18: Union General Grierson's troops clashed with Confederate patrols near New Albany, MS.

CS War Department clerk John B. Jones wrote that bacon fell to $1.50 a pound, butter to $3.25 a pound, and potatoes to $16 a barrel. He believed that foodstuffs were being hoarded to eventually drive up the prices.

April 19: Union forces attacked Fort Huger, VA, capturing the Confederate garrison within. The Federals would withdraw, with their prisoners, the next day.

Union Colonel Grierson's cavalry engaged Confederates near Pontotoc, MS.

April 20: A Union flotilla consisting of four ships attacked Fort Burton at Butte a la Rose, LA, forcing its surrender.

US President Lincoln announced that the breakaway counties of western Virginia would become the State of West Virginia on June 20, 1863.

April 21: In an effort to confuse his opponents, Union Colonel Grierson detached one of his regiments, under Colonel Edward Hatch, and sent them north.

Confederate General John Marmaduke launched a raid into Missouri.

Union Army of the Potomac was preparing for an offensive against the Confederate Army of Northern Virginia near Fredericksburg.

April 22: CS President Davis ordered General Pemberton, commander of Vicksburg defenses, to attack the Union flotilla with fire rafts. Meanwhile, 18 Union ships ran past the defenses with a loss of one transport and six barges.

CS War Department clerk John B. Jones wrote on the following prices: bacon at $1.30 per hog-round, butter at $3.00 a pound, beans at $30 a bushel, corn at $6.50 a bushel, corn meal at $9.00 a bushel, candles at $3.75 a pound, dried apples at $12 a bushel, dried peaches at $18 a bushel, superfine flour at $32 a barrel, extrafine flour at $34 a barrel, regular flour at $36 a barrel, hay at $15 per cwt, lard at $1.70 a pound, Irish potatoes at $10 a bushel, sweet potatoes at $11 a bushel, rice at .33

cents a pound, wheat at $7.00 a bushel, sugar at $1.25 a pound, molasses at $10 a gallon, coffee at $4.50 a pound, salt at .45 cents a pound, whiskey at $35 a gallon, apple brandy at $25 a gallon, and French brandy at $65 a gallon. All prices were in Confederate Dollars.

April 23: Union General Banks' forces engaged Confederates under General Hamilton Bee at Monett's Ferry, LA. The Confederates were driven off.

CS War Department clerk John B. Jones expressed the belief that the war is costing the government CS$60,000,000 a month due to the prices charged for supplies for the armies. (That figure was probably an exaggeration).

April 24: Union Colonel Grierson succeeded in wrecking the main rail supply line into Vicksburg.

Union General Michael Corcoran attacked Confederate General George Pickett's forces near Fredericksburg and was repulsed.

Confederate Congress levied taxes on agricultural goods as well as profits from the sale of goods and services.

Lt Col Freemantle reached San Antonio and got a room in the Menger Hotel, one block from the Alamo.

CS War Department clerk John B. Jones wrote about the belief that the Federal Army will evaporate due to upcoming expirations of terms on enlistment. He does not believe it.

April 25: Confederate General Marmaduke reached the Union garrison at Cape Girardeau, MO.

CS War Department clerk John B. Jones wrote about hearing the news of the Federal invasion of Mississippi. He expressed dismay that CS President Davis would leave the fate of Vicksburg in the hands of a Northerner (General Pemberton, a Pennsylvania native).

Union General Grant's troops engaged the Vicksburg garrison at Hard Times Landing.

April 26: Confederate General Marmaduke attacked Cape Girardeau, MO but was driven back.

Union Colonel Hatch succeeded in drawing Confederates away from General Grierson's forces and with that his troopers headed to Lagrange, TN.

Union General Hooker began his long awaited offensive against Confederate General Lee by marching on Kelly's Ford, VA. Rain hampered the movement.

Lt Col Freemantle took some time off in San Antonio, and saw some of the sights, including Mission San Jose and Mission San Juan.

April 27: Union General Grierson's forces damaged another railroad, this time the railroad line north of Jackson, MS.

Union General Hooker sent three corps across the Rappahannock and Rapidan Rivers, near Fredericksburg.

Lt Col Freemantle left San Antonio and headed for Alleyton (near Houston).

April 28: Road repairs were needed to in order to allow Union General Joseph Hooker's forces to keep going after the rains in Virginia have subsided.

Lt Col Freemantle continued his journey to Alleyton, stopping at Sequin and Gonzales.

April 29: Confederate General Lee ordered General Longstreet to abandon Suffolk, VA and join him. He had just learned that Federal forces were trying to flank him near an area known as the Wilderness.

Union Admiral Porter's ironclads engaged Confederate forts at Grand

Gulf, MS. After sundown, General Grant begins moving his troops across the Mississippi River.

Lt Col Freemantle reached Alleyton where he will catch a train.

April 30: Union General Grant's troops skirmished with Confederates at Bruinsburg, MS.

Union General Hooker had the Army of the Potomac concentrated at Chancellorsville, VA.

CS War Department clerk John B. Jones wrote about General Joseph Hooker's advance and thinks a decisive battle is but days away.

Lt Col Fremantle's train reached Houston and he checked into the Fannin House Hotel.

> *Shoot up everything blue and keep up the scare.*
> *--Confederate Brigadier General Nathan Bedford Forrest.*

May 1: Union General Francis P. Blair Jr's forces continued their engagement at Drumgould's Bluff, MS but withdrew that night.

Battle of Port Gibson, MS: Union commander: General Ulysses S. Grant. Confederate commander: General John Pemberton. Confederate forces tried to stop the Union advance but were repulsed several times until they were forced to withdraw in the early evening. Union victory.

Union General Grierson engaged three Confederate companies at Wall's Bridge, MS, driving them off.

Battle of Chalk Bluff, MO: Union commander: General William Vandever. Confederate commander: General John Marmaduke. While attempting to cross the St Francis River, Marmaduke comes under attack. The Confederates manage to escape the next day, but with heavy losses. Union victory.

May 2: Battle of Chancellorsville, VA: Union commander: General Joseph Hooker. Confederate commander: General Robert E. Lee. Day One: Lee committed his forces in a maneuver that was against all conventional wisdom, he split his army in the face of a numerically superior enemy force. Lee sends ½ of the army, under General Jackson to his left upon receiving intelligence of the Union right flank being exposed and encamped. In the late afternoon, Jackson launched an attack on the Union XI Corps, crushing it. Other Union forces came to the rescue and fighting continued until darkness fell. That night, General Jackson rode ahead of his lines and was mistakenly fired upon by a North Carolina regiment. Jackson was seriously wounded and had his left arm amputated. Cavalry commander J.E.B. Stuart took over Jackson's corps.

Union General Grierson's troops reached Baton Rouge, LA.

Lt Col Freemantle took a train to Galveston and met former Texas Governor Sam Houston while on board.

May 3: Battle of Chancellorsville: Day Two: Confederate General Lee ordered a general attack along his front. Union General Hooker suffered a concussion when his headquarters was hit. The Federals were finally forced to pull back to United States Ford. Battle concludes. Confederate victory.

Union VI and II Corps attacked Confederate positions at Marye's Heights, outside Fredericksburg. The position was captured.

Battle of Salem Church, VA: Union commander: General John Sedgwick. Confederate commander: General Jubal Early. Early was withdrawing from Fredericksburg when Sedgwick attacked. Upon learning of the attack, General Lee sent reinforcements.

Union General Grierson's forces reached Union lines at Baton Rouge.

Lt Col Freemantle returned to Houston.

May 4: Union General Sedgwick was forced to retreat back across the

Rappahannock River under Confederate artillery fire. Battle of Salem Church concludes. Confederate victory.

Union General Hooker ordered the Army of the Potomac back across the Rappahannock River.

CS War Department clerk John B. Jones wrote about receiving reports of the Battle of Chancellorsville and of General Jackson's wounding.

Lt Col Freemantle departed Houston for Shreveport, LA.

May 5: Clement Vallandingham, a leader in the anti-war, pro-Confederate Sons of Liberty group, was arrested.

May 6: Union forces under Admiral Porter captured Alexandria, LA.

Confederate General A.P. Hill was assigned to command General Jackson's corps following Jackson's wounding.

Vallandingham was tried in a military court for treason and sentenced to two years in prison.

CS Navy Commander James Bullock was sent to Europe with $2,000,000 to buy ironclad vessels.

May 7: Confederate General Van Dorn was killed by Dr George Peters, who claimed Van Dorn was having an affair with his wife.

Union Army of the Potomac's morale remained high despite defeat in the Battle of Chancellorsville.

Union forces under General McClernand advanced on Raymond, MS while a corps under General Sherman moved on Dillon's Plantation.

May 8: Union ships shelled Port Hudson, LA.

Confederate General Jackson took a turn for the worst. His wounds were healing, but infection had set in. His wife and daughter were at his side.

CS War Department clerk John B. Jones wrote that good spirits were abound in Richmond as Union General Hooker was no longer threatening the city. Also reported seeing several Federal officers as prisoners.

Lt Col Freemantle reached Shreveport, LA, where he met with Louisiana Governor Moore.

May 9: Confederate General Joe Johnston assumed command of all Confederate forces in the West.

CS President Davis promised the Vicksburg, MS defenders every support, even though Union forces threaten to cut the city off.

Lt Col Freemantle left Shreveport for Munroe in order to cross the Mississippi River and avoid the Federals.

May 10: At 3:15 p. m., Confederate General Jackson died of pneumonia contracted while recovering from wounds suffered at Chancellorsville.

No, no, let us pass over the river and rest under the shade of the trees.
—Confederate Lieutenant General Thomas Jackson's last words.

May 11: Anti-war critic Clement Vallandingham applied for a writ of habeas corpus while in Federal prison.

Anti-war Democrats stormed a Republican newspaper office in Dayton, OH.

CS War Department clerk John B. Jones wrote about hearing of General Jackson's death. He reported that the body will arrive in the afternoon and that flags will be at half-staff. Government offices will also be closed.

May 12: The 54th Massachusetts, an African-American unit, was raised and placed under the command of Union Colonel Robert Shaw, the son of abolitionist parents.

Battle of Raymond, MS: Union commander: General James McPherson. Confederate commander: General John Gregg. A Confederate artillery attack was launched in order to stop the Federals from crossing Fourteen Mile Creek. Despite heavy Union losses, they were reinforced and manage to push the Confederates back. Union victory.

May 13: Confederate General Joe Johnston arrived at Jackson, MS and ordered its evacuation upon learning that two Federal corps were approaching. This maneuver removed any chance of the garrison at Vicksburg getting any reinforcements.

Confederate General Pemberton deployed troops to Edward's Station, MS in order to counter Union General Grant's moves.

CS War Department clerk John B. Jones wrote that the state funeral of General Jackson was held this day.

> *With deep grief the Commanding General announces to the army the death of Lieut.-Gen. T.J. Jackson, who expired on the 10th instant, at 3 ½ p.m. The daring, skill, and energy of this great and good soldier, by the degree of an all-wise Providence, are now lost to us. But while we mourn his death, we feel that his spirit still lives, and will inspire the whole army with his indomitable courage and unshaken confidence in God as out hope and out strength. Let his name be a watchword to his corps, who have followed him to victory on so many fields. Let officers and soldiers emulate his invincible determination to do everything in the defense of out beloved country. R.E. Lee, General*
> *—Confederate General Robert E. Lee, General Orders No. 61*

May 14: Battle of Jackson, MS: Union commanders: Generals Sherman and James McPherson. Confederate commander: General John Gregg. Gregg organized a rear guard action while General Joe Johnston evacuated the Mississippi State capital. At mid-afternoon, Gregg was ordered to disengage and join Johnston. Union victory.

US diplomatic efforts to prevent Great Britain from building warships for the CSA showed signs of succeeding as Confederate Commissioner Bullock decided to move the ships he had bought to France for completion instead of keeping them in Britain.

Lt Col Freemantle headed for Natchez, MS where he could cross the Mississippi River.

May 15: Confederate General Pemberton attempted to cut Union General Grant's supply lines in a bid to halt the Union advance on Vicksburg.

CS War Department clerk John B. Jones wrote about a fire at the Tredegar Iron Works.

May 16: Battle of Champion's Hill, MS: Union commander: General Ulysses S. Grant. Confederate commander: General John Pemberton. Confederates establishing a defensive line east of Vicksburg were attacked by a strong Union force and were forced back after a daylong battle. Union victory.

> *General, the rebels are awful thick up there.*
> —*Unknown Union officer to Major General John Logan.*
>
> *Damn it, that's the place to kill them—where they are thick!*
> —*Logan's reply.*

Lt Col Freemantle was delayed in his journey by the fall of Jackson, MS, but still decided to try and reach the town.

May 17: Union forces under General McClernand engaged Confederates at the Big Black River, east of Vicksburg. 1700 Confederates were captured but the remainder escaped, burning the bridges that they were using.

May 18: Union forces reached the outskirts of Vicksburg.

Lt Col Freemantle reached Jackson, MS with the help of a French boy whose family lived in the area. He got into a spot of bother as local residents mistook him for a spy. Some letters from Confederate officials in Texas that he was carrying saved him from a hanging.

May 19: Union General Grant ordered an assault on the Vicksburg defenses but that attack was repulsed.

US Secretary of War Stanton ordered anti-Union activist Clement Vallandingham banished to the Confederacy.

Lt Col Freemantle breakfasted with Confederate General State Rights Gist.

May 20: Union General Grant ordered his army to entrench themselves around Vicksburg. Between retreating Confederates and the US Navy, the Confederate Navy base at Yazoo City, MS was destroyed along with three warships that were under construction.

CS War Department clerk John B. Jones wrote that butter was now $4 a pound while a sheep costs $50 and a cow $500.

May 21: A Union force from Baton Rouge encountered Confederate troops at Plains Store, LA and drove them off. A second Confederate force arrived and was also driven off. This reestablished General Grant's supply lines and continued the Union advance on Port Hudson.

CS War Department clerk John B. Jones wrote that strawberries were sold this day for $4 a pint. Coal will cost $25 a load and wood for $30 a cord.

May 22: Union General Grant ordered a second attack in the Vicksburg defenses, which also failed. Grant now considered a siege.

Lt Col Freemantle wrote about being able to hear the artillery bombardment that was fired at Vicksburg from his room in Jackson.

May 23: Union General Banks' force reached Port Hudson, LA and began digging in.

Lt Col Freemantle departed Jackson, MS for Mobile, AL.

May 24: Union General Hooker prepared for another Confederate assault near Fredericksburg, not knowing that Confederate General Lee was busy planning an invasion of the North.

Lt Col Freemantle reached Mobile, AL and checked in to the "Battlehouse" Hotel.

Austin, MS burned by US Marines.

May 25: Clement Vallandingham was handed over to Confederate authorities in Tennessee.

May 26: Union General Banks completed his encirclement of Port Hudson, LA.

Lt Col Freemantle departed Mobile on an overnight train for Montgomery, AL.

May 27: Union General Banks launched an attack on Port Hudson, which failed.

CSS *Chattahoochee* was destroyed on the Chattahoochee River, GA. (The remains are at the National Civil War Naval Museum, Port Columbus).

Lt Col Freemantle passed through Montgomery and continued traveling to West Point, GA and on to Atlanta, where he caught another overnight train for Chattanooga, TN.

May 28: The 54th Massachusetts departed Boston, MA for Port Royal, SC.

Union Admiral Porter supplied some heavy guns to assist in reducing the Confederate fortifications around Vicksburg, MS.

Lt Col Freemantle left Chattanooga for Shelbyville, TN. He stopped at

Wartrace, where he met Confederate Generals Hardee and Polk, as well as Clement Vallandigham, recently exiled from the North.

May 29: Union General Burnside offered to resign in protest over the release of Vallandingham. US President Lincoln refused to accept it.

Lt Col Freemantle arrived at Shelbyville and met with Confederate General Bragg.

CS War Department clerk John B. Jones wrote about the following prices: wheat at $7 a bushel, corn at $10 a bushel, oats at $6.50 per bushel, superfine flour at $32 a barrel, extrafine flour at $34 a barrel, regular flour at $37 a barrel, cornmeal at $11 a bushel, bacon at $1.50 a hoground, butter at $3 a pound, lard at $1.60 a pound, candles at $3 a pound, dried apples at $12 a bushel, dried peaches at $18 a bushel, eggs at $1.50 a dozen, beans at $20 a bushel, peas at $18 a bushel, potatoes at $10 a bushel, hay at $12 per cwt, rice at .20 cents a pound, salt at .50 cents a pound, soap at .60 cents a pound, sole leather at $4 a pound, harness leather at, $4.25 a pound, russet and wax uppers at $5.50 a pound, wax kip skins at $6 a pound, calf skins at $325 a dozen, apple brandy at $25 a gallon, whiskey at $32 a gallon, French brandy at $80 a gallon, brown sugar at $1.55 a pound, molasses at $10.50 a gallon, coffee at $4 a pound, and tea at $10 a pound.

May 30: Confederate General Lee reorganized the Army of Northern Virginia into three corps. 1st Corps was commanded by General Longstreet. 2nd Corps was commanded by General A.P. Hill. 3rd Corps was commanded by General Ewell.

Union General Grant prepared for a possible Confederate attack from Jackson, MS, led by General Joe Johnston.

CS War Department clerk John B. Jones wrote about a transaction involving a horse. The offer was for $500 in notes but the seller wanted $250 in gold.

May 31: Falling water levels and the high heat made life difficult for Confederate troops in the trenches at Port Hudson, LA.

CS War Department clerk John B. Jones wrote about the following prices: wheat at $4.50 a bushel, corn at $4 a bushel, oats at $2 per bushel, rye at $3.20 a bushel, superfine flour at $22.50 a barrel, extrafine flour at $34 a barrel, regular flour at $37 a barrel, cornmeal at $4.20 a bushel, bacon at $1 a hoground, salt pork at $1 a pound, butter at $3 a pound, lard at $1 a pound, candles at $3 a pound, dried apples at $3 a bushel, dried peaches at $4.50 a bushel, eggs at $1.50 a dozen, beans at $4 a bushel, peas at $4 a bushel, Irish potatoes at $4 a bushel, sweet potatoes at $5 a bushel, onions at $5 a bushel, and a horse selling for $350.

June 1: There was an impasse between the CSA and the United Kingdom over the ironclad vessels that were supposed to be completed on this date. UK government was considering seizing the vessels.

CS War Department clerk John B. Jones wrote about some Northern newspaper accounts that Union General Grant was killed near Vicksburg. (This was obviously in error, although it might have something to do with an incident in which Grant was thrown from his horse).

June 2: Confederate Army of Northern Virginia received orders to begin marching north.

June 3: Union General Burnside ordered the Chicago *Times* newspaper shut down for its Democratic stance.

Confederate troops, numbering 70,000, departed Fredericksburg and began moving north. The movement was spotted by Union balloon observers but General Hooker, upon receiving the report, was unsure what this meant.

June 4: US President Lincoln ordered the Chicago *Times* reopened, countermanding Union General Burnside's closure order of June 1.

Joint US Army/Navy operation destroyed a foundry at Walterton, VA where cannon shells were being cast.

Confederate Generals Longstreet and Ewell's corps advanced north as

General A.P. Hill's corps remained at Fredericksburg. General Stuart's cavalry was massed around Brandy Station.

Situation was bleak for the Vicksburg defenders as Confederate General Pendleton ordered provisions seized and rationing imposed.

Nadine Turchin, wife of 19th Illinois commander Colonel John Turchin, wrote a letter decrying the role of women in 19th Century America (John Turchin was actually Ivan Turchinoff, a Russian immigrant. His wife's name was Nadia).

CS War Department clerk John B. Jones wrote about getting conflicting reports about the situation in Vicksburg. The dispatches said everything was going well, the Memphis newspapers were saying otherwise.

June 5: Confederate General Lee was concentrating his army near Culpepper, VA while General Stuart held a Grand Review of his cavalry at Brandy Station.

Lt Col Freemantle left Shelbyville, TN for Atlanta, GA.

CS War Department clerk John B. Jones wrote about receiving a dispatch that General Kirby Smith's troops had defeated the Federals at Port Hudson, LA. Except that it was now impossible to cross the Mississippi River. He also wrote about hearing that General Lee's army was on the move.

June 6: Union Colonel Herman Lieb encountered Confederates near Richmond, LA. After beating them away, the Union African Brigade headed for Millikens Bend, LA.

There was contention between Union General Hooker and US President Lincoln over what to do as Confederate General Lee's army moved north. Hooker wanted to invade Virginia and hit Richmond while Lincoln wanted Washington, DC protected.

Lt Col Freemantle traveled from Atlanta to Augusta, GA.

June 7: Confederate forces under General Henry McCulloch attacked Union Colonel Lieb's troops at Millikens Bend, LA. Confederates were almost victorious when two Union gunboats arrived, whose fire help drove the Confederates off.

CS President Davis' plantation, Brierfield, in Mississippi was burned by Union troops.

Mary Ann Loughborough, a Vicksburg resident, wrote about conditions in the city, including the constant shelling that forced most of the residents into caves.

After touring the Powder Works, Lt Col Freemantle left Augusta, GA for Charleston, SC.

June 8: Confederate General Stuart held another cavalry review, this time for General Lee.

Lt Col Freemantle arrived at Charleston but failed to meet Confederate General Beauregard.

June 9: Battle of Brandy Station, VA: Union commander: General Alfred Pleasonton. Confederate commander: General J.E.B. Stuart. Pleasanton launched a surprise attack while Stuart was holding a review. The fight lasts all day in what would become the largest cavalry battle of the war. Pleasonton unexpectedly withdrew from the battle, giving Stuart the victory but the Confederate cavalry leader was embarrassed in that he was surprised to begin with. At this point in the war, Federal cavalry were beginning to gain in efficiency.

Lt Col Freemantle toured Charleston, viewing the forts there.

June 10: Confederate Army of Virginia's II Corps (General Ewell) began their advance up the Shenandoah Valley.

Union ship *Maple Leaf* was forced ashore at Cape Henry, VA by Confederate prisoners who then escaped.

CS War Department clerk John B. Jones wrote that there was fighting on the Rappahannock River. He also reported that there was no news of General Joe Johnston's whereabouts. There was the prevailing feeling in Richmond that the fall of Vicksburg was but a matter of time.

June 11: Despite his exile, Clement Vallandingham was nominated for Ohio governor on the Peace Democrat ticket.

US President Lincoln signed the Conscription Act into law.

June 12: Union General Hooker received intelligence that Confederate troops were on the move towards Pennsylvania.

Rumors of a Confederate invasion caused panic in Pennsylvania as Governor Andrew Curtin called out the state militia, who did not respond very well. A request to New York for help resulted in 26 militia regiments being loaned to Pennsylvania.

Confederate General Ewell's corps moved through Chester Gap, VA undetected by Union cavalry.

June 13: Confederate General Ewell attacked the Federal garrison at Winchester, VA.

June 14: Union General Banks failed in another attack on Port Hudson, LA and was forced to keep up the siege.

Confederate General Ewell's forces captured West Fort at Winchester, surrounding the town and forcing Union troops under General Robert Milroy to withdraw in the night.

Confederate General Longstreet's corps crossed the Potomac River at Sharpsburg. General Lee was with him.

June 15: CSS *Atlanta* sets out from Wilmington, NC.

Confederate General Ewell has his troops make a flanking maneuver that resulted in capturing 2400 Union troops at Winchester (Second Winchester).

Union troops attacked the Vicksburg defenses with no results.

Lt Col Freemantle departed Charleston but was delayed at Florence.

June 16: The Confederate Army of Northern Virginia continued their northward movement toward Pennsylvania.

CS War Department clerk John B. Jones wrote about reading General Lee's dispatch about Winchester.

Union General Grant's strength has reached 77,000, which was over double the 30,000 Confederates that were holding Vicksburg.

Lt Col Freemantle arrived in Wilmington, NC and spent the day in the only active port in the Confederacy.

June 17: CSS *Atlanta* attacked two Union warships at Wassaw Sound, GA, but ran aground and eventually surrendered. (This vessel will be renamed USS *Atlanta*).

Union cavalry under General Judson Kilpatrick attack Confederate cavalry under Colonel Thomas Munford at Aldie, VA. Confederates were forced back. Colonel Munford then regrouped and attacked Union cavalry under Colonel Alfred Duffie, and routed them.

Lt Col Freemantle arrived in Petersburg, VA and caught another train, arriving in Richmond later that morning. He met CS Secretary of State Judah Benjamin and President Davis.

June 18: Union General Grant relieved General McClernand after a message was published questioning the bravery of some units.

Lt Col Freemantle met with CS Secretary of War Seddon and was given letters and a pass to go to Confederate General Lee's army, at this time heading north towards Pennsylvania. It was possible that CS War

Department clerk John B. Jones may have witnessed this, but there seems to be no account of this in his diary.

June 19: Confederate General Stuart's cavalry were forced back at Middleburg, VA by Union cavalry under General David Gregg. They continued to cover the Blue Ridge mountain passes.

Confederate Army of Northern Virginia still advanced northward as the Union Army of the Potomac waited to see which way Lee will go.

Lt Col Freemantle toured Confederate vessels at Drewry's Bluff, VA.

June 20: West Virginia was admitted as the 35th US state.

Battle of Lafourche Crossing, LA: Union commander: Colonel Albert Stickney. Confederate commander: Colonel James Major. An attempt to dislodge Union forces from Port Hudson by causing havoc in the Union rear resulted in an engagement late in the afternoon on the 20th. Two attacks one on the 20th and another on the 21st were both driven back. Union victory.

Lt Col Freemantle departed Richmond for Culpepper, VA.

CS War Department clerk John B. Jones wrote about reading Northern accounts of the panic that was spreading as a result of General Lee's advance.

June 21: Union cavalry attacked Confederate troopers at Middleburg and Upperville, VA driving back Confederate General Stuart to a stronger position at Ashby's Gap.

Lt Col Freemantle crossed into the Shenandoah Valley.

June 22: Confederate cavalry had blocked Ashby's and Snicker's Gaps. This shielded General Lee's forces from Union observation.

Lt Col Freemantle reached Berryville, VA where he met members of Confederate General Lee's staff. He also met Prussian Captain

Scheibert, one of the foreign observers attached to the Army of Northern Virginia.

CS War Department clerk John B. Jones wrote that beef was selling for $1 a pound, bacon was $1.65 a pound, a single cabbage head for $1, and that there were no potatoes to be had. Jones was resorting to a small garden to supplement feeding his family.

June 23: Union General Rosecrans forces feinted toward Confederate General Bragg's left flank at Shelbyville, TN.

Confederate General Stuart received orders to sever Union lines of communication. How it was done and in what direction was left to Stuart's discretion. This action will cut off communication between Stuart and Lee until July 1.

June 24: Battle of Hoover's Gap, TN: Union commander: General George Thomas. Confederate commander: General Braxton Bragg. The Union feint of the previous day masked the main attack on Bragg's right flank. The advance continued until Confederate troops under General Alexander Stewart stopped the movement. Fighting will continue until the 26th when Bragg was forced to withdraw. Union victory.

Confederate General Stuart left the Army of Northern Virginia, still advancing towards Pennsylvania, with three brigades, leaving two to help screen the Confederate movement north.

June 25: Confederate General Stuart ran into the Union II Corps as they were marching toward Frederick, MD. It was determined that the Army of the Potomac was on the move. A message was sent to General Lee but it never arrived.

Union General Hooker was battling General Halleck and Secretary of War Edwin over reinforcements.

Confederate General Bragg's troops remain in place at Shelbyville, TN as the Federal ruse seemed to have worked.

June 26: Confederate General Early's division marched through Gettysburg on the way to York.

June 27: Union General Hooker tendered his resignation as commander of the Army of the Potomac over General Halleck and Secretary Stanton's refusal to allow troops from the Harper's Ferry garrison. This resignation was made in anger but calmly accepted. General George Meade, V Corps commander, was made the new army commander (he will hold this post for the remainder of the war).

Lt Col Freemantle arrived at Confederate General Longstreet's headquarters, 10 miles inside Pennsylvania. That evening he was in Chambersburg.

CS War Department clerk John B. Jones wrote that all able-bodied men under 45 were to meet at Broad Street, Richmond for militia duty in order to prevent the Federals taking advantage of General Lee's army heading north to make a strike on the Confederate capital.

June 28: Union General Thomas moved toward Hillsboro, TN, after Confederate General Bragg's right flank, but Bragg was headed to Tullahoma. Thomas sent General Wilder's brigade to cut the rail lines in Bragg's rear.

Confederate forces attacked Fort Butler at Donaldsonville, LA. but were repulsed by supporting Union gunboats.

A scout named Harrison reached Confederate General Longstreet's headquarters with news that the Union army was on the move. Among the information was the news of the change of command of the Army of the Potomac. This information was passed on to General Lee, who was dismayed that this news was not coming from General Stuart. As a result, Lee starts concentrating his army in Chambersburg, west of Gettysburg.

Union General Meade assumed command of the Army of the Potomac.

June 29: Confederates from Arkansas, commanded by Colonel William Parsons, reached Lane Providence, LA and forced the surrender of the Union garrison.

Meade began his plan to form a defensive line at Pipe Creek, MD, but upon hearing of Lee's movements, he decided to move his forces towards the PA line. At the same time, Union cavalry under General John Buford were conducting a scouting mission in the Gettysburg area.

June 30: Confederate General Stuart attempted to engage Union cavalry at Hannover, PA not only was he repulsed but he was almost captured. He moved to the northeast, further from Lee's army.

Union cavalry spotted Confederate troops on the Cashtown Road, west of Gettysburg. General Buford decided that the main attack would come down the next day and sent a message to the nearest infantry, I Corps under General John Reynolds.

US Marines under General Alfred Ellet were victorious against Confederate troops under Colonel Parsons at Goodrich's Landing, LA.

Confederate General Bragg's forces were pulled back towards Chattanooga.

July 1: Battle of Gettysburg, PA: Union commander: General George Meade. Confederate commander: General Robert E. Lee. Day One: At dawn, Confederates under General Henry Heth attacked a defensive line west of Gettysburg that consisted of two cavalry brigades and one battery of US Regular Artillery. By 10 a.m. Union General Reynolds arrived and had the cavalry hold long enough for his infantry to arrive. At midday, while counterattacking in a wooded area, Reynolds was killed and General Abner Doubleday assumed command. By 12:15 p.m. 11th Corps under General Oliver Howard arrived and assumed command of the battlefield (Oliver outranked Doubleday). This command would soon be taken by General Winfield Hancock by order of General Meade, who was on his way. At 2 p.m. General Lee arrived on the field and assumed operational command from Heth. General A.P. Hill's corps pushed the

Federals to the east while General Richard Ewell's corps moved south from Carlisle. By 3 p.m, Confederate forces outnumbered the Federals. By 4 p.m. the Federals withdrew from the town and formed a line on several ridges to the south. By midnight, the Union forces were solidly entrenched and reinforcements arrived during the night, including General Meade, who arrived at 1 a.m. During the night, several couriers were sent by General Lee in order to find General Stuart.

If the enemy is there, we must attack him.
                                        — General Robert E. Lee.

Lt Col Freemantle heard firing throughout the day while on a tour of the area. He caught up with General Lee west of Gettysburg.

July 2: Battle of Gettysburg: Day Two: General Lee decided to try a flank attack in order to dislodge the Federal Army from the heights south of Gettysburg. He ordered General Longstreet to move his corps to the south and hit the Union left flank. Due to slow planning, those forces were not in place until 4 p.m. Union General Dan Sickles, commanding III Corps, advanced his line forward in violation of General Meade's orders. Meade was in the process of ordering Sickles back when the Confederates attacked. Despite Confederate General John Hood getting wounded by artillery fire, his troops managed to push the Union troops into a rocky area called Devil's Den. While in this area, Army of the Potomac Chief Engineer General Gouverneur Warren noticed two hills that the Confederates could use to reach the Federal rear. General Warren soon found V Corps moving through the area and was able to direct the brigade of Colonel Strong Vincent to the hills. This brigade, consisting of the 16th Michigan, 44th New York, 83rd Pennsylvania and 20th Maine, was placed near the summit of a hill the locals called Little Round Top. Soon the Confederates were through the Devil's Den and attacking the hill. After several attacks, during which Colonel Vincent was mortally wounded, Colonel Joshua Chamberlain, 20th Maine commander, ordered a bayonet charge, breaking up the Confederate attack. Meanwhile, a nearby wheat field (known afterwards as The Wheatfield) was the scene of several failed Union assaults. During one such attack, General Sickles received a cannon ball in the right knee, resulting in that leg being amputated. At 6:30 p.m. an attack was made on Union positions on Culp's Hill, at the Union north end, with no results. Another attack on Cemetery Hill, the apex of the Union line also failed. Firing stopped at midnight.

> *All around, strange, mingled roar—shouts of defiance, rally, and desperation: and underneath, murmured entreaty and stifled moans: gasping prayers, snatched of Sabbath song, whispers of loved names: everywhere men torn and broken, staggering, creeping, quivering on the earth, and dead faces with strangely fixed eyes staring stark into the sky.*
> —*Colonel Joshua Lawrence Chamberlain, commanding officer, 20th Maine, as quoted in* Through Blood and Fire at Gettysburg *in 1913.*

Confederate General Morgan began his raid into Indiana and Ohio.

At Vicksburg, after six weeks of bombardment, white flags appeared on the Confederate lines.

> *On Dit.-That the great Ulysses—the Yankee Generalissimo, surnamed Grant—has expressed his intention of dining in Vicksburg on Saturday next, and celebrating the 4th of July by a grand dinner—and so forth. When asked if he would invite Gen. Jo. Johnston to join he said: "No! For fear there will be a row at the table." Ulysses must get into the city before he dines in it. The way to cook a rabbit is "first catch the rabbit," &c.*
> — Vicksburg Daily Citizen, *letter to the editor.*

July 3: Battle of Gettysburg: Day Three: At 6 a.m. Confederate General Ewell had made another attempt to dislodge Union forces from Culp's Hill with no success. By noon, Ewell had no choice but to pull back. General Lee devised a plan to attack the Union center at Cemetery Ridge. He ordered General Longstreet to assemble his corps for the attack. Longstreet resisted at first but then agreed to Lee's orders. All of the Confederate artillery was set up to deliver a massive fire on the Union center. Three divisions, commanded by Generals Isaac Trimble, Johnson Pettigrew, and George Pickett, were formed in the woods behind the artillery. At 1 p.m. the artillery bombardment began. By 2:55, Union counter fire slackened and the Confederates believed the way was clear for the infantry attack. At 3 p.m. the infantry began the over one mile march towards the Union positions, not knowing that the Union artillery had been resupplied and reinforced. The Union artillery fire smashed whole formations and as soon as the Confederates reached the Emmitsburg Road, they came within range of concentrated Union musket fire. The Confederate troops managed to reach the Union positions but had to withdraw after a sharp fight. General Lee had no choice but to begin to withdraw back into Virginia. Battle of Gettysburg ends. Union victory.

This is a desperate thing to attempt.
> *—Confederate Brigadier General Richard Garnett, hours before he was killed in the Pickett-Pettigrew-Trimble charge.*

General, I have no division
> *—Confederate General George Pickett in response to General Lee's order to prepare for a possible Union counterattack following the Pickett-Pettigrew-Trimble charge.*

When I got close up to General Longstreet, I saw one of his regiments advancing through the woods in good order: so, thinking I was just in time to see the attack, I remarked to the General that, 'I wouldn't have missed this for anything.' Longstreet was seated at the top of a snake fence at the edge of the wood, and looking perfectly calm and impertubed. He replied, laughing, 'The devil you wouldn't! I would like to have missed it very much: we've attacked and been repulsed: look there!
> *—British Lieutenant Colonel Arthur Freemantle, diary entry.*

Two Confederate officers approached the Union lines at Vicksburg offering to surrender. Union General Grant wanted unconditional surrender but Confederate General Pemberton knows that 30,000 prisoners would be impossible to transport. Grant, knowing reality when he saw it, agreed to parole the surrendering army. (Parole was when a captured soldier made a pledge not to take up arms against the enemy until receiving a notice that an enemy soldier had been exchanged for him).

July 4: Confederate General Lee began moving his army south from Gettysburg.

Lt Col Freemantle accompanied General Longstreet during the pullout.

Confederates abandoned most of Tennessee as General Bragg's army reached Chattanooga.

Vicksburg surrendered to Union forces. Upon hearing of criticism over his surrendering, Confederate General Pemberton replied that as a Northerner, he knew that he could get favorable terms on the 4th of July.

Confederate forces under General Theophilus Holmes attacked Helena, AR with no success.

> *Two days bring about great changes. The banner of the Union floats over Vicksburg. Gen. Grant has "caught the rabbit," he has dined in Vicksburg, and he did bring his dinner with him. The "Citizen" lives to see it. For the last time it appears in "Wall-paper." No longer it will eulogize the luxury of mule meat and fricasseed kitten—urge Southern warriors to such diet never more. This is the last wall-paper edition, and is, expecting this note from the types as we found them. It will be valuable hereafter as a curiosity.*
> — *Vicksburg* Daily Citizen, *editorial.*

July 5: Confederate General Morgan captured the Lebanon, KY garrison.

Confederate Army of Northern Virginia was fully withdrawn from the Gettysburg area.

CS War Department clerk John B. Jones wrote, *"We have just received intelligence of a great battle at Gettysburg, Pennsylvania."* This information seems to have come from a truce boat at City Point, VA.

July 6: Union General Meade began his pursuit of General Lee's army.

There was a skirmish between Union General Buford's cavalry and Confederate General Lee's advance guard at Williamsport, MD.

CS War Department clerk John B. Jones wrote about reading some newspaper accounts from the north that actually had Richmonders believing that Lee had won the battle.

July 7: Confederates begin digging in at Hagerstown, MD upon finding the Potomac River too high to cross.

Confederate General Bragg had concentrated his forces around Chattanooga, which left the rest of Tennessee in Union hands.

A Union assault on the Port Hudson, LA was called off as news of the victory at Vicksburg arrived.

Lt Col Freemantle decided to leave the Army of Northern Virginia and received a pass from General Lee for safe conduct through the lines.

July 8: Port Hudson was surrendered to Union forces, which placed the entire Mississippi River under Union control. US President Lincoln would proclaim that, *"the Father of Waters flows again unvexed to the sea."*

At Gettysburg, local farmers were charging high prices to transport wounded soldiers to the rail station and the railroad company that was providing the trains to carry the wounded away had not bothered to clean the cattle cars. US Army Medical Corps officers would soon intervene.

CS War Department clerk John B. Jones wrote that the War Department was notified about the fall of Vicksburg.

July 9: Confederate General Morgan's forces crossed into Indiana, against orders.

Lt Col Freemantle encountered Federal cavalry and was taken to a General Kelly, who allowed him to pass through.

July 10: Union troops under General George Strong landed at Morris Island, SC with the objective of taking Battery Wagner, one of the forts protecting Charleston.

Union General Meade's troops finally made contact with retreating Confederates at Williamsport while General Lee was able to start getting his army across the Potomac. Lee sent the wounded and 4000 Union prisoners across first.

July 11: An initial Union attack on Battery Wagner, SC was repulsed.

Union General Sherman had Confederate General Joe Johnston's troops surrounded at Jackson.

Lt Col Freemantle reached Johnstown, PA where he took a train for Philadelphia.

July 12: Union General Meade's advance force arrived at Williamsport and began to clash with Confederates there, a few miles from the site of the Battle of Sharpsburg.

Lt Col Freemantle reached Philadelphia and switched trains for New York.

July 13: Confederate forces under General Morgan crossed into Ohio.

Draft Riots began in New York as opposition to a planned draft of men into the Union Army exploded into violence aimed at African-Americans.

Since poverty has been our crime
We bow to the decree
We are the poor who have no wealth
To purchase liberty
--A New Yorker's response to the Conscription Act

Lt Col Freemantle observed some of the rioting.

July 14: Union cavalry attacked the Confederate crossing point at Williamsport, taking 500 prisoners and mortally wounding Confederate General Pettigrew.

CS War Department clerk John B. Jones wrote that notification was received about the fall of Port Hudson.

July 15: Draft Riots ended in New York City as Union troops from the Gettysburg battlefield put down the rioters.

Confederate Army of Northern Virginia continued their withdrawal through the Shenandoah Valley.

After much difficulty, Lt Col Freemantle boarded a ship for the UK; his account ends here.

July 16: Confederate General Joe Johnston pulled his troops put of Jackson, MS in the face of advancing Union forces under General Sherman.

At Shepherdstown, MD, there was a cavalry clash at the Potomac River between Union General David Gregg and Confederate Generals Fitzhugh Lee and J.R. Chambliss with no advantage gained by either side.

Confederate General Morgan's troops headed into Ohio after causing havoc in Indiana.

July 17: Battle of Honey Springs, Indian Territory (Oklahoma): Union commander: General James Blunt. Confederate commander: General Douglas Cooper. Union troops made a frontal assault on Confederate positions. Defenders counterattacked several times but were forced to abandon the position. Union victory.

Confederate General Morgan's troops rode through the suburbs of Cincinnati.

Union forces bombarded Battery Wagner, on James Island.

July 18: Union troops made a second attempt to take Battery Wagner, near Charleston. The attack was spearheaded by the all African-American 54th Massachusetts. Despite gaining the ramparts and penetrating the fort's interior, Confederate reinforcements forced the 54th back with heavy losses, including its commander, Colonel Robert Gould Shaw, and most of its officers.

Confederate General Morgan and his troops reached the Ohio River at Buffington Bar, OH. Union forces were closing in.

CS War Department clerk John B. Jones wrote that word was received that Lee had crossed back into Virginia, which confirmed the loss at Gettysburg. Word was also heard of the riots in New York, which delighted Jones.

July 19: Confederate General Morgan's command was encircled at Buffington Bar, but he and 300 others managed to escape.

Union Army of the Potomac crossed over the Potomac in pursuit of the Confederate Army of Northern Virginia.

July 20: Union General George Meade's advance forces reached the Blue Ridge Mountains but had not spotted the retreating Confederates.

Merchants in New York met to discuss compensation for the African-American victims of the recent riots.

O.G. Eiland, a Mississippi planter, wrote CS President Davis advocating the enlistment of slaves into the army in order to save the Confederacy (radical thinking).

July 21: Union General Meade turned his army toward the Shenandoah Valley in order to intercept Confederate General Lee.

July 22: Union III Corps made contact with Confederates at Manassas as the remainder of the Army of Northern Virginia escaped further south.

July 23: Confederate General Morgan and his troopers had spent 20 hours in the saddle in an attempt to shake off Federal pursuers.

CS War Department clerk John B. Jones wrote about the following dispatch received from Charleston, SC, "*Charleston, July 22d, 1863. The enemy recommended shelling yesterday, with but few casualties on our part. We had, in the battle of the 18th inst., about 150 killed and wounded. The enemy's loss, including prisoners, was about 2000. Nearly 800 were buried under a flag of truce. Col. Putnam, acting brigadier-general, and Col. Shaw, commanding the negro regiment, were killed. (Signed) G. T. Beauregard, General*"

July 24: Confederate General Lee's army had passed Front Royal, VA as Union troops entered the town.

July 25: US Navy attempted to clear torpedoes (mines) from the entrance of Mobile Bay, AL.

Union bombardment of Battery Wagner continued. The failure of the Union artillery to reduce the fort's walls was a testimony to the superiority of earthen (sand or dirt) walled forts to masonry (brick) ones.

July 26: Confederate General Morgan and his remaining troops surrendered at Salineville, OH to Union forces, ending Morgan's Raid.

Sam Houston, who commanded the Texas Army in the Texas War of Independence, first president of the Republic of Texas, first US Senator from Texas, and Governor of the state at the time of secession (and who was thrown out of office for refusing to swear allegiance to the CSA), died.

July 27: Skirmishing at Rogersville, KY, Cassville, MO, and Bridgeport, AL.

July 28: Rear areas of the Army of the Potomac in Virginia were being struck by hit and run raids by Confederate partisans under Colonel Mosby.

July 29: Plans were made to construct a Union artillery battery in the marshes of Morris Island, SC.

In London, UK, Queen Victoria reaffirmed the Government's stand on neutrality in response to statements that the British Government was pro-Confederate.

July 30: CS President Davis announced that all African-American troops that were captured would be turned over to State authorities. The problem with that is that it was a State capital crime for an African-American to carry arms, with death as the penalty. The announcement also threatened White officers leading Black troops. US President Lincoln responded with a threat to execute a Confederate soldier for anyone executed by the Confederates. Lincoln added that any Black Union soldier sold into slavery would result in Confederate prisoners forced to do hard labor.

Skirmishes at Grand Junction, TN and Barnwell's Island, SC.

July 31: Both armies had completed their withdrawal from Gettysburg and had taken up positions along the Rappahannock River. The situation in the East had returned to the status quo.

Skirmishes at Paint Lick Bridge, KY and St Catherine's Creek, MS.

US President Lincoln received a letter from Hannah Johnson, whose son was with the 54th Massachusetts and survived the assault on Battery Wagner. She asked for fair treatment for African-Americans serving in the Union Army.

August 1: The army Union General Grant used to take Vicksburg was broken up for occupation duty.

Union and Confederate cavalry skirmished near Brandy Station.

Confederate spy Belle Boyd was once again captured and taken to Old Capital Prison, Washington, DC. (Where she was this time the previous year).

CS President Davis offered amnesty to all Confederate soldiers absent without leave.

Skirmish at Smith's Shoals, KY.

While the blockade was strangling Southern ports, Northern ports, such as Boston and New York were having a boom.

August 2: Plan was submitted that involved mounting a heavy gun at the battery to be constructed at Morris Island that could engage targets in Charleston, 7900 yards away.

August 3: Union troops began building the access road for the new battery at Morris Island.

CS War Department clerk John B. Jones wrote that $12 to $15 Confederate will buy $1 in gold. Flour was selling for $40 a barrel. Bacon is $1.75 a pound. Coal was selling for $25 for a cart full. Firewood could be had for $30 per cord. Butter could be had for $3 a pound.

August 4: At the Morris Island Battery site, Union engineers came under Confederate fire. A dummy site was planned so the Confederates would be distracted.

Skirmishing continued along the Rappahannock River.

August 5: Foundation of Morris Island Battery, named after a Colonel Serrell, was in place.

Confederates strengthened both Battery Wagner and Fort Sumter in order to counter Union moves on James Island.

USS *Commodore Barney* was damaged by an electric (battery powered) torpedo near Dutch Gap, VA.

Skirmishes at Cold Spring Gap, WV, Little Washington, VA, and Muddy Run, VA.

US President Lincoln began his plans on how territory now under Federal control could be reintegrated into the USA.

August 6: US President Lincoln had declared this day a Day of Thanksgiving for the recent victories in Pennsylvania and Mississippi.

Confederate partisans under Colonel Mosby captured a Union wagon train near Fairfax Court House.

At Table Bay, Cape of Good Hope, South Africa, CSS *Alabama* captured the merchant vessel *Sea Bride* to the delight of a crowd of watchers onshore.

CS War Department clerk John B. Jones wrote that the price of flour in Richmond had risen to $30 a barrel with a limit of one.

August 7: US President Lincoln refused a request to suspend the draft in New York.

Skirmish at New Madrid, MO.

August 8: Confederate General Lee, citing the failure of the Gettysburg Campaign and ill health (possibly a mild heart attack, he was suffering from angina) offered to resign as commander of the Army of Northern Virginia. CS President Davis refused to even consider accepting it.

August 9: Siege of Battery Wagner continued as Union troops dug a series of trenches to cover the advance.

August 10: Union force under General Steel left Helena, AR for the state capital of Little Rock.

August 11: Confederate artillery at Battery Wagner shelled Union trenches.

August 12: Union gunboats now patrol the area around Morris Island to protect the new battery under construction.

In a change of policy, US President Lincoln refused to give General McClernand, a "political general" another command.

August 13: Confederate defenders of Battery Wagner managed to keep up a defense despite losing their 32-pounder rifled cannon to a barrel burst. They only have two guns, 10-inch Columbiads, capable of engaging the Union guns on nearby Morris Island.

August 14: The Union battery at Morris Island was almost complete, with 2300 soldiers dumping sandbags to create a stable platform for the guns.

August 15: CSS *H.L. Hunley*, a submarine, arrived by train at Charleston.

At Morris Island, 13,000 sandbags were used to create an artificial island in the middle of a swamp. Now they were ready to place the single gun chosen for this position.

August 16: Union General Rosecrans began his campaign to take Chattanooga.

Union General Burnside left Louisville, KY in order to support Rosecrans.

CS War Department clerk John B. Jones wrote that a new pair of shoes could be had in Richmond for $50. Meanwhile, sugar was selling for $2 a pound.

August 17: At Charleston, the siege continued against Battery Wagner while Union batteries pounded Fort Sumter and Charleston Harbor with no effect. Meanwhile on Morris Island, a single, 8-inch, 200-pounder Parrott rifled cannon was dragged into position. It took all day to carry sufficient powder and shells into the battery, but this action brought Charleston itself into artillery range.

August 18: US President Lincoln test fired a Spencer Repeating Carbine, and ordered 60,000 for the Union army.

An inspector for the US Treasury Department reported on the conditions at a plantation whose owner fled when Federal troops arrived. Report contained descriptions of the appalling condition that slaves were forced to live in.

August 19: Heavy artillery bombardment of both Battery Wagner and Fort Sumter.

August 21: Union troops under Colonel John Wilder began shelling Chattanooga. General Rosecrans also began moving most of his army to the west and south of the city.

Confederate partisan Colonel William Quantrill's forces raided Lawrence, KS and killed 150 men and boys.

[Afterward,] the horrible scene...is thus described by one of the citizens: "I have read of outrages committed in the so-called dark ages, and, horrible as they appeared to me, they sink into insignificance in comparison with what I was then compelled to witness...Our strength failed us [and] many could not help crying like children. Women and little children were all over town, hunting for their husbands and fathers, and sad indeed was the scene when they did finally find them among the corpses laid out for recognition."
　　　—*from* Frank Leslie's Illustrated History of the Civil War

---

Union General Quincy Adams Gillmore demanded that Battery Wagner and Fort Sumter be evacuated or else Charleston would be fired on. Confederate General Beauregard decried this as a violation of the laws of war and asked for several days to evacuate the city. Meanwhile at the Morris Island Battery, the cannon, now christened the "Swamp Angel" was ready for firing.

August 22: CS postal workers went on strike in Richmond, hampering vital war communication.

At 1:30 a.m. the Swamp Angel was fired at Charleston. Upon learning that they had the range to hit the city, 16 more rounds were sent. 12 of those were filled with a flammable liquid concocted by William Parrott and the other four with something called "Short's Solidified Greek Fire." (Perhaps an early form of napalm).

August 23: Confederate General Beauregard protested the shelling of Charleston but the Swamp Angel itself decided the issue; the barrel burst after another 20 shells were fired. (The barrel is now on display in Trenton, NJ).

August 24: CSS *Hunley* attempted to attack USS *New Ironsides* in Charleston Harbor, but the water was too shallow.

Confederate Colonel Alfred Rhett, commander of Fort Sumter, reported that he had only one gun operational and the walls of the fort were now piles of broken bricks.

Confederate Colonel Mosby was making raids in Northern Virginia along the Rappahannock River.

Skirmishes at Barbee's Cross Roads and Coyle's Tavern, VA.

August 25: A Union attempt to take the rifle pits in front of Battery Wagner was repulsed.

Skirmishing continued along the Rappahannock and Chickahominy Rivers in Virginia.

Union General Thomas Ewing issued General Order 11 in retaliation for Quantrill's Raid on Lawrence, KS. This order expelled 20,000 people from Bates, Cass, and Jackson counties. Ewing then ordered all the property and crops in those counties destroyed.

US President Lincoln defended his decision to issue the Emancipation Proclamation in a letter to James Conkling, a Springfield, IL resident and a critic of the measure.

August 26: Troops of the 24th Massachusetts captured the rifle pits outside Battery Wagner.

Union cavalry engaged Confederates at Rock Gap, WV.

Confederate General John Floyd, a Secretary of War in the James Buchanan Administration, died at Abington, VA.

August 27: As Federal troops approach Battery Wagner, they found what was called "sub-terra torpedoes," or in today's terms, land mines.

August 28: Confederate General Beauregard decided to evacuate Battery Wagner.

August 29: CSS *Hunley* accidentally sunk in Charleston Harbor, five crewmembers drowned.

Union troops crossed the Tennessee River at Caperton's Ferry, TN in order to counter moves by Confederate General Bragg.

CS Congress began working on closing loopholes in the draft law that had allowed government clerks to be exempt from military service.

August 30: Confederates began the withdrawal of their remaining operational cannon from Fort Sumter.

August 31: 627 Union shells were fired at Fort Sumter; the Confederates there could no longer fire anything back.

In Washington there was outrage at a $5 a month tax assessed on free African-Americans and several made their displeasure known in a letter to Secretary of War Stanton.

September 1: Confederate troops under General William Cabell ambushed Federals at Devil's Backbone, AR, with no success.

Fort Sumter attacked by USS *New Ironsides* and six monitors.

Most of Union General Rosecrans' army crossed the Tennessee River.

One effect of Northern farmers going off to war is that farm machinery was increasingly in use. The South did not have that luxury.

September 2: Union troops under General Burnside captured Knoxville, TN.

A Union strike denied the Confederates the use of two captured steamers at Port Conway, VA.

September 3: Intelligence was received concerning Confederate cavalry around Greenville, TN. Union troopers were sent to investigate.

Confederate General Early, in response to an order from General Lee, sent General R.H. Anderson's corps to Petersburg, VA. On the way there, they found Union General Sheridan's army going into camp at Berryville, MD. A short attack on the nearby camp of Union General George Crook had no effect.

Spotswood Rice, an African-American serving in the Union Army, expressed hope in a letter to his family that they will be soon reunited as free people.

September 4: Union General Rosecrans' troops had completed the crossing of the Tennessee River, which forced Confederate General Bragg out of his position near Chattanooga, TN.

Union gunboats were launched from New Orleans to conduct operations along the TX/LA coastline.

Union General Grant, at New Orleans, was injured in a fall from his horse, causing allegations from his detractors that he was drunk, a charge that would dog him for the rest of the war.

September 5: Union General Rosecrans had divided his army into three columns for the planned assault on Chattanooga.

Union troops bombarded Battery Wagner.

An international incident was avoided when the British Government ordered two ironclad ships, known as the "Laird Rams," being built for the CS Navy kept in the port of Liverpool.

September 6: At Little Rock, AR, there was a duel between Confederate Generals Lucius Walker and John Marmaduke. Walker was killed.

During the night, Confederates evacuated Battery Wagner and Morris Island, near Charleston.

Confederate General Bragg ordered Chattanooga evacuated.

CS War Department clerk John B. Jones wrote in Richmond that apples were selling for $35 per barrel, bacon for $2.10 pre hoground, butter for $3 per package, cheese for $2 per pound, corn for $9 per bushel, flour for $25 per barrel, onions for $40 per barrel, potatoes for $6 per bushel, oats for $6 per bushel, wheat for $5 per bushel, lard for $1.75 per pound, eggs for $1.50 per dozen, herb seeds for $10 per bushel, clover for $45 per bushel, brown sugar for $2.15 per pound, coffee for $4.75 per pound, molasses for $15 per gallon, rice for .25 a pound, salt for .45 per pound, soap for .80, candles for $3 a pound, corn whisky for $25 a gallon, rye whisky for $40 per gallon, apple brandy for $30 per gallon, and rum for $28 per gallon.

September 7: Union forces secured Battery Wagner.

September 8: Confederate General Bragg pulled back from Chattanooga and headed towards Georgia.

US Marines attempted to storm Fort Sumter but were repulsed.

Confederate General Longstreet's corps was detached and sent to assist General Bragg near Chattanooga.

Union flotilla attempted to sail up Sabine Pass, TX and take Fort Griffin. The attack was halted by 44 Confederates and some very accurate artillery fire.

September 9: Union General Rosecrans' troops advanced on a 40-mile front into Georgia and had separated themselves by as much as a 2-3 day march in mountainous country. Confederate General Bragg had stopped his withdrawal and was preparing to meet Rosecrans.

September 10: Union troops captured Little Rock, AR.

Confederate General Bragg launched an attack on Union General Rosecrans' forces with little success. The Federals pushed on with no idea of the massive Confederate force waiting for them.

September 11: Confederate General Bragg received word that Longstreet's corps from Virginia was en route to reinforce him. Bragg ordered General Polk to attack Federal infantry that were supporting the cavalry screen but nothing was done.

September 12: Union XXI Corps (General Thomas Crittenden) was found isolated southeast of Chattanooga, TN, but Confederate General Polk refused to attack.

September 13: Confederate General Lee withdrew from Culpepper Court House, VA which was then immediately occupied by Federals.

Union General Rosecrans learned that the Confederates were no longer running from Chattanooga and ordered his army concentrated. The farthest away was XX Corps (General McCook) who had to march 57-miles.

At Rodney, MS, several crewmembers of USS *Rattler* were attending church services when they were captured by Confederate cavalry.

September 14: Confederate General Bragg refused to believe that Federal troops were scattered and issued orders to his commanders that were not in line with the situation. Bragg never got along with his subordinates, which contributed to his failing as an army commander.

September 15: Confederate General Bragg planned to maneuver around

Union General Rosecrans' troops and get between him and Chattanooga. Orders to that effect were delayed by his poor performing staff.

September 16: Union General Rosecrans has concentrated his army around Lee and Gordon's Mills on Chickamauga Creek, south of Chattanooga.

September 17: Union General Rosecrans was convinced that Confederate General Bragg would fight. He placed General McCook's troops at Pond Spring (right flank), General Thomas' at Crawfish Springs (middle), and General Crittenden's troops covering the main road to Chattanooga (left flank).

September 18: Confederate General Bragg, now reinforced by General Longstreet and learning of the Federal army concentrating, halted his retreat from Chattanooga and turned to face Union General Rosecrans army. Bragg now has 75,000 to face Rosecrans' 57,000.

September 19: Battle of Chickamauga: Union commander: General William Rosecrans. Confederate commander: General Braxton Bragg. Day One: Union General Thomas sent two brigades against what was believed to be a weak Confederate brigade and ended up engaging Bragg's reserve corps as well as Nathan B. Forrest's cavalry. Reinforcements from both sides pour in and soon control of the battle was lost. At 11 a.m. Union troops formed a command and control structure with Generals Thomas in the middle, Crittenden on the left, and McCook on the right. By noon, a hole had formed in the Union lines which the Confederates tried to exploit, but with no success. Fighting ended at nightfall with no decision. A noted participant was the future novelist Ambrose Bierce, a 1st Lieutenant in the 9th Indiana.

> *We raise one long, loud, cheering shout and charge right upon their breastworks. They are pouring their deadly missiles into our advancing ranks from under their head-logs. We do not stop to look around to see who is killed and wounded, but press right up their breastworks, and plant our battle-flag upon it.*
> --Sam Watkins, Private, 1st Tennessee, CS Army

September 20: Battle of Chickamauga: Day Two: Confederate General Polk launched his attack two hours late. By 9:00 a.m. the Union left was smashed, causing Thomas (now on the left) to call for reinforcements. It was believed that the request was poorly interpreted and a huge hole was created in the Union lines, which the Confederates found quickly. Longstreet launched an assault at 11:15 a.m. with 20000 men and forced a collapse of the Union defense. The Army of the Cumberland was split in two and fell back in panic, except for Thomas' troops, who placed themselves on Snodgrass Hill and held off Confederate attacks for the rest of the day. It was noted that several of Thomas's regiments were equipped with Henry repeating rifles, which were instrumental in holding the Confederates at bay. The Confederates were soon spent and Thomas began an orderly retreat toward Chattanooga, where the Union army would be besieged. Thomas would become known as "The Rock of Chickamauga." Confederate victory, the only such major victory for the CSA in the West. One of those killed in the battle was Confederate General Ben Hardin Helm, brother-in-law of US President Lincoln.

September 21: Union General Rosecrans was collecting his army in Chattanooga while the Confederates wasted time looting captured Federal supplies. It was late afternoon before Confederate General Bragg ordered a pursuit. This angered the cavalry commander, General Forrest, who told Bragg that *"every hour is worth a thousand men."*

September 22: Union General Burnside began the East Tennessee Campaign by attacking Confederate troops at Blountsville, TN, defeating them.

Confederate General Bragg's forces ran into entrenched Union positions near Chattanooga and another chance to destroy the Union force was lost.

News of the Union defeat at Chickamauga had reached US President Lincoln and he was wondering if Rosecrans could even hold Chattanooga.

September 23: US President Lincoln was awakened at the Soldiers'

Home with the news that Secretary of War Stanton had called a Council of War.

September 24: Confederate General Bragg's forces had positioned themselves on Lookout Mountain and Missionary Ridge, effectively cutting Union General Rosecrans' supply lines and sealing his army in Chattanooga.

US President Lincoln met with Secretaries Stanton (War), Seward (State), Chase (Treasury), and General-in-Chief Henry Halleck to discuss the situation in Tennessee.

Recognizing that Chattanooga was the key to any future offensive into the Deep South, Orders were prepared to have Generals Grant and Burnside send reinforcements, as well as 20,000 from the Army of the Potomac.

September 25: Union XI and XII Corps, under General Hooker, began deploying to Chattanooga in order to reinforce General Rosecrans.

Union General Burnside received orders to reinforce General Rosecrans at Chattanooga but instead went to Jonesboro, TN.

September 26: Union General Hooker's troops reached Alexandria, VA to board trains for Tennessee.

The New York *Post* published an article explaining the movement of Hooker's troops to Tennessee, riling up the Lincoln Administration.

September 27: It took the better part of a day, but all of the horses and artillery of Union General Hooker's force were on trains heading for Tennessee.

September 28: Battle of Fordoche Bridge, LA: Union commander: General Napoleon Dana. Confederate commander: General Tom Green. Union forces were marching in support of General Banks' attempt to attack Texas when the Confederates attacked Dana's troops. Skirmishing began at dawn while the battle proper was in full force at mid-day. Union lines were broken and only the cavalry escaped getting captured. Confederate victory.

Union General Rosecrans brought charges against Generals McCook and Crittenden and they were ordered to Indianapolis, IN to stand before a court of inquiry. Since they were all trapped in Chattanooga, all this really accomplished was a lowering of the morale of the besieged troops. This on top of the already short rations.

September 29: Union General Grant received orders to send troops to the aid of the trapped Union force in Chattanooga. General Sherman's corps and most of General McPherson's corps had left Vicksburg and were heading east.

September 30: Confederate cavalry under General Joseph Wheeler began disrupting lines of communication and supply to the Union army now trapped in Chattanooga. The Siege of Chattanooga had begun.

CS War Department clerk John B. Jones wrote that in Richmond, butter sold for $4 a pound, bacon for $3 a pound, lard for $2.25 a pound, beef for $1.25 a pound, lamb for $1.25 a pound, veal for $1.50 a pound, sausages for $1 each, chickens for $7 per pair, ducks for $5 a pair, salted herrings for $4 per dozen, cabbage for $1.50 each, green corn for $2 per dozen, sweet potatoes for $26 a bushel, regular potatoes for .75 a quart, butter-beans for $1.50 per quart, , onions for $1.50 per quart, eggplant for $2 each, tomatoes for $1 a quart, and soap for $1.50 a pound. Buying a pair of boots will take $100, shoes for $60, a mattress will set you back $40, blankets for $40, and sheets for $25 each.

October 1: The Federal supply line from Bridgeport to Chattanooga was cut by Confederate raiders, which left a 28-mile route through mountainous terrain the only remaining supply route. Union General Rosecrans ordered flat-bottomed steamers built to get the supplies to the Federal lines.

October 2: Union General Hooker's troops reached Bridgeport only to find that the only way to get to Chattanooga was that same mountain path. It had taken Hooker's 20,000 men and 3000 horses and mules a week to get to Bridgeport by rail, a distance of 1159 miles.

CS War Department clerk John B. Jones wrote that he managed to get a pair of shoes for $13, while the going price is $75. Boots were now going for $200.

October 3: Union General Hooker established his headquarters near Bridgeport. He had received reports of Confederate cavalry under General Wheeler in the area.

US War Department authorized the enlistment of African-Americans in Maryland, Missouri, and Tennessee.

US President Lincoln proclaimed the last Thursday in November to be a National Day of Thanksgiving. This is the predecessor of today's Thanksgiving Day.

October 4: Union General Hooker observed the construction of steamers at Bridgeport. Union engineers took a flat-bottomed barge and mounted an engine, boiler, and sternwheel. Hooker was impressed and ordered the work to continue, since the supply situation in Chattanooga was getting desperate.

October 5: CSS *David*, a torpedo boat, attacked USS *New Ironsides*, damaging her. The *David* was also damaged and was taking on water. Four of the six crewmembers were captured and the remaining two managed to get the cigar shaped vessel back to Charleston where she ran aground.

Confederate General Wheeler's troopers destroyed the bridge at Stone's River, near Murfreesboro, TN. This made getting supplies to Chattanooga even more difficult.

October 6: Confederate raiders under William Quantrill attacked a Union post at Baxter Springs, KS but were driven off. By chance they spotted a Union column under General James Blunt approaching. The

Confederates attacked, killing many of the Union soldiers including band members. Blount escaped.

In Chattanooga, both sides dug in while putting up with heavy rains.

New York *Herald* printed an editorial criticizing the extravagance shown by the local elites while a war is going on.

October 7: A Union force traveled from the Mississippi River to the Red River, where they managed to capture and destroy two Confederate steamers.

Upon finding that Confederate General Lee was trying to outflank him, Union General Meade ordered the Army of the Potomac to retreat north of the Rappahannock River.

The situation in Chattanooga was even getting bad for the civilians trapped in the city as the wood needed for campfires and shoring up the trenches had come from all the wooden structures in the city.

October 8: Supplies in Chattanooga was getting very short, with most of the Union Army animals eaten. Starvation and the wet weather have resulted in sickness running rampant.

October 9: Confederate General Wheeler's troops have totally wrecked the supply system that was supporting Union General Rosecrans' forces in Chattanooga.

October 10: CS President Davis arrived at General Bragg's headquarters near Chattanooga in order to try and quell the dissent amongst Bragg's senior commanders.

Union and Confederate cavalry clashed near Blue Springs, WV with the Confederates getting repulsed.

Confederate General Lee attempted to force the Union army to withdraw by moving toward Washington, DC. Union General Meade managed to block that maneuver, but still withdrew.

October 11: Union General Sherman left Memphis for Corinth, MS.

October 12: Union Army of Potomac continued their withdrawal as Confederate General Lee approached Manassas.

October 13: Union cavalry almost isolated Confederate General Stuart at Auburn, VA. He escaped.

War critic Clement Vallandingham, in exile in Canada, lost the Ohio governor's race.

October 14: Battle of Bristoe Station, VA: Union commander: General George Meade. Confederate commander: General A.P. Hill. Hill's troops found two Union corps and proceeded to attack. The large numbers of Union troops allowed Meade to hold off Hill and complete a retreat to Centerville. Hill's force sustained heavy losses and had to withdraw. Union victory.

October 15: *H.L. Hunley* sunk in Charleston Harbor. The entire crew including the builder of the submarine, H. L. Hunley, drowned.

October 16: Union District of the Mississippi was created, which united all the armies in the West. Union General Grant was given the command of the district.

Naval assault began on Fort Brooke, near Tampa, FL. This diverted the Confederates attention while a land force-marched to the Hillsborough River where they captured and destroyed two blockade-runners.

Union supply ship at Bridgeport was saved from rising flood waters.

October 17: Confederate General Lee pulled his army back from Manassas to the Rappahannock River.

Union General Grant received two sets of orders from Secretary of War Stanton at a meeting in Indianapolis, IN concerning General Rosecrans. Grant chooses at that point to relieve Rosecrans as commander of the Army of the Cumberland and give that army to General Thomas.

October 18: CS President Davis left General Bragg's headquarters, having failed to resolve the differences among his commanders.

The sunken *Hunley* was located and plans were made to bring the submarine up.

October 19: While maintaining a screen to protect Confederate General Lee's movements, General Stuart encountered Union cavalry under General Kilpatrick. The Union forces gave chase and were lured into an ambush near Buckland Mills, VA. Kilpatrick's forces, once the pursuer, became the pursued as they ran for five miles, all the while being chased by Stuart's troopers in what became known as the "Buckland Races."

October 20: Confederate General Stuart brought his troopers to the Confederate side of the Rappahannock River.

CS War Department clerk John B. Jones wrote that flour was now selling for $61 a barrel, while wood sold for $32 a cord and coal for $30 for 25 bushels.

October 21: Union General Grant departed Nashville and headed for Stevenson, AL.

October 22: Union General Grant arrived at Bridgeport, AL enroute to oversee the situation at Chattanooga.

CS War Department clerk John B. Jones wrote that a woman tried to buy a barrel of flour. The merchant demanded $70. *"My God!"* exclaimed she, *"how can I pay such prices? I have seven children: what shall I do?"* He said, *"I don't know madam unless you eat your children."*

October 23: Union General Grant arrived in Chattanooga.

October 24: Union General Sherman assumed command of the Army of the Tennessee.

US President Lincoln sent a message pressing General Meade to attack Confederate General Lee in Virginia.

October 25: Union General Grant initiated a plan to open a supply line into Chattanooga. This would become known as the "Cracker Line" for the amount of hardtack that was brought in. Meanwhile, the improvised supply steamer was launched at Bridgeport.

Union and Confederate forces clashed near Pine Bluff, AR. Confederates were forced to pull back after several attempts to break the Union line.

October 26: Union General Hooker's troops crossed into Tennessee in order to meet up with the Chattanooga garrison.

October 27: Union forces under General William B. Hazen established a bridgehead across the Tennessee River to form the first stage of the "Cracker Line".

October 28: Union troops under General Hooker moved to secure the bridge head across the Tennessee River and the Wauhatchie Station on the nearby Nashville and Chattanooga Railroad. Confederates were planning a night attack to drive them back.

CSS *Georgia* arrived in Cherbourg, France for repairs.

October 29: Confederate General Longstreet launched an attack on Union troops at Wauhatchie, TN, near Lookout Mountain, at midnight. He tried to communicate by signal flares but that the Federals had cracked the code. Despite this, there was no control over the fighting and the battle sputtered out by sunrise.

October 30: The scratch steamer *Chattanooga* arrived in its namesake city with the first fresh supplies for the beleaguered garrison.

October 31: Union IV Corps moving from Chattanooga to Pulaski, TN.

"The Cracker line is open! Full rations boys!" Supplies were now flooding into Chattanooga.

November 1: Federal siege batteries bombarded Fort Sumter.

Union General Averill led his cavalry on raids behind Confederate lines in WV.

Union General Sherman's forces, enroute to Chattanooga, stopped at Eastport, TN.

November 2: Union General Banks landed his troops at Brazos Santiago in yet another attempt to invade Texas.

US President Lincoln accepted a last minute invitation to say a few words at the dedication ceremony for a new military cemetery at Gettysburg.

CS President Davis delivered a speech to embattled residents in Charleston as Fort Sumter was bombarded again.

November 3: Confederate cavalry attacked Collierville, TN but were forced back to Mississippi when Union reinforcements arrived.

Union General Sherman detached General Dodge's division and tasked them to rebuild the railroad from Memphis, TN to Stevenson, AL.

November 4: Confederate General Bragg ordered General Longstreet to move against Union General Burnside in Eastern Tennessee.

Union troops under General Banks captured Brownsville, TX.

November 5: Confederate Colonel Mosby and his Partisan Rangers continued to cause havoc for Union troops in Northern Virginia.

Union General Grant decided to allow General Burnside to hold Knoxville while he concentrated on driving the Confederates from Chattanooga.

CS War Department clerk John B. Jones wrote that a barrel of flour was sold at an auction for $100, and then sold again for $120.

November 6: Union forces under General Averill defeated Confederates at Droop Mountain, WV, which ended all Confederate attempts to reclaim Western Virginia.

Union forces under General Banks took Point Isabel and Brownsville, TX.

There was a violent reaction to Maryland's approval of a new state constitution in which slavery was outlawed. Local slave owners were refusing to give up their slaves. One of the methods that was being used to keep African-Americans in bondage was to "apprentice" the children for long periods. In other words, the parents were freed but the children were kept.

CS War Department clerk John B. Jones wrote that a common shirt could be bought for $40 per pair. Beef sells for $1.50 a pound and pork for $2 a pound.

Union Sergeant John Ransom, a quartermaster with the 9th MI Cavalry, was captured near Rogersville, TN. He began a documentation of his experiences.

November 7: Union forces captured Lewisburg, WV.

Union troops crossed the Rappahannock River and captured 1600 of Confederate General Early's troops, which forced General Lee to retreat across the Rapidan just as his army was about to settle into winter quarters.

Federal troops departed Fayetteville, AR for an expedition into an area known as Frog Bayou.

November 8: Union General Meade's advance continued with skirmishes at Warrenton and Culpepper Court House, VA.

Skirmishes at Vermillionville and Bayou Junica, LA.

Confederate General Bragg was conducting a purge of all senior commanders in his army. The latest to get his walking papers was General D.H. Hill, who was replaced by General Breckenridge.

November 9: US President Lincoln attended a performance of *Marble Heart*, which starred the actor John Wilkes Booth.

Skirmishing between Union troops and pro-Confederate Indians in the Choctaw Nation, Indian Territory (Oklahoma).

US President Lincoln received a letter complaining that the draft is not being enforced in Pennsylvania.

November 10: Fort Sumter continued to be bombarded at the average rate of 600 shells a day. (Looks like the Federals wanted to erase the fort from existence).

November 11: Confederate General Longstreet and his troops reached the end of the rail line at Loudon, TN. Wagons were used to carry supplies and the men started marching as they advanced on Knoxville.

November 12: Pro-Union delegates had a meeting on how to get Arkansas back into the Union.

November 13: Skirmishing at Palmyra and Blythe's Ferry, TN.

CS War Department clerk John B. Jones wrote that flour was selling for $110 a pound, corn meal for $20 a bushel, bacon for $3 a hoground, lard for $2.30 a pound, butter for $4 a pound, eggs for $2.25 a dozen, regular potatoes for $8 a bushel, sweet potatoes for $12 a bushel, candles for $4 a pound, salt for .45 a pound, coffee for $9 a pound, sugar for $3.25 a pound, molasses for $15 a gallon, rice for .35 a pound, whiskey for as much as $70 a gallon, apple brandy for $50 a gallon, rum for $50 a gallon, French brandy for as much as $100 a gallon, beef and mutton selling for $1.50 a pound, pork for $2 a pound, shoe leather (sole) for $7.50 a pound, shoe leather (uppers) for $8 a pound, harness leather for $6 a pound, hides for $2.75 each, tanning oil for $5 a gallon, and common tobacco for $1.25 a pound.

Union Sergeant Ransom and other Union prisoners reached the Confederate Prison at Belle Island, located in the middle of the James River at Richmond.

November 14: Union General Sherman and 17,000 men arrived at Bridgeport, AL.

A disadvantage of the Confederate Government's decentralized system was made apparent when the threat of force was considered to make North Carolina farmers pay taxes. The farmers felt that they owe more to the state than to the central government. Isn't that what they were fighting for?

A letter from a US Christian Commission member made it plain that not only was it their mission to help soldiers, but lead them to Christ as well.

November 15: Confederate General Wheeler's cavalry joined General Longstreet's army.

Union General Grant planned for the breakout from Chattanooga by using General Sherman and Hooker's troops for the main push.

November 16: Union forces captured Corpus Christi, TX.

Battle of Campbell's Station, TN: Union commander: General Ambrose Burnside. Confederate commander: General James Longstreet. Both armies were on parallel roads but Burnside reached Campbell's Station first. Longstreet responded by attacking both Union flanks, forcing Burnside to retreat to Knoxville, TN. Confederate victory. Longstreet afterwards besieged Knoxville.

An article in the Philadelphia *Press* called for higher wages for workers as the costs of goods and services rose.

November 17: Union troops drove off Confederates on Mustang Island, near Aransas Pass, TX.

US President Lincoln began writing the speech that he would give at Gettysburg.

November 18: US President Lincoln departed Washington, DC for Gettysburg. He was accompanied by Secretary of State William Seward and the Ambassador from France. They would arrive that evening.

November 19: US President Lincoln appeared at the dedication of the first National Cemetery at Gettysburg. After orator Edmund Everett delivered a two and one half hour speech, Lincoln then stepped up and delivered a two-minute speech that became one of the greatest speeches in American history, the Gettysburg Address. The speech was so quick that the photographer did not have time to set up his equipment, so there was no photographic record of the event except for a shot taken afterwards.

November 20: Union General Sherman's movement at Chattanooga was hampered by rain, but they would soon be in place to hit the Confederate right flank.

November 21: US President Lincoln suffered a variola (smallpox) attack.

CS War Department clerk John B. Jones wrote that a suit of clothes could be sold in Richmond for $700 and boots for $200. He also saw an opossum in a butcher's shop sold for $10. $18 Confederate now equals $1 in gold.

November 23: Battle of Chattanooga, TN: Union commander: General Ulysses Grant. Confederate commander: General Braxton Bragg. Day One: Union troops under General Sherman seized Orchard Knob near Missionary Ridge.

November 24: Battle of Chattanooga: Day Two: Union General Hooker's corps stormed Lookout Mountain, with the resulting fight being called "The Battle Above the Clouds." General Sherman attempted an assault on Missionary Ridge but was stopped at a ravine.

November 25: Battle of Chattanooga: Day Three: Union General Joseph Hooker sent his men to the foot of Missionary Ridge but then they proceed up to the summit where they routed the Confederates. A brief counterattack split the Federal line but that did not hold for very long. Bragg had no choice but to run and the Siege of Chattanooga came to an end. Union victory. A noted participant in the Union assault was a First Lieutenant named Arthur McArthur, who won the Medal of Honor. His son was General Douglas McArthur, commander of US forces in the Pacific during World War II.

> *I felt sorry for General Bragg. The army was routed, and Bragg looked so scared. Poor fellow, he looked so hacked and whipped and mortified and chagrined at defeat, and all along the line, when Bragg would pass, the soldiers would raise the yell, "Here is your mule": "Bully for Bragg, he's hell on retreat."*
> —Sam Watkins, Private, 1ˢᵗ Tennessee, describing General Bragg after the battle.

November 26: Confederate General Hood's infantry reached Columbia, TN and began probing Union defenses while looking for a way to cross the Duck River.

Confederate General Wheeler's cavalry engaged two Union cavalry regiments near Atlanta.

Union General Meade was attempting to turn Confederate General Lee's right flank during fighting along the Rapidan River, VA.

Confederate General Patrick Cleburne's troops fought a delaying action at Ringgold Gap, TN in order to cover General Bragg's retreat to Dalton, GA.

November 27: Confederate General Morgan and a few of his officers escaped from a prison at Columbus, OH.

Union General Meade ran into Confederate General Lee's right flank, now along positions Mine Run, VA.

Union Private Sneeden and several assistants were sleeping in an abandoned house near Culpepper, VA when they were captured by Confederates under Colonel Mosby.

November 28: Union and Confederate troops skirmished along Mine Run but nothing else developed. Union General Meade ordered a corps to find a way around Confederate General Lee's southern flank.

November 29: Confederate General Longstreet launched an attack on Fort Sanders, at Knoxville, but stalled after 20 minutes.

November 30: Union V and VI Corps were sent around the Confederate left at Mine Run. When everything was in place, the attack was called off. It did not help either side that freezing rain was also falling.

Union Private Sneeden wrote about reaching Richmond and being placed into Libby prison.

December 1: Union General Meade decided that Confederate General Lee's positions were too strong to attack, so he ordered a withdrawal.

Confederate spy Belle Boyd was released from Old Capital Prison, Washington due to illness.

Confederate General Bragg resigned as commander of the Army of Tennessee and replaced by General William Hardee.

December 2: As Confederate General Hardee assumed command of the Army of Tennessee he was urged by CS President Davis to start another offensive. Meanwhile, a Federal column was marching to assist the Union defenders at Knoxville.

December 3: Confederate General Longstreet decided that it was no longer worth the effort to take Knoxville and ordered his troops to nearby Greenville and into winter quarters.

> *Rumors of exchange to be effective soon. Rebels say we will all be exchanged before many days. It cannot be possible our government will allow us to remain here all winter.* (The prison was an open enclosure and the prisoners had to build their own shelters.) *Gen. Dow is still issuing clothing, but the rebels get more than our men do of it. Guards nearly all dressed in Yankee uniforms.*
> —*Union Sergeant John Ransom, diary entry.*
>
> Clothes were sent by the US Sanitary Commission, but were usually intercepted by Confederate soldiers, whose organizations could barely supply their own troops.

December 4: The previous week has seen 1307 shells strike Fort Sumter.

December 5: Confederate General Longstreet's troops finished their march despite heavy rains that turned the roads into a thick morass.

Union troops departed Little Rock, AR and headed toward Princeton, AR.

December 6: Union General Sherman arrived at Knoxville with orders to relieve General Burnside.

December 7: Seventeen Confederate agents seized the Union steamer *Chesapeake* and sailed her to Nova Scotia.

CS President Davis gave an upbeat speech to the Confederate Congress despite recent reversals in the field.

December 8: US President Lincoln proposed the following: pardon for all Confederates except former officers who resigned their commissions to go south, senior governmental officials, or those who mistreat Union prisoners-of-war. Also announced was the proposal that a state could rejoin the Union with 10% of the citizens taking an oath to the Union and renouncing slavery.

December 9: Union General John Foster replaced General Burnside as commander of the Department of the Ohio.

A mutiny by African-American troops at New Orleans was quickly quelled.

December 10: Union Army of the Potomac in winter quarters.

CS War Department clerk John B. Jones wrote that wheat was selling for $18 per bushel, corn for $15 a bushel, flour for $110 a barrel, cornmeal for $16 a bushel, bacon for $3.25 a pound, lard for $3.50 a pound, beef for $1 a pound, venison for $2.25 a pound, poultry for $2.25 a pound, butter for $4.50 a pound, apples for $80 a barrel, onions for $35 a bushel, regular potatoes for $10 a bushel, sweet potatoes for $15 a bushel, turnips for $6 a bushel, brown sugar for $3.25 a pound, white sugar for $4.50 a pound, English sugar for $5 a pound, molasses for $14 a gallon, rice for .32 a pound, salt for .40 a pound, black pepper for $10 a pound, whisky for $75 a gallon, apple brandy for $50 a gallon, rum for $55 a gallon, gin for $60 a gallon, French brandy for $125 a gallon, a bottle of Hennessy for $180, Scotch whisky for $90 a gallon, champagne for $350 for a dozen bottles, a quart of claret for $100, and ale for $60 a pint or $110 a quart.

December 11: After thousands of shells were fired at Fort Sumter, one finally hit the powder magazine, causing an explosion that killed 11.

December 13: Union General Sheridan was given command of Union forces in the Knoxville area.

December 14: Battle of Bean's Station, TN: Union commander: General James Shackelford. Confederate commander: General James Longstreet. There was skirmishing during the early morning. At daylight, Longstreet launched a series of attacks that failed to break the Union line. At dusk, with Confederate reinforcements arriving, Shackelford decided to pull back to Blain's Cross Roads. Confederate victory.

US President Lincoln gave amnesty to his sister-in-law after she swore allegiance to the Union. Her husband was Confederate General

Benjamin Helm, who died at Chickamauga. This caused a firestorm in the Northern press.

December 15: Confederate General Longstreet chased Union General Shackelford as far as Blain's Crossroads but found that the Federals were too entrenched. Longstreet retired to Russellville, TN and went into winter quarters.

December 16: Confederate General Joe Johnston replaced General Hardee as commander of the Army of the Tennessee.

> *But now, allow me to introduce you to old Joe. Fancy, if you please, a man about fifty years old, rather small of stature, but firmly and compactly built, an open and honest countenance, and a keen and restless black eye, that seemed to read your very inmost thoughts. In his dress, he was the perfect dandy. He ever wore the very finest clothes that could be obtained, carrying out in every point the dress and paraphernalia of the soldier, as adopted by the War Department at Richmond, never omitting anything, even to the trappings of his horse, bridle, and saddle.*
> —*Sam Watkins, Private, 1ˢᵗ Tennessee, describing General Joe Johnston.*

Union General John Buford, considered a hero of the Battle of Gettysburg, died of typhoid.

December 17: US Navy recaptured the steamer *Chesapeake*, but the Confederate agents that took the vessel escaped.

December 18: Union General Sherman, in Knoxville, noticed that the Union troops only have ponchos in which to make winter shelters with.

December 19: Union General Sherman sent a report to the War Department complementing General Burnside for the good fortifications around Knoxville, but also must have mentioned the conditions of the winter camps.

December 20: CSS *Alabama* reached Singapore.

December 21: CS War Department clerk John B. Jones wrote that pound cakes were selling for $100 each and turkeys were going for $40.

Union Sergeant Ransom wrote about a sutler (merchant) who established himself at Belle Island prison and was selling brown sugar for $8 a pound, butter for $11 a pound, cheese for $10 a pound, sour milk for $3 a quart, eggs for $10 a dozen and oysters for $6 a quart.

December 22: Confederate General Longstreet's troops, in winter quarters at Rogersville, TN struggled with pro-Union guerrilla bands who were disrupting their supply trains.

December 23: Federal artillery pounded Fort Sumter.

December 24: Engagement at Bolivar, TN.

December 25: Confederate batteries at John's Island and Stone's River, SC were engaged by Union warships.

Union Private Sneeden wrote that guards at Libby Prison were eating rations that were sent there for the Union prisoners.

Union Sergeant Ransom wrote about a Christmas feast consisting of corn bread and butter, oysters, coffee, beef, crackers, and other items that was purchased for $200 CS or $20 US.

Lay awake long before daylight listening to the bells. As they rang out Christmas good morning I imagined they were in Jackson, Michigan, my old home, and from the spires of the old Presbyterian and Episcopal churches. Little do they think as they are saying their Merry Christmases and enjoying themselves so much, of the hunger and starving here. But there are better days coming.
—Sergeant John Ranson, diary entry.

December 26: Confederate War Department figured about 465,000 were in the Confederate Army. In fact, only 278,000 were in service.

December 27: Union General Grant was in Knoxville and ordered that a rail line be run into east Tennessee in order to better run supplies to Union forces there.

December 28: Union General Sturgis received reports of Confederate cavalry at Dandridge, TN. They left their camp at Mossy Creek to meet them.

December 29: Confederate forces under General Martin attacked the Union forces that were still in the Mossy Creek, TN camp. Union General Sturgis brought his troops back and pushed the Confederates out.

December 30: Union forces seized Fort Esperanza, near Matagorda Bay, TX.

Martha Glover, a slave in Missouri, wrote her husband, who was with the Union Army, about how she wished her husband hadn't left.

1864

January 1: Another shelling of Fort Sumter marked New Years Day in Charleston.

Union Private Sneeden wrote about a fine New Years meal of mule meat and boiled rice, barely edible.

January 2: CS Senate confirmed George Davis as Attorney General.

Union Private Sneeden wrote about inventorying boxes of goods sent from the North to Union prisoners, and taking advantage of the situation to improve their diet.

At Dalton, GA, there was a meeting in which Confederate General Cleburne made a formal proposal to let African-American slaves enlist in the Confederate Army, in exchange for their freedom, in to relieve the very critical manpower situation. The proposal was met with outrage by several of his peers. As a result, Cleburne would no longer see any promotions in rank.

January 3: It was noted this day that the Confederate economy was collapsing, with prices 28 times their 1861 levels.

January 4: Confederate General Lee received authority to take food stocks in order to feed his army. This measure was too little too late due to the fact that Virginia farms could barely support the civilian population, let alone a starving army.

Union General Halleck ordered Generals Banks and Steele to renew the offensive on the Red River in the spring. Problem was the two forces needed for the offensive were 500 miles apart.

Union Private Sneeden helped distribute new clothes to fellow prisoners at Libby Prison, Richmond.

January 5: 1000 African-Americans sent a petition to Washington demanding the right to vote.

January 7: US President Lincoln commuted the death sentence of a Union deserter, not wanting to add to "the butchering business."

CS War Department clerk John B. Jones wrote that beef was selling for $1.25 per pound. He also wrote about meeting an Englishman staying in a Richmond hotel who was living on three British Shillings a day, equal to $20 Confederate.

January 8: Confederate General Morgan arrived in Richmond to a hero's welcome.

Confederate spy David Dodd was hanged at Little Rock, AR.

Military Prison, Little Rock
January 8, 10 o'clock a.m., 1864

My Dear Parents and Sisters:
I was arrested as a spy and tried and was sentenced to be hung today at 3 o'clock. The time is fast approaching, but, thank God! I an prepared to die. I expect to meet all of you in Heaven. I will soon be out of this world of sorrow and trouble. I world like to see you all before I die, but let God's will be done, not ours. I pray to God to give you strength to bear your troubles while in this world. I hope God will receive you in Heaven: there I will meet you. Mother, I know it will be hard for you to give up your only son, but you must remember it is God's will. Goodbye! God will give you strength to bear your troubles. I pray that we may meet in Heaven. Goodbye! God will bless you all.

Your son and brother
David O. Dodd

Federals bombarded Caney Bayou, TX.

January 9: At this point in the war, Confederate General Edmund Kirby Smith's army was totally cut off from any help because Southern Arkansas was surrounded by Union held territory.

Calls went out for volunteers to become officers in Colored Regiments but there was a lack of volunteers, prompting a New England group to offer free military schooling to volunteers. Many white Union officers were themselves racially prejudiced and some were fearful of what would happen to them if they were captured.

CS War Department clerk John B. Jones wrote that beef was selling for $2.50 a pound and therefore he could not buy any. Instead he bought some rice, getting 25 pounds for 40 cents.

January 10: Federals were using fake Confederate money in order to wreck the Southern economy even more. As a result, merchants demanded payment in gold, specie (coins), or foreign currency.

USS *Iron Age* ran aground at Folly Inlet, SC and was destroyed by Confederates.

Union Sergeant Ransom wrote that conditions at Belle Island Prison were killing off prisoners at the rate of sometimes twenty a day.

January 11: A joint resolution was proposed in the US Senate that called for the abolishing of slavery.

CS War Department clerk John B. Jones wrote that a house in Richmond was being rented for $6000 a year.

Union Private Sneeden stole several parts of a Confederate uniform and managed to leave Libby Prison, walking the streets of Richmond and looking for a way to get out of town and back to Union lines. He did not get very far: he was recaptured and taken back to prison.

January 12: A common practice at this time was for a draftee to pay someone $300 (a great sum at the time) to take his place in the ranks. This filled the Union ranks with many who were unfit for service.

US troops entered Matamoros, Mexico to rescue the US Counsel.

January 13: US President Lincoln asked officials in Louisiana and Florida to form pro-Union state governments.

January 14: Union forces advance on Dandridge, TN, which forced Confederate General Longstreet to retreat.

CS President Davis wrote General Joe Johnston and warned him that some of his troops may be needed to defend Alabama and Mississippi in the spring.

January 15: Confederate General Longstreet ordered additional forces to move toward Dandridge.

A new crisis was about to impact the Union war effort. Soldiers who signed up for three-years will have those enlistments expire this year. If they all leave, the Union war effort will effectively end!

January 16: Union cavalry under General Sturgis encountered Confederate troops near Kimbrough's Crossroads, TN and were forced back.

Any remaining shred of hope that the UK and France would recognize the CSA evaporated with both countries directing their attention to a looming war between Denmark and Prussia over the territory of Schleswig-Holstein.

January 17: Confederate General Longstreet attacked Union forces at Dandridge, TN, which forced them to retreat to New Market.

CS War Department clerk John B. Jones wrote that flour was now selling for $200 a barrel and cornmeal for $20 a bushel.

January 18: There was opposition in North Carolina to the CS Government's conscription law, which made all white males 18 to 45 eligible for service.

January 19: Construction began on CSS *Albemarle* in a North Carolina cornfield.

Pro-Unionists met in Little Rock, AR to discuss abolishing slavery in the state.

January 20: US President Lincoln proposed elections in Arkansas so that the state could be readmitted.

Skirmish at Tracy City, TN.

January 21: A pro-Union convention in Nashville, TN proposed an anti-slavery resolution.

Ohio banned the distillation of whisky in order to preserve grain stocks.

January 22: Pro-Unionist Isaac Murphy was installed as provisional governor of Arkansas.

Union General Rosecrans assumed command of the US Federal Department of the Missouri.

January 23: US President Lincoln approved plans to allow freed slaves to be hired by their former masters.

US Department of the Treasury lifted the trading ban on Kentucky and Missouri.

Skirmish at Rolling Prairie, AR.

January 24: Skirmish at Baker Springs, AR.

January 25: Confederate General Longstreet ordered his cavalry to stop Union cavalry from disrupting his supply lines in Tennessee.

Union forces bombarded Fort Sumter without success.

Union troops evacuated Corinth, MS.

Union Sergeant Ransom wrote about a shipment of hams arriving from the north, but the Confederate guards managed to get them. A friend in the cookhouse got a substantial number of the hams into the prison enclosure, at great risk.

January 26: A Confederate force of 600 attacked the Federal garrison, numbering 100, at Athens, AL. The Confederates were repulsed.

US President Lincoln endorsed reopening trade with any Confederate territory that was under Federal control.

January 27: Battle of Kelly's Ford, TN: Union commander: General Samuel Sturgis. Confederate commander: General William Martin. Union forces were victorious but withdrew upon hearing of fresh Confederate troops approaching.

Confederate General Bragg was named CS President Davis' military advisor.

January 28: Skirmish at Tunnel Hill, GA.

January 29: Skirmish at Medley, WV.

CSS *Charleston*, nicknamed "the Ladies Ironclad" because local women raised the funds to build her, was launched in Charleston.

Union steamer *Sir William Wallace* attacked on the Mississippi River.

January 30: Confederate General Pickett moved to attack the Union garrison at New Berne, NC.

January 31: US President Lincoln expressed the opinion that only "loyal, free state men" should have their right to vote restored.

February 1: Union General William Sooey Smith led a cavalry force out of Memphis in order to reach General Sherman at Meridian, MS.

US Congress approved a bill reviving the rank of Lieutenant General. General Grant was the only candidate even considered for the rank.

Octave Johnson, an escaped slave who became a Corporal in the 15th United States Colored Troops, gave an account of his escape to the American Freedmen's Inquiry Commission meeting in New Orleans.

February 2: USS *Underwriter*, a gunboat, was captured and burned by Confederates near New Berne, NC.

February 3: Union General Sherman left Vicksburg for Meridian.

Confederate General Pickett abandoned plans to assault New Berne, NC.

CS President Davis ordered the suspension of *habeas corpus*.

February 4: Union troops under General Sherman now find Confederates under General Polk in the way of their advance into Mississippi.

February 5: Union forces under General Sherman reached Jackson, MS.

Union Sergeant Ransom wrote about a plan to escape Belle Island but the Confederate officers there had found out and had him and the other "escapees" held in confinement for a few days.

February 6: Union General Meade's forces made several crossings at the Rapidan River. This advance was resisted by Confederates under the command of General Ewell.

Confederate Congress banned imports of luxury goods and the circulation of US currency within the CSA.

February 7: Union General Meade's advance stalled, which forced a withdrawal back across the Rapidan River in Virginia.

Union troops under General Truman Seymour land at Jacksonville, FL.

Union General Sherman resumed his march to Meridian, MS.

CS War Department clerk John B. Jones wrote, "*The tocsin is sounding a 9 a.m.*" This was in reference to a report that Union General Butler's troops were marching towards Richmond.

February 8: Union General Smith and his troops were having trouble organizing and had not been able to support General Sherman's march on Meridian.

February 9: 109 Union prisoners tunneled out of Libby Prison in Richmond, 59 of them made it to Union lines.

February 10: Union General Smith completed preparations to launch a cavalry raid in support of General Sherman. Problem was that the raid was supposed to have been launched a week ago. A possible reason was that he had disobeyed orders and waited for reinforcements before leaving Memphis.

CSS *Florida* gets past USS *Kearsarge* at Brest, France.

The Point Lookout, MD newspaper, the *Hammond Gazette*, printed an article about a camp where African-Americans were being recruited to be soldiers.

February 11: Confederate guerillas robbed a train in West Virginia.

Union General Smith's cavalry finally left Memphis, one day past the time he was supposed to be linking up with General Sherman's forces in Mississippi.

CS War Department clerk John B. Jones wrote that bacon is selling for $6 a pound.

February 12: Skirmishes at Chunky Station and Decatur, MS.

Skirmishes at Macon and California House, MO.

CS War Department clerk John B. Jones wrote that sugar was selling for $8 a pound and rice for .85 a pound.

February 13: Expedition underway to clear Confederate forces from Indian Territory (Oklahoma).

A Confederate force under General Joseph Finnegan was assembled at Lake City, FL to counter any Union advance from Jacksonville. Union General Truman Seymour had already left Jacksonville and was headed to the Suwanee River to destroy some bridges.

February 14: Confederate General Polk evacuated Meridian as Union General Sherman's troops enter. General Smith's cavalry still has not showed up.

Union Sergeant Ransom wrote that groups of prisoners were being taken out of Belle Island. Confederates said that they are being sent to Union lines for exchange. Truth was they were headed to a new prison in Georgia.

February 15: Confederate forces formed a defensive line at Ocean Pond, FL along the Olustree River.

February 16: Skirmish at Lauderdale Springs, MS.

February 17: In Charleston Harbor, *H. L. Hunley* attacked and sank USS *Housatonic*. The *Hunley* was lost with all hands. (It was found in 1995 and brought up in 2003. The crew was interred with full Confederate military honors in 2004.) The *Hunley* was a privateer vessel, and as such, despite many accounts, was not officially a Confederate States Ship.

Confederate Government extended the conscription eligibility to cover all white males from 17 to 50.

February 18: Confederate Naval Commander Bullock sent a letter to CS Secretary of the Navy Mallory that the two ironclads that were being built in France would not be allowed to leave.

CS War Department clerk John B. Jones wrote that sugar was selling for $12 a pound.

February 19: Union cavalry under General Smith were moving toward West Point, MS.

February 20: Union General Sherman left Meridian and begins heading back to Vicksburg because he could no longer wait for General Smith's cavalry, who were enroute but dogged by Confederate skirmishers.

Battle of Olustree, FL: Union commander: General Truman Seymour. Confederate commander: General Joseph Finnegan. Union troops attempted to secure North Florida but ran into Confederate defense lines between Jacksonville and Lake City at the rail station of Olustree. Confederate victory as Union line is broken by repeated assaults. Two African-American regiments (54th Massachusetts and 35th US Colored Troops) held off the Confederates, at great risk to their lives, so that their comrades could retreat. Confederate victory.

CS War Department clerk John B. Jones wrote that a ham was sold at a market for $350.

February 21: Union General Smith's troops were drawn into a swamp near West Point, MS. Waiting for them was Confederate General Forrest's troops.

February 22: Confederate troops under General Forrest attacked Union General Smith's troops at Okolona, MS, which forced them to run back to Tennessee.

Union General Seymour's troops reached Jacksonville, FL

Unionist Michael Hamm was elected Louisiana governor.

A paper advocating Salmon P. Chase for president in the upcoming 1864 elections was issued.

Union Private Sneeden wrote about receiving orders to prepare to leave Libby Prison and board rail cars.

February 23: US President Lincoln met with his Cabinet without

Secretary of the Treasury Chase, who was in trouble due to the paper issued the day before.

Union Private Sneeden and other prisoners were on a train and all they knew is they were headed south.

Union Sergeant John Ransom and other prisoners were being held in a building at Richmond, VA after removal from Belle Island.

February 24: CS President Davis appointed General Bragg chief-of-staff of the Confederate Army.

US President Lincoln approved a plan to pay former masters whose slaves enlist in the army at the rate of $300 per former slave.

Union General Thomas ordered a probe of Confederate defense lines at Tunnel Hill, GA.

With the sale of proposed Confederate ironclad vessels to Denmark and Prussia, the effort of the CS Navy to buy warships seems finished.

Union Private Sneeden wrote about reaching the prison at Salisbury, NC.

February 25: Union General Thomas was trying to see if he can break through the Confederate lines at Buzzard's Roost Gap, GA.

Union Private Sneeden wrote about going back on the train at Salisbury, NC and resuming his trip south.

February 26: Union General Smith's troops reached Memphis while General Sherman's forces reached Canton, MS.

CS War Department clerk John B. Jones wrote that pork was selling for $8 a pound.

February 27: First Union prisoners reached Camp Sumter, GA, which will be known by the more notorious name of Andersonville, the name of the town nearest the prison.

CS War Department clerk John B. Jones wrote that sugar was selling for $20 a pound, bacon for $8 a pound, and $12 will buy a pair of chickens.

February 28: Union cavalry under General George Custer made a diversion to allow a raid led by General Judson Kilpatrick and Colonel Ulric Dahlgren to proceed against the prison at Belle Isle.

February 29: Dahlgren's column split from the main body to enter Richmond. (1864 was a leap year)

Union Private Sneeden wrote that he and his fellow prisoners reached Camp Sumter.

Union Sergeant Ransom wrote that the Union prisoners heard about the Dahlgren raid and were hopeful for release.

March 1: USS *St Louis* failed an attempt to capture CSS *Florida* near Funchal, Spain.

Union cavalry under General Kilpatrick skirmished with Richmond defenders and had to withdraw. Colonel Dahlgren paid a visit to the house of CS Secretary of War Seddon and drank some wine with Mrs. Seddon. His troops then rode to the James River and, finding it swollen, executed the African-American who was guiding them for suspected treachery. Dahlgren had lost track of Kilpatrick during all of this.

Union Admiral Porter sent a reconnaissance mission up the Black and Ouachita Rivers. This was done in preparation for the Red River Expedition.

Union Private Sneeden wrote about his first meal at Andersonville, a tin cup of cornmeal which he had to make into a cake! (The corn meal was not only coarse ground, but it had bits of the cob in it, which caused problems for the digestive tracts of whoever ate it).

March 2: Union Colonel Dahlgren was ambushed and killed outside Richmond. Papers found on his body point to an assassination plot against CS President Davis. US officials deny knowledge of any plot.

US Senate formally confirmed the promotion of Grant to Lieutenant General.

CS War Department clerk John B. Jones wrote about paying $20 for a half-cord of wood, $60 for a bushel of white beans, and $8 for a pound of bacon.

Union Private Sneeden wrote about helping a friend build a shelter with whatever they could find. He also began making sketches of the living conditions, which were already becoming horrible.

March 3: In Dayton, OH, fifteen men of the 44th Ohio, on leave, wrecked the offices of the Dayton *Daily Empire* after the newspaper printed a series of anti-Lincoln editorials.

Union General Kilpatrick continued his retreat while Colonel Dahlgren's body was stripped bare (including his wooden leg) by Confederates and sent to Richmond.

March 4: Union General Sherman's forces returned to Vicksburg.

Union General Kilpatrick raided the area near Richmond where Colonel Dahlgren was killed before returning to Union lines.

March 5: A Confederate attack on Yazoo City, MS was repulsed.

Confederate Government ordered that 1/2 of all space on all blockade-runners to be devoted to war materiel. Also authorized was the formation of a fleet of government blockade-runners.

CS War Department clerk John B. Jones wrote that a turkey was sold for $60.

March 6: Both Northern and Southern newspapers printed articles on the recent Kilpatrick raid. Northern papers called it a great victory while the Southern papers decried the raid as barbaric.

March 7: A cargo ship arrived at Halifax, NC with iron for CSS *Albemarle*.

The New York *Times* printed an editorial that depicting the effect that African-American soldiers were having on Northern racial attitudes. Sadly, discriminatory laws were still in effect in the North.

March 8: Union General Grant arrived in Washington, DC.

March 9: Union General Grant was formally promoted to Lieutenant General. After the promotion ceremony, he left Washington, DC to make his headquarters in the field with the Army of the Potomac.

CS War Department clerk John B. Jones wrote that bacon was selling for $15 a pound and cornmeal for $50 a bushel.

March 10: Union Generals Grant and Meade met at Brandy Station, VA. Grant told Meade that he would retain command of the Army of the Potomac, while he would command all Union forces from the field rather than behind a desk in Washington, DC.

March 11: Union commanders planning to advance up the Red River were concerned with river levels. They seem to be lower than expected.

March 12: The Red River Expedition began as Union General Banks launched a joint Army/Navy force against Confederate General Edmund Kirby Smith's Trans-Mississippi Army.

Union General Halleck was relieved as commander-in-chief and named chief of staff.

Union General Grant named General Sherman commander of the armies in the West (Army of the Tennessee, Army of the Ohio, and Army of the Cumberland).

CS War Department clerk John B. Jones wrote that flour was selling for $600 a barrel, cornmeal for $50 per bushel and fresh fish for $5 a pound. His household income was $7200 a year.

March 13: Union troops reached Simsport, LA as part of the Red River Campaign.

Union Sergeant Ransom's train reached Macon, GA. The prisoners have been given *"a pone of corn bread apiece weighing about two pounds, which is liberal on their part."*

March 14: CS Vice President Stephens made a speech to the Georgia Legislature that was critical of CS President Davis.

The Red River Expedition continued as Union troops captured Fort De Russy, LA.

Union Sergeant Ransom wrote that he had reached Camp Sumter.

March 15: Louisiana state government functions were transferred from military to civilian control.

Union flotilla arrived at Alexandria, LA, as part of the Red River Campaign.

Union Private Sneeden wrote about several tunnels that were being dug in order to escape from Andersonville. He also wrote that a barbershop had been set up next to his shanty.

March 16: Union forces were concentrated at Alexandria for a push up the Red River.

March 17: US President Lincoln pressed Maryland to adopt emancipation.

March 18: The US Sanitary Commission finished a fair in Washington, DC which showcased their work. US President Lincoln praised the organization for their accomplishments.

Confederate forces were concentrated at Carroll Jones' Plantation, 36 miles from Alexandria, LA to counter any Union movement up the Red River.

Arkansas voters approved a new state constitution that ended slavery.

CS War Department clerk John B. Jones wrote that most residents of Richmond, VA might average two ounces of meat per day, if there is any. Cornmeal was selling for $50 a bushel and bacon for $7.75 a pound.

March 19: Battle of Laredo, TX: Union commander: General Edmund Davis. Confederate commander: Colonel Santos Benavides. Small Confederate force prevented two Union cavalry units from seizing the Rio Grand River valley. This battle pitted Union Hispanics versus Confederate Hispanics. Confederate victory.

Georgia Legislature voted to press the Confederate Government to offer peace terms. Of course, they were looking nervously at the prospect of a Union invasion from Tennessee.

Union General Bank's forces entered Alexandria, LA..

> *I feel the full weight of the responsibilities devolving on me: and I know that if they are met, it will be due to those armies, and above all to the favor of that Providence which leads both nations and men.*
> —*Newly promoted Lieutenant General Ulysses S. Grant in his acceptance speech.*

March 20: CSS *Alabama* arrived at Cape Town, South Africa.

March 21: US President Lincoln approved recently passed acts allowing the territories of Colorado and Nevada to become states.

A Union advance force captured the 2nd Louisiana Cavalry at Bayou Rapides, 23 miles from Alexandria.

Union Sergeant Ransom wrote that Camp Sumter was fast filling up and wood for fires were already getting scarce. He also met fellow Michiganders among the prisoners.

March 22: Union General Wallace assumed command of the Middle Department, with headquarters at Baltimore.

March 23: Union Generals Banks, Smith and Admiral Porter met at Alexandria, LA.

Union General Grant returned to Washington, DC after allowing General Warren to assume command of V Corps.

March 24: Confederate General Forrest captured Union City, TN.

March 25: Confederate cavalry under General Forrest hit Paducah, KY, causing panic in nearby Ohio.

Union Sergeant Ransom wrote about seeing Confederate Captain Wirz, who recently took command of Camp Sumter.

March 26: Union Army of the Tennessee taken over by General McPherson.

Confederate General Forrest heads for Fort Pillow on the Mississippi River.

March 27: Union General Banks received orders from General Grant to march his army to Mobile, AL while detaching General Thomas Smith's corps to rejoin General Sherman at Vicksburg, MS. This would cause Banks to abandon the Red River Campaign, however, he decided to press ahead with the campaign in the absence of orders from General Halleck canceling the operation.

We have issued to us once each day about a pint of beans, or more properly peas, (full of bugs), and three-quarters of a pint of meal, and nearly every day a piece of bacon the size of your two fingers.
   —Union Sergeant John Ransom describing
        a daily ration at Camp Sumter.

March 28: Union troops under General Banks began their movement toward Shreveport, LA.

A mob of 100 Copperheads attacked Union troops on furlough at Charleston, IL killing 5, wounding 20 and setting off a riot.

March 29: Union General Meade demanded an inquiry after newspapers published articles critical of his leadership at the Battle of Gettysburg. US President Lincoln convinced Meade to withdraw the request.

Federal fleet departed Alexandria, continuing the Red River Campaign.

March 30: Skirmishes at Bolivar, TN, Caperton's Ferry, AL, Monett's Ferry and Cloutierville, LA, and Arkadelphia, AR.

March 31: Union General Banks' troops engaged Confederates at Natchitoches, LA.

Skirmishes at Arkadelphia, AR, Palatka, FL, and Forks-of-Beaver, KY.

April 1: Richmond resident Judith McGuire wrote in her diary about the scarcity of food in the Confederate capital, noting that tea sold for $22 a pound, coffee for $12 a pound, and brown sugar for $10 a pound.

Union Private Sneeden wrote that his shantymate died during the night.

April 2: Confederates destroyed Cape Lookout Light, NC.

Minor skirmishes at Cleveland, TN, and Grossetete Bayou and Crump's Hill, LA.

April 3: Union General Frederick Steele moved from Arkansas into Louisiana to assist General Banks, brushing aside a Confederate attempt to stop him.

Confederate held Fort Sumter bombarded by Union mortars.

April 4: Union General Sheridan assumed command of cavalry units assigned to the Army of the Potomac.

US Congress passed a resolution stating that it would not tolerate the formation of a monarchy in Mexico. This as reports and rumors circulate that French Emperor Napoleon III intends to install the brother of the Habsburg emperor of Austria on a throne in Mexico City.

George F. Davis, a resident of Cincinnati, OH wrote to his Senator, John Sherman (brother of Union General Sherman) to complain about refugees from the south flooding into his city.

April 5: Confederate General Richard Taylor massed 16000 troops in order to prevent Union General Banks from invading Texas.

April 6: State government of Louisiana adopted a new constitution that freed its slaves.

April 7: Battle of Mansfield, LA: Union commander: General Nathaniel Banks. Confederate commander: General Richard Taylor. Taylor established a line near Mansfield. Banks probed but did not attack. Taylor does attack, which caused Banks to withdraw, even though Union reinforcements had arrived. Confederate victory.

Confederate General Longstreet was ordered to return to Virginia from Tennessee.

Union Private Sneeden wrote that a "deadline" had been placed around the prisoner's enclosure at Camp Sumter about 30 feet inside the fence. The Confederate guards had orders to shoot anyone crossing the line. While the line was being built, some tunnels were found, which caused no end to the anger amongst the Confederates.

April 8: US Senate approved the 13th Amendment, outlawing slavery. The measure would be sent to the states for ratification.

Confederate General Taylor repulsed Union General Banks at Sabine Cross Roads, near Mansfield, LA.

CS War Department clerk John B. Jones wrote about paying $25 for a cord of wood.

Union Private Sneeden wrote about a police force, called Regulators, which was formed to keep order and to deal with the Raiders, Union prisoners who robbed and killed fellow prisoners.

April 9: Battle of Pleasant Hill, LA: Union commander: General Nathaniel Banks. Confederate commander: General Richard Taylor. Confederates launched an attack against larger Union forces and managed to drive back their left flank. Taylor was driven off but Banks decided to go back to Alexandria.

Union General Grant issued campaign orders for the Army of the Potomac, putting the Army of Northern Virginia in his sights.

Confederate General Forrest raided Federal communication lines in western Tennessee.

USS *Minnesota* was damaged by torpedo boat CSS *Squib* off Newport News, VA.

Union Sergeant Ransom wrote that the death rate at Camp Sumter was about 30 to 40 daily.

April 10: Battle of Prairie D'Ane, AR: Union commander: General Frederick Steele. Confederate commander: General Sterling Price. Federal forces launched an attack near Moscow, AR, which drove back the Confederates late in the day. Union victory, but Steele was forced to change his line of march.

Archduke Ferdinand of Austria assumed the throne of Mexico as Maximilian I. The Lincoln Administration watched this development with great interest.

April 11: Unionist government was installed in Arkansas with Dr Isaac Murphy as Governor.

CS War Department clerk John B. Jones wrote that potatoes were selling for $1 a quarter, chickens for $35 a pair, and turnip greens for $4 a peck. He also mentions a neighbor who lost all of his pigeons to thieves.

April 12: Confederate cavalry under General Tom Greene attacked Union boats near Pleasant Hill Landing, AR. General Greene was killed and the cavalry was forced back.

Confederate General Forrest attacked Fort Pillow, TN. The fort was taken and 200 of 262 African-American soldiers stationed there were massacred the Union garrison had surrendered.

April 13: The Union convoy that was attacked the previous day managed to deliver supplies to General Banks.

Columbus, KY came under assault by Confederate General Forrest's troopers.

April 14: US Tugboat *Geranium* was fired on by Confederates from Fort Moultrie, SC.

Confederate General Forrest assaulted Paducah, KY.

April 15: The Union Red River fleet was assembled at Grand Ecore, LA. They now have to contend with a lowering river level and Confederate torpedoes, one of which had heavily damaged USS *Eastport*.

April 16: A report was released stating that 146,634 Confederates have been captured since the war began.

Union vessel *General Hunter* destroyed by a Confederate torpedo on the St Johns River, FL

April 17: Union General Grant halted the prisoner exchange program in response to a Confederate refusal to treat African-American soldiers as prisoners of war.

Confederate forces under General R.F. Hoke attacked the Union garrison at Plymouth, NC.

April 18: Confederate General Marmaduke's forces attacked one of Union Colonel Grierson's foraging parties near Camden, AR.

Confederate General Beauregard was relieved of command of the Charleston defenses to assume command of the Department of North Carolina and Southern Virginia.

Federal supply column captured near Poison Springs, AR.

April 19: CSS *Albemarle* attacked Union vessels near Plymouth, NC, driving them off.

April 20: Union garrison of Plymouth surrendered to Confederates.

April 21: Union General Banks ordered his forces withdrawn from Grand Ecore, LA.

Union Private Sneeden wrote about a rainstorm that wrecked most of the shanties in Andersonville Prison.

April 22: CS President Davis expressed the opinion that any African-American soldiers that were captured and turned out to be escaped slaves should be returned to their owners.

Skirmishes at Cotton Plant and Jacksonport, AR.

April 23: Federal troops were hit at Camden, Monett's Ferry, and Swan Lake, AR

April 24: Skirmishes at Decatur, AL, Pineville and Ringgold, GA, and Camden AR.

CS War Department clerk John B. Jones wrote about buying a black coat at an auction for $12. A new coat costs $100.

April 25: Union General Frederick Steele, short of supplies, suffered a setback when a supply train was captured by Confederates at Mark's Mills, AR.

April 26: Union General Grant ordered the garrison at Washington, NC abandoned.

Union General Steele ordered a retreat from Camden, AR, sealing Confederate victory in the Red River Campaign.

Union Sergeant Ransom wrote that he had escaped Camp Sumter on April 21, but was recaptured after only traveling three miles, he was put in a chain gang for two days afterwards.

April 27: Union General Grant began issuing orders for a spring offensive.

CS President Davis dispatched Jacob Thompson to Canada in order to send out peace feelers to supporters in the North.

April 28: Another artillery assault on Fort Sumter.

April 29: Union General Steele continued the retreat from Camden, AR and began to cross the Saline River at Jenkins Ferry, although hampered by the swollen river.

Skirmish at Grand Ecore, LA.

April 30: CS President Davis' son Joe was killed in a fall at the Confederate White House.

Union forces under Colonel Albert Streight engaged Confederate forces under General Forrest in a series of battles beginning at Sand Mountain, AL and ending with the surrender of the Union force at Rome, GA on May 3.

The level of the Red River dropped to the point that Union General

Banks' flotilla was stranded and in danger of capture. Engineers devised a series of dams that would eventually free the flotilla by May 13.

May 1: Skirmish at Stone Church, GA.

Union Private Sneeden wrote about African-American soldiers captured at the Battle of Olustree, FL who were being treated very badly by the Confederate guards.

May 2: CS President Davis addressed the Confederate Congress, admitting for the first time that the hope of foreign recognition, especially from Great Britain and France, has ended. He also blasted the "Total War" policy of the Union armies in which all material means of supporting the war effort, especially farms, had been targeted for destruction.

Union General Sherman's forces engaged Confederate outposts at Tunnel Hill and Ringgold Gap, GA.

CS War Department clerk John B. Jones wrote about seeing tomato plants on sale for $10 a dozen.

Union Sergeant Ransom wrote that a Confederate artillery battery had arrived at Andersonville and was deployed around the prison, aimed into the prison pen! He also reported about 19,000 in the prison with the death rate about 100 daily.

May 3: Despite an attack by Confederate troops, Union General Steele managed to get his command to Little Rock, AR.

Union troops engaged Native-Americans at Cedar Bluffs, Colorado Territory.

May 4: Union General Grant launched the Overland Campaign with the Army of the Potomac crossing the Rapidan River. No longer is Richmond the main objective of the Union effort, the Army of Northern Virginia is.

Union General Sherman prepared to start an advance from Chattanooga, placing the rail center of Atlanta in his sights.

May 5: Union General Butler and his Army of the James landed at Bermuda Hundred, VA and began moving inland.

Battle of the Wilderness, VA: Union commander: General Ulysses S. Grant. Confederate commander: General Lee. Grant launched a flank attack in the same area as the 1863 Battle of Chancellorsville.

Naval engagement on the Alligator River between CSS *Albemarle* and two transports and USS *Mattabasset, Sassacus, Wyalusing,* and *Miami* resulted in one Confederate transport driven off and the other battered. *Albemarle* pulled into Plymouth, NC after damaging *Sassacus* and surviving a hit from *Miami.*

May 6: Union General Butler's advance along the Richmond-Petersburg railroad was halted by Confederate troops at Port Walthall Junction.

At the Wilderness, Federal forces launch a frontal assault on Confederate positions. Confederate General A.P. Hill's forces were about to collapse when General Longstreet's corps arrive. Longstreet was wounded by his own troops five miles from where General Jackson was wounded one year and four days previously. General Lee attempted to lead a charge personally but his own men led him away. The fighting was intense but inconclusive, with the Confederates regaining the trenches. The forest caught fire and hundreds of wounded soldiers burned to death.

A petition was sent to CS President Davis from Randolph County, AL that asked that the county be exempt from providing any more slaves as laborers for the army.

May 7: Union General Grant ended the Battle of the Wilderness by moving the Army of the Potomac to the left, bypassing Confederate General Lee's forces. This took the Confederates off guard as they were used to Union troops marching back north after a defeat.

The Atlanta Campaign began as Union General Sherman's army began marching southeast from Chattanooga.

CSS *Raleigh* attempted to break the blockade at Wilmington, NC but was destroyed after grounding at the harbor entrance.

Union Sergeant John Ransom wrote that bread was now being baked at a cookhouse built outside the stockade at Camp Sumter. The daily ration was now one-quarter of a loaf of bread and five ounces of pork.

May 8: Union General Grant arrived at Spotsylvania Court House to find Confederate General Lee waiting for him.

Union cavalry under General Sheridan went out to raid behind Confederate lines in Virginia.

CS War Department clerk John B. Jones wrote that a cow and calf was sold for $2500.

May 9: Union General McPherson found Confederates entrenched at Resaca, GA.

At Spotsylvania, Union General John Sedgwick was killed by a Confederate sniper after declaring, *"They couldn't hit an elephant at this distance."*

Ambrose Dudley Mann, CS agent in Brussels, Belgium, received a letter of support from Pope Pius IX.

May 10: Union General George Crook burned the New River Bridge, severing the Virginia and Tennessee railroad.

Union General Butler was stopped at Chester Station by Confederate defenders and forced to return to Bermuda Hundred.

Confederate General Stuart took up a position near Yellow Tavern, VA in order to stop Union General Sheridan.

Battle of Spotsylvania, VA: Union commander: General Ulysses S. Grant. Confederate commander: General Robert E. Lee. Federals attacked Confederate entrenchments at the apex of what became known as the "Mule Shoe", also known as the "Bloody Angle."

Union Sergeant Ransom wrote that new prisoners were being robbed by "Raiders", fellow prisoners who preyed on others.

May 11: Battle of Yellow Tavern, VA: Union commander: General Philip Sheridan. Confederate commander: General J.E.B. Stuart. Confederate cavalry launched an attack, which was quickly repulsed. General Stuart was mortally wounded.

May 12: Confederate General Stuart died of injuries suffered at Yellow Tavern.

Confederate General Joe Johnston's army is pulled back from Resaca, GA.

Union General Grant renewed his attack at the "Mule Shoe", near Spotsylvania. A Confederate counterattack resulted in 20 hours of the worst fighting of the war.

Union General Butler moved against Confederate positions at Drewry's Bluff.

May 13: Union General Grant ended the Battle of Spotsylvania by making yet another move to the south.

Union General Butler's attack at Drewry's Bluff was repulsed by Confederate forces under General Beauregard.

May 14: Battle of Resaca, GA: Union commander: General William T. Sherman. Confederate commander: General Joe Johnston. Union forces were repulsed while attacking Confederate entrenchments. Sherman decided to threaten Johnston's supply lines on the 15th, which forcing the Confederates to pull back. Union victory.

In the Shenandoah Valley, Confederate General Breckenridge led a makeshift force to engage Union forces under General Sigel.

Union General Grant, seeking a weakness in Confederate positions around Spotsylvania, ordered General Warren's corps to his left flank.

May 15: Battle of New Market, VA: Union commander: General Franz Sigel. Confederate commander: General John Breckenridge. Federal lines were breached by a smaller Confederate force, which included students from the Virginia Military Institute. Confederate victory. Interesting to note that one of the Confederate units engaged there, the 22nd Virginia, was commanded by Colonel George S. Patton, grandfather of the WWII army commander of the same name.

The cadets did their duty, as the long list of casualties will attest.... Wet, hunger, and many of them shoeless—for they had lost their shoes and socks in the deep mud through which it was necessary to march—they bore their hardships with that uncomplaining resignation which characterizes the true soldier.
        —Lieutenant Colonel Scott Ship, commanding the detachment of VMI cadets at New Market, VA.

General Breckenridge to a VMI Battery: *"Boys, the work you did yesterday will make you famous."*

VMI Cadet Dave Pierce: *"Fame's all right, General, but for God's sake where's your commissary wagon?"*

CS War Department clerk John B. Jones wrote on the following prices: a pair of boots for $200, a coat for $350, a pair of pants for $100, a pair of shoes for $125, flour for $275 a barrel, cornmeal for $80 a bushel, bacon for $9 a pound, chickens for $30 a pair, shad (fish) for $20 each, potatoes for $25 a bushel, turnip greens for $4 a peck, white beans for $4 a quart (or $120 a bushel), butter and lard for $15 a pound, and wood for $50 a cord. There was no beef to be had.

May 16: Confederate forces retreated toward Adairsville, GA

May 17: Union troops under General Howard attacked Confederates near Adairsville. General Joe Johnston ordered a withdrawal as General Sherman's full army arrived.

Union forces under General Banks arrived at the junction of the Red and Atchafalaya Rivers, LA as Confederate troops pursue.

Confederate General Beauregard had Union General Butler all bottled up at Bermuda Hundred.

Union Sergeant Ransom wrote about new prisoners bringing reports on the Union advance on Atlanta.

May 18: Battle of Yellow Bayou, LA: Union commander: General Nathaniel Banks. Confederate commander: General Richard Taylor. Banks detached a part of his force in order to hold off attacking Confederates while bridges were being built. Both sides retired as the foliage was set on fire by the battle.

Union General Grant attempted a flanking attack on Confederate troops near Spotsylvania, which failed.

May 19: There was an unsuccessful attack by Confederate forces under General Richard Ewell at Harris Farm, VA. This action ended the fighting around Spotsylvania.

Confederate forces under General Joe Johnston reach Allatoona Pass, GA.

Union General Sigel was relieved of his army command following his defeat at New Market.

May 20: Union General Banks managed to get his forces across the Atchafalaya River, ending the Red River Campaign in failure.

Union General Grant decided to move his army to the south, away from Spotsylvania.

Union Sergeant Ransom wrote that the population of Camp Sumter was about 20,000. Malnutrition and disease were taking a huge toll on the prisoners.

May 21: In response to Union General Grant's flanking maneuver from Spotsylvania, Confederate General Lee began moving his troops towards the North Anna River.

Confederate General Joe Johnston's forces were now firmly entrenched at Allatoona Pass, GA.

May 22: Union forces under General Sherman reached Allatoona Pass. He decided on another flanking maneuver, this time toward Dallas, closer to Atlanta.

Confederate General Ewell's corps reached Hanover Junction, VA, ahead of Union General Grant's troops, who have reached the North Anna River.

CS War Department clerk John B. Jones wrote that flour was selling for $400 a barrel and cornmeal for $125 a bushel.

Union Sergeant Ransom wrote that he had started a washing business alongside a Minnesota soldier who was running a barbershop. Services were being traded for food, which was the main currency in Camp Sumter.

May 23: Battle of the North Anna River, VA: Union commander: General Ulysses S. Grant. Confederate commander: General Robert E Lee. Confederate troops under General A.P. Hill attacked Union V Corps positions near Jericho Mills with nothing decided.

Confederate General Lee was taken seriously ill during the battle.

Union General Sherman's troops crossed the Etowah River en route to Dallas, GA.

May 24: Union troops crossed the North Anna River at Chesterfield Bridge and Ox Ford.

CS War Department clerk John B. Jones wrote that peas were selling for $10 a half-peck and strawberries for $10 a quart.

Confederate cavalry under General Fitzhugh Lee (one of Robert E. Lee's sons) attacked the Federal supply depot at Wilson's Wharf, VA, but were repulsed.

Confederate General Joe Johnston pulled his army out of Altoona Pass, and headed for New Hope Church.

Confederates under Colonel Colton Green began several attacks on Federal shipping on the Mississippi River.

May 25: Battle of New Hope Church, GA: Union commander: General William T. Sherman. Confederate commander: General Joseph Johnston. A Union attack on Confederate positions resulted in heavy casualties. Both sides entrenched and skirmished throughout the next day. Surviving Federals will call the area the "Hell Hole." This battle will end on May 26 with another Union flanking maneuver.

Union Army of the Potomac received reinforcements led by General Sheridan.

Union General Grant found his way blocked by Confederates and he considered another flanking move.

US Steamer *Lebanon* captured by Confederate Colonel Green's raiders on the Mississippi River.

May 26: Battle of North Anna River ended with yet another Federal flanking maneuver. Technically this gave the Confederates the victory, since they still held the field, but they also noticed that the Federals were flanking deeper into Virginia.

Union General Hunter began his movement in the Shenandoah Valley.

The Confederates who opposed him were commanded by General William "Grumble" Jones.

Union General Sherman's army reached Dallas, GA.

An African-American newspaper printed an article critical of the Lincoln Administration and the Emancipation Proclamation.

May 27: There were cavalry skirmishes along the Pamunkey River, VA as the Army of Northern Virginia began moving to the southeast in order to counter Union General Grant's next move.

Union troops under General Howard were repulsed at Pickett's Mills, near Dallas, GA.

May 28: Battle of Dallas, GA: Union commander: General Sherman. Confederate commander: General Joseph Johnston. Confederate forces under General Hardee attacked Union positions but withdrew after heavy fighting. Union victory.

Battle of Haw's Shop, VA: Union commander: General David Gregg. Confederate commander: General Fitzhugh Lee. Confederate cavalry attacked Union cavalry that was covering Grant's maneuver. Both sides fought to a standstill and began attracting infantry to the area.

New York *Times* printed an article about Union spy Pauline Cushman.

May 29: Battle of Bethesda Church, VA: Union commander: General Ulysses S. Grant. Confederate commander: General Robert E. Lee. Union forces began attacking Confederate positions along the Totopotomoy River. After the Federals failed to break through the lines, Grant was forced to move further south in order to outflank Lee, towards Cold Harbor. Technically a Confederate victory since they still held the line.

Fighting continued at Dallas, GA. Confederates realized that they were losing valuable troops that they could not afford to lose.

May 30: Battle of Bethesda Church ended in a draw as Union forces drove the Confederate left wing back as their left wing was also being driven back. A Union cavalry attack under General Alfred Torbert succeeded in opening a way to Old Cold Harbor.

Confederate General Morgan began his raid into Kentucky in order to disrupt Union General Sherman's supply lines.

Union Sergeant Ransom wrote about an Ohio man, Charlie Hudson, who was shot for attempting to get fresh water by reaching under the "deadline", the barrier at which Confederate guards were authorized to shoot prisoners.

May 31: Union General Sheridan's troops seized the crossroads at Old Cold Harbor.

A split in the Republican Party was evident as radicals were pushing General John Fremont for President.

Union General Sherman's push toward Atlanta had been slowed to a mile a day despite outnumbering the Confederate defenders.

June 1: Union cavalry seized Altoona Pass, opening a supply line to Chattanooga.

Union General Sturgis led his forces from Memphis in pursuit of Confederate General Forrest.

Union General Sheridan's forces at Old Cold Harbor repulsed a Confederate attempt to retake the crossroads.

June 2: The two opposing armies in Virginia have entrenched themselves from Bethesda Church to the Chickahominy River, about seven miles.

Union General Sherman began shifting his advance to the northeast of Atlanta,

June 3: Battle of Cold Harbor, VA: Union commander: General Ulysses Grant. Confederate commander: General Robert E. Lee. A dawn attack on Confederate entrenchments resulted in the bloodiest hour of the war, with 7000 dead and injured within 60 minutes. Grant will later consider this one of two charges he would regret. There would be skirmishing and artillery engagements until June 12.

Union Sergeant Ransom wrote about seeing African-American soldiers of the 54th Massachusetts arriving at Camp Sumter.

June 4: There was a truce at Cold Harbor so that the dead of both armies could be buried.

Confederate General Joe Johnston withdrew to a line covering three mountains in Georgia, Lost, Pine, and Brush, all north of Atlanta.

Federal forces pursued Confederate Generals Morgan and Forrest throughout Tennessee and Kentucky.

June 5: Battle of Piedmont, VA: Union commander: General David Hunter. Confederate commander: General William "Grumble" Jones. Union forces attacked Confederates north of Piedmont, turning a flank and killing Jones in the process. Confederates fled from the area. Union victory.

Confederate General Breckenridge was ordered to rejoin the Army of Northern Virginia. This left a small force in the Shenandoah Valley to counter any Union thrusts.

June 6: Union troops seized Lake Village, AR.

Union troops seized Staunton, VA.

Skirmishing at Raccoon and Big Shanty (Kennesaw), GA as Union General Sherman continued to shift his army around the Confederates.

June 7: National Union Convention met in Baltimore, MD to choose their nominee for President. This group consisted of Republicans and Democrats who supported the war effort.

Union General Sheridan was sent to the Shenandoah Valley to assist General Hunter.

Skirmish at Ripley, MS.

June 8: Confederate General Morgan captured the Union garrison at Mount Sterling, KY. He stole $18,000 in the process.

US President Lincoln received the Union Party nomination for the 1864 Presidential Election. He then chose Andrew Johnson of Tennessee, a Democrat, as his running mate.

Confederate General John Imboden's troops were pushed back, by Union General Hunter's forces, to Waynesboro, VA.

June 9: Union General Sherman found Confederate General Johnston entrenched near Marietta, GA. Performed a series of maneuvers that forced the Confederates to once again withdraw.

Union General Butler's troops attacked Petersburg, VA but were repulsed.

June 10: Battle of Brice's Cross Roads, TN: Union commander: General Samuel Sturgis. Confederate commander: General Nathan Forrest. A Confederate force of 2000 forced back a Union force of 8000. Confederate victory.

Confederate Government authorized military service for 15 to 50 year old males.

June 11: At Cynthiana, KY, Confederate forces under General Morgan captured the Union garrison as well as the reinforcements that were sent to help them.

CSS *Alabama* arrived at Cherbourg, France. Word of this was sent to Union Captain John Winslow, commanding USS *Kearsarge*, at Dover, England.

Union forces captured Lexington, KY.

Battle of Trevilian Station, VA: Union commander: General Philip Sheridan. Confederate commanders: Generals Wade Hampton and Fitzhugh Lee. Union cavalry forced a wedge between the two Confederate cavalry formations, driving both back. Battle will conclude on June 12. During the battle, Sheridan learned that General Hunter, who he was supposed to meet, was not where he was expected, but instead was at Alexandria burning down the Virginia Military Institute.

CS War Department clerk John B. Jones wrote that new potatoes were selling for $160 a bushel.

June 12: Additional Union reinforcements attacked Confederate General Morgan's forces at Cynthiana, KY capturing or killing most of them. Morgan escaped.

Union General Grant ordered his troops to move toward Petersburg, VA while leaving one corps in place at Cold Harbor in order to deceive Lee.

Battle of Trevilian Station ended with Union General Sheridan pulling back.

June 13: Union forces under General Sturgis reentered Tennessee after defeat at Battle of Brice's Cross Roads.

USS *Kearsarge* left Dover for Cherbourg to face CSS *Alabama*.

Confederate General Lee pulled back toward Richmond fearing a direct Union attack. Meanwhile, the Union II Corps (General Hancock) reached the James River at Wilcox Landing, VA.

Confederate General Polk was killed by a cannon ball near Marietta, GA (struck him right in the chest).

June 14: Union transports in position to ferry II Corps across the James River.

USS *Kearsarge* arrived off Cherbourg, France.

June 15: Arlington House, Confederate General Lee's home in Alexandria, VA, was designated a military cemetery. This is now known as Arlington National Cemetery. (This also ensured that the Lee's could no longer occupy their house).

Union troops crossed the James River on pontoon bridges at Weyanoke, VA.

Battle of Petersburg, VA: Union commander: General W.F. Smith. Confederate commander: General Beauregard. Union forces at the head of General Ulysses S. Grant's advance reached Petersburg, only to find Confederates forces waiting for them. The first attack drove the Confederates from their trenches, forcing them to maintain a defensive action while General Lee rushed the rest of his army to the city.

US House of Representatives voted in favor of a resolution abolishing slavery but failed to reach the 2/3 majority required.

Union Sergeant Ransom wrote that his own condition was deteriorating, he was suffering from scurvy. Daily life at Camp Sumter now consisted of dealing with lice, bad water, poor rations, a soaring death rate, oppressive summer weather, and Raiders plundering the camp daily.

June 16: 14,000 Confederate troops were massed to defend Petersburg but the Army of the Potomac, minus VI Corps (General Horaito Wright), had arrived. Confederate General Lee still believed that the main Union thrust will be north of the James River, even though Union forces were south of the river.

Union forces briefly take Bermuda Hundred but were repulsed by Confederates under General Pickett that evening.

June 17: Union General Hunter's forces reached Lynchburg, VA, only to be blocked by Confederate forces under General Ewell.

Confederate General Beauregard launched an attack on Union forces at

Petersburg and discovered that the main Union force was in front of him. That information was passed on to General Lee, who ordered the corps of Generals A.P. Hill and R. H. Anderson to reinforce Beauregard.

June 18: Battle of Petersburg ended in a stalemate. Union General Grant now fell on the same tactics that brought him victory at Vicksburg. The Siege of Petersburg had begun.

Confederate General Joe Johnston moved into prepared positions around Kennesaw Mountain, GA.

Union General Hunter was forced to pull his troops back into West Virginia, leaving the Shenandoah Valley in Confederate hands.

June 19: Battle of Cherbourg, France: Union commander: Captain John Winslow aboard USS *Kearsarge*. Confederate commander: Captain Raphael Semmes aboard CSS *Alabama*. *Kearsarge* was posted outside French territorial waters, effectively trapping the *Alabama* in port. Semmes decided to go out and force an engagement. The two ships meet in international waters and circled each other for over an hour, exchanging broadsides. Because of old ammunition aboard the *Alabama* and defensive chains hanging on the sides of the *Kearsarge*, it was a matter of time before the *Alabama* was finally holed and sunk. Semmes and 13 others escape with the help of an English nobleman. Union victory.

Mary Walker, a Union surgeon, received press backing for her fight for official status while also being critized for wearing trousers, even though they were under her skirts.

June 20: Union General Sherman extended his lines in order to sever Confederate supply lines near Kennesaw Mountain, GA.

Union forces bombarded Fort Sumter.

June 21: Union troops attempted to cut the Weldon Railroad, south of Petersburg.

US President Lincoln visited the newly formed siege lines at Petersburg.

Union General David Birney replaced General Hancock as commander of II Corps.

June 22: Confederate General John Bell Hood, on General Joe Johnston's right flank, attacked Union troops near Kennesaw Mountain, but was driven back with heavy casualties.

Union cavalry under Generals James Wilson and August Kautz severed the South Side Railroad, south of Petersburg.

Confederate troops under General A.P. Hill forced back Union troops to the Jerusalem Plank Road, but the Union siege line was still extended to the west.

June 23: Union cavalry destroyed 30 miles of railroad near Burke Station, VA.

Union cavalry under General Kautz skirmished with Confederates near Burkeville, VA while more Union cavalry under General James Wilson severed the Richmond and Danville Railroad.

Confederate General Hampton tried to recapture the wagons that Union General Sheridan had captured, but failed.

June 24: Maryland voted to abolish slavery.

Union General Sheridan was forced back at St Mary's Church, VA.

Three Union steamers were attacked on the White River, AR. USS *Queen City* destroyed.

June 25: Confederate cavalry under General William H.F. Lee prevented Union cavalry from destroying the Staunton River Bridge.

A tunnel was started from the Union trenches surrounding Petersburg.

This tunnel will eventually be dug under the Confederate lines, filled with explosives, and detonated. The tunnel was being dug by the men of the 48th Pennsylvania, who were coal miners in civilian life.

June 26: Confederate General Early's troops reached Staunton, VA enroute to raid the Washington, DC area so that Union troops would be recalled from Petersburg.

Union Private Sneeden wrote that conditions at Andersonville Prison were getting worse. Several hundred die a day and the dying were being robbed. Rations were cornmeal and bad bacon every day.

Union Sergeant Ransom, either yards away or across the camp from Sneeden, figured about 100 a day was dying. He was also using a cane to get around.

June 27: Battle of Kennesaw Mountain, GA: Union commander: General William T. Sherman. Confederate commander: General Joseph Johnston. Sherman launched an attack in the belief that Johnston's line was spread thin. Union attack was repulsed with heavy causalities. Confederate victory.

All at once a hundred guns from the Federal line opened upon us, and for more than an hour they poured out their solid and chain shot, grape and canister right upon this salient point. Then our pickets jumped into our works and reported the Yankees advancing. The witty man said: "Yes, yonder come forty lines of hard-tack and coffee, and I'm hungry as a dog."
—Sam Watkins, Private, 1st Tennessee, who was at Kennesaw mountain at an area known as the "Dead Angle."

June 28: Union cavalry reached Stony Creek Depot on the Weldon Railroad where they were attacked by Confederate cavalry under Generals William Lee and Hampton. Union forces escaped during the night.

Confederate General Early's troops left Staunton, VA without the needed supplies. They began their movement towards Harper's Ferry.

Confederate General Joe Johnston was planning another defensive line, this time on the Chattahoochee River north of Atlanta.

June 29: Union cavalry under Generals Wilson and Kautz reached Reams Station, VA expecting to find it Union held. Instead they found Confederate infantry, who surrounded them. After abandoning their wagons, both Union cavalry units escaped. Kurtz reached Union lines after dark while Wilson went to the southeast.

June 30: Confederate General Early opened the Second Shenandoah Valley Campaign by moving his forces to New Market. This move threatened both Winchester and Washington, DC.

The Fugitive Slave Act was repealed by Congress.

Union Secretary of the Treasury Salmon Chase resigned.

July 1: Union General McDowell was assigned command to the US Department of the Pacific, headquartered in San Francisco, CA.

US President Lincoln appointed Senator William Fessenden of Maine as Secretary of the Treasury.

Union Private Sneeden wrote about traders in Andersonville selling everything from "goober beans" (peanuts), beer made from cornmeal, even whiskey for .50 a tablespoonful, to tobacco cut in 1-inch squares and selling for .25.

July 2: Confederate General Joe Johnston pulled his troops back from Kennesaw Mountain.

Union General Wilson's troops reached Union lines near Petersburg.

James Island at Charleston was occupied by Union forces.

Confederate General Early received orders to rest and resupply, then try to hit the Baltimore and Ohio lines in Maryland.

Susie King Taylor, an African-American woman with the Union Army as a laundress, wrote about cooking and caring for wounded soldiers.

Union Private Sneeden wrote that his health was deteriorating and was relying on a crutch to get around.

July 3: Union General Sherman moved toward the new Confederate lines at Nickajack Creek, GA.

A Union attack on Fort Johnson near Charleston was repulsed.

Union General Sigel pulled his troops back toward Maryland Heights, MD in the face of Confederate General Early's movement.

July 4: Confederate General Johnson's forces had been pulled back yet again, this time to the Chattahoochee River.

US President Lincoln vetoed a resolution calling for harsh treatment on the South after the war's conclusion.

Confederate forces briefly occupied Harper's Ferry, WV.

Union Private Sneeden wrote that there was a raid on the Raiders shanties, with 125 arrested. There will be a trial planned for some of them.

July 5: Union General A.J. Smith led 14000 troops in a campaign to keep Confederate General Forrest from hitting General Sherman's supply lines.

Confederate General Early crossed the Potomac at Shepherdstown, MD.

New York *Times* editor Horace Greeley received news of Confederate commissioners in Canada with the authority to negotiate. Information was passed on to US President Lincoln.

CS War Department clerk John B. Jones wrote that new potatoes were selling for $4 a quart.

Union Private Sneeden wrote that a court-martial had begun for six of the worst Raiders. Those being tried were identified as William Collins, 88th Pennsylvania, John Sarsfield, 154th New York, Charles Curtis, 5th Rhode Island Battery, Patrick Delaney, 83rd Pennsylvania, John "Terrence" Sullivan, 72nd New York, and Andy Muir, USS *Water Witch*.

Union Sergeant Ransom wrote about witnessing the same trial.

July 6: Hagerstown, MD was captured by Confederate General Early's troops. Early demanded $20,000 ransom from the town.

Union 3rd Division of VI Corps was ordered out of the line at Petersburg in order to help defend Washington, DC. This was one of the objectives of Early's raid.

July 7: Union 3rd Division of VI Corps arrived at Baltimore, MD, enroute to defend the area from Confederate General Early's raid. Meanwhile, Early decided to bypass Union defenders at Maryland Heights and instead heads for South Mountain. He received a break in the form of a shipment of shoes that he had ordered.

Confederates counterattack at James Island, SC as Union cannon continued to batter Fort Sumter.

CS President Davis wrote Confederate General Joe Johnston that no more reinforcements could be sent his way.

July 8: Confederate General Early sent his army through South Mountain, MD in three columns while a makeshift force under Union General Wallace assembled at Frederick.

July 9: Battle of Monocacy, MD: Union commander: General Lew Wallace. Confederate commander: General Jubal Early. Using a cobbled together force and the 3rd Division of VI Corps, General Wallace held off

General Jubal Early while the Washington defenses were strengthened. Wallace was flanked and had to leave the field. Confederate victory. Afterwards, Early demanded $200,000 from the citizens of Frederick.

Union forces cross the Chattahoochee River, north of Atlanta, and forced Confederate General Joe Johnston to pull his forces to Peachtree Creek. That move placed the Army of Tennessee within Atlanta's city limits.

July 10: Confederate General Early's troops reached Rockville, MD where they encamped.

Union General Sherman had decided to besiege Atlanta as he sent cavalry to hit the rail line between Columbus, GA and Montgomery, AL.

Union Private Sneeden wrote that the six Raiders that were on trial were found guilty and sentenced to hang.

July 11: Union cavalry under General Smith reached Pontotoc, MS while Confederate General Forrest has his troops at nearby Okolona, MS.

Confederate General Early reached the outskirts of Washington, DC and found the area reinforced.

Union Private Sneeden wrote that the condemned Raiders were hanged in the stockade. John Collins' rope broke, but new rope was found and the hangings were soon finished. This is also witnessed and accounted by Sergeant Ransom.

July 12: Union General Wright engaged Confederate General Early outside Washington, DC, with US President Lincoln watching. Lincoln was standing on a parapet watching the battle when a Union Captain shouted, "*Get down you damned fool or you will be killed!*" Lincoln replied, "*Captain, I see you already learned how to address a civilian.*" The Captain involved would become Justice Oliver Wendell Holmes of the US Supreme Court.

July 13: Union General A.J. Smith's forces moved to Tupelo, MS.

Union General Wright pursued Confederate General Early as he pulled back from Washington, DC.

July 14: Battle of Tupelo, MS: Union commander: General A.J. Smith. Confederate commanders: Generals Nathan Forrest and Stephen Lee. Confederate forces attacked at 7 a.m. but were not properly controlled, which resulted in both formations being repulsed. Union victory.

July 15: Union Sergeant Ransom wrote that the death rate at Camp Sumter was now about 150 a day.

July 16: Confederate General Jubal Early and his troops retreat from Washington, DC towards the Shenandoah Valley and back into Virginia.

In Atlanta, Union General Sherman advanced his army across the Chattahoochee River.

Confederate General Joe Johnston received a telegram from CS President Davis demanding to know what he was doing about the situation. Johnston planned to hold Atlanta with militia troops and send the field army against Sherman.

Soldiers of the 54th and 55th Massachusetts were refusing pay in protest of unequal pay for African-American soldiers. Whites were paid $13 a month while Blacks were paid $10 a month with $3 taken for clothing. This has gone on for over a year and they wrote US President Lincoln for help.

July 17: Confederate General Joe Johnston was relieved of command of the Army of Tennessee in favor of General John Bell Hood.

Confederate General Early, retreating from Washington DC, received intelligence that a Union force under Generals Hunter and Crook were waiting to attack him.

> *We are not fighting for Slavery. We are fighting for Independence, and that, or extermination, we will have.*
> — *CS President Jefferson Davis to Northern journalist James R. Gilmore*

July 18: US President Lincoln learned from New York *Times* editor Horace Greeley that the Confederate commissioners that he met with at Niagara Falls, NY were only interested in a negotiated settlement that left the CSA independent. Lincoln dismissed any thought of any settlement other than one that restored the Union.

Union troops under General Crook were attacked by Confederates under General Robert Rodes while crossing the Shenandoah River. Crook was forced to withdraw.

July 19: Confederate General Early's force was now headed toward Winchester, VA.

Union General Sherman had divided his army into three segments. The Army of the Cumberland (General Thomas) was holding north of Atlanta, GA, the Army of the Ohio (General Schofield) was positioned to the east, and the Army of the Tennessee (General McPherson) was at Decatur, GA. Confederate General Hood decided to head north and strike Thomas first.

July 20: Battle of Peachtree Creek, GA: Union commander: General George Thomas. Confederate commander: General John Bell Hood. In his first engagement as an army commander, Hood attacked Thomas as his army was crossing the creek. A hasty move into a defensive line prevented Hood from gaining any advantage and forced him to retreat. Hood lost four of his brigadiers in the process. Union victory.

Bombardment of Fort Sumter continues. On this day, the fort's commander was mortally wounded.

Union troops under General Averill attacked Confederate General

Stephen Ramseur at Rutherford's Farm, VA which caused General Early to retreat further south.

July 21: Confederate General Hood sent General Hardee to hit Union General McPherson near Decatur, GA. There were too many delays and the movement would not leave until early the next morning. Meanwhile, General McPherson's troops hit a Confederate position at Bald Hill, east of Atlanta.

July 22: Battle of Atlanta, GA: Union commander: General James McPherson. Confederate commander: General William Hardee. Hood now focused his attention on the Union Army of the Tennessee, having General Hardee send his troops on a 15 mile march, in the very early morning hours, into McPherson's rear area. From the start the Confederates became confused. When Confederate General Walker went forward to see where they were going, he was killed by a Union rifleman. The attack was finally launched at noon, but was repulsed. McPherson was killed when he accidentally rode into a Confederate line held by General Cheatham. Troops under General John Logan forced Hood back with heavy casualties. Union victory, but Hood tried to claim it instead. Truth was the Confederates failed to force Sherman back from Atlanta.

Union troops under General Wright moved to rejoin General Grant at Petersburg.

July 23: Confederate General Early turned his army around and advanced on Union troops near Kernstown, VA.

Union General Smith's troops returned to Memphis as Confederate General Forrest continued his raid.

July 24: Confederate General Early attacked Union General Crook at Kernstown, forcing the Federals back.

July 25: The Union tunneling operation had aroused the suspicion of Confederates at Petersburg. They began some tunneling of their own in an attempt to find the Federal tunnel.

Union General Grant ordered that some of his troops be sent north of the James River, near Petersburg in order to break the rail line between the besieged town and Richmond.

July 26: Union General Crook pulled his army out of the Shenandoah Valley.

The tunnel at Petersburg was declared ready. The plan at this point was that when the gallery at the end of the tunnel was exploded, African-American troops under General Edward Ferrero will go through the breach and take a hill just inside Petersburg.

July 27: A Union Navy boat crew, commanded by Lieutenant J.C. Watson, ran into Mobile Bay, AL to study the depth of the bay and the area where torpedoes might be, in broad daylight!

Union II Corps crossed the James River and headed toward Richmond.

Union General Howard was given command of the Army of the Tennessee, replacing General McPherson who was killed at the Battle of Atlanta. In protest, General Hooker resigned his commission (another political general falls).

Union Sergeant Ransom wrote that he was hanging on despite his illness and that about 200 a day were dying at Camp Sumter. Most of his friends that were imprisoned with him have died.

July 28: Battle of Ezra Church, GA: Union commander: General O.O. Howard. Confederate commander: General Stephen D. Lee. Howard was sent on a mission to cut General Hood's last rail line. General Lee, along with General Alexander Stewart, attacked Howard's troops at Ezra Church. Howard had anticipated this and had already formed a defensive line that resulted in the Confederates withdrawing with heavy losses. Union victory, but Howard was not able to cut the rail line.

Union General Hancock found entrenched Confederates near Four Mile Creek, VA and was forced to withdraw.

July 29: Confederate General Early crossed the Potomac River and headed for Pennsylvania.

Union General Hancock's troops return to their original position south of the James River.

There was a meeting of IX Corps and Army of the Potomac commanders near Petersburg, VA concerning the plans for the follow-on attack after the tunnel was blown up. General George Meade ordered that the African-American troops, who have been training for weeks, not be used for fear of a public backlash if the attack failed. General Grant, agreed and ordered General Burnside to choose another division to spearhead the assault. Burnside called his division commanders and had them draw straws to choose who will go. General James Ledlie, a noted drunkard and coward, drew the short straw.

July 30: Confederate General Early burned Chambersburg, PA after town officials did not pay a $500,000 ransom.

Battle of the Crater, Petersburg, VA: Union commander: General Ambrose Burnside. Confederate commander: General William Mahone. For the past several months, members of a Pennsylvania regiment who were coal miners had been digging a tunnel from the Union lines to a Confederate section of the line known as Pegram's Salient. The end of the tunnel was widened to accommodate several tons of gunpowder. After two fuse lightings, the powder exploded, blowing a huge hole in the Confederate lines. The Federal follow-up attack was un-coordinated and ended up getting bogged down in the crater. An African-American division that was trained for the attack was held back and a white division was the first to go in, with their commander, General James Ledlie, hiding in a bomb shelter and getting drunk. The African-American troops were then sent in as a reserve, but they got bogged down too. Their commander was found in the same shelter as Ledlie. General Mahone rushed reinforcements to the crater and the result was very high casualties among the Union troops. General Grant ordered the assault pulled back, but not until after hundreds of African-American soldiers were massacred by enraged Confederates. General Burnside was relieved of his command and sent home for another assignment, which never came. Confederate victory. **This is the last major Union defeat of the war.**

July 31: Union General Averill's cavalry engaged Confederate cavalry under General John McCausland near Hancock, MD. Confederates flee.

US President Lincoln met General Grant at Fort Monroe, VA to discuss the situation in the East.

August 1: Union General Sheridan was named commander of the Army of the Shenandoah.

Confederate cavalry rode towards Cumberland, MD while pursued by Union General Averill's cavalry. A scratch force under Union General Benjamin Kelly ambushed the Confederates, forcing a withdrawal.

August 2: Union and Confederate cavalry engaged again at Hancock, MD.

Union Commodore George Colvocoresses and 115 men arrested some Confederates at McIntosh Court House, GA who were trying to organize a coast guard.

CSS *Rappahannock* was abandoned at Calais, France after being repaired. The French would only allow a 35-man crew to sail the ship out of port and that was not enough to go out on the high seas. This was another sign of waning support for the Confederacy amongst Europeans.

August 3: Union troops landed on Dauphin Island, AL and besieged Fort Gains.

August 4: Union General Schofield's Army of the Ohio crossed Utoy Creek in an attempt to cut the last rail line going to Atlanta,

A detachment of US Army Signal Corps officers reported in to Admiral Farragut near Mobile Bay. They will maintain communication with ground forces during the attack planned for the next day.

August 5: Battle of Mobile Bay, AL: Union commander: Admiral David Farragut aboard USS *Hartford*. Confederate commander: Admiral Franklin Buchanan aboard CSS *Tennessee*. At dawn, troops under the command of Union General Gordon Granger attacked Fort Gaines while Admiral Farragut's fleet sailed past Fort Morgan, which guarded the east end of the bay opening. The area was covered with a field of torpedoes (mines). At 7:45 a.m. USS *Tecumseh* strikes a torpedo and sank, taking 90 with her. Both fleets engaged each other until 10 a.m. when CSS *Tennessee* surrendered. Union forces controlled the entrance of the bay but not the two main forts yet. Union victory. (It has been noted that Admiral Farragut had ordered when hearing of the torpedoes, *"Damn the torpedoes! Full speed ahead!"* Today there is a debate whether or not he actually said that).

A radical faction of the Republican Party issued a manifesto that accused US President Lincoln of overstepping his power when he vetoed a reconstruction bill.

August 6: Union General Schofield renewed his attempt to sever the rail lines west of Atlanta with no success.

Fort Powell, northwest of Fort Gaines at Mobile Bay, was evacuated.

CSS *Tallahassee* departed Wilmington, NC, the last major Confederate port.

August 7: Confederate General McCausland cavalry was attacked by Union cavalry under General Averill and was routed near Moorefield, VA.

There was an attempt to surrender Fort Gaines but the commander's orders were countermanded.

August 8: Fort Gaines, at Mobile Bay, was surrendered to Union forces.

CS War Department clerk John B. Jones wrote that watermelons were selling for $20 each and corn for $10 for a dozen.

August 9: Union forces began the bombardment of Fort Morgan, on the opposite side of Mobile Bay.

Confederate agents penetrated Union security at City Point, VA and blew up an ammunition barge.

Union General Sherman began his bombardment of Atlanta.

August 10: Confederate cavalry under General Wheeler began a mission to raid northern Georgia and eastern Tennessee.

Union General Sheridan began moving his command toward the Shenandoah Valley. Confederate General Early began his maneuver in order to counter Sheridan's moves.

CSS *Tallahassee* captured seven vessels off Sandy Hook, NJ.

August 11: Confederate General Early began his movement from Winchester to Cedar Creek, VA.

August 12: Skirmish at Cedar Creek.

CSS *Tallahassee* captured six vessels off New York.

Poet Walt Whitman wrote about witnessing one of US President Lincoln's daily outings. He saw Lincoln heading out to the Soldiers Home, where he slept during the summer, since the White House was too hot during that season.

August 13: Fighting at Berryville, VA as Union General Sheridan began to move against Confederate General Early.

Union General Hancock began another maneuver across the James River.

CS War Department clerk John B. Jones wrote that the price of flour had fallen to $200 a barrel, while bacon fell to $6 a pound.

Union Sergeant Ransom wrote about the spring of water that came up in the middle of Camp Sumter after a massive rainstorm.

August 14: Battle of Dalton, GA: Union commander: Colonel Bernard Laibolt. Confederate commander: General Joseph Wheeler. Wheeler demanded the surrender of the Union garrison, which was refused. Laibolt brought his troops into fortifications near Dalton and withstood a day of attacks. The next morning, a Union column under General James Stedman arrived and drove Wheeler off. Union victory.

Union General Sherman continued the bombardment of Atlanta as his troops extended their lines to encircle the Confederate defenders.

August 15: CSS *Tallahassee* captured and burned six ships off New England.

CSS *Georgia* captured by Federals off Lisbon, Portugal. Problem was that the vessel has just been sold to an English ship-owner and had been disarmed.

Union General Sheridan, citing supply problems, retired from Cedar Creek.

Confederate General Richard Taylor was appointed commander, Department of Alabama, Mississippi, and East Louisiana.

CS War Department clerk John B. Jones wrote that the price of flour fell to $175 a barrel and bacon to $5 a pound.

August 16: CSS *Tallahassee* captured and burned five more ships off New England.

Union Cavalry under General Wesley Merritt captured 300 Confederates near Front Royal, VA. A rally by remaining Confederates forced Merritt to withdraw to Cedarville, and then on to Nineveh.

Union General Sheridan's troops reached Winchester, VA.

Union General Hancock attacked Confederate lines at Fussell's Mill, VA. After initial successes, he was forced back.

August 17: CSS *Tallahassee* sailed towards Nova Scotia to resupply with coal, capturing three more vessels enroute.

Confederate General Early's troops advanced from Cedar Creek while Union General Sherman's troops headed for Berryville.

August 18: Union cavalry under General Kilpatrick, on a mission to destroy remaining Confederate supply lines near Atlanta, destroyed part of the Atlanta and West Point Railroad.

Union forces under General Warren seized Globe Tavern, on the Weldon railroad, south of Petersburg, standing up to counterattacks by Confederates under General Henry Heth.

Union General Grant again refused any more prisoner exchanges. This would keep released Confederates from rejoining the army but would also worsen the situation for Union troops held in Southern prisons. The CSA could barely feed its troops, let alone its prisoners.

Union General Sheridan's troops were now heading for Charles Town, WV.

Confederate General Early's army was heading for Bunker Hill, VA.

August 19: Union General Kilpatrick's forces destroyed Confederate supplies at Jonesborough, GA.

Five Confederate brigades under General A.P. Hill drove Union General Warren out of his position at Globe Tavern. He was soon reinforced and managed to recapture the position.

August 20: Union cavalry under General Kilpatrick managed to destroy the Macon and Western Railroad at Lovejoy's Station, GA, but had to flee in order to avoid being captured by Confederate General Cleburne.

Union General Hancock returned to his former positions but maintained a bridgehead across the James River at Deep Bottom, VA.

Union General Warren extended his lines from Globe Tavern to the Jerusalem Plank Road, heading west from Petersburg.

Confederate General Early's troops engaged Union General Philip Sheridan at Berryville, VA.

August 21: Confederate cavalry under General Forrest attacked Memphis in an attempt to free Confederate POWs. Forrest withdrew after two hours.

Confederate General Early splits his forces in two and attacked Union General Sheridan near Charles Town, which forced a Federal delaying action. Sheridan was forced to pull back to Harper's Ferry.

Confederate General A.P. Hill attempted to break Union General Warren's lines to no effect. The extension of the Union lines had severed the rail link between Petersburg, VA and Wilmington, NC.

August 22: Union General Sheridan pulled his troops toward Halltown, VA.

Union forces attacked Fort Morgan, Mobile Bay, from both land and sea. The defenders were not able to respond as their cannon were knocked out. The fort's commander ordered the powder magazine flooded to prevent an explosion, or its capture.

Judith McGuire wrote about the prices she paid during a shopping trip in Richmond. She paid $110 for a pair of ladies' boots, $22 per yard for linen, several spools of thread at $5 a piece, and $5 for a good amount of pins.

August 23: Fort Morgan surrendered to Union forces, giving them control of the entrance to Mobile Bay.

US President Lincoln, believing that he would lose the upcoming election, had his Cabinet sign a memo pledging to cooperate with the incoming administration. He also planed to force the war to a favorable conclusion before the new president, likely McClellan, could make a settlement that would grant the CSA its independence.

August 24: Confederate General Early moved against Union General Sheridan, now in positions along the Potomac River.

Skirmishing along the Weldon Railroad, south of Petersburg.

August 25: Union General Sherman moved six of his seven corps in an effort to encircle Atlanta. Confederate General Hood countered with two corps under General Hardee.

CSS *Tallahassee* reached Wilmington, NC by evading the blockade.

Confederate General Heth overran Union General Hancock's position at Ream's Station, VA.

August 26: Union General Sherman's advance threatened to cut off any avenues of escape form Atlanta. Confederate General Hood was pondering this development while skirmishing took place along the Chattahoochee River.

August 27: Confederate General Early pulled back to Bunker Hill, WV.

Union General Sherman's troops severed another rail link into Atlanta. It was now a matter of time before the city falls.

August 28: Union General Sheridan sets off from Halltown, VA toward Charles Town, WV.

Union forces destroyed 10 miles of the rail line from Atlanta to the Alabama line.

Skirmish at Holly Springs, MS.

August 29: Two Confederate divisions engaged Union cavalry at Smithfield, VA but were stopped by Federal reinforcements.

Democrats begin their convention at Chicago, IL.

August 30: Union troops continued to encircle Atlanta as Confederate General Hood sent the corps of Generals Hardee and Stephen D. Lee (no relation to Robert E. Lee) to Jonesboro to protect the last rail line, the Macon Railroad.

August 31: Democrats nominate Union General McClellan as their nominee for President on a peace at any costs platform, including letting the CSA have its independence.

Confederate General Hardee attacked Union General Sherman's positions near Jonesborough, but was repulsed. During the action, Union troops captured the station at Rough and Ready, severing the Macon Railroad and isolating Atlanta.

CS War Department clerk John B. Jones wrote that salted herrings were going for $16 a dozen and salted shad (fish) for $8 each.

Union Sergeant Ransom wrote that rumors of a prisoner exchange were floating around Camp Sumter.

September 1: Union troops cut Confederate General Hardee's supply and communication lines, which forced a retreat toward Lovejoy's Station, GA. That evening, General Hood ordered Atlanta evacuated.

September 2: A telegram was sent from Union General Sherman to US President Lincoln, "*Atlanta is ours, and fairly won,*" as his army captured the city. The 2nd Massachusetts was the first into the city.

Union General Grant extended his lines to the southwest of Petersburg cutting off more Confederate avenues of supply.

Confederate General Lee proposed the drafting of slaves as a labor force, freeing white laborers for the ranks.

September 3: Around this time, all of the Native-American tribes that were aligned with the Confederacy signed a treaty pledging loyalty to the US.

US President Lincoln declared September 5 as a day of thanksgiving for the recent victories at Atlanta and Mobile Bay.

September 4: At Greenville, TN, Union cavalry caught Confederate cavalry by surprise, resulting in Confederate General John Morgan being killed and most of his troops either killed or captured.

Confederate General Early brought his whole army up to face Union General Sheridan at Berryville, MD, but soon had to pull back.

Union General Sherman ordered the city of Atlanta evacuated.

September 5: Citizens in the Federal occupied areas of Louisiana who had taken a loyalty oath to the US vote to abolish slavery in the state.

Clash between Confederate General Early and Union General Sheridan's troops occurred at Opequon Creek, VA.

> *The loss of Atlanta is a stunning blow.*
> —*John Beauchamp Jones, diary entry.*

September 6: Bombardment of Fort Sumter resumed.

Union Sergeant Ransom wrote that the exchange rumors were this time for real. He now had a chance to leave Camp Sumter.

September 7: Skirmishing continued at Winchester, VA.

Skirmishing at Searcy, AR and Centralia, MO.

The Rev. S.M. Chase, an African-American minister, gave a speech in Baltimore, praising US President Lincoln's work on emancipation.

CS War Department clerk John B. Jones wrote about two English cannon arriving in Richmond.

Union Sergeant Ransom was released from Camp Sumter and taken to a hospital near Savannah, GA.

September 8: George McClellan accepted the Democratic nomination for President, but shied away from the anti-war platform.

September 9: Engagement at Warrensburg, MO.

September 10: Union forces took Fort Hell, a part of the Confederate defenses surrounding Petersburg.

Union General Grant sent a telegram to General Sherman urging him to resume the offensive against Confederate General Hood.

September 11: A 10-day truce was put into effect in order for Atlanta to be evacuated of civilians.

In what is now Oklahoma, pro-Union and pro-Confederate Indians fight each other within the lands of the Cherokee Nation.

Union Private Sneeden wrote that a mass escape took place at Camp Sumter, with about 31 escaping. Most were recaptured after a short time.

September 12: US President Lincoln sent an order to General Grant to reinforce General Sheridan as Confederate General Early was still a threat to Washington, DC and the nearby rail links to the West.

Union General Sherman answered a letter from Atlanta civic leaders who wanted him to rescind the evacuation order. Sherman said that not only he would not rescind the order, but also it was necessary to deny the Confederate Army the use of Atlanta's railroads and industry to continue the war with. Hence, his plan to destroy the city.

September 13: Skirmishing continued at Bunker Hill, VA.

September 14: A Confederate corps under General Richard Anderson left the Shenandoah Valley to join General Lee at Petersburg. The reinforcements were needed because the fighting there was bleeding the Army of Northern Virginia white.

September 15: Union General Grant left Petersburg, to confer with General Sheridan.

September 16: Confederate General Forrest left Verona, MS to raid Union General Sherman's supply lines.

Union Generals Grant and Sheridan met at Charles Town, WV to discuss the situation in the Shenandoah Valley.

Confederate General Hampton attacked a Union supply train heading to Petersburg, VA taking 2400 cows and 300 prisoners.

September 17: Confederate General Early was back in the Shenandoah Valley, planning on hitting the Baltimore and Ohio Railroad near Martinsburg, VA.

Former Union General Fremont withdrew from the 1864 Presidential Campaign.

Union Private Sneeden wrote that he was part of a group of prisoners selected for exchange and had been placed on a train for Savannah, GA.

September 18: Confederate General Early's force was split near Bunker Hill, VA. Union General Sheridan begins moving toward him.

CS War Department clerk John B. Jones wrote that $1 on gold equaled $25 Confederate.

September 19: Confederate General Price led a raid into Missouri with the target being St Louis. This would be a last desperate move since of the 12,000 men who were marching with Price, only 8000 of them were armed.

Battle of Opequon Creek (Third Winchester), VA: Union commander: General Philip Sheridan. Confederate commander: General Jubal Early. Early tried to delay Sheridan's advance toward Winchester. Confederates were thrown back with General Robert Rhodes among the killed. Union victory.

Confederate agents seized the vessel *Philo Parsons* after leaving Detroit, MI. The plan was to free Confederate POWs held at Johnson's Island. The plan fell apart and the agents fled to Canada.

September 20: Union General Sheridan was now in pursuit of Confederate General Early's troops, hitting them at Middletown and Strasburg, VA.

Confederate General Price captured Keytesville, MO.

Confederate General Forrest and his troopers were in Northern Alabama and planned a raid into Tennessee.

September 21: Confederate General Forrest got close to the Union garrison at Athens, TN.

Battle of Fisher's Hill (Cedar Creek), VA: Union commander: General Philip Sheridan. Confederate commander: General Jubal Early. Day One: Sheridan's attack pushed back the Confederate picket line and captured the high ground. Fighting ended at night fall. During the night, Union General Crook's Army of West Virginia moved into concealed positions to wait for morning.

September 22: Battle of Fisher's Hill: Day Two: Union General Crook's troops launched an attack that collapsed the Confederate line. Early retreated toward Rockfish Gap, losing 20 cannon in the process and opened the entire Shenandoah Valley to Sheridan. Union victory.

September 23: Confederate General Early's shattered army fell back towards New Market, VA.

September 24: Union General Sheridan began a scorched earth policy in the Shenandoah Valley. Anything of any value to the Confederacy was burned. It was said at the time that the destruction would be so complete that *"birds flying across the valley would have to carry their own provender."*

Confederate troops under General Price attacked Fayette, MO.

Confederate General Forrest captured Athens, AL.

September 25: Confederate General Early was forced to retreat to Brown's Pass, in the Blue Ridge Mountains.

Confederate General Forrest captured the Sulphur Branch Trestle in northern Alabama, disrupting Federal rail traffic.

CS President Davis met with General Hood at Palmetto, GA to discuss the current situation.

September 26: Skirmishes occur at Port Republic and Brown's Gap, VA as Union General Sheridan's troops pressed Confederate General Early.

Confederate General Forrest struck a Federal garrison neat Pulaski, TN.

Confederate General Price's troops engaged Federals at Arcadia Valley, Shut-in-Gap, and Ironton, MO.

September 27: Confederate General Price attacked the Union garrison at Fort Davidson, MO. He failed to capture the fort but the garrison escaped during the night.

Confederate raiders under William "Bloody Bill" Anderson attacked and killed 24 unarmed Union soldiers at Centralia, MO. He then attacked the Union troops that were coming to reinforce the garrison.

September 28: Confederate General Price resumed his advance toward St Louis, MO.

Atlanta cleared of civilians. Atlanta Campaign ends.

Union Admiral Farragut took sick leave and left Admiral Porter in charge of the Union blockade and Admiral S.P. Lee (a relation to Confederate General Lee) in command of US Naval forces on the Mississippi River.

CS President Davis ordered General Hardee relieved from command of a corps of General Hood's army and reassigned him to command the Department of South Carolina.

Private James Henry Gooding, a private in the 54th MA, wrote US President Lincoln to complain about the lower pay that African-American soldiers were receiving.

September 29: Confederate cavalry under General Forrest skirmished with Federals near Lynchburg, TN.

Confederates in Cuba seized the US vessel *Roanoke* in violation of Spanish neutrality (Cuba at the time was a Spanish possession).

Union General Sheridan and Confederate General Early's troops skirmish near Waynesboro, VA.

Union Generals David Birney and Edward Ord launched an assault on the Richmond, VA defenses. XVII Corps (Ord) managed to take Ft Harrison but X Corps (Birney) was repulsed at Gilmer.

Union forces pushed out from the Weldon Railroad towards the Southside Railroad near Petersburg, VA.

Skirmish at Leesburg and Cuba, MO.

CS War Department clerk John B. Jones wrote about having breakfast with a Mr. Tyler. The meal consisted of two loaves of bread, two cups of coffee and six eggs. The bill came to $16.

September 30: Union General Grant extended his lines southwest of Petersburg, VA, capturing Fort Archer from the Confederates.

Confederate General Lee attempted to take back Fort Harrison from the Federals, but failed. Lee now has only 50,000 troops to cover 35 miles of trenches.

October 1: Union and Confederate troops clashed near Saltville, VA with the Federals being driven off.

Confederate spy Rose Greenhow drowned off the North Carolina coast. The $2000.00 in gold that she was carrying dragged her down.

Confederates under General A.P. Hill attacked Union General Grant's lines southwest of Petersburg but was repulsed.

Union garrisons at Athens and Huntsville, AL attacked by Confederate General Forrest's troops.

Confederate General Hood launched a campaign toward Tennessee in order to bring Union General Sherman out of Atlanta. Sherman responded by sending General John Corse to Altoona.

Orestes A. Brownson published an essay rejecting harsh Reconstruction measures for the South, calling it "New-Englandizing."

October 2: Confederate General Beauregard was named commander of Confederate armies in the West.

Skirmishing at Big Shanty and Kennesaw Water Tank, GA. This resulted in Union General Sherman's communication lines with the North being cut (not that he was worried about it).

Confederates occupied Washington, MO.

CS War Department clerk John B. Jones wrote that he bought a quart of apples for .75. He also mentions that area doctors agreed to charge $30 a visit.

October 3: Union General Sherman ordered General Thomas to

Nashville on the idea that Confederate General Hood was headed there. Those same orders sent General John Schofield to Knoxville.

CS President Davis made a speech at Columbia, SC that called on Southerners to join General Hood and drive Union troops out of Georgia.

Confederate troops under General Price reached Hermann and Miller's Station, MO.

October 4: Confederate General Price abandoned his plan to take St. Louis, MO and headed for Independence, MO.

Confederate General Hood's troops were headed for Dallas, GA, tearing up 15 miles of track in the process.

CS War Department clerk John B. Jones wrote that flour is now $450 a barrel, cornmeal sells for $72 a bushel, and bacon for $10 a pound.

October 5: There was a Confederate attack on the Union garrison at Altoona, GA. Despite repeated attacks, the Federals did not budge and the Confederates were forced to pull back when their ammunition ran short.

October 6: Having completed the destruction of the Shenandoah Valley, Union General Sheridan began his pull out from the valley, despite a cavalry raid by Confederate General Thomas Rosser, which was easily driven off.

The Richmond *Enquirer* published an editorial that called for the enlistment of African-Americans into the Confederate Army. Since the available manpower resources of the Confederacy were now down to teenage boys and old men, this idea was gaining acceptance.

October 7: USS *Wachusett* sailed into Bahia (Salvador), Brazil and engaged CSS *Florida*, capturing the Confederate vessel and towing her out under Brazilian gunfire.

Confederate General Lee attempted to turn Union General Grant's right flank at Petersburg, but was repulsed, with Confederate General John Gregg killed in the process.

October 8: CSS *Shenandoah* left Liverpool, UK to rendezvous with a supply vessel off Madeira, Spain.

October 9: Union and Confederate cavalry clashed at Tom's Brook, VA with a crushing defeat for the Confederates.

October 10: Union General Sheridan positioned his troops near Cedar Creek, VA.

A Union attack on Confederate General Forrest's position near Eastport, TN failed.

October 11: Union General Sherman concentrated his army near Rome, GA.

Supporters of US President Lincoln won state elections in Pennsylvania, Indiana, and Ohio, which gave Lincoln hope for the upcoming Presidential election.

October 12: Union General Sherman and Confederate General Hood's troops clashed near Resaca, GA.

US Supreme Court Chief Justice Roger Taney, who was noted for the Dred Scott Decision, which stated that African-Americans had no rights to citizenship, died at the age of 89.

Union Admiral Porter assumed command of the North Atlantic Blockading Squadron.

October 13: Confederates probed Union General Sheridan's positions around Cedar Creek, VA.

Union forces probed the Richmond defense but had to withdraw due to heavy causalities.

Confederate partisan Colonel Mosby struck a Union payroll wagon near Harpers Ferry. He made off with $175,000.

Maryland adopted a new state constitution that abolished slavery.

Confederate General Hood's troops captured Dalton, GA while tearing up another 20 miles of track.

October 14: Confederate General Price called for recruits to join his army, but this call to the colors was falling on deaf ears.

October 15: Confederate troops from General Price's command attacked Glasgow, MO, in the process they forced the Union garrison, commanded by Colonel Chester Harding to surrender. Earlier that day the Confederates captured Sedalia, MO.

October 16: Skirmish at Ship's Gap, GA.

Confederate troops capture Ridgley, MO.

Union Private Sneeden wrote about reaching a new prison at Millen, GA. His hopes for exchange were dashed.

October 17: Confederate General Hood's army started moving into position at Gadsden, AL in order to invade Tennessee.

Confederate General Price's troops were near Lexington, MO and were facing three Federal forces.

October 18: Confederate General Early prepared to attack Federal positions near Cedar Creek.

October 19: Confederate General Forrest left Corinth, MO and headed to Jackson, TN in support of General Hood's advance.

Battle of Cedar Creek, VA: Union commander: General Philip Sheridan. Confederate commander: General Jubal Early. Early launched an attack on the Union encampment, which sent the Federals into a near rout.

Sheridan at the time was returning from a conference with General Grant. Upon hearing of the attack, Sheridan made an epic ride from Winchester, rallying his troops to counter attack. This counterattack totally smashed Early's army and droves them from the field. Union victory.

Confederate raiders rode from Canada to St Albans, VT. There they robbed three banks of a combined $200,000.

October 20: A Union force under General Blunt engaged Confederate General Price at Lexington, MO but was repulsed. Following the engagement, Blunt established a strong position on the Little Blue River near Independence, MO. Most of his troops were then sent into Independence itself.

Confederate General Early reformed his army ay Fisher's Mill, VA.

The Cleveland *Plain Dealer* endorsed George McClellan for President.

October 21: Battle of Little Blue River, MO: Union commander: General James Blunt. Confederate commander: General Sterling Price. Price took advantage of the weakened Union line and attacked. Blunt returned with the remainder of his army and proceeded to drive the Confederates back. However, Blunt did not have the numbers and had to pull back into Independence, MO. Confederate victory.

Union General Sherman detached part of his army at Gaylesville, AL in order to deal with Confederate General Hood.

October 22: Confederate General Price, who found himself between Union General Samuel Curtis' Army of the Border and Union cavalry under General Alfred Pleasonton, decided to cross the Big Blue River near Westport, MO and attack Curtis' forces before Pleasonton's troopers arrived.

The Washington *Constitutional Union* endorsed George McClellan for President.

October 23: Battle of Westport, MO: Union commanders: Generals Samuel Curtis and Alfred Pleasonton. Confederate commander: General Sterling Price. Price launched four hours of attacks against the entrenched Federal line while Pleasonton pushed back Marmaduke's troops. Price had no choice but to withdraw. Union victory. This ends any more chances that the Confederacy would ever take Missouri.

CS War Department clerk John B. Jones wrote about hearing the news of the St Albans raid.

October 24: Confederate troops under General Price retreated along the Kansas-Missouri line with Federals in pursuit.

Union Sergeant Ransom wrote that he was almost fully recovered from the illnesses that plagued him at Andersonville. He was still in the hospital at Savannah.

October 25: Union General Pleasonton's forces encircled part of Confederate General Price's forces as they retreated from Westport, MO. General Marmaduke, another Confederate general, and 600 soldiers were captured. Another Union detachment caught up with more of Price's army at the Marmilton River, but held off on attacking, which allowed Price to escape.

Battle of Maria Des Cygnes, MO: Union commander, General Alfred Pleasonton. Confederate commander: General Sterling Price. Pleasonton ordered a heavy artillery bombardment, followed by a massed cavalry charge, which broke the Confederate line. Price was forced once again to pull back. Union victory. This effectively ended Confederate operations in Missouri.

Union Sergeant Ransom wrote that he would soon go to a new prison at Millen, GA.

October 26: Confederate partisan William "Bloody Bill" Anderson was killed in an ambush near Richmond, MO.

Confederate General Hood attempted to take his army across the Tennessee River at Decatur, AL, but was stopped by the swollen river.

October 27: A small Union force under Naval Lieutenant William Cushing attacked and sunk CSS *Albemarle* on the Roanoke River, VA.

Union troops under Generals Warren and Hancock attacked the South Side Railroad near Petersburg, VA, but were halted by a strong Confederate defense line commanded by Generals Heth and Mahone.

Union General Butler made an attack on the Richmond, VA defensives, but was repulsed, with 600 of his troops taken prisoner.

October 28: Union Naval Lieutenant Cushing was rescued by USS *Valley City* following the attack on CSS *Albemarle*.

Union General Sherman decided to return to Atlanta. He will leave General Thomas to deal with Confederate General Hood.

October 29: Union gunboats found that sunken hulks had blocked the river channel near Plymouth, NC.

Confederate General Forrest captured the transport *Mazeppa* near Fort Henry, TN.

October 30: Confederate General Forrest captured three more ships, which gave him a small fleet on the Tennessee River.

October 31: Confederate General Hood's army reached Tuscumbia, AL.

Union Sergeant Ransom wrote about being put on a train headed for Millen, GA.

November 1: Confederate General Hood finds the rail line to Decatur, AL neither repaired or that he has received the supplies that he has ordered. This will hamper his operations.

Two divisions of the Union XVI Corps moved to rejoin General Thomas at Nashville.

Union Sergeant Ransom wrote that he had arrived at Camp Lawton, near Millen, GA.

November 2: New York, NY officials were warned of a Confederate plot to burn the city.

Confederate General Forrest's river fleet suffered a defeat at Johnsonville, TN.

November 3: Union IV Corps reached Pulaski, TN. At the same time, one of Confederate General Forrest's gunboats, the *Undine*, repulsed three Federal boats on the Tennessee River.

November 4: Confederate General Forrest attacked the Union supply base at Johnsonville, TN causing $2,000,000 in damage.

Confederate General Breckenridge led a raid into east Tennessee from Virginia.

November 5: Confederate General Forrest began moving his forces in order to rejoin General Hood's army. Meanwhile, Hood was holding a Council of War with his commanders. He wanted to press the advance north while the others were concerned that Union General Sherman would follow them.

November 6: Authorities in Chicago, IL arrested the leaders of a Confederate plot to liberate prisoners at Camp Douglas and burn down the city.

Union Sergeant Ransom wrote about the Presidential election going on up north. He was so mad that Union authorities had suspended the exchange system that, during a mock vote in the prison, he voted for George McClellan.

November 7: CS President Davis made an upbeat address to the

Confederate Congress. Afterwards he sent orders to General Hood to press on to the Ohio River, but Hood was not that optimistic of his chances of success.

November 8: US President Lincoln was elected to a second term.

November 9: Union General Schofield and XXIII Corps passed through Nashville, TN and were heading toward Pulaski, TN.

Union General Sherman began his plans to advance on Savannah, GA. The overall plan was to march to Savannah, then swing north into the Carolinas. The long range goal was to join up with General Grant in Virginia, over 1000 miles away.

November 10: Confederate General Early took one more shot at Union General Sheridan, despite the fact that Early's army was mostly destroyed. Confederates withdrew from New Market, VA.

Confederate General Breckenridge moved his troops into East Tennessee and found Union forces waiting for him at Bull's Gap.

Confederate General Forrest's troopers reached Corinth, MS en route to join General John Bell Hood's army.

November 11: Union and Confederate forces clashed at Bull's Gap, TN which started two days of battles that resulted in Union troops being driven off. Battle ended on November 13 as a Confederate victory.

Union General Sherman's troops began the destruction anything of value at both Atlanta and Rome. His army was amassing as much supplies as the wagons could carry and they planned to live off the land as they marched. It was a major risk in 19th Century warfare to advance more than 100 miles without a supply base. Sherman had decided that there would be no supply bases for his march.

> *You cannot qualify war in harsher terms than I will. War is cruelty, and you cannot refine it. And those who brought war into out country deserve all the curses and maledictions a people can pour out...You might as well appeal against the thunderstorm as against the terrible hardships of war. They are inevitable, and the only way the people of Atlanta can hope once more to live in peace and quiet is to stop the war...*
> —*Union General William Sherman, letter to Atlanta authorities.*

US President Lincoln revealed to his Cabinet in a meeting how he would have handled the situation if he had lost the election. Secretary of State Seward remarked that McClellan would have done nothing during the transition period.

Union Private Sneeden wrote about his refusal to take an oath not to escape from Millen, GA prison.

November 12: Union and Confederate troops skirmished near Cedar Creek, VA.

Confederate General Longstreet's forces were on the move from Loudon, TN.

Union General Sherman's troops began the demolition of most of the structures in Atlanta.

Union Private Sneeden became a clerk with a Surgeon White in the Millen, GA prison hospital.

Union Sergeant Ransom wrote that the prisoners received news of US President Lincoln's re-election.

November 13: Confederate General Early's army was ordered to rejoin General Lee at Petersburg. Union forces now had complete control of the Shenandoah Valley and would keep it for the remainder of the war.

Confederate General Hood established his headquarters at Florence, AL.

Union Sergeant Ransom refused a job as a clerk at Camp Lawton.

November 14: Bad weather forced Confederate General Breckenridge to order his troops back into Virginia from Maryland.

After losing the Presidential Election, George McClellan resigned from the US Army.

Union General Schofield reached Pulaski, TN, which brought the Union force there to 18,000 with 5000 in reserve.

Confederate General Forrest reached Florence, AL and joined General Hood.

Union General Kilpatrick's cavalry left Atlanta while General Henry Slocum's XX Corps departed for Decatur.

November 15: Atlanta was now a wasteland as Union troops prepare to leave.

November 16: March to the Sea began as Union General Sherman severed all communications with the North and began moving his army toward Savannah. The force of 60,000 carried 20 day's rations. Opposing them were 10,000 Confederate infantry, 300 militia, and 10,000 cavalry. The Union force was marching in two columns, one toward Lovejoy Station and the other towards Augusta.

Skirmish at Strawberry Plains, TN.

Union Sergeant Ransom wrote that prisoners were now being taken out of Camp Lawton as word of Union General Sherman's army was known. Rumor was the prisoners were going to Florida.

November 17: CS President Davis denounced any plans by the seceded states to make a separate peace with the Union.

Skirmish at Flat Creek, TN.

November 18: Confederate General Hood finally got his army across the Tennessee River at Florence, AL.

CS President Davis ordered General Howard Cobb to do everything possible to stop Union General Sherman's march in Georgia.

CS War Department clerk John B. Jones wrote that to get groceries for a month would cost him $762.50. Three years ago that amount would buy one year's worth.

November 19: Georgia Governor Joseph Brown called on all men between 16 and 55 to help defend the state. Not many show up.

Confederate General Hood began his invasion of Tennessee.

November 20: Union General Sherman's army continued their advance through Georgia, skirmishing at Clinton, East Macon, and Griswoldville. Confederate defenders could not even slow the Federals down.

November 21: Confederate General Hood was now in a race with Union General Schofield's troops to the Duck River in Tennessee.

CS War Department clerk John B. Jones wrote that $1 in gold would buy $40 Confederate. Oak wood was selling for $100 a cord. Apples were selling for $100 a barrel.

November 22: Union Generals Thomas and Schofield began moving troops toward Columbia, TN in response to Confederate General Hood's movements.

Advance Union units under General Slocum reached the Georgia capital of Milledgeville, southeast of Atlanta. (Atlanta was not the capital at the time).

Union troops under General Charles Walcutt were stopped by Confederate cavalry under General Wheeler near Griswoldville, GA. They managed to hold off repeated attacks until reinforcements arrived.

Union Sergeant Ransom was taken out of Camp Lawton and placed on a train bound for Blackshear, near the Florida line.

November 23: Confederate General Hardee assumed command of the troops trying to oppose Union General Sherman's marching army.

It was interesting to note the method that was used to procure supplies for Sherman's troops. Using volunteers called "bummers": these men would leave the army as the day's marching began, usually on foot. In the evening they would return on a horse or a mule, towing a wagon that was loaded down with chickens, pigs, a cow or two, grain, bread, and vegetables, which were turned over to the quartermaster for that evening's dinner. The horses and mules were employed in pulling wagons and artillery or used as officer's remounts. Other bummers, who were bakers in civilian life, would take over a mill where they would grind grain into flour and then bake soft bread all day long. Afterwards the mill would be destroyed to deny its use to the Confederates. A few of the bummers were thieves in civilian life so it would not have been a surprise if a few valuables were found on their person.

Union Sergeant Ransom escaped from the prison train near Doctortown, GA and hid in nearby woods.

November 24: Union General Schofield's forces reached Columbia, TN and began digging their trenches, all the while being attacked by Confederate General Forrest's cavalry.

Union General Kilpatrick made a feint in order to get Confederate General Wheeler to concentrate his forces near Atlanta.

November 25: Confederate agents attempted to set New York, NY on fire by torching 10 hotels and Barnum's Museum. This ended up as a dismal failure, thankfully. They used a method of "Greek Fire" to start the blaze, but left the windows closed, so the oxygen in the room was used up.

Union Sergeant Ransom wrote that he was receiving help from slaves in the local area.

November 26: Heavy storms were making it difficult for Union General Schofield to cross the Duck River, TN as Confederate General Hood's army arrived.

November 27: Union General Butler's headquarters, the steamer *Greyhound* was blown up with no serious injuries.

Union General Schofield's troops began their crossing of the Duck River in darkness.

Calvary engagement at Waynesboro, GA.

November 28: Hampered by bad weather and having spotted Confederate General Hood's flanking maneuver, Union General Schofield pulled out of Columbia, TN and began their movement towards the nearby town of Franklin.

Confederate General Wheeler engaged Union General Kilpatrick at Buck Head Creek, but was forced to retire after high causalities among his troopers.

Joint Union Army/Navy force landed at Boyd's Landing, SC in order to cut the Savannah-Charleston railroad.

November 29: Confederate General Hood's forces converged at Spring Hill, TN to try and cut off Union General Schofield's troops. Hood failed and Schofield completed his move to Franklin.

Union Private Sneeden wrote about going to Savannah and then onward to Charleston to await exchange.

November 30: Battle of Franklin, TN: Union commander: General John Schofield. Confederate commander: General John Hood. Union forces reached Franklin at dawn and began digging in. Hood arrived late and launched a frontal attack, which broke the Union line but did not drive them off. At the end of the day, Hood lost 6500 men, including six generals. Schofield managed to pull his troops out and move them to

Nashville. Confederates held the field but the army was shattered. Hood decided to continue to advance on Nashville.

> *I cannot describe it. It beggars description. I will not attempt to describe it. I could not. The death-angel was there to gather its last harvest. It was the grand coronation of death.*
> —Sam Watkins, Private, 1st Tennessee, on the
> Battle of Franklin, which he participated in.

Joint Union Army/Navy force engaged Confederates at Honey Hill, SC but pulled back after dark.

Union Sergeant Ransom wrote that he was once again a prisoner, having been betrayed by a local woman to the Georgia Home Guards.

December 1: Union General Thomas concentrated all his army at Nashville. General Schofield had also joined him.

CS War Department clerk John B. Jones wrote about purchasing four yards of cloth at $12 a yard. He believed he could get a government tailor to make a suit for $50. A civilian tailor would charge $300.

December 2: Confederate General Hood sent troops under General William Bate to cut the Nashville-Murfreesboro rail line. At the same time he reached Nashville and set up a line facing the Federals. Union General Thomas received orders from Washington, DC to attack immediately.

Union General Sherman's troops liberated the prison at Millen, GA and discovered the conditions in which Union POWs were being kept.

December 3: Both of Union General Sherman's columns were now converging on Savannah.

December 4: Confederate General Edward Bates attacked Blockhouse No. 7 on the Overall Creek, TN with no success.

Battle of Waynesboro, GA: Union commander: General Judson

Kilpatrick. Confederate commander: General Joseph Wheeler. Kilpatrick decided to take on Wheeler, the only creditable resistance between, General Sherman and Savannah. After several attacks, Wheeler's cavalry fled the area. Union victory.

Union General Thomas received more demands to attack Confederate General Hood's forces. The freezing rain was hampering operations in the Nashville area.

CS War Department clerk John B. Jones wrote about the expenses involved in clothing his family. He received the cloth that he had ordered on December 1. A government tailor had promised to make a suit for $40. His son bought a pre-war coat for $175, which was $15 at the time it was made. One of Jones' daughters made three bonnets from the scraps of old ones because the prices of three brand new ones would cost $700.

December 5: Confederate General Forrest attacked the Union garrisons of Blockhouse No. 4 and a fort at La Vergne, TN. Both garrisons surrendered.

December 6: Confederate General Forrest engaged Federals outside Murfreesboro: TN. Things calmed down during the afternoon as Confederate infantry arrived to reinforce Forrest.

US President Lincoln nominated Salmon Chase, former Treasury Secretary, to be Chief Justice of the Supreme Court.

December 7: Union troops under General Lovell Rousseau engaged Confederate General Forrest's cavalry near Murfreesboro, which forced the Confederates to withdraw.

Union General Butler was relieved of command of the Army of the James and assigned command of an operation to seize Fort Fisher, NC.

CS War Department clerk John B. Jones wrote that tea was selling for $100 a pound and wood for $100 a cord.

December 8: There was skirmishing along Hatcher's Run, VA as both sides begin to settle into winter camps.

Union General Grant had decided to replace General Thomas with General Schofield if Thomas does not attack. Thomas replied that his cavalry was waiting for remounts and would attack when the horses arrived.

December 9: Union General Sherman's lead division reached the outskirts of Savannah.

December 10: An attempt by the CS Navy to send gunboats to the aid of the Savannah defenders failed.

Union General Sherman's army's main body reached the outskirts of Savannah. He found the rice fields flooded so there would be no easy way in.

Union forces made a probe along the Weldon Road, near Petersburg, VA.

December 11: Union General Sherman's troops rebuild the bridge over the Ogeechee River, near Savannah. He was attempting to encircle the city, but failed to cut the road to Charleston.

Union Private Sneeden wrote about being in Charleston and boarding a steamer, which took him to the ship *New York*. There, he and other Union prisoners were handed over to Union exchange agents.

December 12: 4000 Union cavalry under General George Stoneman rode from east Tennessee into southwest Virginia. There were only 1500 Confederates opposing them.

Union General Thomas promised General Halleck that he would drive the Confederates from before Nashville, as soon as the weather broke.

Union Sergeant Ransom wrote about being place into a train, this time heading to Charleston.

December 13: Union General William Hazen's troops captured Fort McAllister, which allowed a supply base to be established as well as communication with the US Navy force offshore.

Confederate General Lee, upon learning that a Union assault force was headed for Wilmington, NC, detached a division to reinforce Fort Fisher.

Union General Grant has decided to travel to Nashville himself and take General John Logan with him to replace General Thomas.

Union General Stoneman defeated a small Confederate force at Kingsport, TN.

Union Private Sneeden and 700 others were transferred to the vessel *Varuna* for the trip north.

Union Sergeant Ransom and two others escaped from the train and were hiding in the woods near Savannah. They were receiving help from friendly African-Americans in the area. Their plan was to reach the column of Union troops that were approaching the city.

December 14: The weather had broken at Nashville and Union General Thomas decided that now is the time to attack Confederate General Hood.

Union General Stoneman defeated another Confederate force at Bristol, TN.

December 15: Battle of Nashville, TN: Union commander: General George Thomas. Confederate commander: General John Hood. Day one: Thomas opened the engagement by assaulting the Confederate right flank, but was forced to pull back. At 10 a.m. General Smith launched an attack that crushed the Confederate left flank. Hood tried a series of defensive positions that did not stand up to the Federal attacks. In the afternoon, an attack by General Schofield freed up the Federal cavalry to hit Hood's rear. Hood ordered a pull back to a shorter defense line as darkness approached.

December 16: Battle of Nashville: Day Two: Union forces continued their advance by battering both the Confederate flanks. In the afternoon, Thomas made a series of feints, followed by a serious attack on the Confederate right, which was driven off. At 3:30 p.m., Union Generals Schofield and Wilson made a withering attack into the Confederate rear area. The Army of Tennessee collapsed and fled south toward Mississippi, no longer a viable force in the West. Union victory.

December 17: The remains of Confederate General Hood's troops still have a little fight in them, as skirmishing at Hollow Tree Gap, TN showed.

Union Private Sneeden reached "Camp Parole" at Annapolis, MD to receive treatment and to await formal exchange with an equal number of Confederate prisoners.

December 18: Union General Stoneman led a force into the Cumberland Gap and was held off by a scratch force under Confederate General Breckinridge at Marion, VA. Stoneman managed to send a detachment to destroy the salt mines.

Confederate General Hardee rejected a call to surrender Savannah. This action was a play for time while an escape route was secured.

December 19: Skirmishing at Columbia, TN as the Federal pursuit of what's left of the Confederate Army of Tennessee continued.

Union Sergeant Ransom wrote that he and his two friends had reached the plantation of a Mr. Kimball, a Georgia Unionist who agreed to help them.

December 20: Confederate defenders of Savannah slipped out of town in the night, which left the city open for the Union.

Union General Stoneman moved his forces to Saltville, VA, in order to destroy the salt works there.

Union Private Sneeden was formally exchanged, given money and sent to Washington, DC.

Union Sergeant Ransom and his two friends were taken to a hiding place along the Big Ogeechee River where they could wait until Federal troops arrive.

December 21: Union General Sherman accepted the surrender of Savannah. This ended the March to the Sea. CSS *Savannah* was destroyed by retreating Confederates in order to prevent capture.

Union Private Sneeden reached Washington, DC where he was reunited with his fellow staff members.

December 22: Union General Sherman made his report on his march to Savannah to US President Lincoln.

> *I beg to present you as a Christmas gift, the city of Savannah, with one hundred and fifty heavy guns, and plenty of ammunition, also about twenty-five thousand bales of cotton.*
> —*Union General William Sherman's message to President Lincoln.*

Confederate General Hood's army once again crossed the Duck River, this time in the other direction.

December 23: Rank of Vice Admiral of the US Navy was created and awarded to Admiral Farragut.

A Federal fleet, consisting of 60 warships plus troop transports, was assembled off Beaufort, NC for the assault on Fort Fisher, NC. That night, the USS *Louisiana* was loaded with explosives, ran aground near the fort, and then exploded. The explosion did not damage the defenses and the Confederates there thought that one of the Union ships had a boiler explosion.

Union Sergeant Ransom wrote that he and his friends made contact with soldiers of the 80th Ohio; they were finally free of the threat of Confederate captivity.

December 24: Union task force arrived off Fort Fisher, NC and began shelling the fort.

Dolly Sumner Lunt, a Georgia resident, wrote on how it would be a bleak Christmas after Union General Sherman's troops came through the area.

Georgia teenager Eliza Andrews wrote in her journal about traveling through the "burnt country" as the area that Union General Sherman's army came through has been named.

Union Private Sneeden wrote that he was officially listed as "missing or killed." That day he took a train for Baltimore, MD so he could catch another train for New York, NY.

December 25: At Fort Fisher, NC, General Butler's troops were landed, however Confederate forces sent by General Lee had arrived and would block any further Union action.

Confederate General Hood's troops reached the Tennessee River at Bainbridge, MS.

Union Sergeant Ransom was reunited with the 8th Michigan Cavalry, whose commander, a Colonel Acker, thought Ransom was dead. Within the hour he was with his old company, who heard his report of other unit members who died at Andersonville. Ranson was soon before Union General Kilpatrick and made his report, not only about Andersonville but also of what he saw at Savannah. The report was sent to General Sherman. It was at this point that the diary ends.

December 26: Union General Butler had decided to give up attacking Fort Fisher and return to Fort Monroe, VA.

Robert Sneeden arrived at his parent's home in New York, NY and was reunited with his family, who believed he was dead. His journal ends at this point.

December 27: Confederate General Hood crossed the Tennessee River and went to Tupelo, MS with the remainder of his army. The Army of Tennessee was no longer in Tennessee and will never return there for the remainder of the war.

December 28: US President Lincoln met with General Grant to discuss the failed Fort Fisher operation and whether or not it was time to remove General Butler from an Army command.

December 29: Discussions continued over the future of Union General Butler: however US President Lincoln, fresh from an election victory, felt he now had the power to remove the political general from command.

December 30: At a Cabinet meeting, US President Lincoln announced that he would remove General Butler from command. This was met with little or no resistance.

December 31: As the New Year approached, the prevailing opinion in the South was that it was only a matter of time before the Union achieved final victory. The war had brought desolation to most of the Confederacy's farmland and the pool of manpower, which was not large to begin with, was almost empty. Two Union armies, General Grant's at Petersburg, VA and General Sherman's at Savannah, GA were poised to deliver the final blow. Many Confederate cities were in ruins and civilians have felt the heavy hand of war. Warfare itself had changed, with rifled cannon, muskets, and repeating rifles forcing a fundamental shift from the Napoleonic tactics of massed infantry and cavalry charges to trenches and fortifications. The only question now was what will happen when the end comes?

January 1: It was during this time that Private Sam Watkins, 1st Tennessee, received a furlough and did not return to active service. His account ends at this point.

January 2: Skirmishing at Franklin and Lexington, MS.

January 3: In Savannah, Union General Sherman was preparing to renew the offensive, with his attention fixed on South Carolina, the "cradle of the Rebellion."

January 4: Union General Grant assigned General Alfred Terry the job of making the assault on Fort Fisher and capture Wilmington, the last open Confederate port.

January 5: Peace feelers were being extended to the South as the Confederacy must have been reading the handwriting on the wall. US President Lincoln issued a pass to Francis Blair to go south and sound out the Confederate leadership about a negotiated settlement. Lincoln's terms: all states back in the Union and slavery abolished.

January 6: Union General Grant asked US President Lincoln to remove Union General Butler as commander of the Army of the James. The "political general's" time had indeed ended and professional soldiers would win the war.

CS War Department clerk John B. Jones wrote that a barrel of flour was selling for $500 a barrel and cornmeal for $75 a bushel.

January 7: An article in *New York World* lamented the availability of weapons in NYC as an effect of the war.

Union General Union General Butler was formally removed from command of not only the Army of the James but also of the Department of Virginia and North Carolina. Those commands were taken over by General Edward Ord.

An ironclad warship that was built in France and sold to Denmark was bought back by France when the Danish Navy could not make payments. The French then off loaded the vessel on the Confederacy. This ship was christened CSS *Stonewall*.

January 8: Union Admiral Porter met General Terry off Beaufort, NC; the two commanders discussed plans to assault Fort Fisher and Wilmington.

January 9: Democratic Party opposition to the proposed Constitutional amendment abolishing slavery begins to crumble.

Tennessee voted to abolish slavery.

CS War Department clerk John B. Jones wrote that flour was now selling for $700 a barrel, cornmeal for $80 a bushel, and coal and wood for $100 a load.

January 10: What was left of the Confederate Army of Tennessee was encamped at Tupelo, MS

January 11: Confederate forces under General Thomas Rosser raided West Virginia, capturing 500 Union troops and destroying tons of supplies.

Missouri voted to abolish slavery.

CS War Department clerk John B. Jones wrote that $60 Confederate will buy $1 in gold.

January 12: Francis Blair met with CS President Davis about starting peace talks. Davis agreed on talks but he was insistent that the only thing he will agree to was Southern Independence.

CS War Department clerk John B. Jones wrote that one gold dollar was equal to $66 Confederate.

January 13: Naval bombardment of Fort Fisher, NC begins. The defense forces in nearby Wilmington were commanded by no other than General Bragg, so no help from the town was coming.

Confederate General Hood resigned his command of the Army of Tennessee.

CS War Department clerk John B. Jones wrote that in Richmond beef was selling for $6 a pound, cornmeal for $80 a bushel, and white beans for $160 per bushel.

January 14: Fort Fisher was rendered unusable by a Union bombardment of 100 shells per minute.

Confederate General Beauregard assumed temporary command of the Army of Tennessee while General Taylor was en route to take permanent command.

CS War Department clerk John B. Jones wrote that a barrel of flour was sold for $1000.

January 15: A force of US Marines and sailors attacked Fort Fisher, and were repulsed with heavy losses. A second attack, led by General Terry, took the fort, placing the entire Confederate Atlantic coast in Union hands as well as making the nearby port of Wilmington vulnerable.

January 16: General Joe Johnston was named commander of the Army of Tennessee while General Beauregard was given command of defense forces in South Carolina, Georgia, and Florida, such as they were.

CS War Department clerk John B. Jones wrote that a gold dollar was now worth $70 Confederate.

Francis Blair met with US President Lincoln and presented CS President Davis' proposal for allowing the Southern states to secure independence.

Davis also proposed joint operations against the Imperial Government in Mexico.

At Fort Fisher, two drunken sailors entered the powder magazine with lighted lanterns. Within moments the magazine blew up, killing 25, injuring 66, and 13 missing. Most of them were of the 169th New York, who was sleeping on the mound covering the magazine at the time.

Confederate General Bragg received a telegram from CS President Davis, ordering him to retake Fort Fisher. That order would not be carried out.

January 17: US President Lincoln rejected a call by CS President Davis for negotiations.

As Union General Sherman ordered his army to prepare to march, he issued Field Order No.15, offering displaced former slaves land along the Georgia coast. This not only created hope in the former slaves, but it also kept him from having to feed the 10,000 that were tagging along with his army.

January 18: Union General Sherman began his march from Savannah to link up with General Grant's forces, currently at Petersburg. Sherman's army is now aimed at South Carolina.

January 19: The prevailing attitude, as General Lee was named General-in Chief of the Confederate States Armies, was that it was far too late for even an experienced soldier like Lee to turn things around.

January 20: Two Confederate blockade-runners captured near Fort Fisher.

Rain hampered Union General Henry Slocum's corps as they were leaving Savannah.

January 21: Union General Sherman's army reached Beaufort, SC.

January 22: Skirmish at Little Rock, AR.

January 23: The Federal headquarters at City Point, VA was attacked by a Confederate fleet of three ironclads, a gunboat, and a torpedo (sea mine) boat. All but one ran aground and brought under fire by Union batteries.

Confederate General Taylor assumed command of the remains of the Army of Tennessee.

January 24: Surviving Confederate vessels from the aborted attack on City Point withdrew. This ended any further Confederate river attacks.

CS Congress authorized the resumption of prisoner exchanges.

CSS *Stonewall* rendezvoused with a tender off Belle Isle, France.

January 25: Skirmishing along the Salkehatchie River, SC.

January 26: Union General Sherman sent troops towards Charleston, while his main army marched on Goldsborough.

CS War Department clerk John B. Jones wrote that beef was selling for $8 a pound and wood is selling for $150 a cord.

January 27: Confederate General Lee communicated with the South Carolina governor about the deteriorating situation in the state.

CS War Department clerk John B. Jones wrote that someone broke into his house and stole two sticks of wood. Wood was selling for $5 a stick.

January 28: Three commissioners, CS Vice-President Stephens, President of the Senate R.M.T. Hunter, and former US Supreme Court Justice John Campbell, were appointed by CS President Davis to hold talks with Union officials.

January 29: Even if the Charleston garrison and General Hardee's forces were combined, there was not much they could do to slow Union General Sherman's army down.

January 30: Union General Pope was given command of the Department of the Missouri.

Skirmish at Champlintown, KY.

January 31: US House of Representatives passed the 13th Amendment and set it to the states for ratification.

February 1: Illinois voted to ratify the 13th Amendment.

February 2: Union ships were sent up the James River to break ice on the river.

Union General Sherman ordered the building of bridges in order to bypass Confederates on the Salkehatchie River, SC.

US President Lincoln traveled to Hampton Roads to meet with the CS commissioners.

Michigan and Rhode Island ratified the 13th Amendment.

CSS *Stonewall* arrived at Ferrol, Spain.

CS War Department clerk John B. Jones wrote that a barrel of flour could fetch about $1000 on the market.

February 3: In South Carolina, two Union brigades used a bypass and launched a flanking attack on Confederate defenses. CS forces under General McLaws were forced to retreat toward Branchville. Main axis of the Union advance was Columbia, the state capital.

US President Lincoln met with the CS commissioners aboard the steamer *River Queen* and told them that the only way to end the war was to agree to Union terms. The meeting, to no one's surprise, ended in failure.

Maryland, New York, and West Virginia ratified the 13th Amendment.

CS War Department clerk John B. Jones wrote that a cord of wood now costs $500.

February 4: Confederate General Beauregard assumed command of the Carolina's defense.

Skirmishes at Angley's Post Office and Buford's Bridge, SC.

Union General Slocum's troops struggle to get cross the Savannah River and cross into South Carolina.

CS War Department clerk John B. Jones wrote, *"Yesterday much of the day was consumed by Congress in displaying a new flag for the Confederacy— before the old one is worn out! Idiots!"* This was in reference to the Confederate Third National flag.

February 5: The latest attempt to break the Petersburg lines began as Union troops took the Boydton Plank Road, extending their lines to the southwest.

As the winter began to fade, the food situation in the Confederate Army of Northern Virginia were beyond critical. Rations were a pint of oatmeal a day. General Lee's efforts to get more food were not succeeding. There were food supplies, but the rail network was almost non-existent, with most of the rail lines in Federal hands. General Lee was heard to say that the Confederate Congress seemed happy to eat peanuts and chew tobacco while his army starved. The situation was so grave that there were 3000 desertions during the winter.

February 6: Confederate Generals Pegram and Mahone launched attacks on Union General Warren's position on the Boydton Plank Road, VA. Pegram was killed and the attack repulsed.

Confederate Secretary of War James Seddon resigned and was replaced by General John C. Breckenridge.

February 7: Maine and Kansas passed the 13th Amendment while Delaware does not.

Union troops were forced back from the Boydton Plank Road by a second Confederate counter-attack, but the line at nearby Hatcher's Run held.

The Confederate Army of Northern Virginia was now in possession of 37 miles of defenses, from Richmond to Petersburg, with only 46,000 men to do it with (About 1243 men per mile.).

February 8: Massachusetts and Pennsylvania passed the 13th Amendment.

Skirmishes at North Platte, Colorado Territory and Rush Creek, Nebraska Territory.

February 9: Union General Schofield was named commander of the Department of North Carolina as he prepared to assault Wilmington.

Confederate General Lee convinced CS President Davis to allow amnesty to deserters who return within 30 days.

February 10: Confederate Naval Captain Semmes assumed command of James River Squadron, part of the Richmond defenses.

Skirmishing at James Island and Johnson's Station, SC as Union troops made contact with the Charleston defenses.

February 11: With Union General Sherman's army about to cut off Charleston, CS President Davis ordered the city defended at all costs while Confederate General Beauregard suggested evacuation.

Tennessee and Alabama were hotbeds of partisan activity, which raised concerns that not all Confederates would surrender when all of the organized armies were defeated.

February 12: Union General Sherman received a letter from Nora Walker, a Union spy, which confirmed Confederate General Hood's resignation and requested payment for her services to the Union.

February 13: Confederate General Hardee withdrew his troops from Charleston as CS Navy vessels in Charleston Harbor were scuttled.

There was a complaint by the UK about the increase in US Navy operations in the Great Lakes. This action, in response to the St Albans raid, was making the Canadians nervous.

February 14: Union General Sherman's army crossed the Congaree River en route to Columbia.

February 15: Union General Sherman's forces approached Columbia as skirmishing took place at Red Bank Creek and Two League Cross Roads.

February 16: Union troops arrived at Columbia. During the afternoon, Confederate General Beauregard ordered the city evacuated.

Confederate General Hardee prepared to evacuate Charleston in order to avoid getting cut off by the Union advance.

Union gunboats shelled Fort Anderson, near Wilmington, NC.

February 17: Columbia, SC was surrendered to Union forces. That night the city was burned to the ground, either by departing Confederates or drunken Union soldiers.

Union forces made a feint towards Charleston, which caused Confederate forces to abandon the remaining forts protecting the city, including Fort Sumter.

CS War Department clerk John B. Jones wrote about buying a bushel of black beans for $65.

February 18: Charleston surrendered to Union forces under General Alexander Schimmelfennig.

Union General Sherman ordered all remaining useful buildings and material in Columbia destroyed.

CSS *Shenandoah* departed Melbourne, Australia and sailed for the North Pacific.

CS War Department clerk John B. Jones wrote that $1 in gold was now worth $100 Confederate.

February 19: Union General Sherman began his movement from Columbia to Fayetteville, NC as his troops wrecked the Columbia rail station and yards.

Union troops attempting to encircle Wilmington were stopped by Confederate defenders, which led to fighting at Town Creek. That night, the Confederates pulled back to the east bank of the Cape Fear River.

February 20: Confederate lines on the Cape Fear River collapsed.

CS House of Representatives approved the use of African-Americans as troops.

February 21: Confederate troops evacuated Wilmington.

CS Senate delayed debate on the bill authorizing African-Americans to enlist in the Confederate Army.

February 22: Confederate General Joe Johnston was assigned command of all CS forces in South Carolina, Georgia, Florida, Tennessee, and North Carolina.

Kentucky rejected the 13th Amendment.

Wilmington, NC fell to Union troops.

February 23: Union gunboats sailed into Georgetown, SC to make contact with General Sherman. Fort White, guarding the port, was already abandoned. Meanwhile, Sherman's troops were approaching the SC/NC line. The only thing that was slowing them down was the rain.

CS War Department clerk John B. Jones wrote on the amassing of Confederate gold in Richmond.

February 24: Confederate General Hampton denied any knowledge that his troops were executing Union General Sherman's "bummers."

CS War Department clerk John B. Jones wrote that beef was selling for $7 a pound, pork for $9 a pound, and butter for $20 a pound.

February 25: Confederate General Joe Johnston once again assumed command of the Army of Tennessee. This time, that army was in North Carolina and had only 25,000 men, including local militia.

February 27: Union General Merritt launched an attack into the Shenandoah Valley. Opposing them were two weak brigades under Confederate General Early.

February 28: Union General Merritt's 10,000 cavalry troopers crossed the North Fork of the Shenandoah River with each man carrying 15 days of rations, as the valley could no longer support an army in the field.

March 1: Union Admiral John Dahlgren lost his flagship to a mine. He escaped injury but was left with only the uniform on his back.

Wisconsin passed the 13th Amendment while New Jersey rejected it.

Confederate General Early began massing his army at Waynesborough, VA in order to counter Union cavalry in the area.

March 2: Confederate General Lee proposed a conference to resolve differences in order to end the war.

Confederate General Early's attempt to retake the Shenandoah Valley ended with his army detachment no longer a threat as a result of an attack by Union General Sheridan at Waynesboro.

March 3: The Freedmen's Bureau, tasked with looking after freed slaves, was established.

Union troops entered Cheraw, SC where they find a cache of vintage wine. The wine was drunk in celebration of its capture.

Union General Grant received orders not to enter into any discussions with Confederate leaders. Army commanders would not be allowed to make political decisions.

CS War Department clerk John B. Jones wrote that his household income rose to $16,000 a year, but that only equaled $300 in gold.

March 4: Union General Sherman's army entered North Carolina.

US President Lincoln was inaugurated for his second term.

> *With malice towards none, with charity for all: with firmness in the right as God gives us to see the right, let us strive to finish the work we are in: to bind up the nations' wounds, to care for him who shall have borne the battle and for his widow and his orphan—to do all which may achieve and cherish a just and lasting peace among ourselves, and with all nations.*
> *—US President Lincoln, Second Inaugural Address.*

CS Congress approved the design for the Third National Flag.

March 5: Confederate General Breckenridge assumed command of Confederate forces in the Appalachian Mountains of Western Virginia.

US President Lincoln named Hugh McCulloch to be Secretary of the Treasury.

March 6: Union General Sherman's troops crossed the Pee Dee River, NC.

Confederate General Joe Johnston was given command of the Department of North Carolina, with an area of responsibility that covered all of NC as well as Virginia up to the Petersburg siege lines.

Meta Morris Grimball, a South Carolina resident, did not share CS President Davis' confidence. She wrote in her diary that current conditions in her home state were getting worse.

CS War Department clerk John B. Jones wrote about buying a cord of oak and green pinewood for $55.

March 7: Union General Jacob Cox's troops established themselves at New Berne, NC.

March 8: Confederate General Bragg made an unsuccessful attack on Union General Cox's position at Kinston, NC.

CS Senate voted to approve the enlistment of African-Americans into the Confederate Army.

March 9: Union General Kilpatrick was surprised at his camp at Monroe's Cross Roads, VA by Confederate Generals Hampton and Wheeler. It was believed that Kilpatrick was so surprised that he ran off without getting dressed.

Vermont passed the 13th Amendment.

The New York *World* printed an editorial that blasted plans for a third draft for the Union armies.

CS War Department clerk John B. Jones wrote that cornmeal was selling for $100 a bushel and bacon for $13 a pound.

March 10: Confederate cavalry, led by General Hampton, were repulsed by rallying Union cavalry under Union General Kilpatrick at Monroe's Cross Roads, VA.

Confederate General Bragg was forced across the Neuse River, withdrawing from Kinston, NC.

Confederate General William Whiting died of injuries suffered in the fall of Fort Fisher.

March 11: Union General Sherman captured Fayetteville, NC.

March 12: Union Naval forces reached Wilmington and established communications with General Sherman at Fayetteville.

March 13: Union General Sheridan's cavalry was involved in a skirmish at Beaver Dam Station, near Richmond.

CS President Davis signed the bill that allowed the enlistment of African-Americans into the Confederate Army.

March 14: Union General Sherman's advance troops skirmished at the Black River while the main body crossed the Cape Fear River, advancing deeper into North Carolina.

March 15: Union General Sherman began moving from Fayetteville towards Goldsborough.

March 16: Battle of Averasboro, NC: Union commander: General Sherman. Confederate commander: General William Hardee. Hardee's troops were set up as a blocking force against Sherman's forces, who were marching from Fayetteville. Union cavalry under General Kilpatrick tried to break the Confederate line, but it took two divisions of infantry to accomplish it. Hardee was forced to withdraw to Bentonville, where the rest of Confederate General Johnston's army was. Union victory.

March 17: Confederate General Hardee's army reached Bentonville, NC and joined General Joe Johnston's force, the only force in the area that might (operative word is <u>might</u>) be able to slow down the Union juggernaught.

Union General Edward Canby began his operations against Mobile, AL.

March 18: Confederate Congress adjourned their legislative session. They will never meet again.

Skirmishing at Bentonville as both Union and Confederate forces are concentrated. The sinking fortunes of the Confederacy are evident in the fact that General Joe Johnston can only muster 17,000 men, while Union General Sherman was fielding 60,000.

Union troops were advancing up the west side of Mobile Bay toward Mobile. This was a diversion: the real attack will come from the east.

March 19: Battle of Bentonville, NC: Union commander: General Henry Slocum. Confederate commander: General Joseph Johnston. Day One: Johnston ordered an attack on a part of the Union XIV Corps, which drove them back. Between thick forests and swamps and the arrival of XX Corps, Johnston' troops had no choice but to return to their original trenches. Sherman rushed the bulk of his army to the area.

Union General Philip Sheridan joined General Grant's command at Petersburg.

Letters from Confederate soldiers in Petersburg expressed knowledge that the entire war effort would fail if they had to pull out of the trenches. Union soldier's letters expressed the feeling that the war will soon be over.

CS War Department clerk John B. Jones wrote that bacon was selling at $20 a pound and cornmeal for $140 a bushel.

March 20: Battle of Bentonville: Day Two: Confederate General Joe Johnston held the line as Union reinforcements approached. Federals begin hitting the Confederate center while fending off cavalry attacks by Confederate General Joseph Wheeler.

CS War Department clerk John B. Jones wrote that a barrel of flour was sold for $1500.

March 21: Battle of Bentonville: Day Three: Federal XX Corps attempted to turn the Confederate left but was stopped by Confederate Generals William Hardee and Wade Hampton. Hardee's 16 year old son, who joined the 8th Texas Cavalry that morning, was killed during a charge. That night, General Joe Johnston pulled his army back to preserve what was left. Battle ended in a Union victory and Confederate forces in North Carolina were no longer able to mount any more offensives.

CSS *Stonewall* tried to start a fight with USS *Niagara* and USS *Sacramento* off Ferrol, Spain, but the Federal warships did not accept the challenge.

March 22: Union General James Wilson sets out on a campaign to take out the last Confederate manufacturing center at Selma, AL.

March 23: At Goldsborough Union General Sherman united his army with those of Generals Schofield and Terry, giving him 100,000 men.

March 24: With Union General Sherman firmly in North Carolina, Confederate General Lee realized that supplies from the south were cut off. He asked General John Gordon to try to open a gap in the Union line so the army can escape and join General Joe Johnston's forces.

March 25: Battle of Fort Steadman, VA: Union commander: General Ulysses S. Grant. Confederate commander: General Robert E. Lee. Confederate forces take a fort within the Union lines in order for the Army of Northern Virginia to escape south and join up with General Joe Johnston's army. A Union counterattack resulted in the capture of 1900 Confederates and a large segment of Confederate entrenchments. This is the last offensive that Lee was able to attempt in the war. Union victory.

Union siege of Mobile, AL, began.

March 26: Union General Sheridan's forces crossed the James River near Petersburg.

Union General Grant planned another extension of his lines with the aim to surround Confederate General Lee's forces and cut off all remaining avenues of retreat.

March 27: Confederate forces were finding the vise tightening around them at Spanish Fort, Mobile, AL.

Union Generals Grant and Sherman, Admiral Porter, and President Lincoln met on board the *River Queen* at City Point, VA where Lincoln advocated for lenient terms for the soon to be defeated South.

March 28: Union General James Wilson's cavalry skirmish with Confederates at Elyton, AL.

Confederate General Lee has managed to amass 50,000 men for a planned breakout. The problem is that he now faced 125,000 Union troops.

March 29: Union General Grant began moving troops toward Dinwiddie Court House, effectively starting the Appomattox Campaign. Confederates abandoned their lines at White Oak Road after a sharp fight.

Confederate General Fitzhugh Lee moved his cavalry to Five Forks, VA in order to support General Pickett's infantry.

March 30: Union General Wilson's cavalry encountered Confederate General Forrest's cavalry at Montevallo, AL.

Union II and V Corps were pressing into the Confederate right flank at Hatcher's Run and Gravelly Run, VA. The Confederate line now stretched razor thin.

CSS *Stonewall* left Tenerife, Canary Islands.

CS War Department clerk John B. Jones wrote about 2,000,000 rations of bread in a North Carolina warehouse but no way to get it to Confederate General Lee's army.

March 31: Confederate General Pickett stopped Union General Sheridan's drive to Dinwiddie Court House, however he was forced to redeploy to nearby Five Forks by superior Union numbers.

At Mobile, AL, the Union assault was delayed because the column coming from Pensacola, FL was delayed by weather.

April 1: Battle of Five Forks, VA: Union commanders: Generals Philip Sheridan and Gouverneur Warren. Confederate commanders: Generals George Pickett and Fitzhugh Lee. At the junction of Five Forks, Sheridan held down the entrenched Confederates while Warren launched a flank attack. At the same time, Fitz Lee and Pickett were having lunch two miles away and did not hear the battle. They returned to their lines in time to see them broken and the Federals advancing. A counterattack was formed, almost stopping Sheridan. Warren was called to assist but arrived late, infuriating Sheridan to the point that he secured permission to relieve Warren of command. General Lee, knowing that his lines were now beyond the breaking point, ordered Pickett relieved of his command. Union victory.

Union General Steele and 13,000 men arrived at Mobile. Now the Federals would be able to besiege the city in earnest.

April 2: Battle of Selma, AL: Union commander: General James Wilson. Confederate commander: General Nathan B. Forrest. Union forces attacked in three prongs, breaking the Confederate line. Forrest escaped but Selma was surrendered. Union victory.

Union General Grant ordered a general assault against Petersburg. During that assault, Confederate General A.P. Hill was killed. The Confederate lines, stretched far beyond their capabilities, were finally broken and General Lee ordered Petersburg abandoned. CS President Davis was informed at a church service of Lee's decision. During the night, Petersburg was abandoned and Lee started moving west in order to get clear of the Federals, and then move south to link up with General Joe Johnston's forces in NC.

> *I THINK IT ABSOLUTELY NECESSARY THAT WE SHOULD ABANDON OUR POSITION TONIGHT.*
> —*Lee's telegram to President Davis.*

Union forces cut Lee's last supply line at White Oak Road.

> *It is true! The enemy have broken through our lines and attained the South Side Road. Gen. Lee has dispatched the Secretary to have everything in readiness to evacuate the city tonight.*
> —*John Beauchamp Jones, diary entry.*

At 11:00 p.m., the Government of the Confederate States of America fled Richmond.

April 3: At 8:15 a.m. Union forces receive the surrender of Richmond. The Confederate capital is now in Union hands. The first troops to enter the city are African-American soldiers under the command of General Godfrey Weitzel. This was a powerful message to the residents of the city, their world had changed.

Cavalry clash between Union General Custer and Confederate General Fitzhugh Lee at Namozine Church, VA.

Confederate General Lee ordered his army to Amelia Court House for supplies.

CS War Department clerk John B. Jones wrote about waking up to explosions in the west end of Richmond. He also reported the following: 7 a.m.: government officials destroyed liquor stocks, causing a riot, 8:30 a.m.: the armory, arsenal, and related facilities are destroyed by explosions that last an hour, 10 a.m.: he reports seeing a Federal battery go by, 11 a.m.: he sees the streets filled with Union African-American troops, and at 9 p.m. he hears about a curfew.

Tuscaloosa, AL fell to Union forces.

April 4: US President Lincoln visits Richmond.

April 5: Confederate Army of Northern Virginia reached Amelia Court House but the promised supplies turned out to be munitions, not the badly needed food.

Confederate cavalry under General Fitzhugh Lee engaged Union forces between Amelia Court House and Jetersville.

CS War Department clerk John B. Jones wrote about his feeling that he will soon end his diary. The CS War Department building was destroyed the day before, so he was out of a job.

April 6: In Virginia, Confederate General Longstreet attempted to break through to the south, but found the Union XXXIV Corps in his way.

Confederate cavalry secured a crossing at the Appomattox River.

Union General Sheridan cut off and captured ¼ of Lee's remaining forces at Saylor's Creek, VA. Eight Confederate Generals were among those captured.

April 7: Confederate General Longstreet attempted to burn the High Bridge across the Appomattox River, but failed. This allowed Union forces to capture the crossing and maintain their pursuit of Lee.

> *General Sheridan says if the thing is pressed, I think Lee will surrender.*
> **Let the thing be pressed.**
> —*President Lincoln, message to General Grant.*

Union troops were repulsed at Farmville, VA.

Union General Grant sent a massage to Confederate General Lee asking him to surrender. Lee answered with a question about terms. Longstreet advised Lee to wait.

Confederate General Forrest's cavalry skirmished with Union forces near Stockton, AL.

The Augusta, GA, *Tri-Weekly Constitution* printed CS President Davis' announcement that he would continue to fight on, despite the fall of Richmond.

April 8: Union General Custer's cavalry sealed off all of the routes out of Appomattox Court House, effectively surrounding the Confederate Army of Northern Virginia. There was discussion about breaking up the army in order to continue the war as an insurgency, but General Lee refused, agreeing finally to meet with Union General Grant.

In Mobile, AL, Spanish Fort surrendered to Union forces.

April 9: Union General Grant and Confederate General Lee had a meeting in the parlor of Wilmer McLean at Appomattox Court House where an agreement for the surrender of the Army of Northern Virginia was signed.

At Mobile, AL, a Union assault at Fort Blakely overran the Confederate defensive lines.

April 10: Word of the surrender reached Washington, DC where celebrations break out. US President Lincoln delivered a speech at the White House, where he requested the song "Dixie" be played.

Pennsylvania Representative Thaddeus Stevens made a speech at Lancaster calling on harsh measures for the defeated Southern states. It seemed that he had not forgiven the Confederates for destroying his steel foundry during the Gettysburg Campaign of 1863.

> *It is true! Yesterday Gen Lee surrendered the 'Army of Northern Virginia.'*
> —*John Beauchamp Jones, diary entry.*

April 11: Last Confederate forts around Mobile Bay surrendered.

In North Carolina, Union General Sherman was now aiming at Confederate General Joe Johnston's forces near Raleigh.

April 12: Confederate General Joe Johnston met with CS President Davis and received authorization to negotiate surrender.

Mobile, AL surrendered to Union forces.

Montgomery, AL fell to Union forces.

Formal surrender of the Army of Northern Virginia took place at Appomattox Court House, VA. Confederate General Lee issued a Farewell Address. Weapons and flags were turned over to Federal authorities. The soldiers were then given parole slips and sent home. This removed a major Confederate army from the field, but there are others.

> *General Order No. 9, After four years of arduous service, marked by unsurpassed courage and fortitude, the Army of Northern Virginia has been compelled to yield to overwhelming numbers and resources. I need not tell the brave survivors of so many hard fought battles, who have remained steadfast to the last, that I have consented to this result from no distrust of them: but feeling that valor and devotion could accomplish nothing that would compensate for the loss that must have attended a continuance of the contest, I determined to avoid the useless sacrifice of those whose past services have endured them to their countrymen. By the terms of the agreement, officers and men can return to their homes and remain until exchanged. You will take with you the satisfaction that proceeds from the consciousness of duty faithfully performed, and I earnestly pray that a merciful God will extend to you his blessing and protection. With an unceasing admiration for your constancy and devotion to your country, and a grateful remembrance of your kind and generous consideration for myself, I bid you all an affectionate farewell. R.E. Lee*

During the formal surrender, as cannon were being parked, muskets stacked, and flags furled, the division of Lieutenant General John Gordon was marching to the spot where they would give up their arms. They were passing a formation of Union troops commanded by one of the officers handling the surrender, Major General Joshua Chamberlain. Chamberlain quickly ordered his troops to attention and then to order arms, raising their muskets in salute to their former enemy. Gordon noticed this and shouted, *"Smarten up boys, the Yankees are saluting our flag."* Gordon then lowered his sword in returning the salute.

Word reached Union General Sherman of the surrender of General Lee.

April 13: Union General Sherman's troops entered Raleigh, NC.

Union General Judson Kilpatrick's cavalry reached Durham Station, NC.

April 14: At Fort Sumter, Union Major General Robert Anderson raised the same flag he had lowered four years before.

US President Lincoln, his wife, and two guests, attended the performance of *Our American Cousin* at Ford's Theatre, Washington, DC. At 10 p.m. John Wilkes Booth, an actor and Confederate supporter, entered the Presidential Box and fired a single shot into Lincoln's head. The President was carried across the street to a boarding house. At the same time, Secretary of State Seward is attacked while another assailant chickens out, sparing Vice-President Johnson.

Well, I guess I know enough to turn you inside out, old gal—you sockdologizing old man-trap...
--The last words Lincoln heard before he was shot.

Sic Semper Tyrannis! The South is avenged!
—John Wilkes Booth as quoted in the New York Times.
(Booth shouted "Sic Semper Tyrannis" as he leapt to the stage after shooting Lincoln. The irony of this was that that is also the motto of the Commonwealth of Virginia. He may not have said the second sentence.)

April 15: Abraham Lincoln, 16th President of the United States, died at 7:22 a.m. At 11:00 a.m., Vice-President Andrew Johnson was sworn in as the 17th President of the United States.

Now he belongs to the Ages.
—US Secretary of War Edwin Stanton as President Lincoln died.

April 16: Confederate General Joe Johnston asked Union General Sherman to meet in order to discuss terms of surrender.

Union troops began a dragnet, looking for the assassin of US President Lincoln.

April 17: Union General Sherman and Confederate General Joe Johnston met at Durham Station to discuss surrender terms.

Union forces captured West Point and Columbus, GA, destroying CSS *Jackson* and capturing 1200 Confederates.

April 18: Union General Sherman and Confederate General Joe Johnston signed an armistice with more liberal terms than Grant gave Lee.

April 19: Union Colonel John Sprague left Cairo, IL to seek Confederate General Kirby Smith in order to discuss a Confederate surrender.

CS President Davis learned of the death of US President Lincoln while at Charlotte, NC.

The body of US President Lincoln lies in state in the Capital.

CS War Department clerk John B. Jones wrote for the last time in his diary. He mentioned the death of US President Lincoln while he was waiting for permission from Federal authorities to move his family to the Eastern Shore of Virginia.

April 20: Union forces captured Macon, GA.

Arkansas passed the 13th Amendment.

April 21: President Lincoln's funeral train left Washington, DC on a route that would reach Springfield, IL on May 3.

Confederate Colonel Mosby disbanded his Partisan Rangers rather than surrender.

April 22: John Wilkes Booth and David Herold, a fellow conspirator in the Lincoln assassination crossed the Potomac River and fled south.

April 24: Union General Sherman was ordered to either demand unconditional surrender from Confederate General Joe Johnston or to resume the offensive.

Assassins Booth and Herold reached Port Conway, VA.

US President Lincoln's body lies in state in New York City.

April 25: Union General Sherman delivered the message he received yesterday to Confederate General Joe Johnston. Johnston wired CS President Davis of the developments, including his intention to surrender.

Union cavalry learn that the assassins of US President Lincoln are hiding in a farm near the Rappahannock River, VA.

April 26: Confederate General Joe Johnston agreed to the same surrender terms that General Lee had agreed to. This removed a second major Confederate army out of the war.

On his 27th birthday, John Wilkes Booth was trapped with David Harold in a barn near Bowling Green, VA. Harold surrendered but Booth was mortally wounded by Sergeant Boston Corbett, who was acting against orders. There were rumors going about that CS President Davis himself ordered Lincoln killed. The truth is that the conspirators acted alone, albeit with some financial assistance from the Confederate Secret Service.

Useless! Useless!—John Wilkes Booth's last words.

The Confederate Cabinet met in Charlotte, NC and agreed to flee west to the Mississippi River. This was their last meeting.

April 27: In what is considered the worst transportation accident in US history, the steamboat *Sultana,* carrying former Union prisoners of war, exploded on the Mississippi River north of Memphis, TN, killing 1450.

CS President Davis continued to flee as his party left Charlotte, NC.

April 28: US President Lincoln's funeral train reached Cleveland, OH.

April 29: With the news of surrendering Confederate armies circulating, many Union soldiers were now demanding immediate demobilization.

April 30: Union General Canby and Confederate General Taylor discussed the surrender of Confederate forces in Alabama and Mississippi.

May 1: US President Andrew Johnson ordered a military commission formed to try those accused of taking part in the Lincoln assassination.

May 2: US President Johnson accused former CS President Davis of being a part of the Lincoln assassination conspiracy and offered a $100,000 reward for his capture.

In Abbeville, SC, CS President Davis conducted a meeting in which he expressed his determination to carry on the war. His remaining military commanders did not express the same optimism.

May 3: Lincoln's funeral train reached Springfield, IL.

Confederate Secretary of State Judah Benjamin left the Davis party and headed for Florida, where he will sail to the Bahamas and then on to Great Britain to begin his exile.

May 4: Confederate General Taylor officially surrendered to Union General Canby at Citronelle, AL.

Abraham Lincoln was buried at Springfield, IL.

Skirmish near Lexington, MO.

May 5: Skirmish at Peche Hill, MO.

May 6: CSS *Stonewall* arrived at Nassau, Bahamas, where its crew learned that the war was over. From there they sailed for Havana, Cuba and turned the vessel over to Spanish authorities. The vessel would serve with the Japanese Navy until the 1880s.

May 7: A detachment of the 4th Michigan Cavalry set out from Macon, GA. This was the force that would capture CS President Davis.

May 8: The trial began of all those involved in the assassination of Lincoln and the attempted assassination of other government officials.

Remaining Confederate troops in Mississippi and Alabama were paroled.

May 9: CS President Davis released the infantry brigades that were escorting him and his family. He still intended to head for the Trans-Mississippi, where he might continue the war.

May 10: US President Johnson declared the rebellion against the US over.

Confederate guerilla William Quantrill was killed near Taylorsville, KY.

Union cavalry captured CS President Davis near Irwinville, GA.

Remaining Confederate flotilla at Mobile, AL surrendered to Union naval forces.

May 11: Confederate General Meriwether Thompson surrendered all of his forces in Arkansas.

May 12: All the accused in the Lincoln assassination trial plead not guilty.

May 13: At Palmito Ranch, TX, there was a skirmish between small units in what turned out to be the last military action of the war. Ironically it's a Confederate victory.

Confederate General Edmund Kirby Smith was advised to surrender by the governors of Arkansas, Louisiana, and Mississippi at a meeting at Marshall, TX.

May 17: Union General Sheridan was named commander of all US forces west of the Mississippi with the aim of both securing Texas and put pressure on the Imperial Mexican government, locked in a struggle with Republican forces under Benito Juarez and supported by French occupation troops.

May 18: Emma LeConte, a resident of Columbia, SC, wrote in her diary her hope of continued Southern resistance despite the capture of former CS President Davis.

May 20: US Vice-Admiral Farragut was appointed to review the Naval Academy, which would lead to reforms.

May 21: CSS *Shenandoah* entered Sea of Okhotsk, Russia in search of Northern whaling ships, unaware that the war was over.

May 22: US President Johnson lifted trade restrictions on Southern ports with the exception of Galveston, La Salle, Brazos Santiago, and Brownsville, all in Texas.

Former CS President Davis was imprisoned in Fortress Monroe.

May 23: In Washington DC, the Grand Review victory parade began with a mass march of the Army of the Potomac.

Pro-Union government of Virginia established in Richmond.

May 24: Union General Sherman's armies marched through Washington DC, ending the Grand Review.

May 25: A warehouse filled with gunpowder exploded in Mobile, AL, causing 300 casualties and widespread damage.

May 26: Confederate General Simon Buckner surrendered his army at New Orleans.

May 27: US President Johnson ordered the release of most of those who were held by Union military authorities.

May29: US President Johnson granted a general amnesty, with few exceptions, to former Confederates.

June 2: Confederate General Edmund Kirby Smith surrendered all troops west of the Mississippi River. Some of those troops refused to surrender and began heading for Mexico.

UK Government withdrew belligerent rights from the CSA.

June 3: Confederate forces on the Red River, LA surrendered.

June 8: Union VI Corps held its own review at Washington, DC.

June 10: CSS *Shenandoah*, its crew still unaware that the war was over, attacked US whaling ships off Japan.

June 17: Edmund Ruffin, the ardent Virginia secessionist and the one who may or may not have fired the first shot at Fort Sumter, SC in 1861, killed himself.

> *I here declare my unmitigated hatred to Yankee rule to all political, social & business connection with Yankees & to the Yankee race. Would that I could impress these sentiments, in their full force, on every living southerner & bequeath them to every one yet to be born! May such sentiments be held universally in the outraged & downtrodden South, though in silence & stillness, until the now far distant day shall arrive for just retribution for Yankee usurpation, oppression, & atrocious outrages & for deliverance & vengeance for the now ruined, subjugated, & enslaved Southern States! May the maledictions of every victim to their malignity, press with full weight on the perfidious Yankee people & their perjured rulers & especially on those of the invading forces who perpetrated, & their leaders & higher authorities who encouraged, directed, or permitted the unprecedented & generally extended outrages of robbery, rapine & destruction, & house burning, all committed contrary to the laws of war on noncombatant residents, & still worse on aged man & helpless women.*
> *—Edmund Ruffin, last diary entry.*

June 22: CSS *Shenandoah* attacked a US whaling fleet in the Bering

Strait. Newspapers found on one vessel told of General Lee's surrender, but also of CS President Davis' intention to fight on. It was decided to seek the rest of the US whaling fleet.

June 23: US President Johnson ordered the naval blockade of Southern ports lifted.

Confederate General Stand Waite, a Cherokee leader, surrendered his command, the last to do so.

July 7: The co-conspirators in the assassination of President Lincoln, Lewis Powell, George Atzerodt, David Herold, and Mary Surratt were executed in Washington, DC. There was considerable protest over the hanging of Surratt, since she was only the owner of the boarding house where the conspirators roomed. US President Johnson was not in the mood to pardon anyone remotely connected with the Lincoln assassination. The minor players in this drama, Michael O'Laughlin, Dr Samuel Mudd, Edward Spangler, and Samuel Arnold, were sentenced to life imprisonment at Dry Tortugas, FL.

August 2: CSS *Shenandoah* hailed a British ship in the eastern Pacific and her crew learned that the war was truly over. Realizing that they could be considered pirates for attacking the US Whaling Fleet, Captain Waddell ordered all arms dismounted and placed in the hold. Then he ordered the crew to sail to England where he would turn her over to British authorities. This journey would make the CSS *Shenandoah* the only Confederate States Navy vessel to circumnavigate the globe.

October 3: Officers commanded by Mexican leader Benito Juarez attended a party organized by US General Sherman. Under the assumption that Juarez was with them, Emperor Maximillian issued the "Black Decree" declaring that all Mexican rebel forces had fled the country and that any further rebellion was punishable with death. In fact, Juarez had not left Mexico.

October 11: US President Johnson pardoned former CS Vice-President Stephens and several Confederate Cabinet members.

November 6: CSS *Shenandoah* surrendered to British authorities at Liverpool, UK.

November 10: Confederate Captain Henry Wirz, superintendent of Andersonville, GA prison, was executed in Washington, DC, the only one from either side to be convicted of war crimes.

December 20: Five years after the secession of South Carolina, the 13th Amendment to the Constitution was fully ratified. Slavery was now illegal anywhere in the US.

Things that any good soldier of the Civil War should know:

What did the infantry and cavalry carry:

Infantry Weapons				
Type	Caliber	Range (in yards)	Weight (in pounds)	Rounds per minute
1855 Enfield Carbine	0.577	350	8	3
1857 Enfield Rifle	0.577	450	9.2	3
US 1835 Musket	0.69	150	11	3
US 1842 Musket	0.69	150	11	3
US 1855 Rifle	0.58	400	10.12	3
US 1861 Rifle	0.52	450	9.75	3
Sharps 1848 Carbine	0.52	350	7	9
Sharps 1848 Rifle	0.52	450	8	9
Spencer Carbine	0.52	450	8.3	20
Henry Rifle	0.435	400	9.25	28

Ok, so how do you load and fire a muzzle loading rifle musket.

Command: "Load"

1. Place the rifle on the ground between your feet, stock down. You should be looking at the muzzle. Hold the rifle with your left hand.

Commands: "Handle Cartridge" and "Tear Cartridge"

2. With your right hand, reach into your cartridge pouch and get one

cartridge. Locate the "tail" at one end. Bite the "tail" and pull the cartridge to open it.

Command: "Charge Cartridge"

3. Pour the powder into the barrel. Tap the rifle gently on the ground as that is being done. Next, drop the bullet into the barrel with the paper, which serves as wadding.

Commands: "Draw Rammer," "Ram Cartridge," and "Return Rammer"

4. Pull out the rammer from its slot under the barrel. Turn the rammer around and tamp the round as far as it will go. Then replace the rammer in the slot. (Don't lose the rammer or you will have only one shot. After you fire, the musket becomes a club.)

Command: "Prime"

5. Bring the rifle level with your right hip. Pull the hammer back one click (half-cock) Reach into the cap pouch and bring out a percussion cap. Place the cap on the nipple. **The rifle will not discharge while it is at half-cock.**

Commands: "Shoulder Arms," "Ready," and "Level"

6. Pull the hammer back one more click (full-cock). Place stock of rifle on your shoulder. Line up your sights on the target. (It's a good idea to aim low.) **The rifle can now be discharged, DO NOT PULL THE TRIGGER UNTIL YOU ARE AIMING AT YOUR TARGET, THESE WEAPONS HAVE NO SAFETY OTHER THAN THE HAMMER AT HALF COCK!!**

Command: "Fire"

7. Pull the trigger when ready or on the command of "fire." (When the trigger is pulled, the hammer comes down onto the cap, crushing it and causing a spark. The spark travels through the touchhole into the barrel. This ignites the powder, causing a small explosion that pushes the bullet out the barrel.)

8. When possible, swab the barrel between shots in order to kill any sparks. This will prevent premature firing while loading.

Oh, by the way, to be good, you need to do this three times a minute!

This is what the artillery used:

Artillery Weapons				
Type	Bore (in Inches)	Range (in yards)	Weight of Piece	Weight of Round/ Charge
US 1841 12 lb Howitzer	4.62	1072	788 pounds	8.9/.75
US 1857 12 lb Howitzer	4.62	1680	1227 pounds	12.3/2.5
US 1861 3" Rifle	3	2788	820 pounds	9.5/1.0
US 1857 6 Pound	3.67	1523	884 pounds	9.5/1.0
US 1863 Parrott	3	2790	890 pounds	9.5/1.0
UK Blakely 12-lb (CS)	3.1	1760	700 pounds	12.0/1.5
UK Whitworth 12-lb (CS)	2.75	800	1100 pounds	12.0/1.75
US 1857 James 14 lb Rifle	3.67	1700	875 pounds	12.0/.75
US 1861 Parrott 20 lb Rifle	3.67	4400	1750 pounds	20.0/2.0
US 1861 Seacoast Mortar	13	4,200	17,000 pounds	215/ukn
CS 1861 Brooke	10	260	22,000 pounds	140/16

OK, now try loading and firing an Artillery Piece:

1. If the gun was already fired, the ventman covers the touch hole with a gloved thumb (thumbstall) as the rammer sponges the barrel to kill any sparks.

2. The ammo carrier gets a round from the caisson and carries it in a pouch similar to a haversack. He gives it to the loader at the front of the gun, who places it into the barrel. The round is attached to a powder bag. (If double canister is called for, one round with powder bag is inserted, then the second round, with the powder bag removed, is added).

3. The rammer pushes the round down into the barrel.

4. The Gunner uses a screw to elevate (up and down) the gun while a crewmember moves the "tongue" to traverse (left and right) the gun. A gun sight is placed on the touchhole for that purpose and is removed once the gun is sighted.

5. The ventman shoves a priming wire into the touchhole, which pierces the powder bag.

6. The Gunnery Sergeant pushes a primer into the touchhole and into the powder bag. A lanyard is attached to the primer.

7. The Gunnery Sergeant pulls the lanyard taunt. At the command "fire" the lanyard is pulled in a sharp, fast manner. The primer is set off, igniting the powder, the explosion causing the round to travel out the barrel and head downrange.

8. The gun lacks a recoil mechanism, so the gun crew must move the gun back into position for the next firing.

9. The Fuse Cutter cuts fuses for shells as needed.

Did you know there were machine guns in the Civil War?

Gatling Gun: .58 caliber, hand cranked, gravity fed, six barrel machine gun which fired 600 rounds a minute. This gun was prone to jamming and was considered too radical for wholesale use.

Union Repeating Gun (The "Coffee Mill" gun): .58 caliber, hand cranked, gravity fed, single barrel machine gun that was prone to overheating. One was used with success on 29 March 1862 at Middleburg, VA.

Or even Hand Grenades?

Ketchum: Designed as a dart, this grenade had a striker that ignited the explosive.

Hanes: A sphere with 12 to 14 percussion caps surrounded by another sphere. On landing, the inner sphere banged against the outer sphere and detonated the grenade.

Adams: Six-pound shell with a paper fuze ignited with a primer attached to an 18-inch lanyard.

Augusta: Confederate copy of the Adams but without the lanyard.

Or even landmines (they called them torpedoes)?

Sea torpedoes were usually kegs or metal barrels filled with powder and detonated with percussion fuzes (contact) or a galvanic battery (electrically).

Land torpedoes were not widely used because it was considered immoral. They were set off by foot pressure that ignited a percussion cap, which detonated the weapon.

Uniforms and Equipment

Or: what the well dressed soldier was issued.

NOTE: Issued was a relative term in this case; while the Union had the industrial base to keep their troops clothed and shod, the system of distribution was not perfected until about mid-war. The Confederacy, however, had neither for very long; the usual method for supplying a Southern regiment was to strip the bodies of dead Union soldiers.

On the other hand, nothing was standardized until months after the war began. At the First Battle of Bull Run (or First Manassas), many Southern units were wearing their blue uniforms while several Northern regiments had arrived wearing their gray militia uniforms, that had to cause confusion to no end.

The following information is for a basic issue needed to keep a soldier able to function. This depended on what was available from the Quartermaster:

A Private's uniform consisted of:
    1 Hat (Slouch or Hardee)
    2 Caps (Kepis)
    1 Cap cover (for when it rains)
    2 Coats (usually Sack Coats)
    3 Pairs of Trousers
    3 Shirts
    1 Blouse (a longer version of the Sack Coat)
    3 Pairs of Drawers (underwear)
    2 Pairs of Shoes

3 pairs of Stockings (socks)
1 Great Coat (perfect for winter)

Personal equipment consisted of:
  1 Belt with Buckle
  1 Baldric (Shoulder Strap)
  1 Cartridge Box with Strap
  1 Cap Box
  1 Bayonet Scabbard with Bayonet
  1 Haversack for rations and extra rounds
  1 Knapsack for carrying other equipment and personal items.
  1 Canteen
  1 Woolen Blanket
  1 Rubber Blanket

Knapsack contained:
  Both Woolen and Rubber blankets rolled together and tied to the top.
  Extra Uniform items
  Mess kit with Plate, Fork and Spoon
  Coffee Boiler
  Tin Mug for coffee
  "Housewife" with needles, threads, and buttons for making repairs
  Shelter Half
  Personal items like combs, toothbrushes, razors, mirror and other items purchased from a sutler

Of course, there is also the matter of feeding the Private:

Rations (not all of these items were received at once; the rations were determined by availability):
  16 ounces of "Hard Bread" (Hardtack)
  22 ounces of "Soft Bread" (Regular)
  20 ounces of salted meat (usually salt pork)
  12 ounces of bacon
  10 ounces of dried beans or peas
  2.6 ounces of rice or hominy
  5.2 ounces of potatoes (when available)

1.3 gills of vinegar
1.6 ounces of green (unroasted) coffee
1.3 ounces of roasted coffee
.25 ounces of tea
2.4 ounces of sugar
1.3 gills of molasses
0.3 ounces of salt
0.04 ounces of pepper
0.2 ounces of candles (actually a small candle)
0.6 ounces of soap

CS Rations usually consisted of corm meal or flour instead of bread. Bacon was the meat of choice in the CS Army

Soldiers could supplement their fare with canned peaches, canned milk, oysters, and candy from the sutler, usually at inflated prices.

Care of Weapons and Equipment (according to the Revised Regulations for the Army, 1862):

1. All arms will be kept in the condition that they were issued. Breakdown of weapons are not allowed except when authorized by a commissioned officer.

2. After firing, wash out the barrel, then run a cloth down the barrel to dry it. After cleaning, put a tampion in the muzzle to keep dirt and water out.

3. Do not have arms loaded in camp unless authorized.

4. Ammunition will be inspected as frequently as possible. Any unauthorized expenditure of rounds will result in the cost of the rounds being docked from the soldier's pay.

5. Do not mix blank and ball rounds.

6. Expose ammunition to the sun to keep them dry.

7. Cartridge boxes and bayonet scabbards will be polished with blacking, not varnish.

8. Mark haversacks with the letter of the company and the number of the soldier. EX: C 57

9. Mark the flap of the knapsack with the unit designation, and company letter, and the soldier's number. EX: 69NY
    C 57

10. Haversacks and canteens will be worn on the left side, canteen over haversack.

Civil War Cooking

Once you were issued your rations, you had to make them edible.

The following are some of the recipes used in the Civil War:

Coffee

(The Union version. The Confederates had to make do with chicory, roasted walnut shells, pecan shells, toasted corn meal, etc)

1. Get some green coffee beans and roast them in a skillet over an open fire, occasionally stirring in water (one ounce per pound of beans) until the beans are a deep brown. Make sure you keep stirring to prevent the beans from burning.

2. Take the beans off and let them cool.

3. Take a handful of beans for each cup of water, place them in a mess tin, and grind them by using the butt of your musket (or a hammer).

4. Place the grounds in the coffee pot and add water. Hang the pot over a fire until the mixture is boiling.

5. Use a cloth to strain the coffee as you pour it into the cup.

6. Add sugar and milk (if available) to taste.

Hardtack

Commonly used as the standard ration.

Ingredients:
4 cups flour
2 teaspoons shorting
1 cup water

1. Combine flour and shorting in a bowl and mix with hands until blended.

2. Add water and knead until dough is stiff and elastic.

3. Place dough on a surface that is dusted with flour and pound it with a mallet until it's about ½-inch thick. Then fold the dough over and repeat pounding. Do this about 5-6 times.

4. Using a rolling pin, roll out the dough until it is ¼-inch thick.

5. Cut the dough into three-inch squares and poke four rows of four holes in each square. Place squares on an ungreased cookie sheet.

6. In the 1860s, they would be made by commercial bakers. The modern day equivalent is to place the cookie sheet in a 325-degree oven for 35 minutes. At that time, turn the oven off and let carryover heat dry out the crackers.

7. Makes 10-12 crackers.

Common names: Army Bread, Sheet Iron Crackers, Hard Bread, Worm Castles, Tooth Dullers.

Cornbread

Commonly used by Confederate troops.

Ingredients:
½ cup cornmeal
Bacon Grease (vegetable oil can do)
Water
Salt

1. Mix the cornmeal in a bowl with one tablespoon of bacon grease. Mix in water until the consistency is about that of runny scrambled eggs. Salt to taste.

2. Coat the bottom of a skillet with bacon grease and heat until the grease almost reaches smoke point.

3. Pour the dough into the skillet and smooth out with a spoon. Make sure the mixture is smaller than the bottom of the pan to allow easier turning.

4. When bottom is browned, turn it over and brown the other side.

5. When both sides are brown, take out and eat.

Salt Pork

Ingredient:
¼ pound of salt pork.

Frying
1. Cut the pork into three parts.

2. Place in pan over a fire and cook until fat is crisp and meat is cooked.
    (If there is no fire, then a cook top will do.)

3. Can be eaten straight or on a piece of hart tack.

Broiling
1. Cut up the meat into three parts and skewer then on a musket's
    ramrod.

2. Position the ramrod over the fire.

3. When done, remove and eat on hardtack.

Boiled
1. Put entire slab into a pot of water and bring it to a boil. Keep it
    boiling until meat is cooked.

2. When meat is cooked, pull the slab out and let the water drain. Then
    cut into portions.

3. Serve on hardtack.

Beef

Broiled
Ingredient:
8 to 10 ounces of beef.

1. Cut beef into chunks and skewer them on a stick or musket ramrod.

2. Position beef over fire and roast until done to preference.

Fried
1. Get some bacon grease and heat in a frying pan.

2. Cut beef into chunks and place in pan.

3. Season with salt (if available).

4. Fry until cooked to preference.

5. Eat with hardtack.

Skillygalee

Ingredients:
One square of hardtack
Water
Bacon grease
Salt

1. Place hardtack in pan and cover it with water until soft (usually 15-20 minutes but it might take you all day).

2. Heat grease in a frying pan.

3. Place soften hardtack in the hot grease and fry until brown.

4. Remove from pan, salt to taste, and eat.

Hell-Fired Stew

Same as Skillygalee but the hardtack is pulverized prior to soaking.

Hardtack Pudding

Ingredients:
One square of hardtack
A cloth bag
Flour
Water
Apples (dried)
Raisins (if available)

1. Put hardtack in the bag and pulverize it. Pour onto a plate and add flour and water and stir until mixture is moistened.

2. Put dough on clean surface and roll it out, using the palms of your hands, until it is 1/8-inch thick.

3. Cover with the dried apples and raisins.

4. Roll up the dough and pinch the ends closed. Wrap that in some clean cloth.

5. Place in a pot of boiling water and boil it for an hour.

6. Remove it from the water, open the cloth, scrape into a mess plate, and eat.

Cush

A favorite amongst Confederate troops.

Ingredients:
One portion of cooked beef (or bacon will do)
Bacon grease
Water
Cornbread

1. Heat up some grease in a frying pan.

2. Add beef (or other meat) and fry for a couple of minutes.

3. Add water and continue cooking for about five minutes.

4. Crumble cornbread into mixture and continue cooking until water is absorbed.

5. Spoon onto a plate and eat.

Confederate Stew

A favorite amongst troops of the Army of Tennessee.

Ingredients:
8 to 10 ounces of beef (usually per person)
Two potatoes
Water
Salt and pepper
½ cup of flour (per person)

1. Cut up beef and potatoes and place then in a pot of water. Season to taste. Boil for 45 minutes.

2. Mix flour and water until almost a liquid (a roux). Add the mixture to the beef and potatoes a little at a time until all is mixed in.

3. When beef and potatoes are soft, spoon out and eat.

Parched Corn
A common short ration

Ingredients:
One or two ears of corn.
Bacon grease
Salt.

1. Remove corn from ears and place in a hot pan of bacon grease.

2. Cover and shake until the kernels have burst.

3. Remove from pan and salt to taste.

4. Eat.

Concerning a soldier's attempt to liven up his rations, *Frank Leslie's Illustrated Newspaper* had this to say about sutlers:

The sutler's store at Harpers Ferry represents one of those apparently inevitable evils which attend even the best-arranged armies. As a study of human life, a sutler's store is full of the most sorrowful reflections, and demands the most earnest care of the superior officers. A little pure stimulant, when administered with the rations, is capable of warding off many ills which flesh is heir to, more especially when under the prostration of fatigue or privation.

Camp life (Life between battles)

At the end of a march or battle, it was important that the troops were encamped as quickly as possible. This would insure that the unit was fully accounted for, as well as providing a dwelling place for the soldiers:

1. The idea area for a camp is a meadow with a slight slope for drainage: a hillside would be better, but not too steep.

2. An area with a stream or river nearby is most ideal. A spot upstream for drinking water, another area for washing and bathing, and a spot downstream for the sinks (latrine). The sinks should not be in an area that would pollute camps downstream. It that becomes a problem, dig a trench at the edge of the camp for that purpose. (**It was known that there was a connection between cleanliness and disease, but not why**).

3. It would be a good idea to locate the field kitchen across the camp from the sinks. This area should also not be near trees in order to cut the risk of fire.

4. Upon arrival at the site, post a company as camp guard to prevent unauthorized departures.

5. Weapons should be stacked in 3s or 4s and a guard placed on them.

6. Spots should be located for the Quartermaster and the Surgeon and their tents set up.

7. Tents for the Colonel, the Lieutenant Colonel, and the Major should

be placed so they can overlook the camp. The Regimental Flags will be placed at the Colonel's tent.

8. The tents of the private soldiers should be arranged in companies, with the Captain's, Lieutenant's, and Sergeant's tents along the outside of the company area. The Private's tents will fill the interior.

9. There should be a "street" between the soldier's tents and the Commanding Officer's. There should also be a large field for drilling, roll call, sick call, etc.

10. Once the tents are pitched, trenches should be dug to provide additional drainage.

Tents (or other shelters):

1. Two-man: each man carried one-half of the shelter, one pole, and some lines. When reaching camp, two would pair off and build the shelter.

2. Sibley: conical tent with an opening at the top so that a stovepipe could be accommodated. Sleeps 6-8.

3. There was also a large, rectangular tent that slept 8, or one Commanding Officer.

4. For winter encampment, a wood floor and short walls would serve as a foundation for the rectangular tent. A stove would be placed in the middle of the floor for heating.

5. If the winter encampment was in a heavily wooded area, log cabins would be built. High-ranking officers (colonels and generals) could requisition a farmhouse for quarters.

Duty Day (when there is no fighting)

1. The duty day starts when the bugle or drum "reveille" is played. This is usually at sunrise, or just after. In hot climates, coffee should be served in order to prevent malaria (yes, they actually believed that).

2. The troops will rise, wash, dress, and present themselves for roll call. The roll is called, absences noted, and those who identify themselves as ill are sent to the Surgeon.

3. Work details are then assigned: camp police (keeping the camp clean), kitchen police (assisting the cook), guard duty, sink duty (cleaning the area around the latrines), etc. Also times for drilling are announced.

4. The bugle or drum call "peas on trencher" announces breakfast.

5. Following breakfast, the work duties should commence.

6. The call "troop" signifies guard mount (beginning sentry duty).

7. To bring the regiment together, sound the "assembly." This is usually for drilling and dress parade.

8. During the duty day, time should be devoted for individual equipment (musket maintenance, leather accouterments, uniforms, etc.).

9. When "roast beef" is called, its dinnertime.

10. All soldiers should be accounted by the time "retreat" is sounded.

They should be in quarters, unless on picket duty, when "tattoo" is sounded.

11. When "taps" (otherwise known as "Butterfield's Lullaby") is sounded, all lights will be out and the troops asleep.

Picket Duty

The system of pickets and sentries are set up as such:

1. Grand Guard: Must consist of at least three platoons (30 soldiers) but can involve an entire regiment. This group is situated closest to the camp and can serve as a rapid reaction force. All other posts are drawn from this group.

2. Picket Guards: Sent forward no further than 600 yards of the Grand Guard line. They are rotated every eight hours. One half of the pickets had to be up at all times.

3. Outposts: Sent forward 200 yards in front of the Picket line. They are up 100% of the time.

4. Sentinels: They are located no further than 50 yards in front of the Outpost line. This is the first line that will see an approaching enemy. They should be rotated every hour.

5. The Officer Commanding is stationed at the Grand Guard line and has overall responsibility for the entire operation. Will go forward to the Picket line at least once during a six-hour period.

6. Senior Officers under the command of the Officer Commanding will be stationed with the flanking companies of the Grand Guard unless there is a situation that requires their presence else ware.

7. Company commanders (lieutenants) are stationed at the Picket line and will visit the Outpost line each hour.

8. Company Non-commissioned officers are stationed at the Outpost line and are responsible for the relief of the Sentinels.

If there is contact with an enemy force:

1. Sentinels will send word to the Outpost line. Meanwhile the sentinels will form a skirmish line and withdraw to the Outpost line.

2. If practicable, both the Sentinel and Outpost lines will fall back to the Picket line where a defensive line will be set up. Otherwise, the Picket line will move forward and the defensive line will be set up at the Outpost line.

3. Grand Guard will then move forward to support the defensive line, either to make a stronger defense or to cover a withdrawal to a stronger defensive line.

4. Report of the contact will be made to either Regimental or Brigade command, depending on the size of the guard. There will be a mounted messenger ready to send any dispatches.

5. If the attacking force is too strong, the guard will make a fighting withdrawal until other regiments can be brought in. The Officer Commanding will make that determination.

Changing of the Guard:

1. When a new guard is ready to take over, the entire guard will be formed in the encampment to be briefed on any orders for the day. Afterwards the guard is marched to where the Grand Guard line is.

2. Grand guard line is relieved first as companies slated to be on the other lines are marched forward.

3. Next to be relived will be the Picket line. Men from the new line are then selected to go to the Outpost line.

4. When the Outpost line is relived, selected soldiers will then go forward to relieve the sentinels.

5. The off going guard will fall back in the opposite manner then the oncoming. Sentinel to Outpost, Outpost to Picket, and Picket to Grand guard.

6. The off going Officer Commanding will brief the oncoming Officer Commanding on all line positions, weak areas (areas that the enemy can exploit), houses or other key areas, and any orders that were received. All on coming officers and non-commissioned officers will receive briefings from their counterparts.

7. When the entire off going guard is assembled, they will be marched back to the camp.

8. Sketches of the area in front of the lines should be made if possible. This should note roads, bridges, towns, wooded areas, terrain features, and distances to same.

Other procedures:

1. No fires will be made farther forward than the Picket line.

2. Houses will not be occupied unless ordered by the Officer Commanding.

3. Officers are responsible for ensuring that each man on the lines knows what his duty is, checks will be conducted at least once during daylight hours and twice at night, once before midnight and the second time between one and four in the morning.

4. Any discrepancies found will be reported to the Officer Commanding.

5. One-half of the officers at the Grand Guard line will be awake at all times.

6. One-half of the officers at the Picket line will be awake at all times.

7. Sleeping is not authorized at the Outpost and Sentinel lines.

8. Sentinels will move up and down their line at all times unless approached. They will make contact with the sentinel to the left and right of him.

9. No one is allowed to pass through unless it is a General Officer or they have a pass. Sentinels cannot judge the validity of a pass: only an officer can do that.

10. Any persons passing through the lines must be stopped and challenged. A sign-countersign will be used. If the individual cannot answer the challenge, then the individual will be held for further questioning by a line officer. If there is no pass, the individual is then arrested and sent back to the Grand Guard line, where he will be detained if he was going out of the line, or to HQ if he was coming in.

11. No one will be moved from any line without the order of the Officer Commanding.

12. No one will abuse any local personnel, not take any property by force.

13. If there is a desertion, all lines will be briefed on the situation and all sign-countersigns will be changed.

14. If movement is heard and/or spotted, a report will be made up the lines immediately.

15. All those on sentry duty will ensure that they have all needed equipment and rations issued.

If the line is approached:

1. Shout the command "HALT." If the individual does not stop, the sentinel is authorized to fire.

2. Never allow a mounted individual to approach the line unless they give the countersign.

3. If contact is made at night, a whistle will be used to alert the other sentinels.

4. If a sentinel must fire, the sentinels on the left and right will support him, then retire towards the Outpost line with fixed bayonets. However the line should hold the enemy as long as possible. At this time, all lines will be under arms.

5. Reports of the contact will be sent by messenger and will be written. To avoid confusion, positions of the movement should be described as being "to our left" or "to our right" of the center of the Sentinel line.

6. If the attack on the lines reaches the Grand Guard line, a request for assistance will be sent to HQ. If possible, use a pre-selected line to form a defensive line so the enemy can be held until reinforcements arrive. If possible, or when reinforcements arrive, an attack should be made as rapidly as possible.

Conduct of Officers

1. If an officer is given temporary command, changing the chain of command was not authorized without the approval of the next higher commander.

2. If an officer takes permanent command of a unit, the outgoing commander will turn over all orders in force, public property, and unit funds.

3. An officer should not correct non-commissioned officers in front of privates.

4. Captains and Lieutenants are responsible for the upkeep and cleanliness of their company areas. They are also responsible for the cleanliness of the men, their uniforms, equipments, and weapons.

5. Officers will be in proper uniform at all times.

6. Company officers and higher will frequently inspect the kitchen areas to ensure sanitation.

7. The Commanding Officer (the Colonel) will set the schedule for the duty day while in camp.

8. No officer should inhabit a house, although vacant, without permission of the brigade or division commanders.

9. Officers in command of the picket line will inspect the line frequently.

10. Officers were responsible for controlling the men while on the march.

Conduct of Non-Commissioned Officers

All Non-Commissioned Officers are chosen by the Colonel, usually with the recommendations of the other Officers.

The 1st Sergeant will conduct the morning roll call. Action to be taken included, noting who is absent, who is sick, assign specific duty, and issue rations and clothing (if needed). Any sick personnel would be sent to the Surgeon. A report of the roll call would be composed for the Colonel.

The NCO had some privileges:

They were not confined with privates in the Guardhouse.

They were not to be used for menial service, or as waiters in an officer's mess.

They could not be reduced in rank except by a court-martial.

They received a certificate of their rank from the Colonel.

They were not transferred to another regiment except with the approval of the Commanding General.

They were allowed to re-enlist during a window of two months prior to one month after the expiration of service.

They assisted the officers in maintaining discipline.

If assigned as Officer of the Guard, they could not leave their post unless visiting sentinel positions, and then only after notifying the duty corporal.

They were not allowed to remove any part of their clothing or equipment while on guard duty.

They ensured the sign/countersign is communicated to the other sentinels.

They were not allowed to use foul language. For the first instance, 1/6 of a dollar (about 17 cents) was taken out of the next pay. On the second, 1/6 of a dollar was forfeited and 24 hours spent in the guardhouse.

They were required to suppress any attempts of mutiny and sedition. Failing to do so would put the NCO on trial.

They had the authority to enforce discipline, even if soldiers from other regiments were involved.

The NCO must be sober, clean, and have strict attention to detail while performing their duties.

Corporals must comport themselves in the same manner as the Sergeants.

From the *Articles of War*

The Articles of War were to be applied to every member of the US Armed Forces, Officer and Enlisted.

Military personnel were encouraged to attend a "divine service." If an enlisted man misbehaved at church, the penalty was forfeiture of 17 cents for the first offence. Additional offensives were penalized by forfeiture of 17 cents plus 24 hours confinement. Officers were penalized one dollar for such offensives.

For the offense of "contemptuous or disrespectful words" against the President, Vice-President, Members of Congress, or State officials, the officer was stripped of his commission and made to leave the service. Enlisted soldiers were court-martialed.

For disrespect to a superior officer, both officers and enlisted were court-martialed.

For mutiny and sedition, the prescribed punishment was death.

For witnessing mutiny and sedition, and failing to attempt to stop it by either reporting it or suppressing it, the prescribed punishment was death.

For striking a superior officer, and/or disobeying a direct order from same, the offender could receive any penalty up to death.

All enlisted personnel had to have the Articles of War read to him within six days of enlistment.

No one was to be released from the Army without a written discharge in his possession.

The Regimental commander had the authority to issue furloughs as needed. Such furloughs were limited to 20 days within a six-month period.

False furlough certificates were punished by a court-martial.

The penalty for a mustering officer receiving money for mustering troops was dismissal from the service and disqualification from holding any Federal office. The same penalty applied for making up muster rolls without having the actual bodies.

The Regimental commander had to provide a report of manning levels at the end of every month.

The penalty for dueling was dismissal for officers, court-martial for enlisted.

Sutlers were prohibited from selling from 9:00 p.m. to Reveille, as well as Sundays during services. They were also held responsible for the quality of their goods. Failure to do so resulted in banishment from the camp.

Officers were required to resolve all problems within the unit. It reflected badly on an officer if higher ups had to deal with it.

Supply personnel who sold, lost, or allowed damage to the supplies they were responsible for were required to pay back the cost of the involved items. Officers were dismissed while enlisted were court-martialed.

Any soldier who sold, lost, or allowed damage to the equipment he was issued had ½ of his pay docked until the value of the equipment was realized, as well as confinement.

Officers found drunk on duty were court-martialed.

Soldiers found asleep on duty were sentenced to death.

Soldiers who "misbehaved before the enemy" were sentenced up to and including death.

Revealing the sign/countersign to unauthorized personnel could result in death.

Helping enemy personnel evade capture could have resulted in death. (Kind of tough on families with sons on both sides.)

Army Engineers were not authorized to perform duties outside their specialty without approval.

If a soldier died while on duty, the Commanding Officer, with two other officers, had to gather the effects of the deceased, arrange for their transport home, and any pay sent to the deceased member's family.

Court-martial:

The board for a General court-martial consisted of five to thirteen officers.

Courts-martial were authorized as low as the Regimental level. The board convened had to consist of at least three officers. If the unit was short of officers, other units could be asked to provide such.

For capital cases, or cases involving officers, the lowest level that could hold the court-martial was at Brigade level.

The Judge Advocate was the prosecutor in the case.

If the defendant remained silent, the court was to go as if he had pled not guilty.

The court had to conduct themselves with decorum. The same court had the power to administer penalties for abusive behavior within the court.

All who gave testimony had to swear to the truth before the court.

Testimonies in non-capital cases were allowed to be sworn before a Justice-of-the-Peace.

Officers could not be tried by those of inferior rank if possible.

Officers charged were confined to barracks, quarters, or tent and made to surrender his sword. Enlisted were confined to the guardhouse. Neither could be held longer than eight days.

If an officer was convicted of cowardice or fraud, information about the incident, charge, and punishment was to be published in the newspapers of the offender's home state. (Especially cowardice since that would cause the offender to lose the respect of family and friends back home. One might as well head west if that happened).

It required a vote of 2/3 of the board to issue a sentence of death or 50 lashes.

The court did have the authority to pardon or lessen a sentence.

Punishments were meted out for the following:

Minor infractions:

Additional duty such as maintaining the sinks (latrines), cleaning out the stables and disposing dead horses.

Theft:

"Buck and Gag": The prisoner's wrists and ankles were tied and a large stick tied to his mouth.

"Standing on the Chines": The prisoner was made to stand on a barrel with the top and bottom removed.

"Wear the Jacket": The prisoner was made to wear a barrel and marched through camp to the ridicule of his fellow soldiers.

"Ride the horse": The prisoner was made to sit on a bar ten feet off the ground as if on a horse, but without the saddle. (Could be painful).

Force the prisoner to march around with a knapsack full of bricks.

Make the prisoner stand on a raised platform without protection from the elements.

Tie the prisoner to a spare wagon wheel. While the wagon is in motion! (Very painful!)

Make the prisoner carry a loaded saddle or a heavy beam all day.

Attach an iron ball to the prisoner's ankle.

Place the prisoner in a "sweat box." (Serious punishment during a Southern summer).

Serious transgressions:

Hanging the prisoner by his thumbs, with the toes just reaching the ground.

Hard labor at harsh places such as the Dry Tortugas, off the Florida coast.

Bread and water punishments were also common.

Cowardice:

The offender was dishonorably discharged, uniform stripped off, head shaved, facial cheeks branded with a red-hot iron (usually the letter C) and finally marched out of the camp, along with the aforementioned notice in the offender's hometown newspaper.

Desertion:

Death by firing squad.

Spying, murder, rape, and treason:

Death by hanging.

Thursday Nov 24th 1864

25 min. after 11 o'clk, the prisoners left Maj. Stevenson's office in the ambulance accompanied by Chaplain McKinnon. They were guarded by the reserve of eight men under a corporal. The officer of Guard & Surgeons accompanied the guard. The battalion was drawn up in two lines facing the prisoners. Light Artillery & Scouts on the right. Infantry battalion under Capt. Munn on the left.

Prisoners arrived at stakes, a prayer was offered by Chaplain. They declined making any remarks and requested not to be tied. They knelt down facing the guards & were blindfolded. There were nine men for each condemned man, one squad under the sergeant and the other under Officer Guard.

At the command "aim," one file fired. The officer of the Guard immediately followed with command "fire," but the discharge was irregular. Allen, who was at the old stake, was instantly killed. Watts was only wounded, but mortally. He groaned distressingly, "Lord have mercy on me," when I immediately ordered up the reserve of four to within two paces of him & he received two shots through the head & he died. Both men were cool, Watts as calm as if he had been on parade, the last thing he did before being blindfolded, was to turn and look at Allen & adjust his arms & hands like his. Allen stood during the Chaplain's prayer & seemed a little affected but as if in prayer. He was praying while shot.

After execution, the troops were broke into columns and marched around the bodies to the dead march. The bodies were carried to Camp Wyatt.

—Colonel William Lamb, describing an execution for desertion at Fort Fisher, NC.

Diversions (Something to do when off-duty)

1. Card games: Poker, euchre, spades, and other card games were popular. Some soldiers were known to throw away the cards just before a battle. If the soldier was killed, he did not want his parents to know he played cards, which was considered a great sin at the time. If the troop survived the battle, he took the first opportunity to search for his cards. (Usually, he could buy a new pack at the sutlers.)

2. Board Games: games like checkers and chess helped pass the time in camp.

3. Cockroach races: place two cockroaches in the middle of a tin plate. After the bets are taken, release the roaches. First roach to the edge wins. Another form of the races involved lice.

4. Dice: dice was rolled and winners and losers were determined by what numbers was rolled. This was considered a particularly evil vice, so much that Confederate General Thomas Jackson authorized severe punishments for his soldiers who were caught playing dice.

5. Baseball: Already a popular sport before the war. There were games between companies, or between regiments. There could also have been the occasional game between Union and Confederate regiments. A friendly game between teams that would see the next day trying to kill each other.

6. Reading: 10 cents at the sutlers could buy a "dime novel" for passing away the time. Other merchants would sell newspapers from New

York, Philadelphia, and Chicago, sometimes as recent as two days old.

7. Letters: A few cents at the sutlers would buy you stationery, envelopes, and postage to send a letter home. If one could not write, a more literate member of the unit could make a few cents writing letters for his mates.

8. Horse Races: A good past time, as well as a good way to keep the horses in shape. The most famous example was the Irish Brigade's Great Steeple Chase of St. Patrick's Day, 1862.

Maneuvering the Regiment

This is how the troops got to and from the battle and how they were moved during the battle:

Formations:

1. Column of Fours: This is the quickest way to get troops from one place to another.
   a. The regiment is formed in a column four across and as many ranks back as possible.
   b. Regimental colors will be at the front with the Color Guard.
   c. Musicians in front of the Color Guard.
   d. Baggage (tents, cooking utensils, supplies, etc.) will follow up in wagons.
   e. Company commanders (usually a Captain) will be at the head of the company while the lieutenant will be at the rear.
   f. Regiment commander (usually a Colonel) will move around and check the formation to ensure all is going well.
   g. The Lieutenant Colonel and Major will also keep things going.
   h. Lieutenants and Sergeants can be posted in the rear to catch stragglers.
   i. There is no talking while marching, so that any commands will be heard.
   j. Once on the move, the command "Route Step" is given, allowing the formation to loosen up and move at a walk.
   k. Halts may be used for rest periods or if something is going on ahead.
   l. When the formation resumes the march, it is at "Attention" until things get going, afterwards it's "Route Step."

    m. If there is a straggler, he must gain permission of an officer to fall out. His musket and knapsack must be left with the formation.

    n. Ensure canteens are full.

    o. Firing of muskets is prohibited on the march.

    p. Ensure no trash is thrown away.

2. Line of Battle: This happens when the enemy is spotted:
    a. The formation is halted.
    b. The companies are spread out into two lines with "A" company on the extreme right and the last company on the extreme left.
    c. Color Guard in the middle of the formation. The flags are used as a guide. (The color guard consisted of a Sergeant or Corporal and eight Privates assigned to protect the National and Regimental flags).
    d. Musicians go to the rear with the Regimental Surgeon to serve as stretcher-bearers.
    e. Lieutenants and Sergeants are behind their companies in order to keep the formation tight.
    f. Guides are posted on the left and right of the formation.
    g. The Sergeant Major is on the left while the Adjutant is on the right.
    h. The left wing (troops to the left of the flag) is commanded by the Major.
    i. The right wing (troops to the right of the flag) is commanded by the Lieutenant Colonel.
    j. The Colonel is in the center behind the formation so orders can be quickly issued.
    k. Staff officers remain with the Colonel in case dispatches need to be sent to Brigade.
    l. If not sent to the rear, Musicians remain with the Colonel.

3. Attack: The methods used to attack an enemy position:
    a. Frontal: This is a straight advance on the enemy position. Using several regiments, brigades, divisions, or even the whole army. This puts a lot of force at a wide point in the enemy's line.
    b. Oblique: This sends the formation at a right angle toward the enemy position.
    c. Flank: This sends the formation directly at the end of the enemy

position. Useful for putting concentrated musket fire at a single point.

d. Rear: If troops can be sent to the rear of the enemy's position without detection, the position can be surrounded and the enemy forced to surrender.

4. Withdrawal: If you have to pull back:
   a. Basic: March the formation backwards until out of enemy musket range. Then have them about face and march to the rear.
   b. Fighting: Have the front rank fire a volley, and then go to the rear of the second rank. That rank fires as the first rank reloads. Then the process is repeated.
   c. Rout: This is everyone for themselves. This means things have gone very, very badly. You want to try to avoid that, since unit cohesion will be lost as everyone runs for the hills.

Manual of Arms

Or, the skills a Private needed:

1. Carrying the musket: Right side of body, barrel pointed up, rammer to the front, barrel resting on the shoulder, right hand gripping the stock below the trigger guard.

2. Support arms: Move the musket from the right to the left, then support the weapon by wrapping the left arm around, allowing the forearm to support the musket at the hammer. The right arm is straight down.

3. Attention: Heels together, feet at an angle, legs straight but do not lock the knees (you will faint), body straight, head straight, eyes front, arms are straight down (if not carrying a musket), hands curled as if holding a roll of specie.

4. Present Arms: Musket is brought in front of the body, held with both hands. This is used as a salute.

5. Order Arms: musket is brought back to the carry position.

6. Shoulder Shift Arms: Musket is brought to where the hammer is at shoulder level and facing out. The weapon is at an angle. The arm is across the stock in order to support the musket.

7. Fix Bayonets: Musket is grounded with the barrel pointed up, supported by the right hand. The left hand grips the bayonet and pulls it out of the scabbard. The bayonet is turned so that the point is straight up. The bayonet is then threaded over the front sight and

the locking ring is turned to the right, locking the bayonet in place. The musket is then returned to the carry position.

8. Charge Bayonet: From the carry position, the left hand grips the barrel between the 1st and 2nd bands. The right hand is holding the stock. The musket is then rotated to about a 45-degree angle, usually accompanied with a shout.

9. Unfix Bayonet: The reverse of #7.

10. Ground: Musket is placed on the ground with the hammer up.

Marching

1. Mark Time: Marching in place.

2. Quick March: Step off with the left foot: each step to be 28 inches.

3. Change Step: Bring feet together, and then resume marching with the foot opposite to the one in step at the time of the command.

4. Squad Backwards: The formation moves backwards while facing forward. This is usually used in a fighting retreat.

5. Double Quick: Formation is running. Good for getting your troops there quickly.

Firing

1. Volley: the entire formation fires their muskets on the command "Fire." In some cases, the front rank would be kneeling. (If this is a new regiment that is about 1000 muskets firing at once.)

2. At Will: after a volley or two, the area in front would be shrouded in smoke. At this point, it is a good idea to have the troops firing as they load.

3. Cease Fire: all troops in the formation will stop firing and place their muskets in the carry position.

4. Firing at the oblique: this is done at the right or left angle of the front of the formation.

5. Fire by File: the right file fires their muskets. As they began reloading, the file next to them fires, and so on, causing ripple fire.

6. Fire by Rank: the first rank fires their muskets. As they began reloading, the second rank fires.

Using the Bayonet

1. Hold the musket at a 45-degree angle with the left hand gripping the forestock and the right hand gripping the shoulder stock behind the trigger guard. This is the **guard** position.

2. Move both hands forward sharply, moving the musket forward and striking the target with the bayonet. This is called the **thrust**.

3. Turn the musket ¼ turn to the right. This will cause further damage to the target.

4. Pull back quickly, removing the bayonet from the target. This is known as **recover**.

Battlefield Medicine

At the beginning of the war, the US Military Medical Department consisted of one Colonel (the Surgeon General), thirty Majors (Surgeons), and 84 Captains and below (the Assistant Surgeons). This was not even close to being adequate for the massive army that was needed to put down the rebellion. Add to this the fact that several doctors were from the South and therefore going with their seceded states, and the US Army had problems operating a Medical Department at first. Of course, the CS Medical Department had to start from scratch.

The Union's doctors were led at the beginning by Thomas Lawson, a veteran of the War of 1812, who had a reputation of being a martinet. He also was dying of cancer, so the Surgeon General position became vacant very fast.

As far as appointing doctors were concerned, it was left to the states to commission those who wanted to be in the Medical Service.

The thing was many of these doctors had just graduated from medical school, at the time not the eight-year course of study, complete with grueling exams and several years residency to top it off. These medical students had two, three, **maybe** four year's worth of education.

It also did not help that many medicines used at the time were just as likely to kill as heal. Medicines such as blue mass and calomel contained mercury, a toxic metal.

For example: Blue Mass contained 33 parts mercury, 5 parts liquorice, 25 parts althaea, 3 parts glycerine, and 34 parts of honey of rose.

Medical science was not as advanced as we have come to know it in the 20th and 21st Centuries: people in the 19th Century knew that there was a connection between sanitation and health, but did not know why. The discovery of bacteria lay years in the future. Doctors also had to put up with regular outbreaks of malaria and yellow fever, but could not figure how it was spread or why there was a "season" for these diseases. That would not be discovered until the Spanish-American War and the discovery by Army Surgeon Walter Reed that mosquitoes were the ones spreading diseases.

Another thing that was considered was water sources, which were mainly streams and rivers. There were no clean water sources, other than wells, and filtration and boiling water were known, but seldom practiced.

As a matter of fact, the basic health advice of the 1860's was thus:

1. Avoid use of ardent spirits (alcoholic beverages).

2. Do not drink very cold water. Cool water is best.

3. Tea, coffee and chocolate are best at meals. (And coffee was supposed to prevent malaria).

4. Do not overeat and limit between meal eating.

5. Wear flannel in all weather conditions.

6. Wash clothes regularly or hang them in the sun.

7. Have a bed of hay, straw, or other such material for sleeping on. Avoid bare ground.

8. Sleep as much as possible.

9. Make sure there is a fire after rain and damp weather.

10. Wash entire body whenever possible with soap and water. (Just make

sure you are NOT washing near the sinks or where drinking water is collected).

11. Wear a white flannel around the bowels if disease prevails (the book never said which disease).

12. Keep in open air but not in direct sunlight.

13. Wear shoes with thick soles.

14. Wear a silk handkerchief in your hat in order to prevent sunstroke.

15. Never eat a heavy meal before a march or a battle.

16. Coffee is a great restorative after a march or battle.

17. Never sleep without a cover.

18. If you must drink brandy, do so after a march or battle.

19. Drink as little as possible, even water.

20. If a wound is jetting blood that means an artery is cut. Tie a handkerchief between the wound and the heart or else the wounded man will die. Use a stick or other thin device to tighten the handkerchief. (Otherwise known as a tourniquet).

21. For a wound in the abdomen, make the wounded man comfortable, for this is fatal.

22. A full beard will give protection against dust and cold. Also will aid perspiration.

23. Avoid fats.

24. Keep your hair cut short and wash the scalp every morning.

25. Wear wool socks and loose shoes.

26. Keep toe and finger nails cut.

27. Wash feet in the evening and the hands and face in the mornings. This will keep the skin soft.

28. When hurt, the best position is on the back with the head elevated.

29. Put a coat on after a march to avoid a cold.

30. Get water to an injured person immediately. If you have no vessel, tie your shirt into a bag and use that.

31. If you are wet, keep moving and you will be all right.

32. If your cooking water comes from a pond or a sluggish stream, boil it, let it cool, and then stir it to get oxygen into it.

33. If you wear garish clothes in battle, you will be more likely to be hit. (A.P Hill liked to wear a bright red shirt in battle).

34. Envelop a canteen with a wet woolen cloth to chill the water.

35. During a rest stop in the march, lie down. You will get more rest.

36. A tablespoon of cornmeal in a glass of water will aid in "evacuation of the bowels." (A laxative?)

37. Loose bowels was the first step toward cholera and the remedy was a diet of boiled rice. If it was an advanced case, wrap the abdomen tightly in flannel.

And with remedies such as these, it's a wonder anybody survived:

1. Thieves Vinegar: Take a handful each of rue, sage, mint, rosemary, wormwood, and lavender and put into a gallon of vinegar to infuse. Let sit in a warm place for four days. Strain the mixture and then add one ounce of camphor. Wash the face and hands with it before exposure in a hospital or sick room. It is called Thieves Vinegar

because of a legend of thieves using this liquid to protect them as they plundered the houses of people sick with Bubonic Plague at Marseilles, France.

2. Prevention of Mosquito Bites: Mix oil of pennyroyal with olive oil and spread on the skin to repel mosquitoes.

3. Sprains and Bruises: mix one pint of train oil, ½ pound of stone pitch, ½ pound of resin, ½ pound of beeswax, and ½ pound of stale tallow. Boil for ½ an hour and skin off any scum. Pour liquid into cups to cool. When needed, spread it on a cloth and apply it to the sprain or bruise.

    In Paris, the treatment for a sprain was to have the doctor grease his thumbs and press them on the sprain for ½ hour. Within one day, the pain was relieved.

    A specific treatment for a sprained ankle was to wash the ankle with salted water and keep the foot as cold as possible. Elevate the foot, don't eat too much, and take a "cooling medicine" until the sprain is cured.

    Another cure for a bruise was to bath the area with water and apply a paper or cloth spread with treacle.

4. Stings: Take a wine glass of vinegar and mix in common (baking) soda. Apply it to the affected areas.

    Another treatment was to apply a plaster of moistened salt. This was to draw out the venom of a bee or wasp sting.

5. Blisters on the feet: Rub the feet with spirits mixed with tallow from a candle.

6. Dirt in the Eye: Place a finger on the affected patients cheek and slightly pull down, exposing the area under the eye. For over the eye, use a knitting needle over the eyelid to hold it up. Use a silk handkerchief to remove the dirt. Bathe the eye and have the patient

stay out of the sun for the day. If there is any inflammation, have the patient take a purgative and apply a cooling lotion.

7. Frostbite: For the feet, apply deer's marrow to the affected area.

    For other areas, take chrome yellow and hog's lard and mix them into an ointment. Apply to affected areas after warming the ointment.

8. Coughs: Take one teacup of molasses, add two tablespoons of vinegar and bring to a simmer. Then add three teaspoons of paregoric and as much refined niter as you can place on a breakfast knife. Take two or three teaspoons before bed and one of two during the day to dispel coughs.

9. Nosebleed: Blow powdered gum Arabic or alum up the nose with a quill to stop the bleeding.

10. Headaches: Use epodeldoe, spirits of wine, and sal ammoniac applied as a lotion to the forehead.

11. Bleeding Wounds: Apply flour and lint to the wound.

12. Infectious wounds: Apply sugar to the wound. Another procedure is to wash the wound with wine, then apply sugar.

13. Warts: Wet the wart with tobacco juice and apply chalk. Another method is to rub the area with fresh beef.

14. Corns: Mix and melt together two ounces of beeswax and two ounces of ammonia. Then add ½ ounce of verdigris. Spread on linen and apply it to the corn.

15. Bunions: If caught early, bind the foot tightly to prevent bunion growth. If inflames, a poultice of twelve grains of iodine and a ½ ounce of lard can be applied. This should be done two to three times daily. If the bunion is enlarged, apply salad oil. Wear lose shoes or slippers.

16. Boils: Treatment is a poultice of molasses or honey mixed with flour. Apply until it disappears. If the boil is painful, a poultice of bread, milk, volatile liniment and laudanum should be used.

Or, when one was sick, these nutritional tidbits:

1. Panada: Take some bread slices, cut off the crust, and boil then in water. After five minutes, take out the bread and pound it in a bowl, adding a little of the water it was boiled in. Mix in butter, sugar, and nutmeg to taste.

2. Toast Water: Take one slice of bread and toast it. Lay the toast in a bowl and pour on boiling water. Cover bowl with a saucer and let cool.

3. Beef Tea: Take one pound of beef and slice it into thin strips. Add salt and boil it in water for an hour. Pour through a strainer into a cup and serve.

4. Broth: Take meat (chicken, beef, or veal), add two tablespoons of rice and boil it until tender. If needed, serve the broth fifteen minutes after boiling, otherwise cover and keep overnight.

5. Water Gruel: Start with two tablespoons of cornmeal or oatmeal with three tablespoons of water. Mix a pint and a half of boiling water slowly to the mixture. Once everything is mixed, put the whole mixture in a skillet and boil it for thirty minutes. Skim the mixture and season with salt. Sugar and nutmeg can also be used.

6. Rice Gruel: Mix one tablespoon of rice, one and a half pints of water, and either a cinnamon stick or lemon peel. Boil it until soft and add a pint of milk. Strain the mixture and add salt, sugar, nutmeg, and butter to taste.

7. Milk Porridge: Same as the gruel but with equal parts of flour, cornmeal, milk and water. The flour, cornmeal and water are cooked first, and then the milk is added prior to boiling.

8. Mutton Custard for Bowel complaints: Take two ounces of mutton suet and shred it. Add cinnamon and nutmeg and boil it in a pint of milk. Skim off any scum that rises. Take a half teacup of this three or four times a day.

9. Bread Jelly: Boil a quart of water and set it aside. Take a 1/3 loaf of bread, cut off the crust, and toast it. Put the toast into the water and boil it slowly until the liquid turns into jelly. Strain the mixture and set it aside. When used, sweeten it with sugar and a little lemon peel.

10. Wine Whey: Boil a ½ pint of milk. Add two glasses of wine and a teaspoon of sugar. After the mixture boils, take it off the fire and set aside. Curds (solids) will form and sink to the bottom of the pot. Pour the whey (liquid) into another pot and add boiling water. Add sugar to taste. Use in cases of typhus.

11. Calves Feet Broth: Take two calves feet and boil them in three quarts of water. When water is half boiled away, take off the fat, season with salt, and serve in a teacup with a spoonful of wine.

12. Rice Jelly: Take ¼ pound of rice, mix in ½ pound of sugar, and add enough water to cover it. Boil until it becomes glutinous. Strain it and set it aside. Season to taste.

13. Hot Lemonade: Cut up a whole lemon, add a teacup of sugar and boiling water. Great for colds.

Some of these "cures" and advice often contributed to killing the patient. For example: Confederate General Thomas Jackson was recovering from having his left arm amputated following his wounding at the Battle of Chancellorsville. He had a stomach complaint that was remedied by wrapping the abdomen with cold, wet towels. This caused the pneumonia that killed him.

Another thing to consider was the advancement of military hardware. Thirty years before the Civil War, the US Army's main long arm was a smoothbore musket with a flintlock ignition system that took a ball slightly smaller than the barrel, which resulted in low accuracy over long ranges. A French officer named Claude Minie developed a bullet that was cone shaped with a base that expanded to fit the barrel when the powder charge was fired. This, plus the addition of rifling and a percussion ignition system, increased the accuracy and lethality of the long arm dramatically. A charging column of infantry could now be hit at longer ranges with relative ease.

When a Minie ball struck a person, the damage was horrific. The bullet did not have a metal jacket around it, so the lead cone turned into a mushroom upon entering the body, causing more damage. This round traveled at speeds slowed than today's supersonic bullets, so heat was not generated, which would have cauterized blood vessels. The slow, tumbling, lead mushrooms smashed bones, pulped organs and tore blood vessels, making death almost certain.

When the round struck bone, it would not break, but shatter laterally. This is why most leg and arm wounds resulted in amputation.

A headshot was usually fatal.

A hit in either the upper or lower torso meant death, but slow and very painful. It was possible to survive that, but it would not have been easy.

Another thing to consider was infection, foreign objects, such as the cloth of a uniform, was dragged into the wound, causing complications. This happened to Union Major General Winfield Hancock. On Day Three of the Battle of Gettysburg, he was on a horse overseeing the defenses at Cemetery Ridge and observing the approaching Pickett-Pettigrew-Trimble charge. During the exchange of musket fire, a Minie bullet struck the pommel of his saddle, tearing off a small nail and a bit of the leather, and drove the mess into Hancock's right hip. He managed to remove the nail, even joking that the Confederates were running out of bullets and resorting to shooting nails, but never fully recovered from the wound.

As the war went on, a system of getting the wounded to medical attention was developed by Dr Jonathan Letterman, the Medical Director for the

Army of the Potomac. For this system to function, an Ambulance Corps was established so patients could be moved quickly from the battlefield to the field hospital. More often than not, friends, or stretcher-bearers who were made up of musicians carried the wounded soldier. There was a position where the ambulance could be found, but the usual case was that the wounded soldier was carried all the way. Sadly, causality collection was not as efficient as claimed, resulting in wounded soldiers lying on the battlefield for as many as 48 hours, many of dying from wounds that would have been survivable if the soldier was taken to the field hospital.

Upon arrival at the field hospital, the wounded was subjected to a triage method that divided them into at least three categories:

1. Those with minor wounds that could wait on treatment.

2. Those with wounds that were survivable with treatment (this was usually the amputations).

3. Those with mortal wounds. No treatment was prescribed except to make the patient as comfortable as possible.

These hospitals were set up in farmhouses, barns, or any shelter that came to hand. The conditions on such places were not ideal, with surgeries being performed on planks or a door placed on sawhorses. The surgery "table" might be washed between operations, but that was not guaranteed. The surgeon's instruments, the scalpels, bone saws, and probes, were usually not sterilized, so infections were passed on from patient to patient. The surgeon's collection of instruments resembled a carpenter's toolbox rather than a doctor's kit. Ether and chloroform was used to put the patient to sleep, but if that was in short supply, that did not stop the doctor. A skilled physician could complete an amputation within 15 minutes, and then be ready for the next one. The limbs were supposed to be burned, but more often than not, they were piled outside. One Union soldier's account told of pigs eating the amputated limbs.

After treatment, the patient could either be returned to duty (minor wounds), or sent out of the area to a regional military hospital. If possible, the soldier could be sent home to fully recover (called recovery leave).

> *The heart-rendering scene at the hospital is one I would like to forget. Piles of dead soldiers were all around, and lying in rows were others who were dying. Doctors and their assistants were moving among the wounded, examining and aiding those who were not beyond help. The screams from the operating table resounded through the woods, for the surgeons were taking off arms and legs of a succession on men carried to them. Teams drawing ambulances were being urged to hasten, hauling the wounded from the field and back to a safer place. Other wagons were collecting and bringing in more wounded. They were being unloaded like so many butchered hogs, and the wagon beds were streaming blood. Once unloaded, the wagons were off to the front again, to collect more unfortunates. Many were dead when unloaded, others die soon afterwards.*
> *—Confederate Lieutenant William C. Thompson, 6th Mississippi, following the battle of Shiloh.*

Both sides organized large-scale hospitals in order to care for the wounded. Union hospitals were established in Washington D.C. as well as many other cities in the North. Washington alone boasted 25 hospitals, both military and private. Add to this the convalescent camps, and the Union had a somewhat decent system in order to treat the wounded.

One innovation that resulted was a Nursing Corps that was staffed by females. Women were already working as government clerks, but wanted to do more. Louisa May Alcott, who would write *Little Women*, worked in a hospital.

Dorothea Dix, a social activist, was instrumental in recruiting women for the Nursing Corps. She did have some rather peculiar qualifications, no women under 30 and they could not be pretty.

Clara Barton did not qualify to work with Dix, but that did not stop her from attaining a position at another hospital. She would go on to create the American Red Cross. She worked with another nurse, Susie King Taylor, who became the only African-American to publish a memoir of her war experiences.

Mary Ann "Mother" Bickerdyke was so successful in the Western Theatre that by order of Major General William T. Sherman, she was the only woman allowed in his hospitals.

Another nurse, this one male, was the poet Walt Whitman, who worked in several hospitals after nursing his wounded brother back to health.

Not only there were women nurses, but at least one woman doctor, Dr. Mary Walker.

The Confederates were not without their own system of helping their wounded. Even hampered with lack of supplies and facilities, they did manage to create a model hospital, Chimborazo, at Richmond, VA.

Southern nurses included Kate Cummings, who defied Southern attitudes towards women to become a nurse, as well as Sally Louisa Tomkins, who was commissioned a Captain in the Confederate Army for her work.

With resources being stretched, it soon fell on private organizations to pitch in and help. The U.S. Sanitary Commission and the U.S. Christian Commission brought food, clothing, and comfort to troops in the field and in the hospital, even running several private hospitals. Several states also formed organizations so that their troops could be helped.

Sadly, beyond a few private organizations, there were no Sanitary Commissions in the CSA.

Common 19th Century Medical Terms:

Ague: Recurring fever as a result of malaria.
Amaurosis: Loss of sight.
Asthenia: Weakness.
Bilious Attack: Nausea, abdominal distress, constipation, and headaches.
Black Vomit: Caused by blood collecting in the stomach due to other conditions.
Bright's Disease: Kidney disorder.
Cardiac Paralysis: What a cardiac arrest was called.
Consumption: What tuberculosis was called.
Cyanche: Sore throat.
Dropsy: Accumulation of fluid in a body cavity or under the skin.
Dyspepsia: Discomfort of the stomach. This seemed to be a common ailment.
Grippe: Influenza.
Mortification: Death.
Necrosis: Dead cells in any part of the body.
Pneumonia: Inflamed lungs.
Prostration: Exhaustion.
Pyemia: Blood poisoning.
Suppuration: Infection with pus.
Syncope: Fainting.
Torpid: Weakness.
Variola: Smallpox.

Soldier Speak

It is amazing that terms used in speaking change from year to year, let alone from a century and a half ago. The following terms were used by both Union and Confederate soldiers:

Absquatulate—to leave in a rush.
Acknowledge the corn—confess to a hoax.
Advertise—to make something public.
Advice—information that was gathered by scouts, spies, or cavalry reconnaissance.
Affair—a small engagement, such as a skirmish.
Aggregate—to gather scattered units into a formation, usually done in the heat of battle.
Amuse—tactic of keeping an enemy occupied without bringing on a general engagement.
Annoy—to harass the enemy.
Ardent—an enthusiastic person.
Argee—bad liquor.
Arkansas toothpick—knife.
Army Grayback—lice.
Artificer—a skilled mechanic.
Avalanche—a derisive term for a two-wheeled ambulance.
Awkward squad—new troops yet to see battle.
Baby waker—the first shot before an artillery bombardment. Usually called a ranging round.
Bait—feed a horse.
Bailed Hay—referred to a block of dried and compressed mixed vegetables issued to soldiers to liven up the diet.
Band Box Regiments—Union regiments that did a lot of drill, but didn't

see battle until late in the war. Its usual reference was to the "Heavy Artillery" regiments that were formed from the units that were stationed at the forts surrounding Washington. Most of them did not keep that reference for long.

Bark Juice—hard liquor.

Barrack Hack—one who avoided drilling. Also referred to a prostitute.

BC—stood for Brigade Commissary. Usually stamped on crates of hardtack.

Beat—a sentry's post. Also referred to a shirker.

Beat up—to dislodge an enemy from a position.

Bee Gun—a hat with a conical top.

Beehive—a knapsack.

Beeves—cattle.

Belly Robber—an army cook.

Bermuda Bacon—this was meat purchased in the North, sent to Bermuda, then transferred to a Confederate blockade-runner, and then on to a Confederate port.

Big ticket—a soldier's honorable discharge.

Birdcage—a gambling game where players bet on the result of a roll of three dice.

Birdie—a prisoner of war.

Blackberry Picker—a straggler. (Probably a reference to green troops on their way to Manassas Junction in 1861, who broke ranks and picked blackberries.)

Blenker—to forage.

Blizzard—heavy musket fire.

Blueback—Confederate currency.

Bluebelly—a Union soldier.

Bog-trotter—a soldier of Irish background.

Bone Yard—the prison cemetery.

Borrowed—referred to theft, foraging, or pillaging.

Bought the Farm—died in battle.

Bounty Jumper—one who would sign up to join a regiment, only to desert after collecting the bounty money.

Bowlegs—a cavalryman.

Boys of the sod—Irish immigrants.

Bragg's bodyguard—lice.

Bread Bag—a rubberized haversack.

Brevet Horse—an Army mule.

Bullpen—an enclosed part of a stockade where prisoners were kept.

Bully—a term of affirmation.

Bully Soup—hot cereal made from corn meal and crushed hardtack.

Bumblebee—bullet.

Bummer—a forager. Made popular during Sherman's March to the Sea.

Bummers Roost—any place safe from the heat of battle.

Busby—an elaborate bearskin headpiece.

Bushwhacker—Confederate guerillas.

Busthead—homemade (or campmade) liquor.

Butcher's Bill—the causality list.

Butternut—Confederate soldier. Also referred to homespun uniforms dyed with walnut shells.

Buzzard—a straggler who was also a thief.

Cabbaging—to steal.

Camp Canard—gossip.

Camp Followers—non-military personnel following an army in the field.

Camp of Instruction—the closest thing to a boot camp either side had.

Canaan—Heaven, the Hereafter.

Candlestick—a bayonet.

Cap-a-pie—informal dress.

Cards—small loaves of cornbread that were the size of playing cards.

Carpet soldier—militia units that managed to avoid front line service.

Cashier—a dishonorable discharge.

Cattle—what Southern soldiers called their Northern counterparts.

Celerity; to be fast.

Change your breath—to drink hard liquor.

Cheese Knife—an officer's sword.

Chicken Guts—braiding on an officer's uniform.

Chicken Heart Disease—battle fatigue.

Chinch—Bedbugs.

Chit—paper currency issued within the army or even a separate unit.

Chuck-a-luck—a gambling game using dice.

Coffee Boiler—a straggler.

Coffee Cooler—another term for a straggler.

Company Bean Boiler—the cook.

Confederate Beef—mule meat.

Contraband—escaped slaves who made it to the Union lines.

Copperhead—Northerners who supported the Confederacy.

Corduroy Road—a road made of logs and/or fence rails laid across a dirt path.

Corked in a bottle—a situation where movement was impossible.

Corncrackers—Kentuckians.

Corn dodgers—cornbread shaped into patties.

Cracker outfits—sutlers.

Critter Company—Southern term for cavalry.

Croaker—a pessimist.

Crooked Shoe—Federal Army footwear fitted to a person's feet. Due to the need to mass produce shoes for the Union, footwear was not shaped to a person's right or left foot.

Cross on Confederate pontoons—to wade across a stream.

Dance—the battle.

Deadbeat—a soldier excused from the fighting.

Dead Cart-an ambulance.

Deadhead—a coward.

Deadwood—a coward.

Desecrated Vegetables— what the block of dried and compressed mixed vegetables issued to soldiers to liven up the diet was usually called.

Desiccated Vegetables— the block of dried and compressed mixed vegetables

Dispatched—killed.

Dog Robber—a cook.

Doodle—what some Southerners called Union soldiers.

Doughboy—what cavalrymen called infantrymen.

Down the line—an area of a town where the brothels were.

Doxy—a mistress.

Draw over the left—to steal.

Drum out—a dishonorable discharge.

Dutch—term for German, derived from *deutsch*.

Eat the dishrag—eating the piece of bread that was used to clean the gravy off a plate.

Embalmed beef—canned beef.

Faith paper—paper currency.

Fast little trick—prostitute.

Feather-bed fighter—a soldier who managed to get the cushy jobs and avoided combat.

Ferryboat—term for a pair of shoes that could be worn on either foot.

Forage—to gather food from the countryside.

Forty Dead Men—a soldier's basic load of 40 cartridges.

Forty-rod—very bad whisky.

French Leave—unauthorized leave in which the soldier returns.

Fresh Fish—new recruits or newcomers to a prisoner of war camp.

Furlough—legal leave of absence.

Furniture—accoutrements.

Galoot—a replacement soldier

Galvanized Confederate—a Union soldier who defects to the Confederacy.

Galvanized Yankees—a Confederate soldier who defects to the Union.

Give the vermin parole—to get rid of body lice without killing them.

Go in search of his rights—a soldier who fled the battlefield.

Gold Brick—a slovenly soldier.

Goober Grabber—a soldier of North Carolina or Georgia. (Goobers are peanuts)

Gopher Hole—bomb shelter, or bombproof.

Government livery—a uniform.

Grab a root—eat potatoes.

Grayback—a Confederate soldier. Also what Union soldiers called lice.

Greenback—Federal currency.

Green Troops—new soldiers with little or no training.

Gump—a fool.

Havelock—white covering for a cap or kepi, did not last too long in service.

Hayfoot/Strawfoot—how some soldiers learned to tell their left foot (hay was tied to the left shoe) and right foot (straw was tied to the right shoe).

Hellmira—what Southerners called the Union prisoner-of-war camp at Elmira, NY.

High Private—a rich person who did not want to wrangle an officer's commission.

Hireling—a Southern term for Union soldiers.

Hog and hominy—a term for Southern food.

Hog drivers—Tennesseans.

Holy Joe—a chaplain.

Hooker—a prostitute. Not attributed to Union Major General Joseph Hooker, but possibly to the red light district of New York City.

Hop, Skip, and Jump—a two wheeled ambulance.

Hornets—bullets (for the buzzing sound they made as they flew past).

Hospital Rat—a soldier who fakes illness.

Hotel de Libby—what Libby Prison in Richmond, VA was called.

Housewife—a sewing kit.

How come you so—an alcoholic beverage.

Hunt gold—to be in combat for the first time.

Instant—refers to a date of the current month (Ex: on the 19th instant).

Johnnies—Confederate soldiers.

Jonah—one with bad luck.

Josh—a Confederate soldier from Arkansas.

Junk—Beef preserved by heavy amounts of salt. Practically inedible.

Katydid—inexperienced soldiers.

Lamp Post—large naval artillery shell.

Layouts—Southerners who hid out to escape conscription.

Lead mine—a dead or wounded soldier with multiple wounds.

Leg case—desertion.

Let her go, Gallagher!!—fire with everything you got.

Lincoln coffee—Northern coffee (the real stuff).

Lincoln hirelings—Southern term for Union soldiers.

Lincoln pie—hardtack.

Lobster Backs—US Marines (even though their uniform was blue with white trousers).

Long Home—grave.

Loose Bowels—surgeon.

Lop-ears—Germans.

Lucifers—matches.

McClellan pie—hardtack.

Metal—courage.

Mossyback—draft dodger.

Mud Heads—Mississippians.

Mud Hook—an anchor.

Mudscows—shoes.

Mud Sills—Confederate term for Union soldiers.

Mugger—a prisoner who attacks fellow prisoners (EX: the Raiders at Andersonville)

Muggins—a scoundrel.

Mule—what we would call Mystery Meat today.

Mustered out-to be formally discharged, usually when a unit was too small to be combat effective and was disbanded. Also occurred when a soldier's term of enlistment expired.

Nationals—Union soldiers.

Niddering—cowardly.

Old Bull—salted horsemeat.

Oldest—term for veterans in a unit.

Old Regular—a soldier who was in the Regular Army prior to the Civil War.

Open the Ball—start the battle.

Oysters—nothing to do with seafood. This was made with cornmeal, eggs, and butter.

Paleface—a new recruit.

Paper Collar Soldiers—soldiers on garrison duty in safe areas.

Peas on a trencher—call for breakfast.

Penny Packet—small quantities.

Pepperbox—a multishot pistol.

Pig sticker—bayonet.

Pigeon Roost—sentry box on a wall or fence.

Play Old Soldier—faking illness.

Pop-skull—illegal whiskey.

Possum Beer—homebrewed beverage made from persimmons.

Powder Monkey—one assigned to carry shells and powder to the artillery piece.

Pumpkin Rind—Union Lieutenant.

Pumpkin Slingers—large caliber Austrian or Prussian muskets.

Quaker Gun—a log painted black and positioned to simulate artillery.

Quickstep—a fast march or diarrhea.

Rag out—formal dress.

Ramrod Bread—bread made by plastering cornmeal on a ramrod and holding it over a fire.

Rations—food.

Razorback—a prisoner of war who was an informer.

Reb—Confederate soldier or civilian.

Rebel Conch—costal Floridian.

Rebel Rag—Confederate Flag.

Red-eye—bad whiskey.

Rodomontade—vain talk.

Robbers Row—where the sutlers set up their shops.

Rogue's March—what was played when one was being drummed out of the service.

Rotgut—bad whiskey.

Running the Blockade—sneaking out of camp, as well as sneaking back in.

Sacred Dust—a corpse.

Salt Horse—beef or pork preserved by salting.

Salt Fish—veterans.

Sandlapper—South Carolinian.

Sauerkraut—German immigrant.

Sawbones—surgeon.

Scratch—test of character.

Scrip—money issued by sutlers for use at the issuers store.

Scuttlebutt—gossip.

Scyugle—a word that could mean anything.

Sea pie—has no seafood. It's a mixture of meat and vegetables in a crust.

Secesh—Northern term for Southern soldiers and civilians.

Secession bread—bread made from rice flour.

See the Elephant—going into battle for the first time.

See Tick Coffee—a Confederate coffee substitute.

Shavetail—a Second Lieutenant.

Shebang—temporary hut of shelter.

Sheep Dip—bad whiskey.

Shellback—a veteran.

Sherman's Neckties—railroad rails that were pulled up, heated over a fire, and wrapped around the nearest pole or tree.

Sherman's sentinels—chimneys left after the house was burned down.

Shinplaster—paper currency.

Short-timer—a soldier whose term of enlistment was about to expire.

Sin away the day of grace—referred to Southerners in Federal occupied territory who still expressed loyalty to the Confederacy.

Sinks—latrines.

Skedaddler—soldier who fled the battlefield.

Skulker—soldier who made it a point to avoid combat.

Slow Bears—Union term for pigs.

Smell powder—to see action.

Snipe—to distract a person so that his food can be stolen.

Soap—money.

Sold—deceived.

Somebody's darling—an unidentified corpse.

Spitfire—musket or rifle.

Spondulics—a quantity of money.

Spotted papers—playing cards.

Squashmolished—a word that combined the words squashed and demolished.

Squirrel Hunters—term for volunteers from rural Ohio.

Stove rat—a prisoner of war who hogged the stove for heat during winter.

Straggler—a soldier who purposely wanders off from his unit in order to avoid combat.

Sunday soldier—insult referring to soldiers of little use.

Swallow the yellow dog—when a Confederate takes the Federal oath of Allegiance.

Taking a twist of the tiger—playing a game of chance.

Taking the cars—taking a train.

Tap-the stump of an amputated leg.

Tar Heel—North Carolinian.

Ticket to Dixie—someone who was drafted into service.

Tigers—Louisianans.

Toad Sticker—a bayonet or sword.

Toothpick—knife.

Tosspot—alcoholic.

Tumbler over—killed.

Turkey driver—Federal Provost Marshall

Turnspit—useless person.

Uhlans—foragers.

Ultimo—refers to a date of the previous month. (Ex: the 25th ultimo).

Used up—a unit that was depleted by combat, sickness, or desertion.

Veal—a soldier that has not seen battle.

Wagon Dog—a soldier who fakes illness in order to avoid combat.

War Horse—a veteran.

Webfoot—a soldier without shoes.

Web-footed cavalry—what the cavalry called infantry.

Wet goods—whisky.

White glove boys—what Eastern Federal soldiers were called by Western soldiers.

Wolfhounds—Confederate soldiers.

Wolverines—Michiganders.

Yaller Dog—a coward.

Yankee—a Northern soldier or civilian. Also a Southern term for lying.

Yankee's devils—Union artillery.

Yankee well—an escape tunnel.

Yellowback—novels sold by sutlers.

Yellow Belly—coward.

Yellow Hammer—Alabamian.

Yunnk—an unpopular individual

It wasn't all done by the Army, you know!

The Navy

Union:

Pre-Civil War strength: 1563 officers and 7500 enlisted were in the US Navy at the outbreak of the Civil War. Of the officers, 321 resigned their commissions when their states seceded.

The pre-CW Navy consisted of:

21 sloops of war (sail powered): 5 in Home Squadron, 4 in the East Indies, 2 in the Mediterranean, 1 near Brazil, 3 patrolling the African Coast, and 6 in the Pacific.

12 steamers (steam powered ships): 4 in Home Squadron, 1 in the East Indies, 1 in the Mediterranean, 1 near Brazil, 4 patrolling the African Coast, and 1 in the Pacific.

3 frigates: 1 in Home Squadron, 1 in the East Indies, and 1 near Brazil.

2 storeships: 1 in the Home Squadron and 1 patrolling the African Coast.

One advantage the North had was the ability to draw upon civilian sources for ships and personnel and they were able to control the possession of the Navy Yards, with their dry docks and maintenance facilities. The Confederates briefly held the Norfolk Navy Yard but they had to give that up in 1862. Pensacola Navy Yard could not be taken as long as the Union held Fort Pickens.

The main problem was that even as President Lincoln ordered the blockade of Southern ports, there were not enough ships to even begin one. It was fortunate that Lincoln had Gideon Welles as Secretary of the Navy. He embarked on a program of not only constructing new ships, but also buying civilian ships for conversion to war vessels. Finding volunteers to crew them were not too hard: many civilians were run off the seas by the presence of Confederate commerce raiders that were already making an influence.

Another advantage that the Union had was the ability to use new technologies, and the industrial base to exploit that advantage. Even though the Confederates were the first to deploy a warship with iron cladding on the outside, the Union was not far behind, and soon overtook the South in iron warship production.

The Blockade:

The coasts of the CSA were segmented into four zones by the time a proper blockade was in place, in 1862.

North Atlantic Blockading Squadron:

Commanders:
Flag Officer Louis M. Goldsborough (1861-1862)
Rear Admiral Samuel P. Lee (1862-1864)
Rear Admiral David Dixon Porter (1864-1865)
Rear Admiral William Radford (1865)

Flagship: *Minnesota*
Ironclad steamer: *Roanoke*
Steamers: *Fort Jackson, Shenandoah, Connecticut, St. Lawrence, Keystone State, Hetzel, Florida, Louisiana, Cambridge, State of Georgia, Mercedita, Maratanza, Morse, Nansemond, Southfield, Niphon, Daylight, Montgomery, Commodore Perry, Mount Vernon, Britannia, Governor Buckingham, Houquah, Lockwood, Underwriter, Calypso, Commodore*

Barney, Commodore Hull, Wyandotte, Mt. Washington, Commodore Jones, Stepping Stones, Lilack, Young Rover, Mystic, Emma, General Putnam, Victoria, Hunchback, Shawsheen, Samuel Rotan, Whitehead, Cohasset, Fab-Kee, and *Seymour.*
Gunboat: *Miami.*
Supply ship: *Newbern.*
Support ship: *Release.*
Sloop: *Granite.*
Tugboats: *Alert* and *Zouave.*
Storeship: *Albemarle.*

Area covered: Coasts of Virginia and North Carolina.

South Atlantic Blockading Squadron:

Commander:
Real Admiral John Dahlgren (1863-1865)

Flagship: *Wabash*
Ironclad Steamers: *Lehigh, Passaic, Nantucket, Montauk, Nahant, Patapsco, New Ironsides,* and *Catskill.*
Steamers: *Canandaigua, Housatonic, Pawnee, Sonoma, Paul Jones, Mahaska, Cimmaron, Nipsic, Chippewa, Unadilla, Ottawa, Huron, Water Witch, Marblehead, Wissahickon, Seneca, Memphis, Lodona, Flambeau, Commodore McDonough, Mohawk, Home, Potomska, Stettin, Iris, Philadelphia, O. M. Pettit, Norwich, Mary Sanford, E. G. Hale, South Carolina, Oleander, Geranium, Larkspur, Daffodil, Jonquil, Carnation, Clover, Dandelion,* and *Columbine.*
Barques: *Ethan Allen, Brazilliera, A. Houghton, Kingfisher, Fernandina,* and *Midnight.*
Schooners: *Hope, Dan Smith, F. A. Ward, Racer, C. P. Williams, George Mangham, Norfolk Packet,* and *Blunt.*
Ordinance sloop: *John Adams.*
Storeships: *Supply* and *Vermont.*

Area covered: Coasts of South Carolina, Georgia, and the East Florida coast to Key West. Main focus was on Charleston, SC.

East Gulf Blockading Squadron (ships assigned as of 1863):

Commanders:
Rear Admiral William Mervine (1861)
Flag Officer William McKean (1861-1862)

Flagship: *St Lawrence.*
Steamers: *San Jacinto, Penguin, Sagamore, Tahoma, Port Royal, Somerset, Lodona, Fort Henry, Huntsville, Magnolia,* and *Stars and Stripes.*
Barques: *Pursuit, Gemshok, James L. Davis, Roebuck, James S. Chambers, Amanda, Ethan Allen,* and *Houghton.*
Sloop of War: *Dale*
Schooners: *Eugenie, Beauregard,* and *Wanderer.*

Area covered: West Florida coast from Key West to the Alabama-Mississippi line.

West Gulf Blockading Squadron:
Commanders:
Rear Admiral David Farragut (1862-1864)
Flag Officer James Palmer (1864-1865)
Real Admiral Henry Thatcher (1865)

Flagship: *Hartford.*
Steamers: *Pensacola, Ossipee, Richmond, Lacawanna, Itasca, Monongahela, Metacomet, Oneida, Princess Royal, Seminole, Octorara, Kanawha, Genesee, Galena, Owasco, Katahdin, Port Royal, Chocura, Pembina, Penobscot, Kennebec, Pinola, Cayuga, Estrella, New London, Aroostook, Sciota, Arkansas, Albatross, John P. Jackson, Virginia, Pengyin, Tennessee, Arizona, Antona, Granite City, Jasmine, Hollyhock, Commodore,* and *Eugenie.*
Steam Frigate: *Colorado.*
Sloops: *Portsmouth* and *Vincennes.*
Barques: *W. G. Anderson, Arthur,* and *J. C. Kuhn.*
Brig: *Bohio* and *Seafoam.*
Support Ships: *Fearnot,* and *Nightingale.*
Barquentine: *Horace Beals.*
Yacht: *Corypheus.*

Schooners: *Maria Wood, Orvetta, John Griffiths, Sam Houston, Sarah Bruen, Henry James,* and *Oliver H. Lee.*
Storeship: *Potomac.*

Area covered: The coast from the Alabama-Mississippi line to the Rio Grande River (Texas-Mexico border).

Mississippi River Squadron:

Flagship: *Blackhawk.*
Ironclad Steamers: *Essex, Eastport, Lafayette, Benton, Louisville, Tuscumbia, Choctaw, Conestoga, Mound City, Lexington, Pittsburg, Chillicothe, Neosho, Carondelet,* and *Osage.*
Steamers: *Moose, Taylor, Forest Rose, Fort Hindman, Hastings, Brilliant, St. Clair, Silver Cloud, Covington, Queen City, Tawah, Key West, Peosta, Reindeer, General Price, General Bragg, Rattler, Exchange, Brown, Linden, Kenwood, Fair Play, Springfield, Fawn, Paw Paw, Naunkeag, Silver Lake, Champion, Alexandria, Great Western, Judge Torrence, New Era, Signal, Prairie Bird, Curlew, Little Rebel, Victory, Tensas, General Pillow, Bobb, Argosy, Ouachita, New National, General Lyon,* and *Samson.*
Hospital Steamer: *Red Rover.*
Tugboats: *Pansy, Fern, Thistle, Laurel, Mignonette, Daisy, Mistletoe, Myrtle, Dahlia, Hyacinth,* and *Ivy.*
Inspection Ship: *Abraham.*

Potomac River Flotilla:

Steamers: *Ella, Yankee, Commodore Read, Currituck, Jacob Bell, Fuchsia, Couer de Lion, Resolute, Freeborn, Anacostia, Wyandank, Tulip, Primrose, Teaser,* and *Dragon.*
Schooners: *Sophonia, Matthew Vassar, Adolph Hugel,* and *William Bacon.*

East India Squadron (Indonesia, Singapore):

Side-wheel sloops: *Saginaw* and *Wyoming.*

West Indian Squadron (Caribbean):
Side-wheel gunboat: *Tioga*.
Screw driven vessels: *Galatea* and *Neptune*.
Sloop: *Macedonian*.
Barque: *Gemsbok*.

Brazil Squadron (South Atlantic):

Screw driven vessel: *Wachusett*.
Side-wheel vessels: *Pulaski* and *Emma Henry*.
Mediterranean Squadron:

Screw driven vessel: *Iroquois*.
Sloop: *Constellation*.

European Squadron (North Atlantic, North Sea):

Frigate: *Niagara*.
Screw driven sloops: *Kearsarge* and *Sacramento*.

Africa Squadron:

Sloop: *Constellation* until 1862, then assigned to Mediterranean Squadron.

Pacific Squadron:

Barques: *Saranac, Fredonia,* and *Massachusetts*.
Side-wheel sloop: *Saginaw*.
Screw driven vessels: *Lancaster* and *Wyoming*.
Double-ended gunboat: *Wateree*.
Side-wheel gunboat: *Monongo*.
Storeships: *Falmouth* and *Relief*.
Sloops: *John Adams, Jamestown,* and *St. Mary's*.

Receiving ships:

These vessels served as basic training centers and never left port:

Allegheny, at Baltimore, MD.
North Carolina, at New York, NY.
Ohio, at Boston, MA.
Potomac, at Pensacola, FL.
Princeton, at Philadelphia, PA.
Clara Rolson and *Grampus*, assigned to the Mississippi River Squadron.
John Hancock, at San Francisco, CA.

Special Squadron:

This group was formed in January 1864 to hunt Confederate commerce raiders:

Steamers: *Mohican, Sacramento, Michigan, Wachusett,* and *Iroquois.*
Steam sloop: *Kearsarge.*
Support ship: *Onward.*
Sloop: *St. Louis.*

Confederate:

The South was not a seafaring region to begin with, but they had to become one in order to keep the field armies supplied. With this in mind, there were a few miracles, such as CSS *Virginia*, an ironclad warship, or the *H. L. Hunley*, a submarine. They did, however, have these insurmountable disadvantages:

Lack of industry: with one major factory and a few minor ones, the industrial base was just not there. Iron for cladding was rolled at the Tredegar Iron Works at Richmond, VA, from salvaged iron, railroad rails, even church bells.

Lack of facilities: The North had all the proper naval facilities, even in Southern territory. The Confederacy held the Norfolk Navy Yard long enough to build the *Virginia*, but had to abandon it. They made up for that by using fields, swamps, and inlets for construction sites.

Lack of trained personnel: Only 321 officers had left the US Navy for Southern service and almost no enlisted. The officers made a good core for the embryonic service, but the enlisted force had to be formed from scratch.

Lack of ships: since there was not a wholesale defection of Navy vessels, the CS Navy had to build that from scratch as well. CS President Davis started that by authorizing Letters of Marque and Reprisal, allowing privately owned ships to be used in military operations against Union shipping. These were considered pirates by the Federals and their crews subject to the death penalty, but not many cases were prosecuted. From these privateers came the commerce raiders that were the bane of the Union.

Ships basically had to be built, bought, or finagled from foreign sources.

All of this, under the auspices of Secretary of the Navy, Stephen Mallory.

Besides commerce raiding, the CS Navy was primarily a costal and river operations force, using small vessels to keep things going.

The vessels mentioned were with these particular fleets at one time or another. Some were destroyed or captured. Others were captured Union naval or civilian vessels.

Texas Costal Flotilla:

Gunboats: *Bayou City, Clifton, General Bee, Josiah H. Bell, Mary Hill,* and *Uncle Ben.*
Steamers: *A. S. Ruthven, Era No. 3, Florida, Grand Bay, Island City, Jeff Davis, John F. Carr, Lone Star, Lucy Gwinn, Neptune, Roebuck,* and *Sun Flower.*
Sail vessels: *Breaker, Dodge, Elma, Fanny Morgan, George Buckhart, Julia A. Hodges, Lecompt, Royal Yacht,* and *Velocity.*

Mississippi Defense Fleet:

Ironclad: *Louisiana*
Gunboats: *A. B. Seger, Anglo-Norman, Anglo-Saxon, Arrow, Barataria, Calhoun, Diana, Dollie Webb, General Quitman, Governor Moore, Ivy, Jackson, A. J. Cotton, James L. Day, McRae, Mobile, Oregon, Pamlico, Tuscaora, Webb,* and *Carondelet.*
Spar Torpedo Boat: *Pioneer.*
Rams: *Colonel Lovell, Defiance, General Beauregard, General Bragg, General Breckinridge, General Earl Van Dorn, General Lovell, General M. Jeff Thompson, General Sterling Price, General Sumter, Little Rebel, Resolute, Stonewall Jackson, Warrior,* and *Web.*
Sail vessels: *Coryphus,* and *Washington.*
Tugboats: *Bell, Algerine,* and *Boston.*
Steamers: *Dan, Darby, Empire Parish, General Quitman, Gossamer, Hart, Landis, Mosher, Music, Orizaba, St. Philip, Star, Texas,* and *W. Burton.*
Side-wheel vessel: *Phoenix.*
Floating Battery: *New Orleans.*

Mississippi River Fleet:

Ironclads: *Arkansas,* and *Missouri.*
Gunboats: *General Polk, Grand Duke, J. A. Cotton, Livingston, Maurepas, Pontchartrain, Queen of the West, St. Mary, Slidell,* and *Tom Sugg.*
Steamers: *Admiral, Alfred Robb, Argo, Argosy, Argus, B. M. Moore, Beauregard, Ben McCullough, Berwick Bay, Bracelet, Charm, Cheney, Clara Dolson, Cotton Plant, Countess, De Sota, Dew Drop, Doubloon, Dr. Batey, Dunbar, Edward J. Gay, Elmira, Emma Bett, Era No. 5, Fairplay, Fred Kennett, Frolic, Gordon Grant, Grampus, Grand Era, Gray Cloud, H. D. Mears, H. R. W. Hill, Hartford City, Hope, J. D. Clark, J. D. Swain, Jeff Davis, John Simonds, John Walsh, Julius, Kanawha Valley, Kaskaskia, Kentucky, Lady Walton, Linn Boyd, Louis D'Or, Louisville, Magenta, Magnolia, Mars, Mary E. Keene, Mary Patterson, May, Merite, Mohawk, Moro, Muscle, Natchez, Nelson, New National, Nina Simmes, Ohio Belle, Osceola, Pargoud, Paul Jones, Prince, Prince of Wales, R. J. Lockland, Red Rover, Republic, Robert Fulton, St. Francis No. 3, Sallie Wood, Sam Kirkman, Samuel Orr, Scotland, Sharp, Sovereign, Starlight, T. D. Hine,* 35th

Parallel, Trent, Twilight, Vicksburg, Victoria, Volunteer, W. W. Crawford, Wade Water Belle, White Cloud, and *Yazoo.*

Mobile Defense Squadron:
Ironclads: Huntsville, *Tuscaloosa* and *Tennessee II.*
Gunboats: *Gaines, Morgan, Baltic,* and *Selma.*
Steamers: *Alert, Crescent, Dick Keys,* and *James Battle.*
Spar Torpedo Boats: *St. Patrick, Mobile II,* and *Gunnison.*
Cutter: *Lewis Cass.*
Transport: *Iron King.*
Tender: *Swan.*
Floating Batteries: *Danube* and *Phoenix.*
Receiving Ship: *Dalman.*

Pensacola Defense Squadron:
Steamers: *Governor Milton, Berosa, Neafie, Helen,* and *Spray.*
Gunboat: *Chattahoochee.*
Transport: *Turel.*
Sloop: *Helen.*
Storeship: *Bradford.*

Savannah Defense Squadron:
Ironclads: *Atlanta* and *Savannah.*
Gunboats: *Macon* and *Isondiga.*
Steamers: *Amazon, Beauregard,* and *Jeff Davis.*
Tenders: *Firefly* and *Resolute.*
Transports: *General Lee, Ida, Leesburg, Robert Habersham,* and *Talomico.*
Sail Vessel: *Gallatin.*
Receiving Ships: *Sampson,* and *Savannah.*
Floating Battery: *Georgia.*

Charleston Defense Squadron:
Ironclads: *Chicora, Palmetto State, Charleston,* and *Columbia.*
Gunboat: *Peedee.*
Steamers: *Chesterfield, Darlington,* and *Lady Davis.*
Spar Torpedo Boat: *David, Midge, Torch, Numbers 1 through 8,* and *H. L. Hunley* (officially listed as a spar torpedo boat, but this was a submarine).

Sail Vessel: *Petrel.*
Tenders: *Catawba, Aid,* and *General Clinch.*
Transports: *Etiwan, Huntress, Marion, Planter, Queen Mah, Sumter,* and *Transport.*
Receiving Ship: *Indian Chief.*

North Carolina Coast and River Fleet:
Ironclads: *Albemarle, Nuese, North Carolina,* and *Raleigh.*
Gunboats: *Fanny, Ellis, Seabird, Uncle Ben,* and *Yadkin.*
Steamers: *Appomattox, Bombshell, Clarrendon, Cotton Plant, Curlew, Currituck, Dolly, Egypt Mills, Equator, Forrest, Governor Morehead, Junaluska, Weldon N. Edwards,* and *Winslow.*
Tender: *Caswell.*
Floating Battery: *Artic.*
Transports: *Albemarle, Colonel Hill, Hawley,* and *Wilson.*
Sail Vessels: *Black Warrior, Jeff Davis, Manassas,* and *Renshaw.*
Storeship: *M. C. Etheridge.*

Virginia Coast and River Fleet (except James River):
Ironclad: *Virginia.*
Spar Torpedo Boats: *Scorpion* and *Squib.*
Gunboats: *Jamestown, Satellite,* and *Teaser.*
Steamers: *Curtis Peck, General Scott, City of Richmond, Harmony, Logan, Northampton, Rappahannock, Reliance: Roanoke, Rondout, Towns,* and *Young America.*
Tugboats: *John B. White* and *Pohowatan.*
Sail Vessels: *Beauregard, Duane,* and *Germantown.*
Receiving Vessel: *Confederate States.*

James River Squadron:
Ironclads: *Virginia II, Richmond,* and *Fredericksburg.*
Gunboats: *Beauford, Drewry, Hampton, Nansemond, Raleigh/Roanoke, Patrick Henry* (CS Naval Academy), and *Torpedo.*
Steamers: *Allison, Beaufort, Schultz, Seaboard,* and *Shrapnel.*
Spar Torpedo Boats: *Hornet* and *Wasp.*
Torpedo Boat Tender: *Torpedo.*
Sail Vessel: *Gallego.*

Commerce Raiders: *Alabama, Alexandria, Florida, Georgia, Georgiana, Nashville, Rappahannock, Shenandoah, Sumter, Tallahassee, Tacony,* and *Tuscaloosa.*

CS Government Blockade Runners: *Bat, Deer, Owl, Stag, Lark, Wren, Condor, Falcon, Flamingo, Ptarmigan, Arizona, Atlantic, Austin, Beauregard, Bahama, Bermuda, Colonel Lamb, Hope, Cornubia, Don, Granite City, Greyhound, Harriet Pickney, Juno, Laurel, Lynx, Magnolia, Matagorda, Merrimac, Phantom, Robert E. Lee, Theodora, Victoria,* and *William G. Hawes.*

How many of you know that these guys were around?

The Marines (The USMC and CSMC)

There has not been much information on the role of the Marines in the Civil War. Their traditional role, ship security and small scale land missions were not called for in the major land battles of the war. Still, US Marines played a part in the eventual Union victory.

Union:

In 1861 the US Marine Corps consisted of the Commandant, usually a Colonel, a Major who had the dual jobs of Adjutant and Inspector, another Major who was the Paymaster, a Quartermaster, another Major, and an Assistant Quartermaster, a Captain, making up the Command Section.

Operations consisted of a Lieutenant Colonel, four Majors, 13 Captains, 20 First Lieutenants, 20 Second Lieutenants, 101 Sergeants, 137 corporals, and 1347 Privates. This was raised to include one additional Colonel, one additional Lieutenant Colonel, one additional Assistant Quartermaster, seven more Captains, 10 more First Lieutenants, and 10 more Second Lieutenants. An additional enlisted strength of 220 corporals, and 2500 privates was authorized.

The US Marine Corps was the size of almost three standard Civil War regiments (a brigade).

Marines played a role in pre-Civil War tensions: it was a detachment of

Marines, led by US Army Colonel Robert E. Lee, who put down John Brown's Revolt in 1859.

The addition of more Marines was authorized after a detachment of 13 Officers and 336 Enlisted were among those running from the battlefield at First Bull Run (Manassas, VA). Some of these additions were used to replace officers who had resigned their commissions and joined the newly created Confederate States Marine Corps.

Noted missions that the Marines were a part of was an assault on Fort Sumter, Charleston, SC on 8 September 1863, an engagement at Honey Hill, SC in 1864, and the assault on Fort Fisher, 15 January 1865 as part of a sailor/Marine force.

Marine uniforms were a little bit different then the Army's. The headgear was the traditional kepi with a badge consisting of an "M" set in a red oval. The blouse was the same as the Army's and was colored the same shade of blue. The trousers were white instead of sky blue. Enlisted rank was noted by upward pointing red chevrons while the officer rank was marked by the use of Russian Knots instead of the rank badges the Army used.

Confederate:

The CS Marine Corps was initially made up of six companies officered by former US Marine officers. The Corps was commanded by a Colonel, with a Lieutenant Colonel, three Majors (adjutant, paymaster, and quartermaster), a Sergeant Major, a Quartermaster Sergeant, and two Musicians in the Command Section.

Operations were conducted at the company level with a total 10 Captains, 10 First Lieutenants, 20 Second Lieutenants, 40 Sergeants, 40 Corporals, and 840 Privates, barely the size of a standard Army regiment.

The companies were assigned thus:

Company A: formed at New Orleans in 1861 and was assigned to Richmond in 1862.

Company B: formed at New Orleans in 1861 and was assigned to Richmond in 1862.

Company C: formed at New Orleans in 1861 and was assigned to Richmond in 1862.

Company D: formed at Memphis and Mobile, assigned to Mobile.

Company E: formed at Savannah, assigned to Charleston in 1864 and sent a detachment to Wilmington.

Company F: formed at New Orleans, moved to Mobile after New Orleans fell.

Parts of these companies were detached to ship duty aboard the following vessels: *Atlanta, Baltic, Charleston, Chicora, Columbia, Dalman, Drewry, Fredericksburg, Gaines, Gallego, Huntress, Indian Chief, Isondiaga, Jamestown, Macon, McRae, Morgan, Nashville, North Carolina, Palmetto State, Patrick Henry, Raleigh, Resolute, Richmond, Sampson, Savannah* (both the steamer and the ironclad vessels), *Tennessee, Time, United States, Virginia, Virginia II, Tallahassee/Olustree, Shenandoah, Georgia, Rappahannock, Stonewall, Artic,* and *Georgia.*

The first CS Marine action was during the attack of CSS *Virginia* on the Federal blockade on 8-9 March 1862. Their last engagement was at Saylor's Creek on 6 April 1865.

CS Marine uniforms copied the US Marine model, except that the overblouse was gray and the enlisted chevrons were brown. Officer rank badges were the same as the CS Army. It is not known if the kepis had any ornamentation, as records were destroyed in 1865. The same white trousers, such as the USMC wore, were used.

Weapons for either side were the standard rifled muskets and sidearms, but specially treated to prevent corrosion while at sea.

Amazing Facts

Or, things that usually do not make it into the history books.

The Issues

The Civil War was not a sudden occurrence; it was a long time in coming. The countdown to Civil War began as the Declaration of Independence was being debated.

If one was to ask, "What caused the Civil War?" it would be like opening up a can of very angry worms. The causes were so various, according to which region one came from, and so contentious that it stirs emotions even today. For the purposes of this book, two of the top issues are mentioned here: Slavery and States Rights.

Any opinions expressed here are those of the writer

Slavery:

This was the #1 issue out of all the issues that had to be dealt with. However, this was not totally a US problem: the African slave trade was in full motion even before there were plans to settle what would one day become the US East Coast. Since 1444 Portugal had been involved in kidnapping Africans and putting them to work, before the New World was discovered.

Spain soon took over and dominated the trade, bringing over Africans to work newly settled lands. Some were with the conquistadors in Mexico and accompanied explorers who discovered the Pacific Ocean. They

417

were also put to work on plantations that produced food for the home markets.

The Dutch wrestled the trade rights from the Spanish and dominated it for fifty years. It is during this time that a certain English colony entered the picture.

August, 1619: A Dutch ship entered the small harbor at Jamestown, Virginia Colony and offloaded 20 Africans that were seized from a Spanish ship. These Africans were designated "indentured servants" and were put to work. This is where the American involvement began.

Crops such as rice and indigo were labor intensive, and there were not enough workers coming over from England so plantation owners jumped at the idea of importing workers. This became popular in the southern colonies, but also a moneymaker for New England merchants. As a result, England took over the slave trade in 1713 and became a slaveholding country.

What developed became known as the Triangle Trade. Ships would depart Boston with fish, grain, rum, and raw materials and sailed for the West African coast. There, they would trade their cargo for newly captured Africans. From Africa, the ships would sail for the West Indies. On arrival, the Africans would be traded for sugar, molasses, and "experienced" slaves. That cargo would be taken to the Colonies, the "experienced" slaves would be sold to the auction houses, the sugar and molasses sold to merchants (usually turned into rum), and the profits went into the pockets of the businessmen backing the venture.

The trip from Africa to the West Indies was known as the "Middle Passage." The newly caught Africans were dense packed into the holds of the slave ships, chained to the deck or to bunks, with the barest of sanitation, if that. Add to that meager food, and you had the ingredients for unimaginable horrors. Deaths from disease and suicide were common on these journeys. Those who were sick or who had died were thrown overboard for the sharks to eat. Even if one survived the trip, there was still the prospect of being sold and put to work for the remainder of ones life.

As the Colonies strove to break away from England, there were paradoxes to the ideas that the colonists were fighting for:

George Washington, commander of the Continental Army and the future 1st President of the United States, had slaves at his Mount Vernon farm. They belonged to his wife and were freed upon his death.

Thomas Jefferson's home, Monticello, was built with slave labor. He did have his reservations about the practice as he was writing, *"all men are created equal."*

Many of the Founding Fathers either had slaves, or were fighting to free them. Many Africans were in the ranks of Washington's army, accepted there without any fuss. (Some say that it was because the British Royal Army planned to increase their ranks with freed slaves).

From 1775 to 1776, the Continental Congress took on the issue while hammering together the Declaration of Independence. There were many precedents to go on:

In 1688, the first anti-slavery demonstration occurred at Germantown, Pennsylvania Colony. In 1700, the first anti-slavery pamphlet, *The Selling of Joseph* was published.

1754: John Woolman, a Quaker minister, published *Some Considerations on the Keeping of Negroes*, another anti-slavery pamphlet.

There were, on the other hand, trouble between Africans and Whites, resulting in a slave revolt in South Carolina in 1739 and riots in New York City in 1741, just to name a few.

In a draft of the Declaration of Independence, there was a charge leveled against England's King George III about the slave trade and that the Crown prohibited the colonies from abolishing the practice. This was opposed by the southern colonies, already heavily involved in agriculture and needing the labor. Under pressure, that language was stricken out of the final draft.

The countdown to Fort Sumter began in Independence Hall.

All was not lost for the anti-slavery forces. Vermont abolished slavery in 1777, with Pennsylvania gradually ending the practice in 1780 and Massachusetts in 1783.

In 1787, as delegates were meeting in Philadelphia for the Constitutional Convention, the Northwest Ordinance had been passed, allowing for new territories like Ohio, Indiana, and Illinois to come into being. These territories, as new states, would be allowed to decide for themselves whether or not to allow slavery.

When the US Constitution was written, slavery continued to be a contentious issue, but a compromise was reached as far as Africans were concerned:

US involvement in the slave trade was to end in 1808.

Slaves, as property, were taxable.

A slave, or Free African, was counted as 3/5 of a person for the purpose of representation in Congress. (This actually gave the slaveholding states fewer representatives than they thought they would get).

As the 19th Century began, some Northern states were considering abolishing slavery as a result of the Industrial Revolution, which began in 1790 and made slavery uneconomical, at least in the North. In the South, any general drift toward emancipation was quashed when Eli Whitney invented the cotton gin, a machine that plucked seeds out of cotton boles, a very labor-intensive activity. This resulted in cotton becoming a cash crop, itself labor intensive and requiring more slaves.

In the South, it was deemed necessary to keep control of the slaves with both legal and physical methods:

A slave marriage was not considered legal, which allowed families to be split up at auctions.

Teaching a slave to read and write was illegal, in many cases punishable by death. Confederate General Thomas Jackson broke that law regularly teaching local slaves to read the Bible.

Minor infractions, like not working hard enough, were punished by whipping.

Escape was highly discouraged: there were professional slave catchers who were assisted by bloodhounds. They were legally backed by the Fugitive Slave Act of 1793, which made escape a Federal offense and prohibited local authorities from assisting runaways. In one of the first cases of civil disobedience in US history, many Northerners ignored this law, helping escaped slaves to British North America (Canada).

But then, who would blame the slave for trying to escape, they lived in crude log cabins, wore the most basic (and cheapest) clothes, fed usually meager food (learning how to make do with what they had actually led to several types of cuisine that people enjoy today, but at the time it was not so hot), woke up and were in the fields at the crack of dawn and worked until after sundown (not the idyllic condition depicted in the movie *Gone With the Wind*), punished for the least infraction, could be sold at the Master's whim, killed, and, basically, condemned to a life of hard work.

There were slaves who were freed by a process called manumission, but there were restrictions on even that, a Freeman could not vote, hold public office, usually had poor jobs at little pay, and had to deal with the racial prejudices of neighbors, even in the North.

There was also the issue of political power: the South was leery of Northerners getting more power in Congress, and of course the North was wary of the opposite happening. There was a compromise that came out of the Northwest Ordinance, for one state that allowed slavery to enter the Union, that had to be followed by one state that did not allow the practice, and vice versa.

Example: 1803: Ohio entered the US as a Free State.
　　　　1812: Louisiana entered the US as a Slave State.

There were other methods being considered to tackle the question of slavery, in 1816, the American Colonization Society was formed with the aim of sending freed slaves to Africa. There was one problem with that, most of these persons were second and third generation African-Americans who probably never heard of Africa, but facts sometimes fail to trump good intentions. The colony was called Liberia and its capital was called Monrovia, after President James Monroe. This colony, which became a republic in 1847, was the only independent nation on the African continent at the time, the rest of Africa having been carved up into European possessions.

The first half of the 19th Century became very combative: groups were organizing in the North to press for a political solution while the South tried to expand the practice westward, especially into new lands such as Texas. The Southern view was reinforced by revolts such as Denmark Vesey in 1822, or Nat Turner in 1831. The Northern view was reinforced by people like William Lloyd Garrison publishing the *Liberator* and the New England Anti-Slavery Society forming in Boston, MA.

Violence became part of the discourse, in places as diverse as Charleston and Boston. In New York, an anti-slavery rally was broken up by those who did not want to see Blacks and Whites mingling. In Georgia, it became a death penalty offence to advocate abolition, or in their minds, "inciting a slave insurrection."

The political discourse was not much better (sounds familiar); in 1837 Congress passed a Gag Rule, prohibiting discussion, resolutions, or petitions mentioning slavery until 1844! When it was lifted, the North pounced with an anti-slavery petition while the South presented a resolution calling for the disbanding of the United States. A stricter Gag Rule was then put into place. This prevented former President John Quincy Adams from offering 350 petitions calling for the abolishment of slavery. Adams would go on to represent a group of slaves who captured the Spanish slave ship *Amistad*. He would win the case and the would-be slaves were returned to Africa.

Even as the Congress, and the nation, was embroiled in the Mexican War, there was another attempt to limit the spread of slavery: David

Wilmot, Representative from Pennsylvania, introduced a proviso to prohibit any land taken as a result of the war to allow slavery. Not only was that shot down, but also Senator John C. Calhoun of South Carolina put forward the provision that Congress had no right to limit the spread of slavery.

The response to that was the idea of "popular sovereignty," that is, let the states decide whether or not to have slavery. This would bypass Congress entirely, but would open up more troubles.

Congress did try to establish a balance on the issue with the Compromise of 1850, allowing California to enter the Union as a Free State, establishing the New Mexico and Utah Territories, set the borders of Texas, strengthening the Fugitive Slave Act, and finally abolishing the slave trade (but not slavery) in the District of Columbia.

In several Southern states, it was resolved to hold the North to a very high standard concerning the Compromise of 1850, or else secession would be on the table.

Some of the public conducted what would be called activism today, in the form of the Underground Railroad, a system of safe houses that runaway slaves could go to in order to get food, medical attention, and protection on their journey north. This was done at great risk to those running the operation, prison under Federal law or death under State law. Harriet Tubman, a runaway slave herself, became the most famous of the "conductors."

Another method of activism was the written word. There were several anti-slavery publications, but a series of stories began to appear in the *National Era* under the title, *"Uncle Tom's Cabin or Life Among the Lowly."* These stories, soon published as a novel, caused cheers in the North, where it became a best-seller, and a firestorm in the South, where it was banned. Its author, Harriet Beecher Stowe, wife of abolitionist Henry Beecher, became both a celebrity and a villain overnight.

Then came Kansas.

There was the Kansas-Nebraska Act, which opened areas west of Missouri to settlement. Both pro and anti-slavery forces rushed people to the area in order to influence a future vote on whether or not to allow slavery into the territory. These settlers were usually well armed so that the other side could be intimidated.

In 1855, Kansas voted to allow slavery and expelled dissenting opinion from the new Kansas Legislature. Anti-slavery elements met in Lawrence and declared their own Legislature, setting the stage for armed conflict.

On the political front, a new party was emerging: the remains of the old Whig Party, plus smaller parties such as the Know-Nothings and the Wide-Awakes, joined together to become the Republican Party, which became the anti-slavery party.

In 1856 the Republicans attempted to win the White House with the explorer John Fremont, but lost to Democrat Franklin Buchanan.

1857 saw a momentous decision from the US Supreme Court: *Dred Scott vs. United States.*

Dred Scott was a slave owned by a US Army officer, who took him to Minnesota during his career. After the officer died, his widow planned to sell Scott. He made an attempt to sue for his freedom, citing his residence in Minnesota, a Free State. The Supreme Court ruled that as a slave, he had no right to sue in Federal courts, neither was he (and by extension all African-Americans) afforded the rights of any citizen. The court also ruled that the Federal Government could not deprive citizens of their property rights, including slaves.

In the Mid-Term Election of 1858, a one-time Congressman and self-taught lawyer named Abraham Lincoln won the Republican nomination for the Illinois Senate seat held by Democrat Stephen Douglas. They both embark on a series of debates from 21 August to 15 October. Lincoln took the anti-slavery position while Douglas pressed for popular sovereignty. Douglas won the election.

> *A house divided against itself cannot stand. I believe this government cannot endure, permanently half slave and half free.*
> —*Abraham Lincoln, 16 June 1858*

Throughout the nation, the strains of the slavery issue were stretching to the breaking point. There were conventions calling for secession and court cases that either upheld current laws, or called then unconstitutional, depending on what side the judge was on. (Sound familiar?)

Then there was Harpers Ferry.

16 October 1859: Abolitionist John Brown, leading a group of Blacks and Whites, seized the Federal Arsenal at Harpers Ferry, VA. Their plan was to seize the arms and give them to slaves in order to ferment a revolt. They ended up blockaded in the main building and were overcome by a force of US Marines led by Army Colonel Robert E. Lee and Lieutenant J.E.B. Stuart. Brown was tried for treason by the State of Virginia and sentenced to be hanged. On 2 December, as he was led to the gallows, he declared that only blood could wash the stain of slavery away.

1860: the Presidential Election was in full swing, the Republicans, after several ballots, nominated Abraham Lincoln. The Democrats, however, were another matter: their party was split along regional lines, with the Northern faction selecting Stephen Douglas, and the Southern faction selecting John Breckenridge, Buchanan's Vice-President. As the campaign progressed, several Southern states declared that if Lincoln was elected, Articles of Secession would be considered.

6 November 1860: Abraham Lincoln was elected President.

20 December 1860: South Carolina voted to secede.

The nation was running down the road to war.

Slavery would die, first by the Union victory, and then by the 13th Amendment, outlawing the practice. Anything beyond that would take another century.

States' Rights

The second most mentioned issue was States' Rights. The premise here was that a state could better decide what to do within their borders than the Federal Government.

Prior to the Civil War, a US citizen though of themselves as a citizen of their state first, then of the nation. For example: Robert E. Lee was a Colonel in the US Army at the beginning of 1861. When he was offered command of the entire Union war effort, he had to decide between the nation and his state. When Virginia seceded, Lee felt he had no choice but to resign his commission and go with his state. He was expressing a common attitude at the time.

It was the same as far as the relationship between the State and Federal Governments were concerned. The USA started out with the Articles of Confederation, which created a weak central government and strong state governments. This created problems in matters such as defense and taxation. Finally, the Constitution was written, granting exact powers to a central, or Federal, government, such as, defense, taxation, interstate commerce, and relations with other countries. The 10th Amendment spelled out that any powers not granted to the Federal Government were reserved to the States.

Herein was the conflict. When Congress passed a law, usually the states went along with it. Sometimes, the states were not happy when the Federal Government did something that they did not agree with.

For example:

December 1814 to January 1815: A convention of New England Federalists met at Hartford, CT to consider secession over the War of 1812. Nothing came out of this meeting.

19 May, 1828: Congress passed a tariff on imported goods from Europe, making those imports more expensive then US made goods. This "Tariff of Abominations" was greeted with anger in the agricultural South, who needed such imports. John C. Calhoun, at the time Vice-President in

the Andrew Jackson Administration, wrote an article blasting the tariff as unconstitutional and called on his home state, South Carolina, to nullify, or refuse to enforce, the tariff. Calhoun ended up resigning the Vice-Presidency over the issue.

January 1830: Senator Daniel Webster asserted in a series of debates that the states derived their power from the Constitution and that the Federal Government was the final authority. That did not sit well with most Southerners.

24 November 1832: Congress passed another Tariff Act. South Carolina responded by issuing an Ordinance of Nullification against it. President Jackson threatened to order Federal troops to Charleston in order to enforce the law. The Governor of South Carolina called for 10,000 militia to repel what was being called a "Federal invasion." Calhoun, at this point a Senator, met with Senator Henry Clay and the two hammered out an agreement, which managed to avoid a civil war. The following year, the Compromise Tariff of 1833 was passed, which reduced the tariffs, and South Carolina followed suit, repealing their nullification ordinance.

In the North, many citizens, and some politicians, had a beef with the Fugitive Slave Law, which made escape from slavery a Federal offense and gave the Federal authorities power to assist in catching runaway slaves. Many citizens organized to impede those efforts, hiding runaways and blocking slave catchers and bailiffs from carrying out their duties, at risk of jail time themselves (today, they are called Acts of Disobedience, or Social Activism).

> *I will not obey it, by God!*
> —*Ralph Waldo Emerson on the Fugitive Slave Act.*

In the South, many people saw the conflict over slavery as a Federal intrusion into their lives. Many politicians believed that it was State business to decide if slavery was to exist (pity they did not want Missouri and Kansas to have that choice), not the Federal Government. During the 1850s, as the Republican Party was on the ascendant (and adopting an anti-slavery platform), people in the South believed that they would be forced to give up their slaves at the point of a bayonet. Almost all of the Deep South states resolved to secede if a Republican was elected President, which happened in 1860.

As the South began to secede, President Franklin Buchanan felt that even though the states could not leave the Union, the Constitution did not address what the Federal Government could do about it. He was right, the addition of new states was provided for (there were 36 states at the time) but nothing on what it a state wanted to express their rights and leave.

Because of a perceived violation of their "rights," the Southern States began to break away.

Did the South have a chance?

The North had a solid industrial base, with about 100,000 factories and 1,100,000 workers. The South had 20,000 factories and 100,000 workers.

Replacing Union war material lost on the battlefield could be accomplished within a week. The South had to make do with captured material a lot of the time.

The North had 20,000 miles of railroads to move goods and passengers. The South had only 9000.

A train trip from Chicago to New York took about four days. A trip from New Orleans to Richmond could take two weeks with several train changes due to different track gauges. Also, about 91% of the US railroad equipment was held in the North. (It was little wonder that the South resorted to stealing locomotives in order to keep things going).

The North's population was 22,000,000. The South's was 9,000,000. This allowed the Union to field armies of 100,000 without straining the population while the South had manpower shortages from the start.

Even with horrific causalities, the North could refill its ranks despite occasionally resorting to a draft. In the South, one soldier killed or wounded was a giant blow to the army. The South's population included 4,000,000 African-American slaves that the CSA was not willing to tap for combat manpower.

The North had a good strategy and, after Lincoln found Grant, Sherman, and Sheridan, the leadership to carry it out.

Jefferson Davis interfered in his General's operations. There was talent, but it was not used properly.

The North presented a mostly united front.

The Confederacy set as its cornerstone the concept of States Rights. State governors took advantage of that by withholding troops and supplies needed for the defense of the nation. The CSA never fully concentrated combat power like the Union could.

The North had a seafaring tradition and held most of the yards needed to build a navy. The South seized one yard and did not hold that very long.

All the sea faring expertise was in New England, not New Orleans. There were ports in the South, just not the dry docks needed to maintain ships.

The North was changing almost daily with the influx of immigrants. The South was in a kind of stasis with its agricultural, slaveholding system.

The North was looking forward, the South backward.

The North had ready reserves of gold and specie to finance the war. The South's economy was tied up in cotton and slaves, with losing either causing a collapse.

This despite the introduction of "greenbacks" and a temporary income tax by the North.

It seemed that the South was doomed from the start. Without a large population, resources, industrial might, and the ability to transport goods (without resorting to blockade runners), the South might have had one chance to win, perhaps if they were organized enough to press the attack after First Manassas.

In short, they simply ran out of time.

> *You people of the South don't know what you are doing. This country will be drenched in blood, and God only knows how it will end. It is all folly, madness, a crime against civilization! You people speak so lightly of war; you don't know what you're talking about. War is a terrible thing! You mistake, too, the people of the North. They are a peaceable people but an earnest people, and they will fight, too. They are not going to let this country be destroyed without a mighty effort to save it... Besides, where are your men and appliances of war to contend against them? The North can make a steam engine, locomotive, or railway car; hardly a yard of cloth or pair of shoes can you make. You are rushing into war with one of the most powerful, ingeniously mechanical, and determined people on Earth—right at your doors. You are bound to fail. Only in your spirit and determination are you prepared for war. In all else you are totally unprepared, with a bad cause to start with. At first you will make headway, but as your limited resources begin to fail, shut out from the markets of Europe as you will be, your cause will begin to wane. If your people will but stop and think, they must see in the end that you will surely fail.*
> —*William T Sherman to Professor Daniel F. Boyd upon hearing of South Carolina's secession.*

The war's numbers:

On 1 January 1861, the US Army stood at 16,267 men to include Infantry, Cavalry, Artillery, Engineers, Quartermaster, and other functions.

By 1865, the Union Army had up to 2,750,000 men under arms while the Confederate Army had up to 1,250,000 (estimated).

There were 10,455 "campaigns, battles, engagements, combats, actions, assaults, skirmishes, operations, sieges, raids, expeditions, reconnaissances, scouts, affairs, occupations, and captures."

The Monetary Price of the Civil War

Total expenditures of the US, both Federal and State governments: $2,300,000,000.00

Total expenditures of the CS, both Confederate and State governments: $1,000,000,000.00

The destruction of national capital (wealth) was negligible in the North, but the South lost $1,490,000,000.00

The National Debt of the Union in 1860 was about $65,000,000.00 or $2.06 for every person in the North. In 1865, it was $2,000,000,000.00 or $75.06 for each person.

It did not help the Confederacy that the CS Dollar had devalued from the day they started issuing currency.

To bolster the Southern economy, Confederate raiding parties would seize a town and demand a ransom, or else the town would be sacked. This is what happened to Chambersburg, PA in 1864.

When Richmond was evacuated in 1865, it was estimated that as much as $350,000 in gold bullion and specie (coins) rolled out with the fleeing Confederate Government. A large chunk of that went missing and has not been seen since.

The last Confederate coins handed out as pay was $1.00 silver coins given to General P.G.T. Beauregard and each of his staff.

The Blood Price of the Civil War:

Bloodiest Multi-day Battle: Gettysburg, PA,

Dead: Union, 3155. Confederate, 3903
Wounded: Union, 14,529. Confederate, 18,735
Missing: Union, 5365. Confederate, 5425
Total: Union, 23,049. Confederate, 28,063
Total Causalities: 51,112

Bloodiest Single Day Battle: Antietam (Sharpsburg, MD)

Dead: Union, 2108. Confederate, 2700
Wounded: Union, 9549. Confederate, 9024
Missing: Union, 753. Confederate, 2000
Total: Union, 12,140. Confederate, 13,724
Total Causalities: 26,134

Bloodiest Hour: Cold Harbor, VA.
Total Union causalities of 12,000, with 7000 in the first 20 minutes of the battle.

The high casualties were caused by tactics not catching up with technology; officers on both sides were taught Napoleonic style tactics at West Point, while the lethality of the weapons were improved by Industrial Age methods.

Units who paid a high price: (Unit/Percentage of unit lost/Battle)

Union:
1st Minnesota—82%—Gettysburg
141st Pennsylvania—75%—Gettysburg
101st New York—73%—Second Manassas
25th Massachusetts—70%—Cold Harbor
36th Wisconsin—69%—Bethesda Church
20th Massachusetts—68%—Fredericksburg
8th Vermont—67%—Cedar Creek
81st Pennsylvania—67%—Fredericksburg
12th Massachusetts—67%—Antietam
1st Maine Heavy Artillery—66%—Petersburg

Confederate:
1st Texas—82%—Antietam
21st Georgia—76%—Second Manassas
26th North Carolina—71%—Gettysburg
6th Mississippi—70%—Shiloh
8th Tennessee—68%—Stones River
10th Tennessee—68%—Chickamauga
Palmetto Sharpshooters—67%—Glendale
17th South Carolina—66%—Second Manassas
23rd South Carolina—66%—Second Manassas
44th Georgia—65%—Mechanicsville

Total Union losses: 360,222.

Total Confederate losses: 258,000

The total death toll was 618,222; which is 92,180 less than all other US wars combined, including Iraq and Afghanistan (as of 2010).

Articles of Secession

South Carolina: 20 December 1860

We the people of South Carolina, in convention assembled, to declare and ordain, and it is hereby declared and ordained, that the ordinance adopted by us in convention on the twenty third day of May in the year of our Lord one thousand seven hundred and eighty eight, whereby the Constitution of the United States of America was ratified, and also all acts and parts of acts of the General Assembly of this State, ratifying amendments of the said Constitution, are hereby repealed: and the union now subsisting between South Carolina and other States, under the name "United States of America" is hereby dissolved. Done at Charleston the twentieth day of December in the year of our Lord one thousand eight hundred and sixty.

Mississippi, 9 January 1861

The people of Mississippi, in convention assembled, do ordain and declare, and it is hereby ordained and declared, as follows, to wit:

SEC 1: *That all the laws and ordinances by which the said State of Mississippi became a member of the Federal Union of the United States of America be, and the same are hereby repealed, and that all obligations on the part of the said State, or the people thereof, be withdrawn, and that the said State does hereby resume all the rights, functions, and powers which by any of the said laws and ordinances were conveyed to the Government of the United States, and is absolved from all the obligations, restraints, and duties incurred to the said Federal Union, and shall henceforth be a free, sovereign, and independent State.*

SEC 2: *That so much of the first section of the seventh article of the Constitution of this State, as requires members of the Legislature and all officers, both legislative and judicial, to take an oath to support the Constitution on the United States, be, and the same is hereby abrogated and annulled.*

SEC 3: *That all rights acquired and vested under the Constitution of the United States, or under any act of Congress passed in pursuance thereof, or any law of this State, and not incompatible with this ordinance, shall remain in force, and have the same effect as if the ordinance had not been passed.*

SEC 4: *That the people of the State of Mississippi, hereby consent to form a Federal Union with such of the States as have seceded or may secede from the Union of the United States of America, upon the basis of the present Constitution of the United States, except such parts thereof as embrace other portions than such seceded States.*

Florida, 10 January 1861

Whereas, all hope of preserving the union upon terms consistent with the safety and honor of the slaveholding States, has been fully dissipated by the recent indications of the strength of the anti-slavery sentiment of the free States: therefore,

Be it enacted by the people of Florida, in convention assembled, *That it is the right of the several States of the Union, at such time, and for such cause as in the opinion of the people of such States acting in their sovereign capacity, may be just and proper, to withdraw from the Union, and, in the opinion of this Convention, the existing causes are such as to compel Florida to proceed to exercise this right.*

We, the people of the State of Florida, in convention assembled, *do solemnly ordain, publish, and declare that the State of Florida hereby withdraws herself from the Confederacy of States existing under the name of The United States of America, and from the existing Government of the said States: and that all political connections between her and the Government of said States ought to be, and the same is hereby totally annulled, and said Union of States dissolved: the State of Florida is hereby declared a sovereign and independent nation: and that all ordinances heretofore adopted, in as so far as they create* or recognize said Union, are rescinded: and all laws, or parts of laws, in force in this State, in so far as they recognize or assent to said Union be and they are hereby repealed.

Alabama, 11 January 1861

An Ordinance to dissolve the Union between the State of Alabama and other States united under the compact styled "The Constitution of the United States of America"

Whereas, the election of Abraham Lincoln and Hannibal Hamlin to the offices of President and Vice-President of the United States of America, by a sectional party, avowedly hostile to the domestic institutions and to the peace and security of the people of the State of Alabama, preceded by many and dangerous infractions of the Constitution of the United States by many of the States and people of the Northern section, is a political wrong of so insulting and menacing a character as to justify the people of Alabama in the adoption of prompt and decided measures for their future peace and security:

Therefore, Be it declared and ordained by the people of the State of Alabama in convention assembled, That the State of Alabama now withdraws, and is hereby withdrawn from the Union known as "the United States of America" and henceforth ceases to be one of said United States and is, and right ought to be, a sovereign and independent State.

SEC 2: Be it further declared and ordained by the people of the State of Alabama in convention assembled, That all of the powers over the territory of said State, and over the people thereof, heretofore delegated to the Government of the United States of America, be and they are hereby withdrawn from said Government, and are hereby resumed and vested in the people of the State of Alabama.

And as it is the desire and purpose of the State of Alabama to meet the slaveholding States of the South who may approve such purpose, in order to frame a provisional as well as a permanent government upon the principles of the Constitution of the United States.

Be it resolved by the people of Alabama in convention assembled, That the people of the States of Delaware, Maryland, Virginia, North Carolina, South Carolina, Florida Georgia, Mississippi, Louisiana, Texas, Arkansas, Tennessee, Kentucky, and Missouri, be, and are hereby, invited to meet the people of the State of Alabama, by there delegates, in convention, on the 4th of February, A.D. 1861, for the purpose of consulting with each other as to the most effectual mode of securing concerted and harmonious action in whatever measures may be deemed most desirable for our common peace and security.

And be it further resolved, That the president of this Convention be, and is hereby, instructed to transmit forthwith a copy of the forgoing preamble, ordinance, and resolutions, to the Governors of the several States named in said resolutions.

Done by the people of the State of Alabama in Convention assembled, at Montgomery, on this, the 11th day of January, A.D. 1861

WM.M. BROOKS, President of the Convention.

Georgia, 19 January 1861

An Ordinance to dissolve the Union between the State of Georgia and other States united with her under the compact of Government entitled "The Constitution of the United States"

We the people of the State of Georgia, in Convention assembled, do declare and ordain, and it is hereby declared and ordained, that the ordinance adopted by the people of Georgia in Convention in the year 1788, whereby the Constitution of the United States was assented to, ratified, and adopted, and also all acts and parts of acts of the General Assembly ratifying and adopting the amendments to the said Constitution, are hereby repealed, rescinded, and abrogated: and we do further declare and ordain, that the Union now subsisting between the State of Georgia and other States, under the name of the United states of America, is hereby dissolved: and that the State of Georgia is in full possession and exercise of all those rights of sovereignty which belong and appertain to a free and independent State.

Louisiana, 26 January 1861

An Ordinance to dissolve the Union between the State of Louisiana and other States united with her under the compact of Government entitled "The Constitution of the United States of America"

We, the people of the State of Louisiana, in Convention assembled, *do declare and ordain, and it is hereby declared and ordained, that the Ordinance passed by us in Convention on the 22nd day of November, in the year 1811, whereby the Constitution of the United States of America, and the amendments of said Constitution, were adopted, and all laws and ordinances by which the State of Louisiana became a member of the Federal Union, be, and the same are hereby, repealed and abrogated: and that the union now subsisting between Louisiana and other States, under the name of the "United States of America," is hereby dissolved.*

We do further declare and ordain, that the State of Louisiana hereby resumes all rights and powers heretofore delegated to the Government of the United States of America: that her citizens are absolved from all allegiance to said Government: and that she is in full possession and exercise of all those rights of sovereignty which appertain to a free and independent State.

We do further declare and ordain, that all rights acquired and vested under the Constitution of the United States, or any act of Congress or treaty, or under any law of this State and not incompatible with this ordinance, shall remain in force, and have the same effect as if this ordinance had not been passed.

The undersigned hereby certifies that the above ordinance is a true copy of the original ordinance adopted this day by the Convention of the State of Louisiana.

Given under my hand and the great seal of Louisiana, at Baton Rouge, this 26th day of January, in the year of our Lord, 1861.

A. MOUTON: Pres. of the Convention.

J. Thomas Wheat, Secretary of the Convention.

Texas, 1 February 1861

An Ordinance to dissolve the Union between the State of Texas and other States united with her under the compact of Government styled "The Constitution of the United States of America"

SEC 1: Whereas the Federal Government has failed to accomplish the purposes of the compact of union between these States, in giving protection either to the persons of our people upon an exposed frontier, or to the property of our citizens: and whereas the action of the Northern States is violative of the compact between the States and the guarantees of the Constitution: and whereas the recent developments in Federal affairs make it evident that the power of the Federal Government is sought to be made a weapon with which to strike down the interests and property of the people of Texas and her sister slaveholding States, instead of permitting it to be, as was intended—our shield against outrage and aggression: therefore "We, the people of the State of Texas, by delegates in the Convention assembled, do declare and ordain that the ordinance adopted by out Convention of delegates on the (4th) day of July, A.D. 1845, and afterwards ratified by us, under which the Republic of Texas was admitted into the Union with other States, and became a party to the compact styled 'The Constitution of the United States of America' be, and is hereby repealed and annulled.

That all the powers which, by the said compact, were delegated by Texas to the Federal Government are resumed. That Texas is of right absolved from all restraints and obligations incurred by said compact, and is a sovereign State, and that her citizens and people are absolved from all allegiance to the United States or the Government thereof.

SEC 2: This ordinance shall be submitted to the people of Texas for their ratification or rejection, by the qualified voters, on the 23rd day of February 1861: and unless rejected by a majority of the votes cast, shall take effect and be in force on or after the 2nd day of March, A.D. 1861. Provided that in the representative district of El Paso said election may be held on the 18th of February, 1861.

Done by the people of the State of Texas, in convention assembled, at Austin, the 1st day of February, A.D. 1861.

Virginia, 17 April 1861

An ordinance to repeal the ratification of the Constitution of the United States of America, by the State of Virginia, and to resume all the rights and powers granted under said Constitution.

The people of Virginia, in the ratification of the Constitution of the United States of America, adopted by them in Convention, on the 25th day of June, in the year of our lord one thousand seven hundred and eighty-eight, having declared the that the powers granted under the said Constitution were derived from the people of the United States, and might be resumed whensoever the same should be perverted to their injury and oppression, and the Federal Government having perverted said powers, not only to the injury of the people of Virginia, but to the oppression of the Southern slaveholding States.

Now, therefore, we, the people of Virginia, do declare and ordain, that the Ordinance adopted by the people of this State in Convention on the twenty-fifth day of June, in the year of our Lord one thousand seven hundred and eighty-eight, whereby the Constitution of the United States of America was ratified, and all acts of the General Assembly of this State ratifying or adopting amendments to said Constitution are hereby repealed and abrogated: that the union between the State of Virginia and the other States under the Constitution aforesaid is hereby dissolved, and that the State of Virginia is in the full possession of all the rights of sovereignty which belong and appertain to a free and independent State. And they do further declare that said Constitution is no longer binding on any of the citizens of this State.

This Ordinance shall take effect and be an act of this day, when ratified by a majority of the votes of the people of this State, cast at a poll to be taken thereon on the fourth Thursday in May next, in pursuance of a schedule hereafter to be enacted.

Done in Convention in the city of Richmond, on the seventeenth day of April, in the year of our Lord one thousand eight hundred and sixty-one, and in the eighty-fifth year of the commonwealth of Virginia.

A true copy.

JON. L. EUBANK
Secretary of Convention

Arkansas, 6 May 1861

Whereas, in addition to the well-founded causes of complaint set forth by this Convention, in resolutions adopted on the 11th March, A.D. 1861, against the sectional party now in power in Washington City, headed by Abraham Lincoln , he has, in the face or resolutions passed by this Convention, pledging the State of Arkansas to resist to the last extremity any attempt on the part of such power to coerce any State that seceded from the old Union, proclaimed to the world that war should be waged against such States until they should be compelled to submit to their rule, and large forces to accomplish this have by this same power been called out and are now being marshaled to carry out this inhuman design, and to longer submit to such rule or remain in the old Union on the United States would be disgraceful and ruinous to the State of Arkansas.

Therefore, we, the people of the State of Arkansas, in Convention assembled, do hereby declare and ordain, and it is hereby declared and ordained, that the "ordinance and acceptance of compact" passed and approved by the General assembly of the State of Arkansas, on the 18th day of October, A.D. 1836, whereby it was said General Assembly ordained that, by virtue of the authority vested in said General Assembly, by the provisions of the ordinance adopted by the convention of delegates assembled at Little Rock, for the purpose of forming a constitution and system of government for said State, the propositions set forth in "an act supplementary to an act entitled an act for the admission of the State of Arkansas into the Union, and to provide for the due execution of the laws of the United States within the same, and for other purposes, were freely accepted, ratified, and irrevocably confirmed articles of compact and union between the State of Arkansas and the United States," and all other laws and every other law and ordinance, whereby the State of Arkansas became a member of the Federal Union, be, and the same are hereby in all respects and for every purpose herewith consistent repealed, abrogated, and fully set aside: and the Union now subsisting between the State of Arkansas and the other States, under the name of the United States of America, is hereby forever dissolved.

And we do further hereby declare and ordain, that the State of Arkansas hereby resumes to herself all rights and powers heretofore delegated to the Government of the United States of America—that her citizens are absolved from allegiance to said Government of the United States, and that she is in full possession and exercise of all the rights and sovereignty which appertain to a free and independent State.

We do further ordain and declare that all rights acquired and vested under the Constitution of the United States of America, or of any act or acts of Congress, or treaty, or under any law of this State, and not incompatible with this ordinance, shall remain in full force and effect, in nowise altered or impaired, and have the same effect as if this ordinance had not been passed.

Adopted and passed in open Convention on the 6th day of May, A.D. 1861

North Carolina, 20 May 1861

We, the people of the State of North Carolina, in Convention assembled, do declare and ordain, and it is hereby declared and ordained, that the ordinance adopted by the State of North Carolina, in the Convention of 1789, whereby the Constitution of the United States was ratified and adopted, and also all acts and parts of acts of the General assembly, ratifying and adopting amendments to said Constitution are hereby repealed, rescinded, and abrogated.

We do further declare and ordain that the Union now subsisting between the State of North Carolina and the other States, under the title of the United States of America, is hereby dissolved, and that the State of North Carolina is in the full possession and exercise of all those rights of sovereignty which belong and appertain to a free and independent State.

Done at Raleigh, 20th day of May, in the year of our Lord, 1861.

Tennessee, 8 June 1861

Declaration of Independence and Ordinance dissolving the Federal relations between the State of Tennessee and the United States of America.

1st. We. the people of the State of Tennessee, waiving an expression of opinion as to the abstract doctrine of secession, but asserting the right as a free and *independent people to alter, reform, or abolish our form of Government in such manner as we think proper, do ordain and declare that all the laws and ordinances by which the State of Tennessee became a member of the Federal Union of the United States of America, are hereby abrogated and annulled, and that all obligations on put part be withdrawn therefrom: and we do hereby resume all the rights, functions and powers which by any of said ordinances were conveyed to the Government of the United States, and absolve ourselves from all the obligations, restraints, and duties incurred thereto: and do hereby henceforth become a free, sovereign, and independent State.*

2nd. We furthermore declare and ordain, that Article 10, Sections 1 and 2 of the Constitution of the State of Tennessee, which requires members of the General Assembly, and all officers, civil and military, to take an oath to support the Constitution of the United States, be and the same are hereby abrogated and annulled, and all parts of the Constitution of the State of Tennessee, making citizenship of the United States a qualification for office, and recognizing the Constitution of the United States as the supreme law of this State, are in like manner abrogated and annulled.

3rd. We furthermore ordain and declare that all rights acquired and vested under the Constitution of the United States, or under any act of Congress passed in pursuance thereof, or under any laws of this State, and not incompatible with this ordinance, shall remain in force and have the same effect as if this ordinance had not been passed.

Noted Persons of the Civil War

Adelbert Ames was the last surviving Union General Officer when he died in 1933.

James Andrews, whose mission led to the Great Locomotive Chase, was one of the first to receive the Medal of Honor (posthumously).

Prince Albert of the United Kingdom was working on calming matters following the *Trent* incident when he died. He toned down the rhetoric in the diplomatic letter that was sent to President Lincoln, paving the way for a resolution to the crisis.

One of the Confederate cavalry units that were harassing General William T. Sherman's forces in the Carolinas was led by a New Yorker, William W. Allen.

Lewis Armistead was expelled from West Point for hitting fellow cadet (and future fellow Confederate general) Jubal Early with a plate.

John Jacob Astor, Jr. was a volunteer aide to Major General George McClellan. He received a brevet promotion to Brigadier General for services during the Peninsular Campaign, but no one knows what for.

Union Brigadier General Henry Barnum was wounded at the Battle of Malvern Hill. He was heard to have said, *"Tell my wife that in my last thoughts were blended herself, my boy, and my flag. God bless the old fla........"* He then fell silent and was believed to be dead. That was not the case and he was promoted to Major General.

Francis Bartow is believed to be the first Confederate officer killed in battle (First Manassas).

Ordinary Seaman Philip Bazaar was part of the mixed Navy/Marine force that attacked Fort Fisher on 15 January 1865. He was one of six who managed to get in the fort before the Union attack was repulsed. His actions resulted in Bazaar becoming the second Hispanic-American in the US Navy to receive the Medal of Honor.

Erastus Beadle published small books called "dime novels" for the entertainment of Union troops. The paperback novel is it's descendent.

Rhode Islander Lloyd J. Beall resigned from the US Army to become a Confederate Colonel. He would go on to become the Commandant of the Confederate States Marine Corps.

George Beardslee improved mass communications by inventing a mobile telegraph wagon, allowing communications centers to be set up anyplace there was a wire.

Pierre Gustave Toutant Beauregard was Superintendent of the United States Military Academy at West Point—for only four days. He was relieved of his duties for his secessionist views.

Beauregard had to learn English while he was growing up (he was a Creole who spoke French).

Beauregard was the star pupil in Robert Anderson's artillery tactics class at West Point, the same Anderson that he fired on at Fort Sumter.

Robert Todd Lincoln Beckwith was listed as the last confirmed descendant of Abraham Lincoln when he died in 1985.

Dr. Henry Ward Beecher was a minister who became involved in the abolition movement. He helped get weapons to anti-slavery forces in Kansas, contributing to the situation that became "Bleeding Kansas." The Sharps rifles that were sent were nicknamed "Beecher's Bibles."

The Reverend Henry Bellows organized several women's aid organizations into what would become the US Sanitary Commission, the largest group aiding Union soldiers in the field.

Colonel Santos Benavides was the highest ranking Hispanic in Confederate service.

George Benninsky, a Polish immigrant, was paid $150 to take the place of future President Grover Cleveland in the ranks.

A military hospital in St. Louis was noted for having "three maiden ladies from Philadelphia" on the staff as nurses. These ladies were from one of the richest families in the US at the time, grandnieces of James Biddle, a naval hero of the War of 1812.

Ambrose Bierce shouldered a musket throughout the war. His war experiences led him to write *"Devil's Dictionary."*

One of Bierce's Civil War stories, *"Incident at Owl Creek Bridge,"* became an episode of *The Twilight Zone.*

Lyman Blake invented a stitching machine that allowed mass production of shoes, allowing Union troops to be well shod.

Edwin Booth was the most famous actor of his day, but it was his brother John Wilkes who would steal the fame by assassinating Abraham Lincoln. (A little known fact was that Edwin saved the life of Robert Todd Lincoln at a train station a few months before his brother's infamous act).

John Wilkes Booth borrowed a militia uniform so he could witness the hanging of abolitionist John Brown.

Gail Borden invented condensed milk in 1856, but his product did not become popular until the Civil War, when it became a staple for Union troops. His Eagle Brand milk is available on store shelves today.

Elias Boudinot assisted Stand Waite in signing up fellow Cherokees to the Confederate colors. His actions resulted in the Five Civilized

Tribes getting stripped of lands and rights. That land is now the State of Oklahoma.

Matthew Brady's pictures were made mostly by assistants that he sent into the field. His eyesight was failing and could not go into the field himself. He did, however, take full credit for the assistant's work. One of his most noted exhibits was "The Dead of Antietam," shown a few short weeks after the battle.

John C. Breckenridge was Vice-President in the Buchanan Administration, the Southern Democrat candidate for President in 1860, a Confederate Senator from Kentucky, a Confederate Brigadier General, and finally CS Secretary of War. He is remembered as the only Vice-President of the United States who took up arms against the US.

Confederate Captain John Bryan was the first combatant to use a balloon to conduct a reconnaissance of enemy lines. The balloon was lifted by "smoke," or hot air, because the Confederacy did not have the means to produce hydrogen, which is how the Federals got their balloons to rise.

John Burns was a retired constable and cobbler, as well as a veteran of both the War of 1812 and the Mexican War. When the Civil War came to his town of Gettysburg he grabbed his flintlock musket and ran for the nearest Union formation, the 150th Pennsylvania. After enduring some ridicule, he received a more modern musket and participated in several volleys, during which he was wounded. He was one of the first people that Abraham Lincoln wanted to see when he arrived for the dedication of the new National Cemetery.

Ambrose Burnside's wild whiskers were the inspiration for the term "sideburns."

Captain Van Buskirk was noted as the tallest man in the Union Army; at 6' 10 ½ "(the average height at the time was 5' 8"). The shortest man was an unidentified 192nd Ohio member who rose to 3'4".

Benjamin Butler actually pushed for the nomination of Jefferson Davis as the Democrat Party candidate for President of the United States.

Butler had two nicknames; "Beast," because of how Southerners felt about his administration of New Orleans, and "Spoons," because of an allegation that he had stolen silver spoons from several well to do houses.

It has been said that following the issuing of Order No. 28 that someone in New Orleans began selling chamber pots with Butler's picture painted on the inside of the pot.

Daniel Butterfield liked to write bugle calls. One of his works, *"Butterfield's Lullaby"* is known today as *"Taps."* (He was buried at West Point, NY, although he never attended the Military Academy).

Andrew Carnegie was an aide to a division superintendent to a railroad when he was hired to handle rail and telegraph lines for the Federal war effort. He used that experience to go into the iron and steel business in 1865 and became very wealthy. He used that wealth to create charitable endeavors. Carnegie Hall in New York City is named for him.

William H. Carney was the first African-American to earn the Medal of Honor, awarded in 1900.

Henry Carter did not want to follow in his family's glove making business. Instead, he accumulated a set of engraving tools and, while learning to become a businessman in London, submitted sketches to various London publications under the pseudonym Frank Leslie. After a successful career at the *London Illustrated News*, he moved to the US, legally changed his name to Leslie, and, after working for showman P.T. Barnum, launched *Frank Leslie's Illustrated Newspaper* in 1855. The Civil War would make the paper popular.

Salmon Chase, US Secretary of the Treasury, advocated the use of non-interest bearing bonds as currency. These were unpopular at first, but after Congress passed a law retiring the bills, public uproar caused them to relent. Since then, paper currency is still issued in the US.

Colonel William Christian received a brevet promotion to Brigadier General three years after he was forced to resign for cowardice.

Christopher Columbus Clark joined the Enrolled Missouri Militia on his 21st birthday (30 April 1864) and served 51 days. One of his descendants became the first African-American President of the United States, Barack Obama.

John Clem was 10 when he enlisted in the US Army as a drummer boy. He ended his career in 1916 at the rank of Major General.

Samuel Clemens served briefly in a pro-Confederate unit before deciding that being a newspaper reporter was better. He is better known by the pseudonym Mark Twain.

William Cody was a Union scout following a stint with the Pony Express. However, it would be his post war experiences that would put "Buffalo Bill" in the history books.

New Jersey native Samuel Cooper resigned his position as US Army Adjutant General in order to accept the same position with the CS Army. His record-keeping skills contributed to the *Official Records*.

In 1845, a Chinese boy was found on a cargo ship bound for Massachusetts. He was adopted by the ship's captain and welcomed into his family. He repaid his adopted family's kindness by joining the 23rd Massachusetts. Private Joseph Day Cahota fought at Drury's Bluff and Cold Harbor, one of an estimated 50 Chinese-Americans to don Union blue. Sadly, the Chinese Exclusion Act of 1882 prevented him from becoming a citizen, despite serving his country for 30 years.

Stephen Crane, born after the war, wrote one of the greatest stories of the Civil War, *The Red Badge of Courage*.

Commander Tunus A.M. Craven stepped to one side in order to allow his helmsman to escape and went down with his ship, USS *Tecumseh*, in Mobile Bay.

Pleasant Crump, a private with the 10th Alabama, became the last confirmed Confederate veteran when the claims of four others were debunked. Crump died in 1951.

Kentucky Senator John Crittenden's family was a symbol of the fractured nation, one son, Thomas, became a Union Brigadier General, while the other, George, became a Confederate Major General.

Lieutenant Thomas Custer won two Medals of Honor during the Civil War, but would share the fate of his brother, George, at the Little Big Horn.

Jefferson Davis was a compromise candidate for provisional Confederate President.

Davis emptied his own pockets in order to quell the Richmond Bread Riots. Militia who were aiming their muskets at the crowd backed him up.

At Irwinville, GA on 10 May 1865, a party of Federal cavalry entered Davis' camp. As he was trying to escape, his wife, Varina, threw a shawl over him. This led to cartoons as well as a display at P.T. Barnum's Showhouse depicting him in a dress.

On the third day of the Battle of Gettysburg, Corporal Joseph H De Castro won a struggle with the color bearer of the 19th Virginia and captured the flag. De Castro became the first Hispanic in the US Army to be awarded the Medal of Honor (the medal was automatically awarded for capturing an enemy flag).

There was a popular story about Lieutenant George Dixon being hit in a leg by a minie ball during the Battle of Shiloh. That ball was deflected by a $20 gold coin that was in his pocket. He kept the bent coin as a lucky piece and had it with him when he commanded *H.L. Hunley* on its famous mission, from which he never returned. The story was confirmed when, following the raising of the submarine in 2000, an archaeologist found the coin next to Dixon's skeleton.

Abner Doubleday may have been a good artillerist, but he did not invent baseball. That sport was already popular before the Civil War. He is credited with firing the first return shot from Fort Sumter.

Frederick Douglass was a slave who escaped his bonds to become a writer and advocate for abolition. He was one of the first to advocate the recruitment of African-Americans, long before the US government warmed up to the idea.

Stephen Douglas was the first candidate to personally campaign nationwide while he was the Northern Democrat candidate for President in the 1860 Election.

James Dunkenfield never received fame as a private in the 72nd Pennsylvania Fire Zouaves, leaving service after losing the fingers of his left hand. His son, William Claude, would achieved fame, not in the military, but on the stage and in the early days of movies, as the star W.C. Fields.

James Eads had no formal schooling, or shipbuilding experience, when he designed and built eight ironclad river steamers for the Union. These vessels were instrumental at places like Forts Henry and Donelson and Island No. 10. He also invented the diving bell.

Daniel Decatur Emmett, a New Yorker, composed the song "Dixie."

Edward Everett, a famous orator of the time, was the headline speaker at the dedication of the new National Cemetery at Gettysburg. President Lincoln was also invited to say a few words (almost as an afterthought). Everett's speech took 2 ½ hours. Lincoln's took 2 ½ minutes. Everett complemented Lincoln on his speech. Lincoln thought that his speech was a failure. Today, no one remembers what Everett said that day while schoolchildren have memorized Lincoln's Gettysburg Address for decades.

Admiral David Farragut was the highest ranking Hispanic in Federal service (his father was Spanish).

John T. Ford, owner of Ford's Theater, was jailed during the hysteria that followed the Lincoln Assassination.

Nathan Bedford Forrest was known to have had 29 horses shot from under him. He also was known as a founding member of the Ku Klux Klan, which he regretted on his deathbed.

When secessionists attempted to seize the Federal Arsenal at St Louis, they were led by New Yorker Daniel Frost.

The pardoning of Confederate Private Paul Fusz (for smuggling drugs through the lines) is considered by some to be Abraham Lincoln's last official act as President.

When Port Hudson, LA fell on 8 July 1863, the Confederate garrison was led by New Yorker Franklin Gardner.

James Garfield served as Lieutenant Colonel of the 42nd Ohio until promoted to Major General in September 1863. Three months later, he resigned his commission to take a seat in Congress. He would become the 20th President of the United States, as well as the second President to be assassinated while in office.

William Lloyd Garrison was named in an arrest warrant, issued by the State of Georgia, for his anti-slavery writings.

Garrison was also an advocate for women's rights, expressing that view when he walked out of an anti-slavery convention in London, UK, when a group of women abolitionists were barred entry.

Garrison publicly burned a copy of the Constitution to protest the fact that it protected Slavery.

Richard Gatling was so horrified by the carnage of war that he developed a hand-cranked, multi-barreled weapon in order to make wars unwageable. The system of rotating barrels is used to this day.

Indiana native William Gilham was an instructor at the Virginia Military Institute when war broke out. After leading a brigade at Cheat Mountain in 1861, he went back to the school. Some of his students were at New Market in 1864.

The system of prisons in Richmond was run by a Californian, Archibald C. Godwin. Getting killed in the Third Battle of Winchester might have saved him from the same fate as Henry Wirz, commandant of Andersonville.

Archibald Gracie Jr's father must have regretted sending his son to run the Mobile, AL branch of his mercantile business, since he repaid his father's kindness by siding with the South and becoming a Confederate general. That decision was paid for when he was killed at Petersburg. (The Gracie Mansion is now the residence of the Mayor of New York City).

When the Civil War began, Ulysses S. Grant was employed as a clerk in his father's tanning shop.

Grant had a dislike for fancy uniforms. When he showed up at the McLean house to accept Robert E. Lee's surrender, he was wearing a slouch hat, a private's blouse with his rank sewn on the shoulders, mud splattered pants, and carried no sword.

Grant sent a letter and a silver service to Confederate Major General George Pickett in order to commemorate the birth of Pickett's son. (Grant and Pickett were friends before the war).

Grant received 10,000 cigars from across the country after capturing Forts Henry and Donelson. (He liked smoking cigars, which most likely contributed to his death from throat cancer).

Lemuel Grant was a Maine native who designed and built the defense lines around Atlanta.

Edward Everett Hale would have been forgotten if he had not written, *"The Man Without a Country."* The story was inspired by the tale of Clement Vallandigham, who was one of the major opponents to the Union war effort.

Lieutenant Colonel Charles Hamilton of the 7th Wisconsin was a grandson of the first US Secretary of the Treasury, Alexander Hamilton.

Vice-President Hannibal Hamlin served two months as a Private.

Colonel Benjamin Harrison of the 70th Indiana, the grandson of President William Henry Harrison would himself become President in 1888. His war experience included the Atlanta Campaign and the Battle of Nashville.

Tyler Henry, working at the New Haven Arms Company at the outbreak of the war, developed a rim-fire copper cartridge and a mechanism for loading them into the breech of a rifle. The Henry rifle was not bought by the War Department, but individual soldiers, as well as several regiments, purchased their own Henry rifles. The rifle became so popular that Henry's boss, Oliver F. Winchester, began to mass-produce them. The resulting Winchester rifles became a staple in the post-war West.

James Hickok was a Union scout who would have been lost to history had he not became known as the gunman "Wild Bill" Hickok.

A.P. Hill must have been valuable to both Thomas Jackson and Robert E. Lee: both of them were giving orders to Hill while on their deathbeds.

Winslow Homer was an artist for *Harper's Weekly*, during which he had sketched one of the most famous Civil War drawings, *Sharpshooter*. After the war, he devoted his artistic talent to seascapes.

Jedediah Hotchkiss, mapmaker to Confederate General Thomas Jackson, was from New York. His maps were instrumental in the Shenandoah Valley Campaign of 1862, and many of them were printed in the *Official Military Atlas of the Civil War*.

Even after his father was ousted from the Texas Governorship, Sam Houston Jr. served in the 2nd Texas and was wounded at Shiloh.

Elias Howe, a private in the 17th Connecticut, perfected a sewing machine that was popular in Europe. He won a gold medal at the Paris Exposition of 1867 and soon after became acclaimed in the US.

Daniel Hough became the first Union soldier to die in the war when a spark ignited some powder bags during a cannon salute at Fort Sumter, following the Federal surrender in 1861. No one today knows where he his grave is.

Amos Humiston, a sergeant in a New York regiment was killed on 1 July 1863 at Gettysburg. In his hand was a picture of his three children. The photo was copied and circulated until the family was found. The picture became so popular that interest in the plight of children of Union soldiers killed in the war was generated. This led to the founding of a home for such orphans. Humiston's widow became that home's first matron.

One of the Confederate purchasing agents in Europe was Caleb Huse, from Massachusetts.

Private John Ingraham, 1ˢᵗ Confederate Regiment, Georgia Volunteers, is the only known body buried on the Chickamauga battlefield. All others were moved in order to develop the park.

Thomas Jackson did not like the nickname "Stonewall." He felt it was more deserved by the brigade he led at First Manassas.

Jackson was known for teaching African-Americans to read the Bible, despite a Virginia law prohibiting him from doing so.

Before First Manassas, to help rest his troops, Jackson was the sole person on picket duty.

If Jackson could help it, he never attacked on a Sunday. First Manassas was an exception, which was also his wife's birthday.

Jackson never put pepper on his food, claiming that it hurt his left leg.

Jackson wanted to adopt a "total war" approach towards the North, attacking farms, factories, and infrastructure, however, President Davis did not feel the same way. It is unknown if Davis regretted that decision when he heard that Union General Sherman was using the same tactic while marching through Georgia.

In the end, Jackson was buried in two places, his amputated arm at Ellwood Manor, and the rest of him on the grounds of the Virginia Military Institute.

William Jackson was not as famous or successful as his cousin Thomas. Thomas was known as Stonewall while William was called Mudwall.

Another William Jackson was a coachman for CS President Davis. He was also a Union spy.

Jesse James, and his brother Frank, rode with the pro-Confederate Missouri Home Guard in 1861, but soon they were working for William Quantrill. They are more noted for being outlaws after the war.

Robert Tyler Jones, a grandson of President John Tyler, led a color guard at Gettysburg.

Bushrod Johnson, who led Confederate troops at Chickamauga, came from Ohio.

Six years before dying at Shiloh, Confederate General Albert S. Johnston led US troops in putting down a rebellion of Mormons in Utah.

Joseph Johnston was a pallbearer at the funeral of his old friend and former enemy William T. Sherman. His respect for the Union General was such that he took his hat off. Problem was it was cold and rainy. Johnston caught a cold, which turned into pneumonia, and died several weeks later.

The family of the man who wrote what became the National Anthem supported secession.

Manning Kimmel resigned his commission and joined the Confederate Army right after First Manassas. His son, Husband, was the Navy commander at Pearl Harbor, HI on 7 December 1941.

Curtis King was the oldest known enlisted man in the Union Army, joining the 37th Iowa in 1862 at the age of 80.

Robert E. Lee's father, "Light-Horse Harry" Lee led the first US response against insurgents during the Whiskey Rebellion of 1794.

Lee is noted to have received no demerits while a cadet at West Point, a feat that has not been duplicated since.

One of Lee's pre-Civil War commands was the Department of Texas, headquartered in San Antonio. He was a noted guest of the Menger Hotel, one block from the Alamo.

Sidney Smith Lee Jr., a nephew of the famous Confederate General, served aboard CSS *Shenandoah*.

Virginia Governor John Letcher was a staunch Unionist, at least until President Lincoln's call for troops.

Eli Lilly served the Union as a Colonel. While he was bypassed for post-war honors, his small pharmaceutical business became one of the worlds largest within a century.

Abraham Lincoln was also the name of a private in the 1st Virginia Cavalry. (He must have taken a lot of grief).

President Abraham Lincoln was in favor of shipping freed slaves to Africa until talked out of that view by men like Frederick Douglass.

President Lincoln was elected an honorary citizen of the Republic of San Marino.

President Lincoln lost more elections than he won.

Presidents Lincoln and Davis were born less than 100 miles apart.

Robert Todd Lincoln, son of the President, became an aide to Lieutenant General Ulysses S. Grant due to political pressure. After the war he was Secretary of War (in the Garfield and Arthur Administrations) and Ambassador to Great Britain before becoming the Chief Executive

Officer of the Pullman Car Company, a maker of railroad sleeping cars.

Edouard Manet, a noted French painter, witnessed the battle between USS *Kearsarge* and CSS *Alabama*. His rendering of the battle is noted as one of his best paintings.

Lunsford L. Lomax, from Rhode Island, led the 11th Virginia Cavalry at Gettysburg, where he would one day become a Commissioner of the Military Park.

Not only did Confederate General James Longstreet become a Republican after the war, he took a job as President Grant's Minister to the Ottoman Empire (Turkey).

Mansfield Lovell gave up a career as a New York City Deputy Street Commissioner to wear the stars of a Confederate Major General.

Thaddeus Lowe flew in one of his balloons from Cincinnati and landed at Charleston, several days after Fort Sumter. He was almost arrested as a spy, but was put on the first train north after proving he was a scientist.

Lieutenant Arthur MacArthur Jr won the Medal of Honor for his part in storming Missionary Ridge. His son, Douglas, won the Medal of Honor for his part in defending the Philippines in WWII.

Karl Marx, the father of Communism, wrote articles for the New York *Tribune*. He never stepped foot in North America, but was interested in the social implications of the Civil War.

Matthew Maury was already an US Navy oceanographer of note when he switched sides. He was noted for his work involving the Gulf Stream.

Rhode Island native John McAnerny Jr. set up the ambush that led to the death of Union Colonel Ulrich Dahlgren.

George McClellan was an observer of the Crimean War.

McClellan did not find out about his removal from command of the Army of the Potomac until reading about in a day-old newspaper.

McClellan developed a saddle that was used in operations by the US Army until WWII, and is still used by ceremonial units.

Catholic Priest Father Thomas Mooney was rebuked for christening an artillery piece.

Thomas Nast worked for *Frank Leslie's Illustrated Newspaper* before the Civil War. Already noted for his sketches, he was hired by *Harper's Weekly* and sketched many Civil War battles. Post-war, he became famous for creating the symbols of the Democratic and Republican Parties, the donkey and elephant.

John O'Connor became known for enlisting in 32 regiments. Right after he collected the enlistment bounty, he deserted and went to another regiment to enlist. He was caught when a recruitment officer recognized him.

Eli Parker was rejected by the Governor of New York when he raised a regiment to fight for the Union. It was through his friendship with Ulysses S. Grant that he was able to don Union blue, becoming a member of Grant's staff and eventually writing the Articles of Surrender that was signed at Appomattox. Parker was a leader of the Seneca Nation.

Jacob Parott was the very first Union soldier to receive the Medal of Honor. He participated in the mission that resulted in the Great Locomotive Chase.

John C. Pemberton, commander of the Vicksburg, defenses, was a Pennsylvanian. In 1864, he resigned his general's commission and reverted to the rank of Lieutenant Colonel in an artillery unit, and did quite well.

The Reverend William Pendleton, as a Confederate Brigadier General, commanded an artillery battery of four guns in 1861, which he named "Matthew," "Mark," "Luke," and "John."

Galusha Pennypacker was the youngest Brigadier General on either side, being promoted before turning 21.

At Christmastime, a favorite song is"Jingle Bells." The writer of that song, James Lord Pierpont, was a Massachusetts native who served in the 1st Georgia Cavalry.

Perhaps if Lewis Powell, a Private in the 2nd Florida, had not been wounded and captured at Gettysburg, he might not have gotten mixed up with John Wilkes Booth after his escape from a hospital. Powell was assigned the task of killing US Secretary of State Seward, which he failed to accomplish.

Seaman John Ortega became the first Hispanic in the US Navy to win the Medal of Honor for bravery during several raids in the Charleston, SC area.

William Quantrill, the Confederate partisan who led the sack of Lawrence, KS, was from Ohio.

Paul Joseph Revere was commanding the 20th Massachusetts when he was mortally wounded at Gettysburg. His grandfather was Paul Revere, who made the famous Midnight Ride in 1775.

George Rains, a Confederate explosives expert, invented a sensitive percussion cap, making land and sea mines possible.

Union Colonel Charles Ripley, head of the US Army Ordnance Department in 1861, refused to buy breech loading or repeating rifles because he feared that it would result in the soldiers wasting ammunition.

Ohio native Roswell Ripley commanded the cannons at Fort Moultrie while Fort Sumter was being shelled in 1861.

Felix Robertson was the last surviving Confederate General Officer when he died in 1928.

Future President Theodore Roosevelt watched President Lincoln's funeral procession in New York City. He was six at the time.

In London, Baron Rothschild was asked who he though would win the war. His answer; "The North," because "it has the largest purse."

William Howard Russell's articles for the London *Times* were criticized by both sides.

Union General Winfield Scott served in uniform during the administrations of 14 Presidents (Jefferson to Lincoln).

Commanding the 46th Mississippi at Chickasaw Bluffs was Massachusetts native Claudius F. Sears.

Union Navy Captain Thomas Selfridge should never have been assigned to any vessels: He was a Lieutenant on USS *Cumberland* when the warship was attacked by CSS *Virginia*, he commanded USS *Cairo* when the gunboat struck a torpedo in the Yazoo River, and then he commanded USS *Conestoga* during a collision with another Federal warship. However, during the disastrous Red River Campaign, he managed to get USS *Osage* out of a sticky situation. Finally, he commanded USS *Huron* during the Fort Fisher Campaign, which he got through unscathed.

Philip Sheridan paid a 25 cent toll as he was riding toward Winchester in September, 1864.

William T. Sherman hated newspaper reporters (that's nothing new).

Sherman's most famous quote: *"War is Hell"* was not said during the war but at an address made to the Michigan Military Academy on 19 June 1879.

As a youth, Sherman tried to dye his red hair, turning it green.

Union Major General Dan Sickles liked to visit his amputated leg, which was given to the Army Medical Museum. Today, it is at the National Museum of Health and Medicine.

Confederate Commissioner to France, John Slidell, was once a New York businessman.

The New Orleans, Vicksburg and Mobile Defenses were built by New Yorker Martin Smith.

Henry Stanley, a private in the 6th Arkansas, was captured at the Battle of Shiloh. While at Camp Douglas, IL, he swore an oath to the US and served in the Union army (called a "galvanized Yankee," these troops were posted in the West) until illness forced his discharge. He soon joined the US Navy, but deserted in 1865. Stanley would have been lost to history if he did not lead an expedition to find the presumed lost David Livingston in Africa.

John Staples was paid $500 to enlist in the place of President Lincoln.

One of the six Confederate generals to die at Franklin, TN was the Ohioan Otho Strahl.

Union General George "Rock of Chickamauga" Thomas was a Virginian.

David Twiggs was a hero of the War of 1812, the Black Hawk War, the Seminole war, and the Mexican War. All that was wiped away with one act of treachery; the turning over of all Federal property to Texas secessionists in 1861.

Clement Vallandigham was not only banished from Union territory, but the Confederates deported him as well.

Cornelius Vanderbilt donated five of his steamships to the US Navy.

Confederate General Earl Van Dorn was a womanizer who paid for his being "a dedicated romantic" when he was shot by a Dr. Peters, the husband of one of Van Dorn's presumed lovers.

James Waddell, following his time as commander of CSS *Shenandoah*, became commander of the Maryland Oyster Police, tasked with protecting Maryland's oyster beds from poachers.

Stand Waite, a Cherokee leader, was the last Confederate General to surrender his command.

Senator Daniel Webster's son Fletcher formed the 12th Massachusetts. He was killed at the Second Battle of Manassas.

Gideon Welles had no naval experience when he became the US Secretary of the Navy.

Henry Wirz was the only individual from either side executed for war crimes. He ran the prison camp of Camp Sumter, otherwise known as Andersonville.

Walt Whitman wrote poetry between shifts as a volunteer hospital nurse in Washington, D.C.

Maxwell Woodhull allowed subordinates aboard USS *Connecticut* to experiment with using an ice filled room to preserve fresh beef. This resulted in cold rooms becoming a common feature in meat packing plants across the nation.

Albert Woolson was the last surviving member of the Union Army when he died in 1956. Since the claims of four men to be Confederate veterans have been debunked, and the last confirmed Confederate soldier died in 1951, Woolson can be considered the last Civil War veteran.

It has not been confirmed whether or not Union General Thomas Williams was killed at Baton Rouge, LA by his own troops who grabbed his arms and held him to the muzzle of a cannon, which was touched off.

Walter Williams was listed as the last surviving member of the Confederate Army as well as the last Civil War veteran when he died in 1959, two years before the Centennial. Since his death, that has been debunked.

Future President Woodrow Wilson was eight when he saw Jefferson Davis ride through his town as a Federal prisoner.

Zebulon York went with his adopted state of Louisiana rather than his home state of Maine.

Count Ferdinand von Zeppelin, father of the rigid airship, observed Union balloons.

Felix Zollicoffer, who was nearsighted, left his glasses behind when he rode into battle at Mill Springs, so he was not able to see that it was a Union officer he was shouting orders to, or that the same officer was pointing his sidearm at the Confederate General.

Foreigners in Civil War Service

Name, Rank, and Unit (if known)

Union:

Austria:
Henry Bornstein, Colonel, 2nd Missouri

Canada:
Joseph Scott, Colonel, 19th Illinois

England:
James Ashworth, Colonel, 121st Pennsylvania
Edward Baker, Colonel, 1st California (69th Pennsylvania)
John Fitzroy de Courcy, Major
Edward Molineaux, Colonel, 159th New York
Sir Percy Wyndham, Colonel

France:
Comte de Paris, Observer on Major General McClellan's staff
Philippe Regis de Trobriand, Brigadier General
Charles A. de Villiers, Colonel, 11th Ohio
Duc de Chartres, Observer on Major General McClellan's staff
Alfred Duffie, Brigadier General
Charles W. Le Gendre, Colonel, 51st New York
Nikolas Greusel, Colonel, 36th New York
Prince de Joinville, Brigadier General

Germany (Prussia):
Fritz Anneke, Colonel, 34th Wisconsin

Adolph August, Brigadier General
Valentine Bausenwein, Major
Ludwig Blenker, Brigadier General
Heinrich Bohlen, Brigadier General
Adolph Buschbeck, Colonel, 27th Pennsylvania
Joseph Conrad, 15th Missouri
Frederick Fuger, Sergeant, Battery A, 4th New York Artillery
Joseph Gerhardt, Colonel, 46th New York
William Heine, Colonel, 103rd New York
Friederich Hocker, Colonel, 24th Illinois
August Kautz, Brigadier General
Leopold Kazinski, Colonel
Konrad Krez, Colonel, 27th Wisconsin
William Kuffner, Colonel, 149th Illinois
Leopold Matthies, Brigadier General
George Mindel, Colonel, 27th New York
August Moor, Colonel, 28th Ohio
Peter Osterhaus, Major General
Carl Salomon, Colonel, 5th Missouri
Edward Salomon, Colonel, 82nd Missouri
Friederich Salomon, Brigadier General
Friedrich Karl von Schirach, Major
Karl Schurz, Major General
Albert Sigel, Colonel, 5th Missouri Militia
Franz Sigel, Major General
Ludwig von Blessing, Colonel, 37th Ohio
Frederick Wilhelm von Egloffstein, Brigadier General
Leopold von Gilsa, Colonel, 41st New York
Felix von Salm-Salm, Colonel, 8th and 68th New York
George W. von Schack, Colonel
Alexander von Schimmelfennig, Brigadier General
Friederich Baron von Steinwehr, Brigadier General
Hugo von Wangelin, Colonel, 12th Missouri
Max von Weber, Brigadier General
August von Willich, Brigadier General
Louis Wagner, Colonel, 88th Pennsylvania

Hungary:
George Amsberg, Colonel, 55th New York
Alexander Asboth, Brigadier General
Peter Paul Dobozy, Lieutenant Colonel, 4th United States Colored Heavy Artillery
John Fiala, Colonel
Philip Figyelmessy, Colonel
Cornelius Fornet, Colonel, 22nd New Jersey
Frederick Knefler, Colonel, 79th Indiana
Gabriel Korpanay, Lieutenant Colonel, 7th New York
Eugene Kozlay, Colonel, 54th New York
Geza Mihalotzy, Colonel, 24th Illinois
Joseph Nemeth, Colonel, 5th Missouri Cavalry
Nicholas Perczel, Colonel, 10th Iowa
Anthony Pokorny, Lieutenant Colonel, 7th New York
George Pomutz, Lieutenant Colonel, 15th Iowa
Robert Rombauer, Colonel, Missouri Reserve Corps
Julius Stahel-Szamwald, Major General
Emery Szabad, Colonel
George Utassy, Colonel, 39th New York "Garibaldi Guards"
Joseph Vandor, Colonel, 7th Wisconsin
Gustav Waagner, Colonel, 2ne New York Heavy Artillery
Charles Zagonyi, Hungarian, Colonel
Ladislaus Zsulavsky, Colonel, 82nd United States Colored Troops

Ireland:
Michael Bryan, Colonel, 175th New York
Richard Byrnes, Colonel, 28th Massachusetts
Thomas Cahill, Colonel, 9th Connecticut
Andrew Caraher, Colonel, 28th Massachusetts
Howard Carroll, Colonel, 105th New York
Thomas Cass, Colonel, 9th Massachusetts
Michael Corcoran, Brigadier General
George Gray, Colonel, 6th Michigan Cavalry
James Gwyn, Colonel, 118th Pennsylvania
Patrick Kelly, Colonel, 88th New York
W.H. Lytle, Colonel, 10th Ohio

Thomas Meagher, Major General
Robert Minty, Colonel, 4th Michigan Cavalry
St. Clair A. Mulholland, Colonel, 116th Pennsylvania
James Mulligan, Colonel, 23rd Illinois
Patrick O'Rorke, Colonel, 140th Pennsylvania
Robert Patterson, Brigadier General
William Sewell, Colonel, 5th New Jersey
Robert Nugent, Colonel, 69th New York
James Shields, Major General
Thomas Smyth, Major General
Thomas Sweeny, Major General

Italy:
Luigi Palma de Cesnola, Colonel, 4th New York Cavalry
Achille de Vecchi, Colonel, 9th Massachusetts Battery
Albert Maggi, Colonel, 33rd Massachusetts
Luigi Navone, Colonel

Norway:
Hans Heg, Colonel, 15th Wisconsin

Poland:
Joseph Karge, Colonel, 1st New Jersey Cavalry
Wladimir Krzyzanowski, Colonel, 58th New York
Ladislaus Koniusjewski, Major, 26th Missouri
Alexander Raszewski, Major, 31st New York
George Sokalski, Lieutenant Colonel, 26th Missouri
Albin Scheopf, Brigadier General

Russia:
Ivan Turchinoff, Brigadier General

Scotland:
David Ireland, Colonel, 137th New York

Spain:
Edward Ferrero, Brigadier General

Sweden:
John Ericsson, Designer and builder of USS *Monitor*
Ernst Holmstedt, Colonel, 74th United States Colored Troops
Oscar Malmborg, Colonel, 55th Illinois
Hand Mattson, Colonel, 3rd Minnesota
Palle Rosencrantz, Colonel
Charles Stohnbrand, Brigadier General
Ernst Mattais Peter von Vegesack, aide-de-camp to Union General John Wool
Adolph Warberg, Major

Switzerland:
Samuel Brodbeck, Colonel, 12th Iowa
John Kuhn, Colonel, 145th Illinois
Hermann Lieb, Colonel, 5th United States Colored Troops
Joseph Mosch, Colonel, 83rd New York
Arnold Sutermeister, Colonel

One interestingly diverse Union regiment:

39th New York, the "Garibaldi Guards"
Commander: Colonel George Utassy, a Hungarian.
Its Lieutenant Colonel was an Italian.
The Regimental Surgeon was a Prussian.
There were three companies of Hungarian Hussars.
Three companies were of Prussian Infantry.
One company was of Italian Carabineers.
One company was Swiss.
One was of the French *Chasseurs a Pied.*
One company was of Spaniards.
One company was of Portuguese.
The rest of the ranks were made up of English, Croats, Bavarians, Cossacks, Garribaldians, Sepoys, Prussians, and Algerians.

Confederate:

Belgium:
George Auguste Gaston de Coppens, Lieutenant Colonel, 1st Louisiana Zouaves
Henri Honori St. Paul, Lieutenant Colonel

Canada:
William G. Robinson, Colonel, 2nd North Carolina Cavalry

Cuba:
A.J. Gonzalez, Colonel
Loreta Janeta Velazquez, Lieutenant

England:
William Alexander, Lieutenant in 21st Alabama and one of the engineers who built the *H. L. Hunley.*
George Campbell, Colonel
George St. Leger Grenfel, Lieutenant Colonel, Aide to Major General John Morgan
John Cassons, Captain, Staff officer for Major General Evander Law
George Jackson, Colonel
Colin Leventhrope, Brigadier General
John Mallet, Lieutenant Colonel

France:
P.F. de Gourney, Lieutenant Colonel, 12th Battalion Louisiana Artillery
Camille Armand Jules Marie de Polignac, Major General
Xavier Debray, Brigadier General
Aristide Gerald, Colonel, 13th Louisiana
Louis Lay, Lieutenant Colonel, 6th Louisiana
Pierre Soule, Brigadier General

Germany (Prussia):
Robert Bechem, Brigadier General
Augustus Buchel, Colonel, 1st Texas Cavalry
John Emrich, Lieutenant Colonel, 8th Alabama
B.F. Eshleman, Lieutenant Colonel, Louisiana Artillery
B.W. Frobel, Lieutenant Colonel, Artillery
Augustus Reichard, Colonel, 12th Louisiana
Heros von Borck, chief-of-staff to Major General J.E.B. Stuart.
Henry von Everstein, Sergeant, 7th North Carolina
Victor von Schelila, Lieutenant Colonel, Aide to Major General Simon B. Buckner
Leon von Zinken, Colonel, 20th Louisiana
John Wagener, Brigadier General

Hungary:
Adolphus Adler, Colonel, Engineers
Bela Estvan, Colonel

Ireland:
William Browne, Brigadier General
A.R. Blakely, Louisiana Artillery
Patrick Cleburne, Major General
Joseph Finnegan, Brigadier General
Michael Grogan, Lieutenant Colonel, 2nd Louisiana
Andrew Gwynne, Lieutenant Colonel, 38th Tennessee
James Hagen, Brigadier General
Joseph Hanlon, Lieutenant Colonel
Walter Lane, Brigadier General
Joseph McGraw, Lieutenant Colonel, Artillery
William Monaghan, Colonel, 6th Louisiana
Patrick Moore, Brigadier General
James Nelligan, Lieutenant Colonel, 1st Louisiana
Michael Nolan, Lieutenant Colonel, 1st Louisiana
James Reily, Colonel, 4th Texas Mounted Rangers
Henry Strong, Colonel, 6th Louisiana
Jack Thorington, Colonel, Hilliard's Alabama Legion

Poland:
Arthur Grabowski, Colonel
Hypoite Oladowski, Colonel
Frank Schaller, Colonel, 22nd Mississippi
Valery Sulakowski, Colonel, 14th Louisiana
Ignatius Szymanski, Colonel, Louisiana Militia

Scotland:
Peter Alexander, Brigadier General
J.G. Campbell, Lieutenant Colonel, 6th Louisiana
James Duff, Colonel, 33rd Texas Cavalry
Peter Alexander Selkirk McGlashan, Brigadier General (the last one commissioned at that rank, the papers were signed while President Jefferson Davis was fleeing Richmond, VA)
George Morton, Lieutenant Colonel, 2nd Tennessee Cavalry

Sweden:
Eric Erson, Lieutenant Colonel
August Forsberg, Colonel, 51st Virginia

The Irish

Of the myriad nationalities that immigrated to the United States prior to the Civil War, the Irish were one of the most prominent. The 1860 Census had counted 1,611,304 Irish-born immigrants living in the US, mostly in the Northeast, but many moved inland towards the South and the West.

There was a tradition of Irish serving in various armed forces around the world, such as Napoleon's *Grande Armee*, several South American revolutionary armies, and on both sides of the Mexican War. It seemed that this was the only way Irishmen were able to get any respect beyond the menial jobs that they held. Of course, they were facing anti-immigrant and anti-Catholic discrimination on top of their image as bunch of fighting drunkards who were not smart enough to do anything better.

There were a good number if Irish soldiers in the Regular Army when the Civil War broke out. There were also many Irish who were in militia units around the country who formed the nucleus of many regiments, both Union and Confederate.

As the guns at Fort Sumter fell silent, US President Abraham Lincoln issued a call for 75,000 volunteers to put down the rebellion in the South, thousands of Irish flocked to the colors:

Recruitment officers met many of these immigrants just as they were getting off the boat from Ireland. Others were recruited from the factories, wharves and farms throughout the North.

Many Irish nationalists enlisted in, or formed regiments, in the hopes that they would receive valuable combat experience in case of an attempt to free Ireland from British control.

One such was Thomas Meagher, born on 3 August 1823 in Waterford, Ireland. He was involved in Irish revolutionary activities, including the Rebellion of 1848, for which he was arrested and sentenced to death. That sentence was commuted to life at a penal colony in Tasmania. He escaped from there and made his way to California, and then to New York, where he became a US Citizen and a member of the Irish community there.

As the war started, he raised a company of the 69th New York and got his first taste of battle at First Bull Run (Manassas, VA). He assumed the leadership of the regiment when his commander was captured during the battle. During the winter of 1861-62, Meagher assembled the Irish Brigade, consisting of his 69th New York along with the 63rd and 88th New York, the 28th Massachusetts, and the 116th Pennsylvania.

Their battle honors were legendary:

At Seven Pines the brigade smashed the flank of a Confederate advance near the Adams House, near the Chickahominy River.

At Gaines' Mill Meagher's troops stopped another Confederate assault, which allowed Union baggage trains to get away.

The brigade captured a Confederate battery near Meadow Station.

At Malvern Hill the brigade supported Berdan's Sharpshooters, who were acting as skirmishers.

At Antietam the brigade was part of the assault on a Confederate line at the sunken road that became known as "Bloody Lane."

At Fredericksburg the Irish Brigade were sent up Marye's Heights in the face of horrific cannon and musket fire. They ended up exchanging fire with fellow Irishman of the 24th Georgia.

At Chancellorsville they rescued the guns of the 5th Maine Artillery when the gun crews were killed.

At this point, the brigade had dropped to under 500 men, about half a regiment. Meagher asked to take his brigade home and recruit more regiments and was refused. In response, Meagher resigned his commission on 8 May 1863. Colonel Patrick Kelly, from Kerry, Ireland, became the new commander.

At Gettysburg the Irish Brigade was part of an attack on The Wheatfield, resulting in the brigade's further decimation.

The Irish Brigade was listed as "combat ineffective," meaning that there were not enough troops to even maintain a defensive line, let alone attack. Even as such, they did take part in the Mine Run Campaign in late 1863.

In January 1864, the remains of the Irish Brigade re-enlisted almost to a man and were sent home to recruit new members. St. Patrick's Day, 1864, saw the reorganized brigade back in the field, in time for the Overland Campaign, under the command of Colonel Thomas Smyth. Smyth would go on to be the last General Officer killed in the war, just hours before the Confederate surrender.

The new Irish Brigade distinguished themselves at the Wilderness during the savage fighting along the Brock Road.

At Spotsylvania, they were part of the assault on the Mule Shoe. After that battle, Colonel Richard Byrnes was given command of the brigade.

At Cold Harbor, as the Union assault was getting shredded, the Irish managed to penetrate a portion of the Confederate line. Byrnes was mortally wounded and Colonel Kelly resumed command.

Kelly himself was killed on 16 June 1864 during the assault on the Confederate lines at Petersburg.

The Irish Brigade was once again decimated to the point that it was disbanded and incorporated with other brigades. However, that was not the end.

On 2 November 1864, the Irish Brigade (Reorganized) was assembled under the command of Colonel Robert Nugent, one of the few surviving officers of the original Irish Brigade. That brigade would take part in the Siege of Petersburg as well as the Appomattox Campaign. Colonel Nugent was the one who carried the first letter to Confederate General Robert E. Lee suggesting surrender.

The Irish Brigade marched in the Grand Review before heading home and finally disbanding on 30 June 1865.

Meagher was brought back into Union service, serving in Major General William T. Sherman's command. After again resigning his commission, he was appointed the territorial secretary of Montana Territory and served as Acting Governor. He died on 1 July 1867 after falling off a riverboat on the Missouri River, supposedly drunk. The body was never found.

The other great Irish commander in Union service was Michael Corcoran.

He was born on 21 September 1827 in Carrowkeel, County Donegal and had trained to be a policeman. While a part of the Irish Constabulary, he joined a revolutionary organization called the Ribbonmen. Fleeing charges of treason, he went to New York, where he worked first in a tavern, then as a school inspector and finally in the post office. He became part of the 69th New York Militia, enlisting as a private and soon becoming its colonel. When the Civil War broke out, the 69th New York Militia became the 69th New York Infantry. They were sent to Washington and assigned to the brigade of William T. Sherman. At First Bull Run, Corcoran was wounded and captured, becoming a national hero for refusing to be exchanged for a Confederate prisoner.

Corcoran was exchanged on 14 August 1862, but could not resume his old position because Meagher was given the command. Corcoran decided to raise a brigade of his own. The 155th, 164th, 170th, and the 184th New

York became Corcoran's Legion. The Legion was assigned to the Suffolk, VA area before being assigned to the Washington Defenses.

Corcoran was not able to do too much more: he was killed on 22 December 1863 in an accident involving his horse.

Other Irishman of note in Federal service:

Major St. Clair Mulholland commanded the 116th Pennsylvania while holding a rear-guard action at Chancellorsville, earning the Medal of Honor.

Father William Corby was the chaplain of the 88th New York, having come from a small Catholic boarding school that would become Notre Dame University. At Antietam, he rode up and down the Irish Brigade's line of battle, granting absolution to those who would die bravely in battle. At Gettysburg, he granted mass absolution to those who were headed for the Wheatfield. A passing general was moved by the event, none other that II Corps commander Winfield Scott Hancock.

Major James Quinlan received the Medal of Honor for his actions at Savage Station, VA.

1st Lieutenant George W. Ford captured a Confederate flag at Saylor's Creek, earning a Medal of Honor.

1st Lieutenant Louis Sacriste led the effort to save one of the 5th Maine Artillery's cannon at Chancellorsville, earning his Medal of Honor.

Private Timothy Donoghue carried a wounded officer, while wounded himself, off Marye's Heights, earning a Medal of Honor.

In all, 76 Irish-born soldiers won the Medal of Honor, of which six were in the Irish Brigade. This out of the 1196 awarded.

While Irish soldiers were making a name for themselves in the Union Army, there were others in whom fate sent to Charleston, rather than New York.

Irish Confederate commanders included:

Patrick Cleburne, born on 16 March 1828 at Ovens, County Cork. He joined the British Army after failing medical school, and had served for over three years when he bought his discharge and moved to Arkansas, becoming a druggist and then a lawyer. When the Civil War broke out, he sided with his fellow Arkansans and joined the Yell Rifles as a private. His military experience was noted and he was quickly promoted to Captain. He participated in the fighting at Shiloh, Perryville, and Murfreesboro where he was promoted to Major General. He then fought at Chickamauga, Missionary Ridge, and Ringgold Gap. He almost trashed his military career by suggesting that slaves could be armed in support of the Confederacy. He would not rise above division commander for that. Still, he served throughout the defense of Atlanta and on with the Army of Tennessee's advance into Tennessee. He was killed during the Battle of Franklin, 30 November 1864, one of six generals to fall.

Joseph Finegan was born on 17 November 1814 at Clones, County Monaghan. Seeking his fortune, he immigrated to Florida in 1835 where he started a family and a lumber business at St. Augustine. At the time Florida seceded, Finegan was in the Legislature and had voted to leave the Union. He was made state director of military affairs and was instrumental in forming regiments for Confederate service as well as state defense.

On 8 April 1862, he was in Confederate service himself as a Brigadier General. His battle experiences included, St. John's Bluff, Olustree, Cold Harbor, Globe Tavern, the siege lines of Petersburg, and finally Hatcher's Run before transferring back to Florida prior to the Confederate surrender. His last act as a Confederate general was to help Secretary of War John C. Breckenridge escape to Cuba. Finegan served in the Florida Senate before dying on 29 October 1885.

The Civil War cemented the Irish into the American experience, establishing respect for them at places such as Shiloh and Fredericksburg. After the war, their energies were used for more peaceful purposes, such as building the Transcontinental Railroad.

African-Americans

There can never be any look at the Civil War without noting the contributions of African-Americans in the conflict.

The whole idea of having African-Americans fight for their freedom was a sticky issue from the start. Freed slaves had fought in the American Revolution as full-fledged members of George Washington's Continental Army as well as several units that fought in the War of 1812. Most noted were the African-Americans who fought with Andrew Jackson's army at the Battle of New Orleans.

By the time the Mexican War (1846-1848) began, Blacks had been barred from military service; their past service being forgotten amid racial prejudices. There was one exception, the Navy. In filling out crew rosters for their warships, Navy recruiters were not picky about who served as powder monkeys (boys who hauled bags of gun powder to the cannon), cannoneers, or riggers (needed for sail-powered ships).

As the Civil War began, many Northern African-Americans heeded President Abraham Lincoln's call for volunteers and rushed to recruiting stations, only to be turned away.

> *Why does the government reject the negro? Is he not a man? Can he not wield a sword, fire a gun, march and countermarch, and obey orders like any other?....If persons so humble as we can be allowed to speak to the President of the United States, we should ask him if this dark and terrible hour of the nation's extremity is a time for consulting a mere vulgar and unnatural prejudice?...We would tell him that this is no time to fight with one hand, when both are needed: that this is no time to fight with your white hand, and allow your black hand to remain tied...Men, in earnest don't fight with one hand, when they might fight with two, and a man drowning would not refuse to be saved even by a colored hand.*
> —*Frederick Douglass, August 1861.*

In the South, there was no question about Blacks serving in the Confederate Army, it was not happening. Officially, slaves could be rented to the armies as teamsters, cooks, manual laborers, wagon drivers, and other support functions. Unofficially, many of these African-Americans held muskets and stood in volley lines, keeping up as good a fire as their White counterparts. When Major General Patrick Cleburne suggested that slaves should be allowed to serve in the army in exchange for their freedom, he was ripped apart in the realm of popular opinion and ended up losing promotion opportunities.

> *Over 3,000 Negroes must be included in this number [Confederate troops]. These were clad in all kinds of uniforms, not only in cast-off or captured United States uniforms, but in coats with Southern buttons, State buttons, etc. These were shabby, but not shabbier or seedier than those worn by white men in the rebel ranks. Most of the Negroes had arms, rifles, muskets, sabers, bowie-knives, dirks, etc.....and were manifestly an integral portion of the Southern Confederate Army.*
> Dr Lewis Steiner, Chief Inspector of the US Sanitary Commission, account of his observation of Confederate General Thomas Jackson's occupation of Frederick, MD in 1862

In New Orleans, a group of Free Blacks got together and began drilling as a unit. They were named the Louisiana Native Guards, a militia unit that pledged to help the defense of the city, an obvious target for a Union invasion. This group of African-Americans pledged their services to the

Confederacy, however, local defenders were not interested and abandoned the Native Guards to the advancing Federals. As a result, they switched allegiances to the Union. Among their duties was the garrisoning of Ship Island, off Gulfport, MS, a major Union base in the region.

In February of 1862 there was the first major attempt to put African-Americans in uniform. Union Major General David Hunter had been placed in command of the Union Department of the South, which covered the coastal areas of South Carolina, Georgia, and northeast Florida with 18,000 troops. Hunter felt that that was not enough to do the job, and Washington was not sending reinforcements any time soon.

13 April 1862: General Hunter issued a declaration that all slaves of "enemies of the United States" were to be confiscated and declared free. The main object was to deprive local plantations of needed labor. This also gave him a pool to tap for manpower. Later that month, Hunter ordered able-bodied Blacks gathered in order to raise a regiment, named the 1st South Carolina (US) Infantry (African Descent). They were initially used as labor, but was intended to be a combat unit, that is, if the US Government would recognize the unit and fund it. This proved to be a problem because President Lincoln had already quashed the declaration. Since the government refused to pay and equip the unit, the experiment fell apart with its disbanding on 10 August 1862.

27 September 1862: The Louisiana Native Guards was officially accepted into Union service as the 1st Regiment Louisiana Native Guards. What was amazing at the time was that the line officers (Captains and Lieutenants) were Black.

12 October 1862: The 2nd Regiment Louisiana Native Guards was mustered into service.

29 October 1862: The 1st Kansas (Colored) Volunteer Infantry took part in a skirmish at Island Mound, MO. This unit was locally raised but not in Federal service. This was the first time that Blacks fought in Missouri as a unit, rather than as individuals as they had been since the fighting began. That unit would receive Federal recognition on 1 January 1863.

24 November 1862: The 3rd Regiment Louisiana Native Guards was mustered into service.

Around that same time, the 1st and 2nd Regiments took part in operations in the Bayou La Fourche, south of New Orleans.

It was not until 1863 that the Federal Government, and especially Lincoln, saw the necessity of allowing Blacks into the Army: their numbers would be sorely needed. This action was a result of two things: pressure from several African-American groups and the need to put the war on a more moral footing. That second item stemmed from the issuance of the Emancipation Proclamation, which changed the object of the war from preserving the Union to that of ending Slavery once and for all. Blacks knew from that point that it was their fight too. Lincoln authorized the addition of 100,000 African-Americans to the army with one provision: all the officers had to be White.

Finding officers to command these new units were problematic at first; some Northerners were just as prejudiced as Southerners and would have no part in this enterprise. However, many officers, and a few enlisted enticed with the promises of a commission, decided to volunteer.

When this news hit the Confederacy, reaction was intense. The Confederate Congress quickly passed a law that allowed captured Black troops to be "returned to a state of slavery" (even if that soldier was a Free Black to begin with) and any officers who were captured while in command of African-American troops were to be subject to execution for "inciting servile insurrection." Still that did not deter the Northerners.

As 1863 dawned, the commander of Union forces in Louisiana at the time, Major General Banks, succumbed to pressure from locals, who believed that the presence of Black troops would cause problems, sent the 2nd Regiment to Ship Island and the 1st to the old Confederate forts of Jackson and St. Philip. The 3rd was used in operations around Baton Rouge between February and May of 1863. Other operations included a skirmish at Pascagoula, MS on 9 April 1863 and an assault on Port Hudson, LA on 27 May 1863.

These actions began to answer a question that was in the minds of the Northern public (as well as a few generals and politicians): Will the Black Man fight? The answer to that question was a resounding YES!

In Massachusetts, there was another effort to raise an African-American regiment. They put out a call for volunteers and received a response from not just Massachusetts men, but from all over the US. This group included Northern Free Blacks as well as those who just escaped slavery in the South. This group was designated the 54th Massachusetts and command was given to Robert Gould Shaw, a son of a prominent abolitionist family. Shaw had troubles from the start, getting his green troops trained for battle amid rumors that they would only be used only for manual labor and as garrison troops, getting his troops the equipment they needed from reluctant supply officers, and, the biggest insult of all, the pay.

Union Privates received a monthly pay of $13.00 a month and their clothing was taken care of. The War Department declared that African-Americans would receive $10.00 a month, with $3.00 taken for uniforms. In a world in which $10.00 was a small fortune, that was a lot of money lost. In order to quell a possible riot, Shaw and his officers pledged not to receive their pay until the inequality was addressed.

28 May 1863: The 54th Massachusetts paraded through the streets of Boston, to the delight of both Blacks and Whites, and boarded transports to South Carolina. They soon arrived at St. Simeon's Island and Shaw reported to the garrison commander, Colonel James Montgomery.

11 June 1863: Elements of the 54th Massachusetts and the 2nd South Carolina (US) African Descent marched to Darien, GA where a raid that Colonel Montgomery was carrying out resulted in the town being burned down. Shaw was not happy at the operation and felt that the honor of the 54th was dirtied. He managed to have his regiment transferred to Charleston.

8 July 1863: The 54th Massachusetts began moving to James Island, where they would take part in operations against Confederate defenses there.

11 July 1863: Shaw and his troops arrived.

16 July 1863: The 54th got their first taste of combat. While performing picket duty on Sol Legare's Island, about 300 Confederates attacked. The purpose of this attack was to capture the camp of the 10th Connecticut and as many soldiers as possible. The African-Americans held their ground in order to give the 10th CT time to get away. Their losses were 14 killed, 18 wounded, and 13 missing (those missing were found to have been captured and executed).

Having proved that his men can fight, Shaw volunteered for another mission. There had been an attempt to take a Confederate artillery position called Battery Wagner. This position was at the north end of Morris Island and covered the harbor entrance to Charleston. On 10 July, Federal forces were savaged an attempt to take the fort. The Union commander, Brigadier General Quincy Gilmore, decided to soften up the place with both land-based and naval bombardment. As plans were made to assemble another ground assault, Gilmore would have heard of the request to include the 54th Massachusetts and approved their transfer.

18 July1863: 9:00 a.m.: As the 54th Massachusetts arrived on Folly Island, south of Morris Island, the bombardment was already in progress. Gilmore thought that after he was through, units like the 54th would only need a mopping-up operation to secure the fort.

Gilmore had experience in battering down forts; he was the one who took out Fort Pulaski, near Savannah, GA. There was a difference: Pulaski was a brick fort that could be battered down. Wagner was a sand and earth fort that swallowed incoming shells while its garrison rested in shelters called bombproofs.

5:00 p.m.: Shaw and his troops were ferried across to Morris Island, where he was offered the honor of being the first regiment into the attack. The 54th would be backed up by the 6th Connecticut, 48th New York, 3rd New Hampshire, 9th Maine, and 76th Pennsylvania. Three artillery batteries backed them up.

The entire formation would have to march up a narrow strip of sand between a marsh and the Atlantic Ocean. As they approached the fort, they would be subject to artillery fire from the Confederate defenders.

About 6:00 p.m., the formation began to advance.

First thing the Federals found out was that not all the Confederate guns were destroyed: solid cannon shells began to pound the approaching formations. Shaw told his men to lie down among the dunes until darkness fell.

7:45 p.m.: Shaw gave the order, *"Move in quick time until within a hundred yards of the fort, then double quick and charge."* With that he yelled "FORWARD!" The formation moved as one, despite the shell and grapeshot that began to pepper the Federals. Every hole that appeared in the line was quickly filled in as the 54th approached the wall, where they found a moat that had to be crossed before the wall could be climbed. On the wall were troops of the 31st, 51st, and 61st North Carolina, firing down into the mass of Union troops.

The 54th was not the only ones there: the 6th Connecticut and 48th New York were at the southeast corner trying to get in as well.

Sergeant William Carney found his unit's National Flag next to its fallen color bearer. He picked it up and, despite being wounded several times, kept the flag up in the face of the enemy. In 1900, he would become the first African-American to receive the Medal of Honor.

Shaw rallied his men to the top of the fort's wall, where he was fatally wounded. The other top officers were either killed or wounded. Captain Louis Emilio became the de-facto commander of the 54th MA and rallied his men to the top of the wall.

The first wave of the assault was hung up along the wall and there was a delay in sending in the second. When they were finally sent in, that wave was also stopped. The assault was finally repulsed by Confederate reinforcements.

When everything was finished, the 54th Massachusetts lost 256 in the assault, including most of the officers.

Shaw was buried with several of his soldiers. The Confederates refused to send his body across the lines, stating, *"We buried him with his n*****s."* Shaw's father considered that an honor.

The heroics of the 54th Massachusetts proved to be the spark that opened the way for more African-Americans to join the US Army. So many units were being formed that a new designation was created: United States Colored Troops.

In 1864, there were other opportunities for African-American troops to prove their worth.

20 February 1864: Olustree, FL: The 54th Massachusetts was in battle again, along with the 35th US Colored Troops, the 1st North Carolina (US) Colored and the 2nd South Carolina (US) African Descent. Union forces were attempting to push their way from Jacksonville to Tallahassee when 1200 Confederates under Brigadier General Joseph Finnegan repulsed them. The African-American troops covered the retreat, buying time with their lives.

12 April 1864: A garrison of African-Americans and Tennessee Unionists were overrun at Fort Pillow, on the Mississippi River, by Confederates under Lieutenant General Nathan Bedford Forrest. Whether it was done after the surrender, or because they refused to surrender, most of the garrison was massacred.

As the fighting progressed, there arose the issue of African-American soldiers who became prisoners of war. The official Confederate position was that African-Americans in uniform were not to be afforded POW status. There were Black troops in prisons like Andersonville, GA and Belle Island, VA, but they were used for manual labor. Lieutenant General Ulysses S. Grant, in his capacity as Commander-in-Chief of all Union forces, stopped the practice of prisoner exchanges until his African-Americans were given the same status as White troops.

During the Overland Campaign against the Confederate Army of Northern Virginia, African-Americans made up two brigades of IX Corps and fought from the Wilderness to Petersburg.

In contrast, Major General William T. Sherman's Western armies did not have a single Black soldier. It seemed that Sherman had no use for them.

30 July 1864: The Battle of the Crater: The original plan for when the mine was detonated had both African-American brigades spearheading the assault: they had trained for a straight month while the mine was being dug. Sadly, General Ulysses S. Grant had ordered the IX Corps commander, Major General Ambrose Burnside, not to send in the Black troops for political and public relations reasons. An unprepared brigade, led by a drunkard and coward, was sent in first. The African-Americans were sent in later, after the assault had bogged down, losing scores in the process.

Despite the bravery of the African-Americans in that battle, only one, Sergeant Decatur Dorsey, 39th US Colored Troops, received the Medal of Honor.

On the Confederate side, the debate about using Black troops was not decided until it was becoming too late. Despite protests from hard-liners, the Confederate Congress approved the enlistment of African-Americans into the Confederate Army. Two regiments of mixed White and Black troops drilled to the delight of Richmond residents, but it was too little, too late.

As Richmond fell on 3 April 1865, the first Union troops to enter the former Confederate Capital were members of the 28th US Colored Troops. This spoke volumes to the defeated Confederates. Other units were involved in the Appomattox campaign, which ended with the surrender of the Army of Northern Virginia.

The last engagement of the Civil War, at Palmito Ranch, TX (11-12 May, 1865) saw the last use of African-American soldiers in the Civil

War as the 62nd US Colored Troops made up a large part of the Union force that was repulsed.

Following the war's conclusion, African-African troops made up a large part of the force needed to police the former Confederate States, leaving bad feelings amongst the local population that contributed to the Black Codes that were enacted following the end of Reconstruction. They were also involved in operations along the Rio Grand River that were conducted to keep Imperial Mexico from invading.

Even so, the pace of disbanding Black units was not as fast as the White ones, but in the course of time, the volunteer regiments were disbanded. Those who wanted to continue in the Army were assigned to the 9th and 10th US Cavalry, who would become known as "Buffalo Soldiers" and would see large-scale battle again in the Spanish-American War (at times alongside former Confederates). The 24th and 25th US Infantry was also authorized.

African-Americans earned their citizenship at places like Fort Wagner and the Crater. Sadly, that reward was not realized until the 1960's, one hundred years after their battles. In total, 180,000 African-Americans served in 163 units and 1/3 of them fell in battle.

We, the colored soldiers, have fairly won our rights by loyalty and bravery shall we obtain them? If we are refused now, we shall demand them.
—Sergeant Major William McCeslin: 29th U.S.C.T.

Women

There is another aspect of the Civil War that should be included in every history, the contributions and impact that women made in the conflict. Many of these women were not the stay at home types who saw their husbands, fathers, and brothers march off to war. They maintained farms, worked in factories, nursed the wounded, clerked in government offices and, in about 1250 cases, donned a male disguise and carried a musket.

Many left diaries that gave insights into civilian life on the Home Front as well as when the front reached their home. They chronicled the struggles of life while the men were away, especially the struggle to get food on the table while armies were stripping the farms bare and their insights into the political issues at the time. There might have been a few Scarlett O'Hara types, with their parasols and saying, "fiddle-de-de," but a good look at the women of the period would find that they were a lot tougher than popular literature suggested. Especially since some of these women were African-Americans, with the added burden of being slaves.

(Author's note: I listed the women here, instead of with the other Noted Persons listed earlier because the Women of the Civil War deserve their own spotlight).

Union:

Louisa May Alcott worked in a Georgetown, MD hospital helping wounded Union soldiers. She wrote letters to her family, which described her experiences working there. Those letters became *Hospital Sketches*.

She is more famous for her post-war novels, *Little Women* and *Little Men.*

Susie Baker was a slave in Georgia who managed to learn to read and write. She put those skills to good use while a laundress with the 33rd United States Colored Troops. After the war, she helped organize part of the Women's Relief Corps, as well as becoming a nurse.

Clara Barton started her working life in the US Patent Office. She soon took up nursing and, after the war, was instrumental in founding the America Red Cross.

> *In all this vast assemblage I saw no other trace of woman-kind. I was faint, but could not eat: weary, but could not sleep: depressed, but could not weep. So I climbed into my wagon, tied down the cover, dropped down in the little nook I had occupied so long, and prayed God with all the earnestness of my soul to stay the morrow's strife, or send us victory—and for my poor self—that he impart somewhat of wisdom and strength to my hart—nerve to my arm—speed to my feet, and fill my hands for the terrible duties of the coming day—and heavy and sad I waited its approach.*
> *—Clara Barton, writing on her experiences at Antietam.*

Mary Bickerdyke served as a nurse in 19 engagements in the West while an agent of the Sanitary Commission. Her assistance was such that Major General William Sherman made her the only civilian woman allowed in his area of operations. At the end of the war, she was allowed to ride at the head of a group of Sanitary Commission agents at the Grand Review. Post-war she worked on securing pensions for Union veterans, including hers. She was known to the troops as "Mother" Bickerdyke.

Elizabeth Blackwell put her status as the first female medical doctor to good use, helping to establish the Sanitary Commission, which was a great help to many Union soldiers, in camp or in the hospital.

Mary Elizabeth Bowser was an African-American servant working in the Confederate White House. She was a well-educated woman who picked up lots of information that the Union was able to use, right from the desk of CS President Jefferson Davis!

Kady Brownell was a color-bearer in the 1st Rhode Island at the First Battle of Manassas, the unit her husband was serving in. She was officially on the rolls as a "Daughter of the Regiment," as well as a vivandiere, or sutler. The couple also served with the 5th Rhode Island.

Florena Budwin enlisted in the Union Army with her husband. Both were captured and sent to Andersonville, where he died. She was transferred to the Florence, SC prison, where she died.

Frances Clayton followed her husband into the Union Army, participating in 18 engagements until her husband was killed in the Battle of Stones River in 1862. She was wounded in the same battle and her gender was discovered as she was being treated. She was one of about 1000 women who disguised themselves was men and followed the Union colors.

Lizzie Compton never gave up trying to enlist as a Union soldier. She claimed to have been in seven different units.

Pauline Cushman tricked some Confederate sympathizers in New Orleans by accepting $300 just to go on a stage and present a toast to the CSA. She made the toast, received the money, and used it to start her career as a Union spy.

Frances Day entered the 126th Pennsylvania as Sergeant Frank Mayne in order to be near her sweetheart. She deserted after her beau died of illness.

Dorothea Dix broke gender barriers by becoming the first female superintendent of US Army nurses. As a matter of fact, the demands placed on manpower by the war effort led to women being hired by many departments of the Federal Government.

One of Dix's requirements for new nurses was that none could be younger than 30, she was afraid that younger women would only become nurses in order to find husbands (Clara Barton was one of the rejects).

A little girl named Emily disguised herself as a boy and joined a Michigan regiment. She died at Lookout Mountain, outside Chattanooga, TN.

Anne Etheridge followed her husband into Union service, but did not follow him when he deserted. She became a "Daughter of the Regiment" in the 2nd, 3rd, and 5th Michigan before the war's end.

Ella Gibson was elected chaplain of the 1st WI Heavy Artillery.

Cornelia Hancock started her nursing career in the camp hospitals that sprang up following the Battle of Gettysburg.

Albert Cashier was injured in an automobile accident in 1911. In the hospital, it was found that "Cashier" was actually a woman named Jennie Hodgers who disguised herself as a man, served in the 95th Illinois Infantry, and kept the deception well into the 20th Century.

Clara Harris was a close eyewitness to the Lincoln Assassination.

Julia Ward Howe was taking a carriage ride with her husband when she spotted a group of Union soldiers singing "John Brown's Body." She remarked that there should be better words to that tune. That night, she could not sleep and began writing a poem that she felt was better suited for the music. The poem became "The Battle Hymn of the Republic" and was a great hit with the troops. Sadly, the *Atlantic Monthly* only paid her $4 for the poem.

Elizabeth Keckley, an African-American seamstress, was the close confidant of First Lady Mary Lincoln. She also worked at one time for Confederate First Lady Varina Davis.

Mary Livermore bucked more traditional women's roles to co-direct the Chicago office of the Sanitary Commission.

Ellen "Nellie" Marcy rejected the marriage proposal from A.P. Hill and accepted the one from George McClellan, which was why some Union troops were heard to yell during one of Hill's attacks, *"My god, Nellie, why didn't you marry him?"*

In 1864, near Florence, AL, Confederate troops captured a Federal soldier named Frank Miller, shooting him in the leg as he tried to escape. Upon searching him, it turned out that he was a woman, named Frances Hook. She had enlisted with her brother, only to see him die at Shiloh.

Mary Siezgle was another woman who enlisted in the Federal Army in order to be near her husband. They served in the 44th New York Infantry.

Harriet Beecher Stowe's book, *Uncle Tom's Cabin*, was first published as a serial in the *National Era*. The following year it was released in book form. It sold 1,000,000 copies, a mega-best seller in its time. During the war, President Lincoln met Stowe and remarked to her, *"So you are the little woman whose book started this war."* (Really interesting was that the villain, Simon Legree, was a Northerner.)

Mary Tepe, known as French Mary, was a vivandiere. She sold pies, tinned meat, personal care items, and sometimes whiskey. She also mended and washed soldiers' uniforms. She became a vivandiere when her husband enlisted in the 114th Pennsylvania. At Fredericksburg, she was wounded while tending a group of wounded. She was decorated for braving 13 battles while serving her husband's unit.

Franklin Thompson enlisted in the 2nd Michigan Infantry during the first call up of volunteers by the Lincoln Administration. After demonstrating to the surgeon the ability to handle a musket and tear a cartridge (and not much else) he was mustered in. There were two reasons he did not have to serve in the Union Army, he was a Canadian, and he was she named Sarah Emma Edmonds. Following the war, her comrades campaigned successfully for her to receive a pension.

Several Union soldiers noticed the peculiar way John Thompson was putting on his socks. Further investigation discovered that "Thompson" was female.

Harriet Tubman, an escaped slave, became the most well known "conductors" in the Underground Railroad, the system of safe houses that assisted escaped slaves. She also served as a scout for the Union Army in South Carolina.

Residents of Richmond, VA took no notice of the woman who was wondering the streets, talking to herself. "That's just Crazy Bet," they would say with contempt for the local Unionist. In fact, Elizabeth Van Lew's insanity was an act covering the fact that she was running a spy ring that extended into the office of President Jefferson Davis himself.

Elizabeth Cooper Vernon trained male volunteers in military methods at the start of the war.

Ginnie Wade was the only civilian killed during the Battle of Gettysburg, having been struck by a stray bullet while baking bread on 3 July 1863.

Private Lyons Wakeman died of illness during the Red River Campaign. The 153rd New York soldier was really Sarah Rosetta Wakeman.

Mary Walker, M.D., was the only female surgeon in the Union Army. She was also the only woman to receive a Medal of Honor during the Civil War. (It was revoked in 1919 and reinstated in 1977)

Confederate:

Two brothers, Sam and Keith Blalock, members of the 26th North Carolina, were seen to have a really close relationship. It was because "Sam" was actually Keith's wife, Malinda.

Belle Boyd made sure Major General Thomas Jackson knew about Federal troop movements in the Shenandoah Valley.

Mary Chesnut was the wife of James Chesnut Jr, a Confederate Congressman. She began writing a diary about what she saw and heard throughout the war. She witnessed the bombardment of Fort Sumter from a rooftop and documented everything until the war came to an end. Her diary is considered one of the most detailed personal accounts of the period.

Mary Ann Clark was one of 250 known Southern women who disguised themselves as men and fought for the Cause. She was a Lieutenant under Braxton Bragg.

Kate Cumming's diary of her experiences as a nurse was published in 1866 as *"A Journal of Hospital Life in the Confederate Army of Tennessee."*

Rose O'Neal Greenhow was a spy for the Confederacy who informed Richmond of Federal movements that resulted in the First Battle of Manassas. After a period of house arrest (during which she still sent messages South) she was taken to the Old Capital Prison (named such because it was where Congress met while the Capital was being rebuilt following the Sack of Washington during the War of 1812) and held until May of 1862. She was sent to Europe in 1863 to talk with leaders there. The quest for diplomatic recognition failed but she was given money for the Cause. On the way back, her ship was caught in a storm and floundered. She was placed in a lifeboat and was being rowed to shore when the boat was swamped and Greenhow fell into the water. She might have survived if she had undone the belt containing the $2000.00 in gold that she was wearing.

Mrs. Judith Henry became the first woman to die in the war when her house was hit by Federal artillery during the First Battle of Manassas.

Charlie Hopper looked to be about 16 to the members of the 1st Virginia Cavalry. It is not known if they ever found out if "Hopper" was really Charlotte Hope.

Sarah Morgan was another diarist whose detailed accounts provided a look at how things went in the South.

Sarah Jane Ann Perkins served in a Confederate artillery battery until captured at Hanover Junction.

Mary Pittman, disguised as a Lieutenant Rawley, rode with Nathan Bedford Forrest. She took up spying, but defected to the Union.

Sally Tompkins became the only woman commissioned in the Confederate

Army. It was a reward for running the most successful hospital in the Confederacy, with only 73 patients out of 1300 dying under her care.

Loreta Janeta Velazquez, over her husband's objections, followed him into Confederate service. She took the name Harry T. Buford and was identified as a Lieutenant. In her memoirs, she detailed her participation in battles as diverse as Ball's Bluff and Shiloh.

The most famous love letter of the war.

On 14 July, 1861, Sullivan Ballou, a Major in the 2nd Rhode Island, took some time as his regiment was preparing to head into Virginia to write a letter to his wife, Sarah:

July the 14th, 1861
Washington D.C.

My very dear Sarah:
The indications are very strong that we shall move in a few days—perhaps tomorrow. Lest I should not be able to write you again, I feel impelled to write lines that may fall under your eye when I shall be no more.

Our movement may be one of a few days duration and full of pleasure—and it may be one of severe conflict and death to me. Not my will, but thine O God, be done. If it is necessary that I should fall on the battlefield for my country, I am ready. I have no misgivings about, or lack of confidence in, the cause in which I am engaged, and my courage does not halt or falter. I know how strongly American Civilization now leans upon the triumph of the Government, and how great a debt we owe to those who went before us through the blood and suffering of the Revolution. And I am willing—perfectly willing—to lay down all my joys in this life, to help maintain this Government, and to pay that debt.

But, my dear wife, when I know that with my own joys I lay down nearly all of yours, and replace them in this life with cares and sorrows—when, after having eaten for long years the bitter fruit of

498

orphanage myself, I must offer it as their only sustenance to my dear little children—is it weak or dishonorable, while the banner of my purpose floats calmly and proudly in the breeze, that my unbounded love for you, my darling wife and children, should struggle in fierce, though useless, contest with my love of country?

I cannot describe to you my feelings on this calm summer night, when two thousand men are sleeping around me, many of them enjoying the last, perhaps, before that of death—and I, suspicious that Death is creeping behind me with his fatal dart, am communing with God, my country, and thee.

I have sought most closely and diligently, and often in my breast, for a wrong motive in thus hazarding the happiness of those I loved and I could not find one. A pure love of my country and of the principles have often advocated before the people and "the name of honor that I love more than I fear death" have called upon me, and I have obeyed.

Sarah, my love for you is deathless, it seems to bind me to you with mighty cables that nothing but Omnipotence could break: and yet my love of Country comes over me like a strong wind and bears me irresistibly on with all these chains to the battlefield.

The memories of the blissful moments I have spent with you come creeping over me, and I feel most gratified to God and to you that I have enjoyed them so long. And hard it is for me to give them up and burn to ashes the hopes of future years, when God willing, we might still have lived and loved together and seen our sons grow up to honorable manhood around us. I have, I know, but few and small claims upon Divine Providence, but something whispers to me—perhaps it is the wafted prayer of my little Edgar—that I shall return to my loved ones unharmed. If I do not, my dear Sarah, never forget how much I love you, and when my last breath escapes me on the battlefield, it will whisper your name.

Forgive my many faults, and the many pains I have caused you. How thoughtless and foolish I have often been! How gladly would I wash *out with my tears every little spot upon your happiness, and struggle with all the misfortune of this world, to shield you and my children from harm. But I cannot. I must watch you from the spirit land and hover near you, while you buffet the storms with your precious little freight, and wait with sad patience till we meet to part no more.*

But, O Sarah! If the dead can come back to this earth and flit unseen around those they loved, I shall always be near you: in the garish day and in the darkest night—amidst your happiest scenes and gloomiest hours—always, always: and if there be a soft breeze upon your cheek, it shall be my breath: or the cool air fans your throbbing temple, it shall be my spirit passing by.

Sarah, do not mourn me dead: think I am gone and wait for thee, for we shall meet again.

As for my little boys, they will grow as I have done, and never know a father's love and care. Little Willie is too young to remember me long, and my blue-eyed Edgar will keep my frolics with him among the dimmest memories of his childhood. Sarah, I have unlimited confidence in your maternal care and your development of their characters. Tell my two mothers his and hers I call God's blessing upon them. O Sarah, I wait for you there! Come to me, and lead thither my children.

Sullivan

Major Ballou was killed at the First Battle of Bull Run. The letter was never mailed, but was delivered with Ballou's personal effects. The letter might have been lost to history if Ken Burns had not found it and used it as a quote in his miniseries *The Civil War* in the 1990's.

Other things one normally doesn't see in the history books...

Each side had a different way of naming a battle: the Confederates named a battle after the nearest town, while the Federals named it after the closest river or creek. For example: what the South called the Battle of Sharpsburg, after Sharpsburg, MD, the North called the Battle of Antietam, after Antietam Creek, which ran nearby.

On the other hand, Union armies were named after rivers (Army of the Potomac, Army of the Tennessee, Army of the Ohio, Army of the Cumberland, etc.), while Confederate armies were named after states or regions (Army of Northern Virginia, Army of Tennessee, Army of the Trans-Mississippi, etc.).

The Arizona Rangers (CSA) under John R. Baylor, briefly occupied Tucson. They pulled out when a strong Union force under James H. Carleton came out of California. Carleton became the first governor of the newly created Arizona Territory.

The Philadelphia Brigade, the 69th, 71st, 72nd, and the 106th Pennsylvania, were financed by the State of California and were originally designated the 1st, 2nd, 3rd, and 5th California.

Colorado Territory formed four infantry regiments and one brigade of light artillery. Their only Civil War engagement was at Glorieta Pass.

Dakota Territory (present-day North and South Dakota) formed two cavalry companies but neither saw action in the war. They were created to replace Regular Cavalry who were brought east. Their mission in the area was to guard against raids by Lakota tribes.

Delaware was a Slave state. It took the 13th Amendment to the Constitution to abolish the practice there.

In what would become the State of Oklahoma, there was a civil war within a civil war as the Five Civilized Tribes (Choctaw, Creek Cherokee, Seminole, and Chickasaw) split over their tribal leaders pledge to join the Confederacy. Some members of these tribes owned slaves. The Cherokees switched loyalties and freed their slaves in 1864.

There was a 1st Nebraska Infantry Regiment at the Battle of Shiloh.

A Confederate flag flew briefly over Virginia City, Nevada but the silver out of the Comstock Lode went into the Federal Treasury. As in the Dakota Territory, Nevada formed units to replace Regular troops who were pulled to serve in the East. Nevada became a state on 31 October 1864 (which is why the words "Battle Born" appear on the Nevada state flag).

Oregon created ten cavalry companies, but were only used in the state, and even that was supported by California troops.

Utah Territory's involvement was limited to protecting the Overland Mail route and telegraph lines.

Washington Territory had to worry more about Shoshoni raids than any possible Confederate incursion.

The nation's westward mail was served by the Pony Express from 1860 to 1861.

One of the largest news agencies that would report on the Civil War, the Associated Press, had already been in existence since 1848.

One of the greatest naval battles of the Civil War did not take place in US waters, but in the English Channel. (USS *Kearsarge* vs. CSS *Alabama*)

Contrary to popular belief, the Gettysburg Address was not written on an envelope during the train ride to Gettysburg. The rattle of the rail cars over the tracks would have prevented smooth writing. Most known drafts were written on Executive Mansion stationary.

The nation's tax system had its genesis in the Internal Revenue Act of 1864. The income tax died after the war, but was revived thanks to the 16th Amendment in 1913. On top of a 3% tax on income, there were taxes on liquor, cigars, pipe tobacco, jewelry, licenses, and even inheritances.

"In God we Trust" was first stamped on coins in late 1864.

The US War Department at first refused to purchase repeating weapons because they thought that the rapid rate of fire would waste ammunition.

The town of Winchester, VA changed hands 76 times.

The Union had a submarine of their own, the *Alligator*.

The flag of the 20th Tennessee was made from a ladies silk dress. Not just any lady, but the wife of General John C. Breckenridge.

The State of Georgia never yielded sovereignty to the CSA. Governor Joseph Brown originally wanted to issue their own currency, keep their troops in the state, and even attempted to back up a dispute against the Confederate Government by force.

US Navy vessels that were stationed on the Mississippi River were initially manned by Army troops.

Baltimore did not have a rail line through the town. Passengers traveling through the city had to be hauled by horse-drawn cars through the town from the President Street Station to the Washington Street Station. This presented an opportunity for Southern sympathizers to create trouble when the 6th Massachusetts was on their way to Washington. That trouble resulted in a fight that left four soldiers and twelve civilians dead.

It was a group of volunteer firefighters who committed the first act of what would become the New York Draft Riots.

New painkillers, such as morphine and opium, were used to such an extent that the first generation of drug addicts in the US was created.

When the CSA made its last ditch attempt to stave off defeat by allowing slaves to enlist, it was decreed that the African-Americans would receive equal pay as their White counterparts, something the North did not do.

Orders for the commanding officer of Fort Barrancas (Pensacola, FL) arrived in the form of a pink, scented envelope. Taken for a letter from a lady, the Confederates let the letter through. The letter, actually, was orders to relocate the Federal garrison to Fort Pickens. The move delayed the flashpoint of the war until the bombardment of Fort Sumter, three months later.

Two state governors died at Pittsburg Landing: Wisconsin's Louis Powell Harvey fell into the Tennessee River and drowned while delivering medicine and Kentucky's Secessionist Governor George W. Johnson was mortally wounded during an assault.

The town of Newburgh, IN surrendered to the Confederates, who fooled the Federals by mounting stovepipes to look like cannon.

Confederate defenders at Vicksburg were spooked by the sudden appearance of the USS *Black Terror*, and shot up a lot of ammunition in the process. The *"Black Terror"* was actually a raft made up to look like an ironclad steamer. The vessel flew a skull and crossbones as well as a Union flag. The message painted on the side read, "Deluded Rebels— Give In." Its appearance forced the Confederates to scuttle the USS *Indianola*, captured the day before. It cost the Federals $8.63 to put the vessel together, just a little bit more than the cost of one of the shells thrown at it (a good return on that investment).

A Union scout mistook a farmer's wife's clothesline with the family washing for a Confederate camp.

Thomas's Legion, a Confederate unit made up of primarily Cherokees, defeated a Union garrison at Waynesville, North Carolina on 6 May 1865, and then surrendered to the Federals!

Confederate officers brought their own horses to war, while Union officers were issued their animals. The Federal officer's pay was docked 40 cents a day for the use of the horse.

In order to make money with minimum effort, some Northern clothing manufacturers used a material called shoddy to make uniforms. Shoddy was created by recycling rags and reweaving the fibers. This material easily tore and a uniform made with such tended to come apart in the rain. The practice became so widespread that the period became, "The Age of Shoddy." This also gave the English language a term for anything of inferior quality.

The first reason given for the blockade of Confederate ports was that there were no Federal customs taxes being collected.

Many regiments offered bounties, up to and sometimes more than a years pay, to recruits.

To this day, no one knows the identity of the Confederate officer who wrapped three cigars in a copy of Special Order 191, and then lost it.

Fort Sumter, while in Confederate hands, was hit with nearly one million pounds of iron before it was surrendered. Amazingly, only two Confederates were killed and 50 wounded throughout the bombardments.

The Confederate States Marine Corps was smaller than a regiment.

Regardless of the length, it seemed that a well-built Federal pontoon bridge could stand up to 7865 pounds.

The Federal causalities suffered in the Battle of the Wilderness (1864) were more than the US war deaths in both the War of 1812 and the Mexican War.

A lot of military intelligence that the Federals received was courtesy of African-Americans who were, sadly, lost to history.

The largest support of the Union from another nation came in the form of two Russian fleets that wintered in New York and San Francisco. One of the things they did to show their goodwill was to buy heating fuel for New York's poor that winter. It was revealed in 1914 that the "goodwill visit" was, if fact, a repositioning of the fleets in case of war with the UK or France.

The Confederacy enacted a conscription law before the Union did.

3% of total firearms production in the United States in 1860 was in the South.

Free African-American males who became prosperous resorted to owning their wives and children in order to prevent their abduction by slave catchers.

The gallows on which abolitionist John Brown was hanged was cut up and the pieces were sold for $1.00 each.

The Richmond Howitzers, a Confederate artillery unit, buried a pet crow with full military honors.

It was believed that in 1860 25% of Whites in the South had at least one African-American ancestor.

There was such a shortage of trained military instructors in the CSA that cadets from schools such as VMI were pressed into duty as drill instructors.

On a dark night in 1861, pickets guarding the camp of the 3rd New York Artillery halted a coach. They were surprised to find President Lincoln, Secretary of State Seward, and General McClellan, who were out on a tour of the camps.

The 7th New York Militia, the first to reach Washington in 1861, did not suffer any combat deaths in the 150 days it was active.

Someone on either side found out that a musket barrel could hold a pint of whiskey.

According to Confederate Army Regulations, if two officers in a unit had the same date of rank and no prior US or CS service, seniority was to be determined by lottery.

In what is now West Virginia, a German immigrant in Confederate service shot at a German on the Federal line when he learned that the Federal was from Bavaria. Sectional fighting was not unique to the US.

Some Confederate artillery units started out with captured British guns from the War of 1812.

The US Marine Corps ran from the field only once in its history, at the First Battle of Manassas.

The 55th Illinois had 91 pairs of brothers when it was first mustered.

There were 10 US Army officers at Fort Sumter when it was shelled in 1861. Six of them became Major Generals, one rose no higher than Colonel, and three died, including the one who resigned his commission and joined the Confederate Army.

The first volunteers for North Carolina service learned their drill lessons from a manual printed at a school for the deaf.

1/3 of the causalities at First Manassas were from New York City.

The first Civil War monument was erected in September of 1861 on the First Manassas battlefield.

The 9th Pennsylvania Cavalry was armed with lances until 1863.

The 3rd Maine, as they left for Washington, received about 10,000 doughnuts, courtesy of the ladies of Augusta.

The 5th Pennsylvania Cavalry was composed of mostly Jewish personnel, the largest such unit in US Army history.

USS *Monitor* was the first warship in the US Navy to have flush toilets.

Confederate troops were prepared for the winter of 1862 with the nearly 60,000 overcoats taken from the Federals during the Peninsula Campaign.

The surrender of Federal troops (12,000) at Harper's Ferry on 15 September 1862 was the largest body of US troops surrendered until the Japanese capture of the Bataan Peninsula on 9 April 1942 (40,000).

In Washington City, there were about 450 places where a Union soldier could partake in "horizontal refreshment." (You can figure what that meant for yourself).

The 131st, 133rd, 161st, 173rd, and the 174th New York Infantry, as well as the 14th New York Cavalry, were raised by the NYPD.

The 53rd New York Infantry lacked discipline to the extent that it was disbanded seven months after it was formed.

If you hold an American Express card, you are a customer of a company that was an express mail service at the time of the Civil War.

While McClellan commanded the Army of the Potomac, there were 28 wagons for every 1000 soldiers.

The yacht *America*, which won the Queens Cup in 1851 (creating the America's Cup) became a blockade-runner.

The Novelty Iron Works made the turret of USS *Monitor*.

A Union warship shelled a heard of cattle on the North Carolina coast.

Troops of the 6th Iowa found a mixed breed dog for a mascot. The dog was named after the Confederate President.

During the winter of 1862, near Fredericksburg, VA, a Federal band was playing for their fellows. After a few popular Northern tunes, a Confederate picket shouted, "Now play some of ours." The band fulfilled with the request, afterwards playing "Home Sweet Home" to the delight and tears of both sides. The same thing occurred at Murfreesboro, TN on New Year's Day, 1863.

Some Confederate troops had captured an artillery piece at Pea Ridge, AR and decided to burn it rather than take it with them. They should have checked the barrel first, it was loaded and the resulting explosion wounded many of them.

The Union's most noted mascot was "Old Abe," a bald eagle who survived the war with the 8th Wisconsin Infantry.

At Chickamauga, a Confederate chaplain was reminding the troops that those killed would eat supper in Heaven. One soldier yelled, "Come along and take supper with us."

As Confederate Major General John Hood's Texas Brigade was marching through Chambersburg, PA, a local woman was watching the scene with a Union flag pinned to her chest. A passing soldier yelled, *"Take care, madam, for Hood's boys are great at storming breastworks when the Yankee colors is on them."* She fled back into her house.

The CSA issued 582 types of paper currency.

At Cemetery Ridge, near Gettysburg, the gate to the cemetery had this sign: *All persons found using firearms in these grounds will be prosecuted with the utmost rigor of the law.*

31 Confederate battle flags were captured at Gettysburg, the largest such capture that did not involve the surrender of an army.

Each side lost five generals during that same battle. (Union: Farnsworth, Reynolds, Vincent, Weed, and Zook. Confederate: Armistead, Barksdale, Garnett, Pender, and Semmes).

Facing each other at Vicksburg, MS was 39 regiments from Missouri. 22 were Federal, 17 were Confederate.

Even though the uniform regulations of both sides required them, most soldiers never saw a cravat.

In order to join the 16th New York Cavalry, one had to bring his own horse.

The 7th Tennessee (Confederate) was captured at one point of the war by the 7th Tennessee (Union).

Lawyers accounted for 129 of 425 Confederate generals while 126 of 583 Federal generals were of that profession.

Washington D.C. was the heaviest fortified city in the world during the 1860s, with 807 cannons and 98 mortars spread across 75 forts of various sizes.

The American Bible Society distributed 800,000 Bibles to the troops. 100,000 of those went to Confederates, which was not a bad thing.

At Petersburg, VA, as a captured Confederate soldier was being taken past a Federal artillery park, he was heard to exclaim, *"By, God, you fellows have almost as many guns marked 'US' as we do."*

At the end of 1864, the combined strength of the 3rd and 18th Tennessee Infantry was 12 men, an indication that the Confederacy had no more to give.

Even in the midst of war, the schoolchildren of the South were still being taught. In one schoolbook, there was this math problem: *If one Confederate soldier can whip 7 Yankees, how many Confederate soldiers can whip 49 Yankees?*

Northern children read stories like *The Little Corporal, The Spy of Atlanta, Vicksburg Spy,* and *War Trails.* Southern Children read stories like *The Young Confederate Soldier* and *Story of a Refugee.*

One of the most dangerous jobs in the Confederacy was not working in a powder mill or even as a soldier, it was as an agent of the Conscription Bureau. 38 were killed by resisters while in the course of their duties, which was finding men for the Confederate Army.

The 55th Illinois Infantry traveled 11,965 miles from its initial muster in Chicago to its disbandment following the Grand Review in 1865.

Researchers now believe that at least 50 Chinese-Americans were in the Union ranks at battles such as Gettysburg and Cold Harbor.

The CSA never established a Supreme Court.

Only two of the original officers were present for duty when the 20th Massachusetts Infantry disbanded in 1865.

Of the estimated 2000 blockade-runners that were active, there were only 150 when the war ended.

The Duchy of Saxe-Coburg-Gotha was the only country to extend diplomatic recognition to the CSA.

The only Confederate soldiers to receive any mustering out pay at the end of the war was the 500 soldiers in San Antonio, TX who grabbed $80,000 in silver and divided it amongst themselves. Each one received about $160.00.

Old Jim was the last surviving horse of the Civil War when he died in 1894.

Almost the entire student body of the University of Mississippi left school to form both the University Grays and the Lamar Rifles.

The kepi, even though widely issued, was not as popular as the forage cap or the slouch hat: the kepi could not shield its wearer from sun and rain.

A nickname for Confederate soldiers, butternuts, came about because some soldiers wore homespun clothes dyed with walnut shells.

There were more battles fought in Virginia than any other state in the Civil War.

Even while fighting the Federals, the CS Navy actually got the chance to fight a foreign enemy, in the form of Moroccans who objected to the presence of CSS *Georgia* off their coast in March 1863. One volley of cannon fire from the warship decided the matter in favor of the Southerners.

The US Navy got into their own foreign incident when USS *Wyoming*, on watch for the possible appearance of CSS *Alabama*, was called to take on three Japanese warships and six shore batteries that were being used to harass foreign merchant shipping in the Shimonoseki Strait. The Federals took out the ships and batteries with a crew that had never been in battle before!

Would the Battle of Five Forks have ended differently if George Pickett had not gone to that shad bake?

The Napoleon cannon was named after Emperor Napoleon III, not Napoleon Bonaparte.

CSS *Alabama* never put into any port of the state the raider was named after.

An estimated 3500 Hispanics fought on both sides during the war.

Copperheads

As with any other war in US history, the Civil War had its own anti-war opposition. There was a small, vocal, and sometimes violent group that took it upon themselves to work against the war policies of the Lincoln Administration. This group primarily consisted of a faction of the Democratic Party known as Peace Democrats and would be considered quite radical today. They were assisted by several northern newspapers and had the support of lawyers and other professionals.

There are two stories of the origin of the name for their group, Copperheads. The most popular one was that some members cut the Goddess of Liberty images out of copper pennies and fixed them to the lapels of their coats to identify themselves to each other. The other one was they were described by their Republican opponents as venomous snakes, such as the Copperhead snake.

There was not a single organization called Copperhead, the anti-war opposition actually consisted of several groups:

Knights of the Golden Circle

The Knights of the Golden Circle was an already established group (established in 1854) that wanted to maintain the balance of Slave and Free states. One of their goals was to expand the US into Mexico and the Caribbean in order to keep that balance. The group planned what was called filibustering expeditions to countries like Cuba. They planned to raise and equip a small armed force, invade said country and take over its government, and then turn that country over to the US as a new territory, usually with the aim of creating a Slave state. These plans never got beyond the discussion stage. In 1861, they had some involvement in Kentucky's secession movement, but beyond that, there was not too much that they were able to do. Actions they did take included resisting the draft and harassing Union patrols looking for deserters. One popular tactic was to entice Union soldiers to desert by providing civilian clothes, maps to safe houses, and train tickets. Not many took up the offer. The group came to an end in 1865 amid allegations that they assisted in the Lincoln Assassination.

Order of American Knights

Established in 1850 by Phineas C. Wright, the Order of American Knights was much feared throughout the Civil War, mostly for imagined reasons. This organization patterned themselves after the Knights of the Golden Circle in their Southern sympathies as well as their tactics. Their base of membership stretched throughout the North, however, their true numbers were inflated. One thing that caught the attention of Union authorities was a meeting held in December, 1863 in Chicago, where they denounced the Lincoln Administration's activities as unconstitutional and called for the Peace Democrats to prepare to take up arms against a looming dictatorship. The same group met in February 1864 and, expressing misgivings about Wright's views and tactics and actually voted to dissolve the organization. Wright himself was arrested and imprisoned for the remainder of the war. He spent the immediate post-war years trying to establish Democrat exile communities in South America.

Sons of Liberty

The Sons of Liberty was a new group to the anti-war movement, conceived in 1863 and was fully formed the following year when the former Order of American Knights was dissolved and their members renamed themselves the Sons of Liberty. This organization is not the same as the Sons of Liberty formed before the American Revolution, although their members probable thought they were. This group was a little more active, organizing themselves into military style formations in response to the Conscription Act of 1863, planning to take over sever state governments in the Northwest and secede from the Union, and to form mutual protection societies for their members. They went so far as to plan (with some help form the Confederacy) to free Confederate prisoners from Camp Douglas, Chicago, IL, arm them, and then seize control of Illinois, Indiana, Missouri, and Kentucky. Democratic Party authorities in Illinois found out and demanded they stop. This, coupled with reports from a government detective that had infiltrated the group, which was published in several Republican newspapers, ended the plot and the leaders were arrested. They were tried before a military commission, found guilty of inciting insurrection and giving aid and comfort to the CSA, and sentenced to death. One leader, Lambdin Milligan, appealed his conviction on the grounds that a military commission could not try civilians. In a Supreme Court decision known as *Ex Parte Milligan*, the court overturned the convictions and set them free. At the end of the war, the organization fizzled out.

These organizations were at their strongest when Union was prospects were at their lowest. Union defeats on the battlefield were usually followed by calls for negotiations with the Confederacy with the aim of just ending the war, even if it meant victory for the South. When 1864 brought Union victories, especially the capture of Atlanta, their calls fell on increasingly deaf ears.

One view that they had was that the war was supposed to be fought strictly for the preservation of the Union. When President Lincoln issued the Emancipation Proclamation in 1863, they expressed their view that emancipation was unconstitutional and the aim of the war had been changed to a social one, namely freedom for African-Americans. Their racist views were widely published in various newspapers and proclaimed in speeches.

Another view that had was that President Lincoln was a despot who trampled on the rights of dissenters, closed Democrat newspapers, suspended *habeas corpus*, and was leading the nation into a military dictatorship. They believed in their hearts that a Republican controlled Congress threatened their way of life. When the Conscription Act was enacted, some of that opposition took form in the New York City Draft Riots.

The most vocal of the dissenters was Ohio Congressman Clement Vallandingham, who was a Supreme Commander of the Sons of Liberty. On 14 January, 1863, he made a speech on the floor of the House of Representatives that not only called the war illegal and immoral, but claimed that it would eventually lead to the secession of the Northwest States.

Later that spring, Major General Ambrose Burnside, at the time commander of the Military District of Ohio, published General Order No. 38, declaring that support for the Confederacy in the district would no longer be tolerated. Vallandingham openly defied the order by making speeches on 5 May 1863 and was arrested. He was tried with "expressing treasonous sympathy" and sentenced to prison for the duration of the war. Lincoln stepped in the commuted the sentence to banishment to the CSA. He was soon turned over to Confederate authorities, but they had no use for him. He soon relocated to Canada, where he could still maintain some sort of activity.

In the Election of 1864, Vallandingham was placed on the ballot as the Peace Democrat candidate for Ohio Governor. He soon returned to the US, where he aided in the writing of the Peace Plank of the party platform. His views that the war was a failure, however, lost its punch in the light of Union victories as well as their candidate, former Major General George McClellan, rejecting the Peace Plank. Vallandingham even lost in the Ohio Governor's race. Vallandingham himself met an ignoble end, post-war he had returned to the law profession and, while demonstrating to a friend how the victim was shot, forgot to check that the pistol he was using was loaded, and shot himself.

With the re-election of President Lincoln and the prospect that the war would soon end with total Union victory, the Copperheads soon faded from importance.

Exiles

As the Civil War was winding down, many Confederates, seeing the writing on the wall, resolved not to allow themselves to be placed back under Federal laws. Some, like Edwin Ruffin, chose to commit suicide, while others chose exile:

4 July 1865: Confederate Brigadier General Joseph Shelby led a group that included former Governors Pendleton Murrah (Texas), Charles Morehead (Kentucky), and Henry Allen (Louisiana). Also among this group were Generals John Magruder, Thomas Hindman, and Sterling Price. They crossed the Rio Grande to establish a colony in Mexico.

Major Washington Goldsmith, who commanded Georgia troops, helped establish a colony in British Honduras (now Belize).

John Taylor Wood, a Confederate Navy Captain, relocated to Nova Scotia, rather than swear an oath to the United States.

A Confederate community in Ontario, Canada hosted Jubal Early, John Hood, James Mason (CS Commissioner to the UK), and John Breckenridge.

A very large Confederate colony was formed north of Sao Paulo, Brazil. This community still exists in the form of the town of Americana, populated with descendents of the founders.

Matthew Maury, former US Navy oceanographer and former Confederate Navy purchasing agent in Europe, directed the Imperial Mexican Observatory.

Judah Benjamin, former CS Secretary of State, became a Queens Counsel for Lancashire, England.

Others who lived in England, included Louis Wigfall and Robert Toombs.

Many of the estimated 10000 exiles did return to the US, but only after taking the oath of loyalty to the United States. Others were staunch Confederates to the end and never returned.

Reconstruction

There can never be a look at the Civil War without looking at its aftermath. It was not as simple as both sides turning in their arms, one in victory and the other in defeat, and heading home to their shops and farms, which is what the common soldier wanted to do, but what happened politically to the former CSA.

President Lincoln wanted a kind and gentle reunion of the states. Problem was he was dead from an assassin's bullet. His successor, Andrew Johnson, was a War Democrat who was on the Union ticket as Vice-President until that bullet thrust him into the center of the post-Civil War maelstrom.

Johnson, former Military Governor of Tennessee, had some of his own ideas that would have played better in the South than in the North. On the subject of the recently free slaves, he was against equal rights for African-Americans. He also wanted to let the states handle their own affairs.

This did not sit well with the most powerful faction in Congress, the Radical Republicans. They wanted harsh measures placed on the South, even demoting those states to Territorial Status. They were able push through a plan to split the former CSA into military districts and to have the US Army maintain control.

District 1: Virginia, Commanded by Major General John Schofield.

District 2: North Carolina and South Carolina, Commanded by Major General Daniel Sickles.

District 3: Alabama, Georgia, and Florida, Commanded by Major Generals John Pope and George Meade.

District 4: Mississippi and Arkansas, Commanded by Major General Edward Ord.

District 5: Louisiana and Texas, Commanded by Major Generals Philip Sheridan and Winfield Hancock, who also had the job of securing the border with Imperial Mexico.

Tennessee, Johnson's home state, was not in any district.

Even as these plans were put into place, Congress and President Johnson were already on a collision course over several issues:

Johnson had issued a proclamation allowing whites-only conventions to elect members of Congress from the South. Congress retaliated by refusing to seat those elected.

Congress also passed laws (over the President's veto) to strengthen the Freedmen's Bureau, an organization dedicated to help freed slaves adjust to their new life. Part of that help was to establish small farms, which ended up under the control of landlords (usually their former masters) who saddled the African-Americans with a debt that few could repay. Other services included education and legal help.

There were plans in the works for readmitting the Southern States: all they had to do was to ratify the 13th Amendment to the Constitution. As soon as that was accomplished, the state was readmitted, but the military government would still be in place.

1866: Tennessee was readmitted and not placed within any military district.

1868: South Carolina, North Carolina, Florida, Alabama, Louisiana and Arkansas were back in.

1870: Virginia, Georgia, Mississippi, and Texas were finally reunited.

Another sticking point was what to do with former Confederates. Most were receiving pardons in exchange for swearing a loyalty oath to the United States. Many of the Radical Republicans wanted men like former President Jefferson Davis and former General Robert E. Lee tried for treason. Davis was already in jail after being captured during his attempt to flee the country. Lee had returned to private life and had accepted an offer to become president of Washington College in Lexington, VA. Neither would come to trial, but Davis would suffer two years behind bars before his release.

Eventually, Congress voided the Constitutions of the Southern states, instead mandating that new conventions, this time staffed with African-Americans and Whites who did not support the Confederacy, elect new members of Congress. This would be a condition of lifting the military rule. As a result, two Senators and 15 Representatives were African-American.

Things finally came to a head when Congress passed a law limiting President Johnson's ability to control the actions of the military in the South, this being in response to Johnson preventing military commanders from protecting African-Americans from assault. Johnson responded by firing Secretary of War Edwin Stanton, a Radical Republican. In February of 1868, Congress responded by drawing up, and then approving, Articles of Impeachment. This is a Constitutionally approved method to remove a President, believed to be guilty of "high crimes and misdemeanors," from office. When the House of Representatives approved the articles, the Senate moved to hold the formal trial. When the final Senate vote was called, it fell one vote short of the 2/3 needed to find Johnson guilty, and remove him from office. This did have an affect on the Election of 1868, returning the Republicans to the White House with the election of General of the Armies Ulysses S. Grant.

Grant continued the policies of the Radicals, pushing the 14th Amendment, which granted US Citizenship to African-Americans, and prohibited states from limiting the rights of citizens, and the 15th Amendment, which granted all male citizens (including African-Americans) the right to vote.

All of these rules and requirements were hard on former Confederate citizens: these changes that were overturning their world was being enforced by the bayonets of garrison troops, many of then African-Americans, and assisted by both Northerners and African-Americans acting as agents. They were known by their luggage, which was made of the same material that carpets were made of. These agents were called "Carpetbaggers" as a term of derision.

Some Southerners decided on direct action, starting with assaulting Blacks whenever possible, and then banding into groups to terrorize and intimidate African-Americans from exercising their new rights. The most notorious of these was the Ku Klux Klan, with former Confederate General Nathan Bedford Forrest a reputed founder. These groups launched several attempts to stop African-Americans from voting, which resulted in several states imposing martial law and using their militias to attack the Klan. Congress responded by making it a Federal offense to prevent someone from voting. President Grant used that law in 1871 to enforce voting rights and to target Klan members in South Carolina.

During Grant's second term, public opinion turned against these harsh measures in the hopes that Westward migration would help meld the two regions. The Grant Administration was also beset with scandals that lessened its effectiveness. A crisis in South Carolina resulted in Grant sending in Federal troops, but it was seen as unpopular.

Even though the 15th Amendment had been approved, many Northern states had instituted literacy tests on order to keep several minority groups from voting, a measure that would soon take place in the South.

Reconstruction came to an end with the Election of 1876. Rutherford B. Hayes, a former Union general, was declared the winner of a highly contested election when he agreed to remove all Federal troops from the South, disband the military governments and return the states to civilian control, known as the Compromise of 1877.

Without the influence of Federal troops and other Federal intervention, the Southern States soon voted in Democrat majorities and the few gains that African-Americans had made were quashed, not to be revived for nearly a century.

The Union was once again whole, a set of problems was solved, but a new set of problems had arisen. These problems would not be addressed until the mid 20th Century.

Here is a good way to end this book, with a roll call:

Before and After the Civil War
(Those who survived the conflict)

Union

Adelbert Ames—Division Commander
Before: Seaman aboard Clipper Ships, West Point class of 1861.
After: Governor of Mississippi. Senator from Mississippi, Flour merchant, Textile manufacturer, served in Spanish-American War.

Robert Anderson—Commander at Fort Sumter.
Before: West Point Class of 1825, Regular Army Officer.
After: Relocated to France for health reasons.

Sandor Asboth—Division Commander
Before: Political Refugee.
After: US Minister to Uruguay.

William Averill—Cavalry Commander
Before: West Point Class of 1855, Regular Army Officer.
After: Managed an oil and coal company, US minister to British North America (Canada).

Romeyn Ayres—Division Commander
Before: West Point Class of 1847, Regular Army Officer.
After: Remained on Active Duty until his death in 1888.

Nathaniel Banks—Army Commander
Before: Cotton mill worker, Newspaperman, Speaker of the

Massachusetts House of Representatives, Speaker of the US House of Representatives, Governor of Massachusetts.
After: Congressman, State Senator, Unites States Marshall.

Francis Barlow—Division Commander
Before: Lawyer
After: Lawyer

Clara Barton—Nurse and Relief Worker
Before: Clerk in the US Patent Office.
After: Founder of the American Red Cross.

Hiram Berdan—Sharpshooter Corps Commander
Before: Engineer.
After: Inventor.

William Birney—Division Commander
Before: Lawyer, Journalist.
After: Lawyer.

Francis Blair—Corps Commander
Before: Regular Army Enlisted, US Representative from Kentucky.
After: Planter, US Senator.

Montgomery Blair—US Postmaster General
Before: West Point Class of 1835, Lawyer, US District Attorney for Missouri, Mayor of St. Louis, Judge.
After: Democratic Activist, Member of the Maryland Legislature.

James Blunt—District Commander
Before: Doctor
After: Doctor, Civil Servant.

Don Carlos Buell—Army Commander
Before: West Point Class of 1841, Regular Army Officer.
After: Worked in the coal and iron industries.

Ambrose Burnside—Corps and Army Commander
Before: West Point Class of 1847, Regular Army Officer.
After: Governor of Rhode Island, US Senator.

Benjamin F. Butler—Army Commander
Before: Lawyer.
After: US Representative from Massachusetts, Governor of Massachusetts.

Daniel Butterfield—Division Commander and composer of "Taps."
Before: Businessman with American Express.
After: Returned to business.

Edward Canby—District Commander
Before: West Point Class of 1835, Regular Army Officer.
After: Remained on Active Duty.

Christopher "Kit" Carson—Battalion Commander
Before: Explorer, Guide, Saddler, Indian Agent.
After: Rancher

Joshua Lawrence Chamberlain—Brigade Commander.
Before: College Professor.
After: Writer, President of Bowdoin College, Governor of Maine.

John Corse—Division Commander
Before: Lawyer, Politician.
After: Tax Official.

Darius Couch—Corps Commander.
Before: West Point Class of 1846, Worked in copper industry.
After: Politician.

Thomas Crittenden—Corps Commander
Before: Diplomat.
After: Remained on Active duty.

George Crook—Division commander
Before: West Point Class of 1852, Regular Army Officer.
After: Remained on Active Duty.

Samuel Curtis—Army Commander.
Before: Civil engineer, Lawyer.
After: Railroad inspector.

George Custer—Cavalry Commander
Before: West Point Class of 1861
After: Remained on Active Duty (until meting his fate at Little Big Horn, MT, in 1876).

Lysander Cutler—Iron Brigade Commander
Before: Teacher and businessman.
After: Died after the war ended.

John Dahlgren—Naval Commander
Before: Regular US Navy Officer.
After: Remained on Active Duty.

Napoleon Dana—Corps Commander
Before: West Point Class of 1842, Regular Army officer, Banker.
After: Trader, Pension Official.

Philippe de Trobriand—Division commander
Before: Novelist, Lawyer, Poet, Duelist.
After: Remained on Active Duty until he was made a Baron.

John Dix—Department Commander.
Before: Regular Army Officer, Lawyer, US Senator, Secretary of the Treasury.
After: Diplomat, Governor of New York.

Grenville Dodge—Division Commander.
Before: Civil Engineering
After: Railroad builder, US Representative from Massachusetts.

Abner Doubleday—Corps Commander.
Before: West Point Class of 1842, Regular Army Officer.
After: Remained on Active Duty, Took out patent for cable railway while stationed in San Francisco.

Percival Drayton—Commander USS *Hartford*.
Before: Regular US Navy Officer
After: Shore assignment until his death in August 1865.

David G. Farragut—US Navy Admiral
Before: Regular US Navy Officer.
After: Remained on Active Duty.

Edward Ferrero—Division Commander
Before: Dance instructor.
After: Dance instructor.

William Franklin—Corps Commander
Before: West Point Class of 1843, Topographical Engineer.
After: Civil Engineer, Director of Colt Firearms Co.

John C. Fremont—Army Commander
Before: Explorer, US Senator from California, First Republican Presidential Candidate.
After: Territorial Governor of Arizona.

William French—Corps Commander.
Before: West Point Class of 1837, Regular Army Officer.
After: Remained on Active Duty.

William Gamble—Cavalry Commander.
Before: US Army Enlisted, Civil engineer.
After: Regular Army Officer.

James Garfield—Brigade Commander
Before: Teacher, Ohio State Senator, Lawyer.
After: US Senator from Ohio, 20th President of the United States.

John Gibbon—Corps Commander.
Before: West Point Class of 1847, Regular Army officer.
After: Remained on Active Duty.

Ulysses S. Grant—Commander in Chief of the Union Army
Before: West Point Class of 1843, Regular Army Officer, Businessman,
Farmer, Real Estate Agent, Clerk in family leather goods shop.
After: First 4-Star General, 18th President of the United States,
Businessman, Writer.

George Greene—Brigade Commander
Before: West Point Class of 1823, Regular Army Officer, West Point
Instructor.
After: Civil Engineer.

David McM. Gregg—Cavalry Commander.
Before: West Point Class of 1855, Regular Army Officer.
After: Farmer, Diplomat.

Benjamin Grierson—Cavalry Commander
Before: Music Teacher, Merchant.
After: Remained on Active Duty.

Charles Griffin—Corps Commander.
Before: West Point Class of 1847, Regular Army officer.
After: Remained on Active Duty.

Henry W. Halleck—Army Commander.
Before: West Point Class of 1839, Regular Army Officer, Lawyer.
After: Remained on Active Duty.

Winfield S. Hancock—Corps Commander
Before: West Point Class of 1844, Regular Army Officer.
After: Remained on Active Duty.

Benjamin Harrison—Brigade Commander
Before: Lawyer, Politician.
After: US Senator from Indiana, 23rd President of the United States.

Herman Haupt—Supervisor of US Military Railroads.
Before: West Point Class of 1835, Civil Engineer.
After: Civil Engineer (mainly railroads).

Rutherford B. Hayes—Brigade Commander.
Before: Lawyer.
After: US Representative from Ohio, Governor of Ohio, 19th President of the United States.

Samuel Heintzelman—Corps Commander.
Before: West Point Class of 1826, Regular Army Officer.
After: Remained on Active Duty.

Joseph Hooker—Corps and Army Commander
Before: West Point Class of 1837, Farmer
After: Remained on Active Duty.

Oliver O. Howard—Corps Commander
Before: West Point Class of 1854, Mathematics instructor.
After: Educator, Writer.

Henry Hunt—Artillerist
Before: West Point Class of 1839, Regular Army officer.
After: Remained on Active Duty.

David Hunter—District Commander
Before: West Point Class of 1822, Regular Army Officer.
After: Remained on Active Duty.

Stephen Hurlbut—Corps Commander
Before: Lawyer, State Legislator.
After: Diplomat.

Rufus Ingalls—Quartermaster
Before: West Point Class of 1843, Regular Army Officer.
After: Remained on Active Duty.

August Kautz—Division Commander.
Before: US Army Enlisted, West Point Class of 1852, Regular Army Officer.
After: Remained on Active Duty.

Erasmus Keyes—Corps Commander
Before: West Point Class of 1832, Regular Army Officer.
After: Winemaker, Banker, Operated a mine.

Judson Kilpatrick—Cavalry Commander
Before: West Point Class of 1861.
After: US Minister to Chile.

Nathan Kimball—Division Commander
Before: Doctor, Voluntary Army Officer during Mexican War.
After: State Treasurer, State Legislator, Surveyor General of Utah.

Rufus King—Division Commander, First commander of Iron Brigade.
Before: West Point Class of 1833, Civil Engineer.
After: Customs official.

Wladimir Krzyzanowski—Brigade Commander
Before: 1848 Revolutionary, Civil Engineer
After: Treasury agent.

James Ledlie—Brigade Commander. (He was the one who hid in a bomb shelter while his men were being slaughtered at The Crater, Petersburg, VA.)
Before: Civil Engineer, Railroad Engineer.
After: Civil Engineer, Railroad Engineer.

Samuel Lee—Naval Commander. (Distant Relative to Robert E. Lee)
Before: Regular Navy Officer.
After: Farmer.

Eli Lilly—Cavalry Officer
Before: Pharmacist.
After: founder of Eli Lilly and Company.

John Logan—Division and Corps Commander.
Before: Lawyer.
After: US Representative from Illinois.

George McClellan—Army Commander.
Before: West Point Class of 1846, Regular Army Officer, Railroad Engineer.
After: Governor of New Jersey.

John McClernand—Army Commander
Before: Lawyer, State Legislator, US Representative from Illinois.
After: Lawyer, Judge, Politician.

Alexander McCook—Corps Commander.
Before: West Point Class of 1852, Regular Army Officer, West Point Instructor.
After: Remained on Active Duty.

Anson McCook—Division Commander.
Before: Lawyer.
After: Lawyer, US Representative from Ohio.

Edward McCook—Cavalry Commander.
Before: Lawyer.
After: Diplomat, Territorial Governor of Colorado.

Roderick McCook—Naval commander.
Before: Annapolis Class of 1859.
After: Served on Lighthouse Duty.

Irvin McDowell—Army Commander.
Before: West Point Class of 1838, Regular Army officer.
After: Remained on Active Duty.

William McKinley—23rd Ohio Enlisted and Officer.
Before: Teacher.
After: US Representative from Ohio, 24th President of the United States.

George Meade—Army Commander.
Before: West Point Class of 1835, Civil Engineer, Regular Army Officer.
After: Remained on Active Duty.

Thomas Meagher—Commander of Irish Brigade.
Before: Irish Revolutionary.
After: Acting Territorial Governor of Montana.

Montgomery Meigs—Quartermaster General.
Before: West Point Class of 1836, Regular Army Officer.
After: Remained on Active Duty.

Solomon Meredith—Commander, Iron Brigade.
Before: State Legislator.
After: Surveyor General for Montana Territory.

Wesley Merritt—Cavalry Commander.
Before: West Point Class of 1860.
After: Remained on Active Duty.

Robert Milroy—Division Commander.
Before: Lawyer, Volunteer Army Officer.
After: Canal Manager, Indian Agent.

Richard Oglesby—Division Commander.
Before: Lawyer, Volunteer Army Officer.
After: US Senator, Governor of Illinois.

Edward Ord—Army Commander.
Before: West Point Class of 1839, Regular Army officer.
After: Remained on Active Duty.

Ely Parker—Assistant to General Ulysses S. Grant.
Before: Civil Engineer, Trained as a lawyer but was not allowed to practice law.
After: Indian Commissioner in Grant Administration, Businessman.

Henry Pleasants—Brigade Commander. (He commanded the digging of the mine that led to The Crater.)
Before: Mining Engineer, Railroad Engineer.
After: Mining Engineer.

Alfred Pleasonton—Cavalry Commander.
Before: West Point Class of 1844, Regular Army officer.
After: Railroader.

John Pope—Army Commander
Before: West Point Class of 1842, Regular Army Officer.
After: Remained on Active Duty.

David D. Porter—Naval Commander
Before: Regular Navy Officer.
After: Remained on Active Duty.

Fitz-John Porter—Corps Commander.
Before: West Point Class of 1845, Regular Army Officer.
After: Mining, Construction, Merchant, Police Commissioner of New York City, Fire Commissioner of New York City, Public Works Commissioner of New York City.

Benjamin Prentiss—Division Commander.
Before: Militia Officer, Lawyer.
After: Lawyer, Pension Agent, Postmaster.

John Rawlins—Aide to General Ulysses S. Grant.
Before: Lawyer.
After: Secretary of War in Grant Administration.

William Rosecrans—Army Commander.
Before: West Point Class of 1842, Businessman.
After US Representative from California, US Minister to Mexico.

John Schofield—Corps Commander.
Before: West Point Class of 1853, Regular Army Officer, West Point Instructor.
After: Remained on Active Duty.

Carl Schurz—Corps Commander.
Before: 1848 Revolutionary.
After: Writer, Political Activist.

Winfield Scott—Commander in Chief
Before: Lawyer, Regular Army Officer.
After: Honored Retirement.

Philip Sheridan—Cavalry Commander.
Before: West Point Class of 1853, Regular Army officer.
After: Reconstruction Governor of Texas and Louisiana, General in Chief, Helped create Yellowstone National Park.

William T. Sherman—Army Commander.
Before: West Point Class of 1840, Regular Army Officer, Banker, Lawyer.
After: General in Chief.

James Shields—Division Commander.
Before: Lawyer, Land Commissioner, Volunteer Army Officer, US Senator.
After: US Senator.

Daniel Sickles—Corps Commander.
Before: US Representative from New York, Secretary of US Legation, London UK.
After: Chairman of the New York State Monuments Commission, US Minister to Spain.

Franz Sigel—Corps Commander.
Before: 1848 Revolutionary, Teacher.
After: Pension Agent.

Henry Slocum—Corps Commander.
Before: West Point Class of 1852, Regular Army Officer, Lawyer.
After: US Representative from New York.

Robert Smalls—Harbor pilot at Charleston, SC.
Before: Slave.
After: US Representative from South Carolina.

William "Baldy" Smith—Corps Commander.
Before: West Point Class of 1845, Regular Army Officer, West Point Instructor.
After: Civil Engineer.

William Sooy Smith—Division Commander.
Before: West Point Class of 1856, Railroad Engineer.
After: Civil Engineer.

Julius Stahel—Division Commander.
Before: Austrian Army officer, 1848 Revolutionary.
After: Diplomat.

Edwin Stanton—US Secretary of War.
Before: Lawyer.
After: Named US Supreme Court Justice but died before taking the seat.

James Steadman—Division Commander.
Before: State Legislator (Ohio), Gold Prospector (California).
After: State Legislator, Journalist.

George Stoneman—Cavalry Commander.
Before: West Point Class of 1846, Regular Army Officer.
After: Railroader, Governor of California.

Samuel Sturgis—Corps Commander.
Before: West Point Class of 1846, Regular Army Commander.
After: Remained on Active Duty.

George Sykes—Corps Commander.
Before: West Point Class of 1842, Regular Army Officer.
After: Remained on Active Duty.

Alfred Terry—Corps Commander.
Before: Lawyer.
After: Remained on Active Duty.

George Thomas, the "Rock of Chickamauga"—Army Commander.
Before: West Point Class of 1840, Regular Army Officer.
After: Remained on Active Duty.

John Basil Turchin—Brigade Commander.
Before: Graduate of Russian Imperial Military School.
After: Civil Engineer.

Emory Upton—Corps Commander.
Before: West Point Class of 1861.
After: Remained on Active Duty.

Adolph Wilhelm August Friedrich von Steinwehr—Division Commander.
Before: Prussian Army Officer.
After: Topographical Engineer, Geographer, Teacher.

Lewis Wallace—Corps Commander.
Before: Volunteer Army officer, Lawyer.
After: Governor of New Mexico Territory, Diplomat, Writer.

Gouverneur K. Warren—Corps Commander.
Before: West Point Class of 1850, Regular Army Officer.
After: Remained on Active Duty.

Alexander Webb—Corps Commander.
Before: West Point Class of 1855, Regular Army officer.
After: President of City College of New York.

Godfrey Weitzel—Corps Commander.
Before: West Point Class of 1855, Regular Army officer.
After: Remained on Active Duty.

Gideon Welles—US Secretary of the Navy
Before: Journalist, State Legislator.
After: Writer.

Charles Wilkes—Naval Commander.
Before: Regular Navy Officer.
After: Retired from Active Duty.

August von Willich—Brigade Commander.
Before: 1848 Revolutionary.
After: Public Official.

John Winslow—commander, USS *Kearsarge*.
Before: Regular Navy Officer.
After: Remained on Active Duty.

John Worden—commander, USS *Monitor*.
Before: Regular Navy Officer.
After: Remained on Active Duty.

Horatio Wright—Corps Commander.
Before: West Point Class of 1841, Regular Army Officer.
After: Remained on Active Duty. Helped complete Washington Monument.

Confederate

Edward P. Alexander—Artillery Chief
Before: West Point Class of 1857, Engineer Corps, West Point instructor, Developed flag signal system.
After: College professor, Planter, Railroad investor.

George "Tige" Anderson—Brigade Commander
Before: Planter, Regular Army Captain.
After: Police Chief of Atlanta, GA.

Richard "Fighting Dick" Anderson—Division and Corps Commander
Before: West Point Class of 1842, Regular Army Officer.
After: Failed in several ventures.

Pierre Gustave Toutant Beauregard—Army Commander
Before: West Point Class of 1838, Regular Army Officer, Superintendent of West Point.
After: Director of the Louisiana Lottery, Adjutant General of Louisiana.

Judah Benjamin—CS Secretary of State
Before: Lawyer, State Legislator, US Senator from Louisiana.
After: Lawyer, Queen's Counsel (a high rank of judicial official in the UK)

Henry Benning—Brigade Commander
Before: Lawyer, Georgia Supreme Court Justice.
After: Lawyer.

Milledge Bonham—Brigade Commander
Before: Regular Army Officer, US Representative from South Carolina. (Brief break in service in order to serve as Governor of South Carolina)
After: Lawyer, Planter.

Belle Boyd—Spy
Before: No career.
After: Actress on the English Stage.

Braxton Bragg—Army Commander
Before: West Point Class of 1837, Regular Army Officer, planter.
After: State Engineer of Alabama.

John Breckinridge—Division Commander and CS Secretary of War
Before: Lawyer, Volunteer Army Officer (Mexican War), US Representative from Kentucky, Vice-President of the United States.
After: Lawyer, President of a railroad and an insurance company.

Franklin Buchanan—Naval Commander
Before: Regular Navy Officer.
After: College President, Insurance Agent.

Simon Bolivar Buckner—District Commander
Before: West Point Class of 1844, West Point Instructor, Real Estate Agent.
After: Newspaperman, President of an insurance company, Governor of Kentucky.

James Bulloch—Naval Agent in the UK.
Before: Regular US Navy Officer.
After: Writer, Maritime Lawyer.

Benjamin Franklin Cheatham—Corps Commander
Before: Farmer
After: Farmer, Prison Official, Postmaster.

Jefferson Davis—President of the Confederate States of America.
Before: West Point Class of 1848, Regular Army Officer, Planter, Volunteer Army Officer ("Mississippi Rifles"), US Representative from Mississippi, US Senator, Secretary of War.
After: Writer.

Jubal Early—Corps Commander
Before: West Point Class of 1837, Regular Army Officer, Lawyer, Member of the Virginia Legislature.
After: Lawyer, Founder of the Southern Historical Society, connected with the Louisiana Lottery.

Richard Ewell—Corps Commander.
Before: West Point Class of 1840, Regular Army Officer.
After: Farmer.

Nathan Bedford Forrest—Cavalry commander.
Before: Slave trader, plantation owner.
After: Farmer, Railroader, Early leader of the KKK.

Birkett D. Fry—Division Commander.
Before: Virginia Military Institute Graduate, Regular Army Officer, Cotton Mill manager.
After: Alabama cotton mill manager.

John Gordon—Division commander.
Before: Coal mine management.
After: Governor of Georgia, US Senator from Georgia.

Josiah Gorgas—CS Ordinance Chief.
Before: West Point Class of 1841, Regular Army Officer.
After: Engaged in the iron business, Teacher.

Wade Hampton—Cavalry Commander.
Before: Plantation owner.
After: Governor of South Carolina, US Senator from South Carolina.

William J. Hardee—Army Commander.
Before: West Point Class of 1838, Regular Army Officer, Wrote *Hardee's Tactics*.
After: Plantation owner, Railroad President.

Henry Heth—Division Commander.
Before: West Point Class of 1847, Regular Army Officer.
After: Insurance Agent.

Daniel H. Hill—Corps Commander
Before: West Point Class of 1842, Regular Army Officer, Educator.
After: Educator, Writer.

Thomas Hindman—Corps Commander
Before: Lawyer, State Legislator, US Representative from Tennessee.
After: Lawyer.

John B. Hood—Army Commander
Before: West Point Class of 1853, Regular Army officer.
After: Merchant.

Jedediah Hotchkiss—Mapmaker
Before: Teacher.
After: Businessman.

John Imboden—Cavalry Commander
Before: State Legislator.
After: Businessman, Lawyer.

Alfred Iverson—Cavalry Commander
Before: Regular Army Officer.
After: Citrus Farmer

Bushrod Johnson—Corps Commander
Before: West Point Class of 1840, Military School teacher.
After: Educator.

Joseph E. Johnston—Army Commander
Before: West Point Class of 1829, Regular Army Officer.
After: US Representative from Virginia, Federal railroad commissioner.

Catesby Jones—Commanded CSS *Virginia* during the battle with USS *Monitor*.
Before: Regular Navy Officer
After: Businessman.

James Kemper—Division Commander
Before: Lawyer, State Legislator.
After: Governor of Virginia.

Joseph Kershaw—Division Commander.
Before: Volunteer Army Officer, Lawyer, Politician.
After: Lawyer, State Senator, Judge, Postmaster.

Evander Law—Brigade Commander
Before: Military Academy Instructor.
After: Educator, Journalist.

Fitzhugh Lee—Cavalry Commander
Before: West Point Class of 1856, Regular Army Officer.
After: Farmer, Governor of Virginia, Diplomat, Volunteer Officer in the Spanish-American War.

George Washington Lee—Division Commander
Before: West Point Class of 1854, Regular Army Officer.
After: President of Washington College (succeeded his father).

Robert E. Lee—Army Commander, Commander in Chief of Confederate Armies.
Before: West Point Class of 1829, Regular Army Officer, West Point Superintendent
After: President of Washington College (now Washington and Lee College).

Stephen D. Lee—Corps Commander
Before: West Point Class of 1854, Regular Army officer.
After: Farmer, State Legislator, College President.

William H. Lee—Cavalry Commander.
Before: Regular Army officer, Plantation manager.
After: Farmer, State Senator, US Representative from Virginia.

Armistead Long—Artillerist.
Before: West Point Class of 1850, Regular Army Officer.
After: Civil Engineer.

James Longstreet—Corps Commander
Before: West Point Class of 1842, Regular Army Officer.
After: US Minister to Turkey, Railroad Commissioner.

William Loring—Division Commander.
Before: Lawyer, State Legislator, Volunteer Army Officer in Mexican War.
After: Division commander in Egyptian Army.

David G. McIntosh—Artillerist.
Before: Lawyer.
After: Lawyer.

Lafayette McLaws—Division Commander.
Before: West Point Class of 1842, Regular Army Officer.
After: Insurance Agent, Tax Collector, Postmaster.

John Maffitt—Commander CSS *Florida*.
Before: Regular Navy Officer.
After: Farmer.

John "Prince John" Magruder—District Commander.
Before: West Point Class of 1830, Regular Army Officer.
After: Lecturer.

William Mahone—Division Commander.
Before: Educator, Railroader.
After: Railroader, Politician.

Stephen Mallory—CS Secretary of the Navy.
Before: Customs Inspector, Lawyer.
After: Lawyer.

John Marmaduke—Cavalry Commander.
Before: West Point Class of 1857, Regular Army officer.
After: Insurance Agent, Governor of Missouri.

Samuel Maxey—Division Commander.
Before: West Point Class of 1846, Regular Army officer, Lawyer.
After: Lawyer, US Senator.

John S. Mosby—Partisan Ranger
Before: Lawyer.
After: Lawyer, US Counsel to Hong Kong.

William C. Oates—Commander 15th Alabama. (Led the charge up Little Round Top, Gettysburg, July 2, 1863.)
Before: Wanderer, Lawyer.
After: US Representative from Alabama, Governor of Alabama, Returned to Active Duty for the Spanish-American War.

John C. Pemberton—Army Commander.
Before: West Point Class of 1837, Regular Army Officer.
After: Farmer.

Edmund Pettus—Brigade Commander.
Before: Lawyer.
After: US Senator.

George Pickett—Division Commander.
Before: West Point Class of 1846, Regular Army Officer.
After: Insurance Agent.

Gideon Pillow—Division Commander.
Before: Lawyer, Volunteer Army Officer.
After: Lawyer.

William Poague—Artillerist.
Before: Lawyer.
After: Farmer, Teacher, State Legislator, VMI Treasurer.

Camille Armand Jules Marie, Prince de Polignac—Division Commander.
Before: French Army Officer
After: Mathematician, Economist.

Sterling Price—Army Commander.
Before: Lawyer, Farmer.
After: Leader of exiles in Mexico.

George W. Rains—CS Ordinance Officer.
Before: West Point Class of 1842, Regular Army Officer.
After: Businessman, College Professor.

Thomas Rosser—Division Commander.
Before: West Point Class of 1861.
After: Farmer, Railroader, Returned to Active Duty for the Spanish-American War.

Alfred Scales—Division Commander.
Before: Lawyer, US Representative from North Carolina.
After: Lawyer, US Representative from North Carolina, Banker, Governor of North Carolina.

Raphael Semmes—Commander CSS *Alabama.*
Before: Regular Navy Officer.
After: Lawyer, Writer.

Scott Shipp—Led VMI Cadets at New Market, VA.
Before: Commander of Cadets, VMI.
After: Superintendent, VMI, Lawyer.

Henry Sibley—Army Commander.
Before: West Point Class of 1838, Regular Army Officer.
After: Artillery Commander in Egyptian Army, Lecturer.

Edmund Kirby Smith—Army Commander.
Before: West Point Class of 1845, Regular Army officer.
After: Educator, Operated a telegraph business.

William "Extra Billy" Smith—Brigade Commander.
Before: Governor of Virginia, US Representative from Virginia.
After: State Legislator.

William Taliaferro—Division Commander.
Before: Lawyer.
After: State Legislator, Judge.

Heros Von Borcke—Cavalry Commander.
Before: Prussian Army Officer.
After: Returned to Prussian Army Service.

James Waddell—Commander, CSS *Shenandoah.*
Before: Regular Navy Officer.
After: Ocean Liner Captain.

Stand Watie—Commander of Confederate Cherokee troops.
Before: Planter, Journalist.
After: Planter, businessman.

Joseph Wheeler—Cavalry Commander.
Before: West Point Class of 1859.
After: US Representative from Alabama, Brigadier General during Spanish-American War.

Cadmus Wilcox—Division Commander.
Before: West Point Class of 1846, Regular Army Officer.
After: Civil Servant.

Those who answered the call to the colors and fell.

Union

Edward Baker—Brigade Commander
Died: 21 October, 1861 of wounds received at Ball's Bluff, VA.

George Bayard—Cavalry Commander.
Died: 14 December, 1862 of wounds received at Fredericksburg, VA.

Hiram Berry—Division Commander.
Died: 3 May, 1863 of wounds received at Chancellorsville, VA.

Daniel Bidwell—Brigade Commander.
Died: 19 October, 1864 of wounds received at Cedar Creek, VA.

William Bradford—Commander of Fort Pillow.
Died: 14 April, 1864, having been executed by Confederates following the Fall of Fort Pillow.

Hiram Burnham—Brigade Commander.
Died: 29 September, 1864 of wounds received at Fort Harrison, near Petersburg, VA.

James Cameron—Commander, 79th New York "Highlanders"
Died: 21 July, 1861 of wounds received at Manassas, VA.

Tunus Craven—Commander, USS *Tecumseh*.
Died: 5 August 1864 when his vessel struck a mine and sunk at Mobile Bay, AL.

Edward Cross—Brigade Commander.
Died: 2 July 1863 of wounds received at Gettysburg, PA.

Alonzo Cushing—Artillerist.
Died: 3 July 1863 of wounds received at Gettysburg, PA.

Benjamin F. Davis—Cavalry Commander.
Died: 9 June 1863 of wounds received at Brandy Station, VA.

Charles Ellet Jr. —Naval Commander.
Died: 21 June, 1862 of wounds received at Memphis, TN.

Ephraim Ellsworth—Commander, 11th New York "Ellsworth's Fire Zouaves."
Died: 24 May, 1861 of wounds received at Alexandria, VA.

Elon Farnsworth—Cavalry commander
Died: 3 July, 1863 of wounds received at Gettysburg, PA.

John Grebel—Artillerist.
Died: 9 June, 1861 of wounds received at Big Bethel, VA.

Pleasant Hackleman—Brigade Commander.
Died: 3 October, 1862 of wounds received at Corinth, MS.

Charles Harker—Brigade Commander.
Died: 27 June, 1864 of wounds received at Kennesaw Mountain, GA.

Alexander Hays—Division Commander.
Died: 5 May, 1864 of wounds received in The Wilderness, VA.

Charles Hazlett—Artillerist.
Died: 2 July, 1863 of wounds received at Gettysburg, PA.

Hans Heg—Brigade Commander.
Died: 19 September, 1863 of wounds received at Chickamauga, TN/ GA.

Joshua Howell—Division Commander.
Died: 14 September, 1864 of wounds received at Petersburg, VA.

Conrad Jackson—Brigade Commander.
Died: 13 December, 1862 of wounds received at Fredericksburg, VA.

Philip Kearny—Division Commander.
Died: 1 September, 1862 of wounds received at Chantilly, VA.

Patrick Kelly—Brigade Commander.
Died: 16 June, 1864 of wounds received at Petersburg, VA.

Edmund Kirby—Artillerist.
Died: 3 May, 1863 of wounds received at Chancellorsville, VA.

Edward Kirk—Brigade Commander.
Died: 21 July, 1863 of wounds received at Murfreesboro, TN.

John Kitching—Division Commander.
Died: 10 January 1865 of wounds received at Cedar Creek, VA.

Abraham Lincoln—16th President of the United States
Died: 15 April 1865 of wounds received from assassin John Wilkes Booth.

Charles Lowell Jr. —Brigade Commander.
Died: 20 October 1864 of wounds received at Cedar Creek, VA.

Nathaniel Lyon—Army commander.
Died: 10 August, 1861 of wounds received at Wilson's Creek, MO.

Daniel McCook Jr.—Brigade Commander.
Died: 17 July, 1864 of wounds received at Kennesaw Mountain, GA.

Robert McCook—Brigade Commander.
Died: 5 August, 1862 of wounds received in a guerilla attack near Decherd, TN.

James McPherson—Corps Commander.
Died: 22 July, 1864 of wounds received at Atlanta, GA.

Joseph Mansfield—Corps Commander.
Died: 18 September, 1862 of wounds received at Sharpsburg, MD.

Patrick O'Rourke—Commander, 140th New York
Died: 2 July, 1863 of wounds received at Gettysburg, PA.

Everett Peabody—Brigade Commander.
Died: 6 April, 1862 of wounds received at Pittsburg Landing, TN.

Jesse Reno—Division Commander.
Died: 14 September, 1862 of wounds received at South Mountain, MD.

Paul Joseph Revere—Commander, 20th Massachusetts. (Grandson of Paul Revere)
Died: 4 July, 1863 of wounds received at Gettysburg, PA

John Reynolds—Corps Commander.
Died: 1 July, 1863 of wounds received at Gettysburg, PA.

James Rice—Division Commander.
Died: 10 May, 1864 of wounds received at Spotsylvania, VA.

Israel "Fighting Dick" Richardson—Division Commander.
Died: 3 November, 1862 of wounds received at Sharpsburg, MD.

David Russell—Division Commander.
Died: 19 September, 1864 of wounds received at Winchester, VA.

John Sedgwick—Corps Commander.
Died: 9 May, 1864 of wounds received at Spotsylvania, VA.

Robert G. Shaw—Commander, 54th Massachusetts.
Died: 18 July, 1863 of wounds received at Battery Wagner, SC.

Joshua Sill—Division Commander.
Died: 31 December, 1862 of wounds received at Murfreesboro, TN.

George Strong—Brigade Commander.
Died: 30 July, 1863 of wounds received at Battery Wagner, SC.

William Terrill—Artillerist.
Died: 8 October, 1862 of wounds received at Perryville, KY.

Strong Vincent—Brigade Commander.
Died: 2 July, 1863 of wounds received at Gettysburg, PA.

James Wadsworth—Division Commander.
Died: 8 May, 1864 of wounds received in The Wilderness, VA.

William H. L. Wallace—Division Commander.
Died: 10 April, 1862 of wounds received at Pittsburg Landing, TN.

Fletcher Webster—Commander, 12th Massachusetts. (Son of Daniel Webster)
Died: 30 August, 1862 of wounds received near Manassas, VA.

Stephen Weed—Artillerist.
Died: 2 July, 1863 of wounds received at Gettysburg, PA.

Amiel Whipple—Division Commander.
Died: 7 May, 1863 of wounds received at Chancellorsville, VA.

Bayard Wilkeson—Artillerist.
Died: 1 July, 1863 of wounds received at Gettysburg, PA.

George Willard—Brigade Commander.
Died: 2 July, 1863 of wounds received at Gettysburg, PA.

John Williams—Private.
Died: 13 May, 1865 of wounds received at Palmito Ranch, TX. (He was the last Union soldier to be killed.)

Thomas Williams—Brigade Commander.
Died: 5 August, 1862 of wounds received at Baton Rouge, LA.

Samuel Zook—Division Commander.
Died: 3 July, 1863 of wounds received at Gettysburg, PA.

Confederate

George Anderson—Brigade Commander
Died: 16 October, 1862 of wounds received at Sharpsburg, MD

Lewis Armistead—Brigade Commander
Died: 5 July, 1863 of wounds received at Gettysburg, PA.

Turner Ashby—Cavalry Commander.
Died: 6 June, 1862 of wounds received at Harrisonburg, VA.

Isaac Avery—Brigade Commander.
Died: 2 July, 1863 of wounds received at Gettysburg, PA.

William Barksdale—Division Commander.
Died: 3 July, 1863 of wounds received at Gettysburg, PA.

Francis Bartow—Brigade Commander.
Died: 21 July, 1861 of wounds received at Manassas, VA.

Robert Beckham—Artillerist.
Died: 5 December, 1864 of wounds received at Franklin, TN.

Bernard Bee—Brigade Commander.
Died: 21 July, 1861 of wounds received at Manassas, VA.

Lawrence Branch—Brigade Commander.
Died: 17 September, 1862 of wounds received at Sharpsburg, MD.

John Brown—Artillerist.
Died: 6 May, 1864 of wounds received at The Wilderness, VA.

Henry Burgwyn, the "Boy Colonel"—Commander, 26th North Carolina.
Died: 1 July, 1863 of wounds received at Gettysburg, PA.

John Carter—Division Commander.
Died: 10 December, 1864 of wounds received at Franklin, TN.

John Chambliss—Cavalry Commander.
Died: 16 August, 1864 of wounds received at Deep Bottom, near Richmond, VA.

Langdon Cheves—Balloonist.
Died: 10 July, 1863 of wounds received during a bombardment at Charleston, SC.

Patrick Cleburne—Corps Commander.
Died: 30 November, 1864 of wounds received at Franklin, TN.

Thomas Cobb—Division Commander.
Died 13 December, 1862 of wounds received at Fredericksburg, VA.

Peyton Colquitt—Brigade Commander.
Died: 20 September, 1863 of wounds received at Chickamauga, TN/GA.

Stapleton Crutchfield—Artillerist.
Died: 6 April, 1865 of wounds received at Saylor's Creek, VA.

Junius Daniel—Brigade Commander.
Died: 13 May, 1864 of wounds received at Spotsylvania, VA.

James Deshler—Brigade Commander.
Died: 20 September, 1863 of wounds received at Chickamauga, TN/GA.

George Dixon—Commander, CSS *H.L. Hunley*.
Died: 17 February, 1864 when the *Hunley* sunk following its successful attack on USS *Housatonic*.

George Doles—Division Commander.
Died: 2 June, 1864 of wounds received at Bethesda Church, VA.

Marcellus Douglass—Brigade Commander.
Died: 17 September, 1862 of wounds received at Sharpsburg, MD.

John Dunovant—Brigade Commander.
Died: 1 October, 1864 of wounds received at Petersburg, VA.

Samuel Fulkerson—Brigade Commander.
Died: 27 June, 1862 of wounds received at Gaines' Mill, VA.

John Fulton—Division Commander.
Died: 4 July, 1864 of wounds received at Petersburg, VA.

Samuel Garland—Brigade Commander.
Died: 14 September, 1862 of wounds received at South Mountain, MD.

Richard Garnett—Brigade Commander.
Died: 3 July, 1863 of wounds received at Gettysburg, PA.

Robert Garnett—Army Commander.
Died: 13 July, 1861 of wounds received at Carrick's Ford, VA. (First General Officer to die in the Civil War.)

Thomas Garnett—Division Commander.
Died: 2 May, 1863 of wounds received at Chancellorsville, VA.

Victor J. B. Girardey—Brigade Commander.
Died: 16 August, 1864 of wounds received at Fussell's Mill, VA.

States Rights Gist—Brigade Commander.
Died: 30 November, 1864 of wounds received at Franklin, TN.

Adley Gladden—Brigade Commander.
Died: 12 April, 1862 of wounds received at Pittsburg Landing, TN.

Archibald Godwin—Division Commander.
Died: 18 September, 1864 of wounds received at Winchester, VA.

James Gordon—Cavalry Commander.
Died: 12 May, 1864 of wounds received at Meadow Bridge, VA.

Hiram Granbury—Brigade Commander.
Died: 30 November, 1864 of wounds received at Franklin, TN.

Martin Green—Division Commander.
Died: 26 June, 1863 of wounds received at Vicksburg, MS.

Thomas Green—Cavalry Commander.
Died: 12 April, 1864 of wounds received at Blair's Landing, LA.

John Gregg—Division Commander.
Died: 7 October, 1864 of wounds received near Petersburg, VA.

Maxcy Gregg—Division Commander.
Died: 13 December, 1862 of wounds received at Fredericksburg, VA.

Richard Griffith—Division Commander.
Died: 29 June, 1862 of wounds received at Savage Station, VA.

Roger Hanson—Brigade Commander.
Died: 4 January, 1863 of wounds received at Murfreesboro, TN.

Robert Hatton—Brigade Commander.
Died: 31 May, 1862 of wounds received at Seven Pines, VA.

Benjamin Helm—Brigade Commander.
Died: 21 September, 1863 of wounds received at Chickamauga, TN/
GA.

Ambrose P. Hill—Corps Commander.
Died: 2 April, 1865 of wounds received at Petersburg, VA.

Thomas J. Jackson—Corps Commander.
Died: 10 May, 1863 of wounds received at Chancellorsville, VA.

Albert Jenkins—Cavalry Commander.
Died: 9 May, 1864 of wounds received at Cloyd's Mountain, WV.

Micah Jenkins—Brigade Commander.
Died: 6 May, 1864 of wounds received at The Wilderness, VA.

Albert S. Johnston—Army Commander.
Died: 6 April, 1862 of wounds received at Pittsburg Landing, TN.

William "Grumble" Jones—Cavalry commander.
Died: 5 June, 1864 of wounds received at Piedmont, WV.

John Kelly—Brigade Commander.
Died: 2 September, 1864 of wounds received near Franklin, TN.

Joseph Latimer—Artillerist.
Died: 1 August, 1863 of wounds received at Gettysburg, PA.

Lewis Little—Brigade Commander.
Died: 19 September, 1862 of wounds received at Iuka, MS.

Ben McCulloch—Division Commander.
Died: 7 March, 1862 of wounds received at Pea Ridge, AR.

James McIntosh—Cavalry Commander.
Died: 7 March, 1862 of wounds received at Pea Ridge, AR.

John Hunt Morgan—Partisan Ranger.
Died: 4 September, 1864 of wounds received at Greenville, TN.

Jean Jacques Alfred Alexander Mouton—Division Commander.
Died: 8 April, 1864 on wounds received at Mansfield, LA.

George S. Patton—Brigade Commander.
Died: 19 September, 1864 of wounds received at Winchester, VA.

John Pegram—Cavalry Commander.
Died: 6 February, 1865 of wounds received at Hatchers Run, VA.

William Pegram—Artillerist.
Died: 1 April, 1865 of wounds received at Five Forks, VA.

John Pelham, the "Gallant Pelham"—Artillerist.
Died: 17 March, 1863 of wounds received at Kelly's Ford, VA.

William Pender—Division Commander.
Died: 18 July, 1863 of wounds received at Gettysburg, PA.

Abner Perrin—Division Commander.
Died: 12 May, 1864 of wounds received at Spotsylvania, VA.

James Pettigrew—Division commander.
Died: 17 July, 1863 of wounds received at Falling Waters, MD.

Leonidas Polk—Corps and Army Commander.
Died: 14 June, 1864 of wounds received at Pine Mountain, GA.

Carnot Posey—Brigade Commander.
Died: 13 November, 1863 of wounds received at Bristoe Station, VA.

William Quantrill—Guerilla
Died: 6 June, 1865 of wounds received at Bloomfield, KY.

James Rains—Brigade Commander.
Died: 31 December, 1862 of wounds received at Murfreesboro.

Stephen Ramseur—Division Commander.
Died: 19 October, 1864 of wounds received at Cedar Creek, VA.

Robert Rhodes—Division Commander.
Died: 19 September, 1864 of wounds received at Winchester, VA.

William Scurry—Division Commander.
Died: 30 April, 1864 of wounds received at Camden, AR.

William Starke—Division Commander.
Died: 17 September, 1862 of wounds received at Sharpsburg, MD.

James Ewell Brown (Jeb) Stuart—Cavalry Commander.
Died: 12 Mat, 1864 of wounds received at Yellow Tavern, VA.

Lloyd Tilghman—Brigade Commander.
Died: 16 May, 1863 of wounds received at Vicksburg, MS.

Edward Tracy—Brigade Commander.
Died: 1 May, 1863 of wounds received at Port Gibson, LA.

Robert Tyler—Brigade Commander.
Died: 16 April, 1865 of wounds received at Fort Tyler, West Point, GA.

Earl Van Dorn—Army Commander.
Died: 7 May, 1863 of wounds received in a duel at Spring Hill, TN.

John Villepigue—Brigade Commander.
Died: 9 November, 1862 of ill health.

Francis Walker—Division Commander.
Died: 22 July, 1864 of wounds received at Atlanta, GA.

William Walker—Division Commander.
Died: 22 July, 1864 of wounds received at Atlanta, GA.

Edward Warren—Brigade Commander.
Died: 6 May, 1864 of wounds received at The Wilderness, VA.

Richard Weightman—Brigade Commander.
Died: 10 August, 1861 at Wilson's Creek, MO.

Chatham Wheat—Commander, "Wheat's Louisiana Tigers."
Died: 21 July, 1861 of wounds received at Manassas, VA.

William Whiting—Commander Fort Fisher, NC.
Died: 10 March, 1865 of wounds received at Fort Fisher, NC.

Jesse Williams—Brigade Commander.
Died: 12 May, 1864 of wounds received at Spotsylvania, VA.

Edward Wills—Brigade Commander.
Died: 30 May, 1864 of wounds received at Bethesda Church, VA.

Charles Winder—Brigade Commander.
Died: 9 August, 1862 of wounds received at Cedar Mountain, VA.

Felix Zollicoffer—Brigade Commander.
Died: 12 January, 1862 of wounds received at Mill Springs, KY

> *A little waif of a drummer boy, who had somehow drifted up the mountain in the surge, lies there, his pale face upward, a blue spot on his breast. Muffle the drum for the poor child and his mother!*
> *—Unknown correspondent, Chickamauga.*

Bibliography

Arnold, James and Wiener, Roberta: *The Timechart History of the Civil War*, Lowe & B. Hould Publishers, 2001

Alexander, Bevin, *How The South Could Have Won The Civil War: The Fatal Errors That Led To Confederate Defeat*, Crown Publishers, 2007

Author Unknown, *The Military Handbook and Soldiers Manual of Information including the Official Articles of War*, Originally printed by Beadle and Company Publishers in 1861. The version I used is a reprint but no clue as to who reprinted it.

Baldwin, John and Powers, Ron, *Last Flag Down: the Epic Journey of the Last Confederate Warship*, Crown Publishers, 2007

Bishop, Chris, Drury, Ian, and Gibbons, Tony: *1400 Days: The US Civil War Day by Day*, JG Press, 1998

Brewer, Paul, *The Civil War, State by State*, Thunder Bay Press, 2004

Bruun, Erik and Crosby, Jay, *Our Nation's Archive: The History of the United States in Documents*, Tess Press, 2009

Butterfield, Daniel, *Camp and Outpost Duty for Infantry*, Stackpole Books, 2003 (Original by Harper and Brothers, 1862)

Cadwallader, Sylvanus, *Three Years with Grant*, Bison Books, 1996 (Original by Alfred A Knopf, Inc., 1955)

Caren, Eric C, *Civil War Extra: A Newspaper History of the Civil War, Volume I: Nat Turner to 1862 and Volume II: 1863 to 1865*, Castle Books, 1999.

Cartmell, Donald, *The Civil War Up Close*, Barnes and Noble Books, 2006

Davis, Kenneth C. *Don't Know Much About the Civil War*, HarperCollins, 1996

Dickson, Keith D., *The Civil War for Dummies: A Reference for the Rest of Us!*, IDG Books, 2001

Fisher, Garry, *Rebel Cornbread and Yankee Coffee: Authentic Civil War Cooking*, Sweetwater Press, 2001

Flood, Charles B., *Grant and Sherman: The Friendship that won the Civil War*, Farrar, Strauss, and Giroux, 2005

Freemantle, Arthur J.L: *Three Months in the Southern States*, Greenhouse Publishing Reprint, 2000 (Original by William Blackwood and Sons, 1863)

Gallman, J. Matthew: *The Civil War Chronicle*, Crown Publishers, 2000

Garrison, Webb: *True Tales of the Civil War*, Gramercy Books, 1988

Gleeson, Ed: *Erin Go Gray, An Irish Rebel Trilogy*, Guild Press of Indiana, 1997

Hardee, W. J., *Hardee's Rifle and Light Infantry Tactics*, Invictus Publishing Reprint, 1997 (Original by J. O. Kane Publishers, New York, 1862)

Heidler, David S, and Heidler, Jeanne T: *Encyclopedia of the American Civil War*, W.W. Norton & Company, 2000

Hood, John B., *Advance and Retreat: Personal Experiences in the United States and Confederate States Armies*, Bison Books, 1996 (Originally published in 1880 for the Hood Orphan Memorial Fund, New Orleans, LA)

Hyslop, Stephen G and Kagan, Neil: *Eyewitness to the Civil War, The Complete History From Secession to Reconstruction*, National Geographic, 2006.

Johnson, Clint: *Civil War Blunders*, John F. Blair, Publisher, 2003

Jones, John Beauchamp: *A Rebel War Clerks Diary, Part I*, Time Life Reprint, 1982 (Original 1866)

Jones, John Beauchamp: *A Rebel War Clerks Diary, Part II*, Time Life Reprint, 1982 (Original 1866)

Katcher, Philip: *Brassey's Almanac: The American Civil War*, Brassey's, 2003

Konstam, Angus, *The Civil War: A Visual Encyclopedia*, Barnes and Noble Books, 2004

Kunhardt, Dorothy M and Philip B. Jr, *Twenty Days: A narrative in Text and Pictures of the Assassination of Abraham Lincoln and the Twenty Days and Nights that followed—The Nation in mourning, the Long Trip Home to Springfield*, Castle Books, 1993 (Originally printed in 1965)

Madden, David: *Beyond the Battlefield: The Ordinary Life and Extraordinary Times of the Civil War Soldier*, Simon and Schuster, 2000

McDonald, Joanna M. *The Faces of Irish Civil War Soldiers*, Rank and File Publications, 1999

McPherson, James M: *The Atlas of the Civil War*, Macmillan, 1994

McPherson, James M and the New York *Times*, *The Most Fearful*

Ordeal—Original Coverage of the Civil War by Writers and Reporters of the New York Times, St. Martins Press, 2004

Murray, Stuart A.P., Editor, *Witness to the Civil War: First Hand Accounts from Frank Leslie's Illustrated Newspaper,* HarperCollins, 2006

Nofi, Albert, *A Civil War Treasury,* Castle Books, 1992

Nofi, Albert, *The Civil War Notebook: A Collection of Little-Known Facts and Other Odds-and-Ends about the Civil War,* Combined Books, 1993

Norris, David A, *Life During the Civil War,* Moorshead Magazines Ltd, 2009

Orso, Allen, Publisher, *Armchair Reader: Civil War, Untold Tales of the Blue and Gray,* West Side Publications, 2007

Philips, Charles and Axelrod, Alan, *Portraits of the Civil War in Photographs, Diaries, and Letters,* Barns and noble Books, 1998 (Originally published as *My Brother's Face* by Zenda, Inc, in 1993)

Pritchard, Russ A. Jr: *Civil War Weapons and Equipment,* The Lyons Press, 2003

Pritchard, Russ A. Jr: *The Irish Brigade, A Pictorial History of the Famed Civil War Fighters,* Courage Books, 2004

Ranson, John: *John Ransom's Andersonville Diary,* Berkley Books Reprint, 1994 (Original 1881)

Sinclair, Arthur: *Two Years on the* Alabama, Tantallon Press, 2004 (Original 1895)

Sneeden, Robert Knox: *Eye of the Storm,* The Free Press, 2000

Tenney, W. J.: *The Military History of the Rebellion in the United States,*

Stackpole Books reprint, 2003 (Original printed by D. Appleton and Company, 1866)

Tsui, Bonnie, *She Went to the Field: Women Soldiers of the Civil War*, The Globe Pequot Press, 2003

Tucker, Spencer C: *Raphael Semmes and the Alabama*, McWhiney Foundation Press, 1998

United States War Department: *The 1863 U.S. Infantry Tactics*, Stackpole Books, 2003 (Original printed by J.B. Lippincott and Company, 1863)

Wagner, Margaret: *The American Civil War: 365 Days*, Harry N. Abrams, Inc, 2006

Watkins, Sam, *Company Aytch, or, A Side Show of the Big Show*, Plume Books, 1999 (Original published in 1882.)

Welsh, Jack D., M.D., *Medical Histories of Union Generals*, Kent State University Press, 1996

Winik, Jay, *April 1865: The Month that Saved America*, Harper Collins, 2001

Woodward, C. Vann and Muhlenfeld, Elisabeth: *The Private Mary Chesnut*, Oxford University Press, 1984

Wright, John D., Editor, *The Oxford Dictionary of Civil War Quotations*, Oxford University Press, 2006.

Websites:

http://americancivilwar.com
www.civilwarhome.com
www.historychannel.com
www.loc.gov
www.history.navy.mil
www.archives.gov
www.civilweek.com
www.patrickcleburne.com
http://civilwar.si.edu/
http://userpages.aug.com/captbarb/femvets2.html
http://www.cwartillery.org/adrill.html
http://www.19th-century-us-history.com
http://home.triad.rr.com/aom/civil.htm
http://kms.kapalama.ksbe.edu/projects/2002/civilwar
http://www.7thtexas.info/uniform_og_utstyr.htm
http://www.usgennet.org/usa/mo/county/stlouis/blackcs.htm
www.wikipedia.org
http://www.defense.gov/news/newsarticle.aspx?id=44949

Shon Powers has been a Civil War Buff and a student of that conflict since 1994. His interest, however, has been there since a visit to Gettysburg in 1974. This interest has been extended into the world of reenacting and to being an amatuer historian. He is married and lives in San Antonio, Texas where he retired from the US Air Force and works as a Facilities Safety Specialist for West Corporation. This is his second book, having published a book called "Lord, I'm In A Really Weird Place," a book of short stories and narratives.